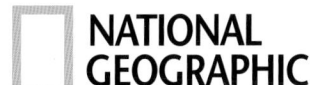
NATIONAL GEOGRAPHIC

PHOTO BASICS

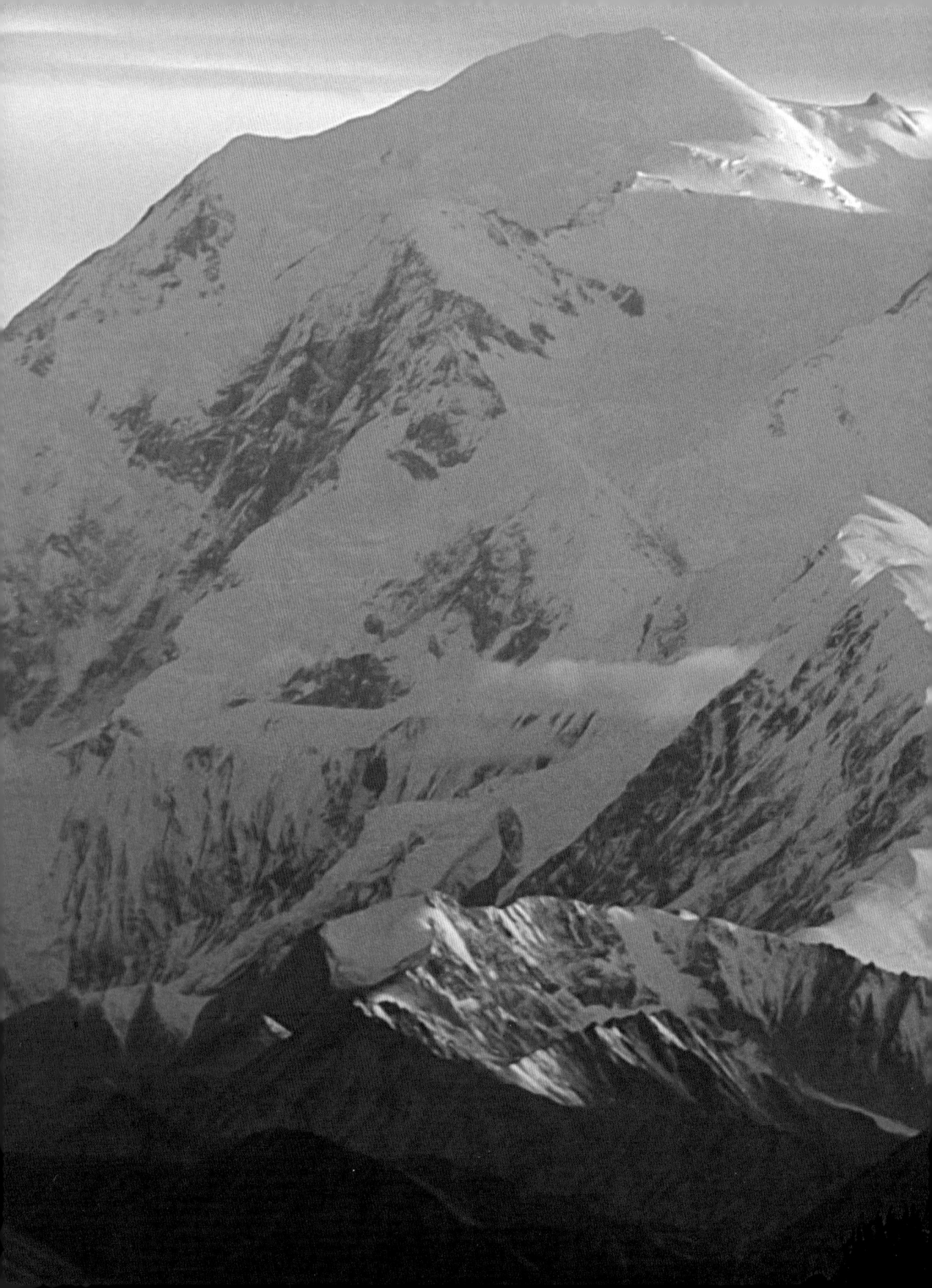

NATIONAL GEOGRAPHIC

PHOTO BASICS

The Ultimate Beginner's Guide to Great Photography

JOEL SARTORE
WITH HEATHER PERRY

NATIONAL GEOGRAPHIC
WASHINGTON, D.C.

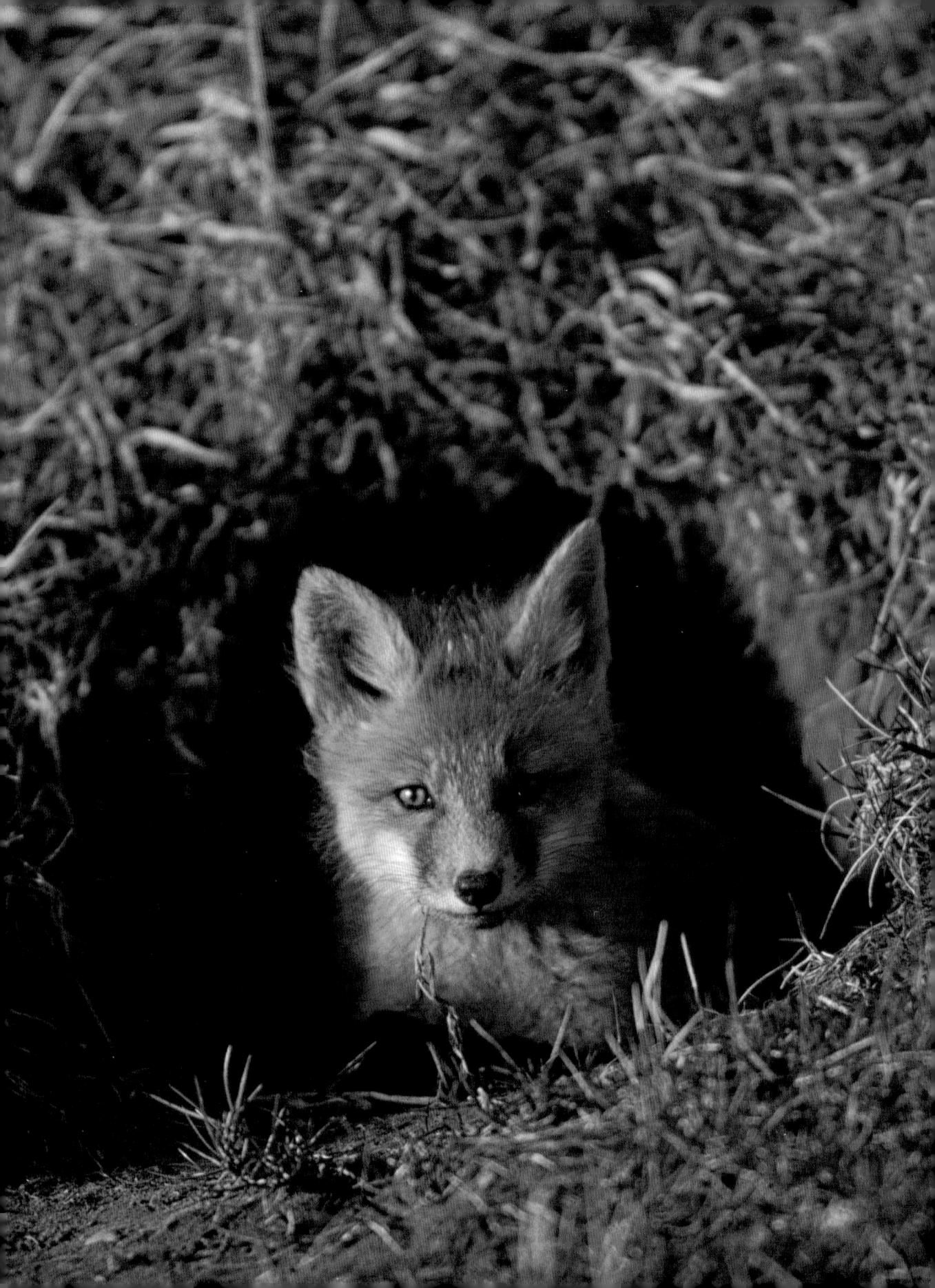

CONTENTS

An arctic fox cub peers out of its burrow in Prudhoe Bay, Alaska.
Previous pages: A hiker photographs the view of Mount McKinley in Alaska's Denali National Park.

INTRODUCTION

For decades, I've been traveling the world in search of great pictures. And you know what I've discovered? Most of the time, I feel like I shouldn't be taking pictures at all.

I say this because it's a very rare thing when everything comes together—great light, a perfect background, and just the right moment. In fact, it can be a bit like finding a needle in a haystack.

But don't be discouraged, dear readers! It just takes vision and patience, and practice, practice, practice.

Many years ago, when I was just starting out, I asked the photo director of a student newspaper, "What's the secret to building a great portfolio?" He said simply, "Run a lot of pictures through your camera, Joel." At the time I thought he was being a bit snarky. But now I see how right he was.

Some 40 years later, I'm still learning that the more you shoot, the better you get. This is because you're seeing what works and what doesn't with each situation—success or failure is apparent within each frame. We really do learn things best when we're made uncomfortable, and boy have I been made miserable by my failures when shooting new things. But, looking back now, I see that each image has led to me getting better the next time.

Why does this all seem so hard? To start, there's that 500-page instruction manual that came with your camera.

St. Basil's Cathedral stands bright at night in Moscow's Red Square.

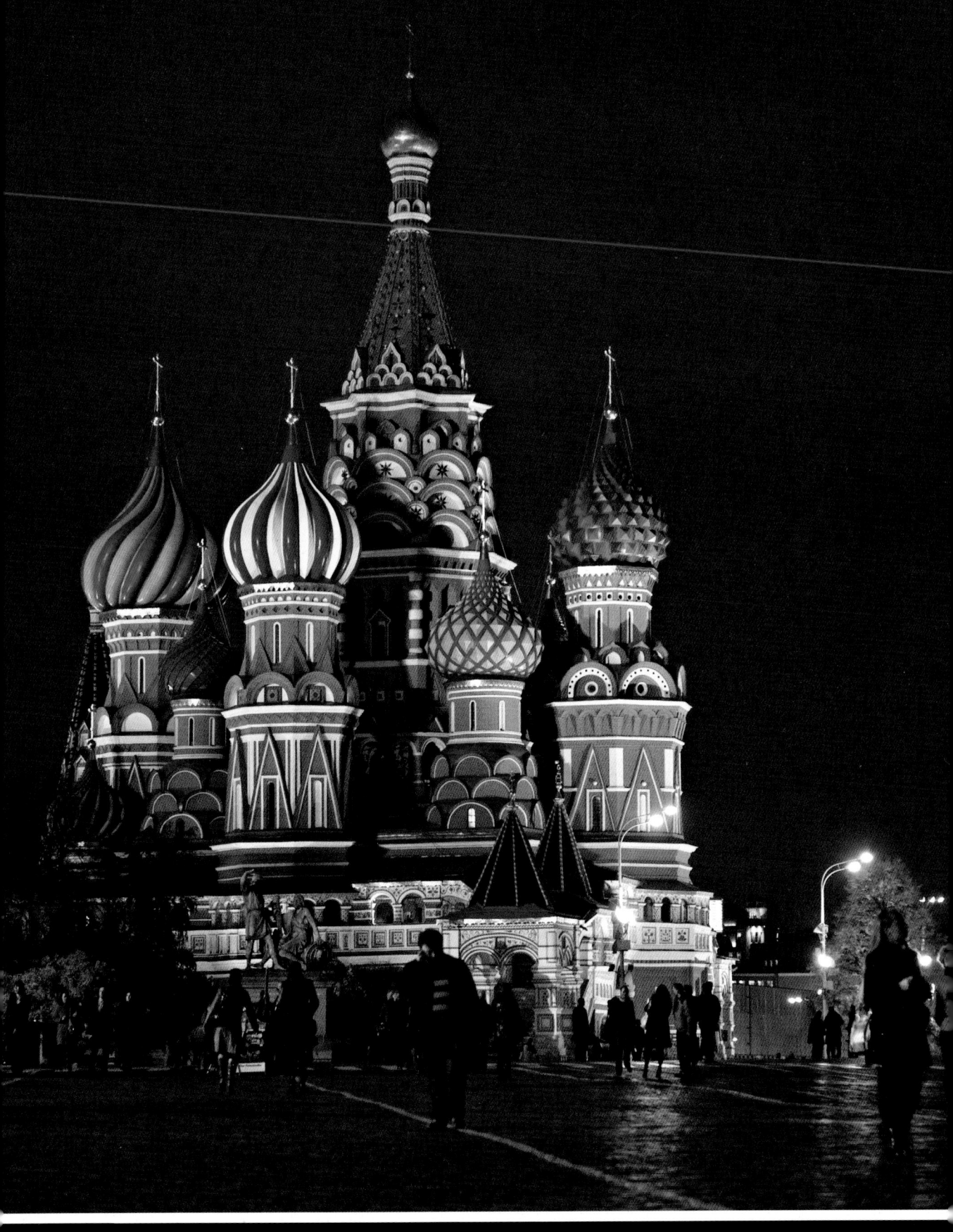

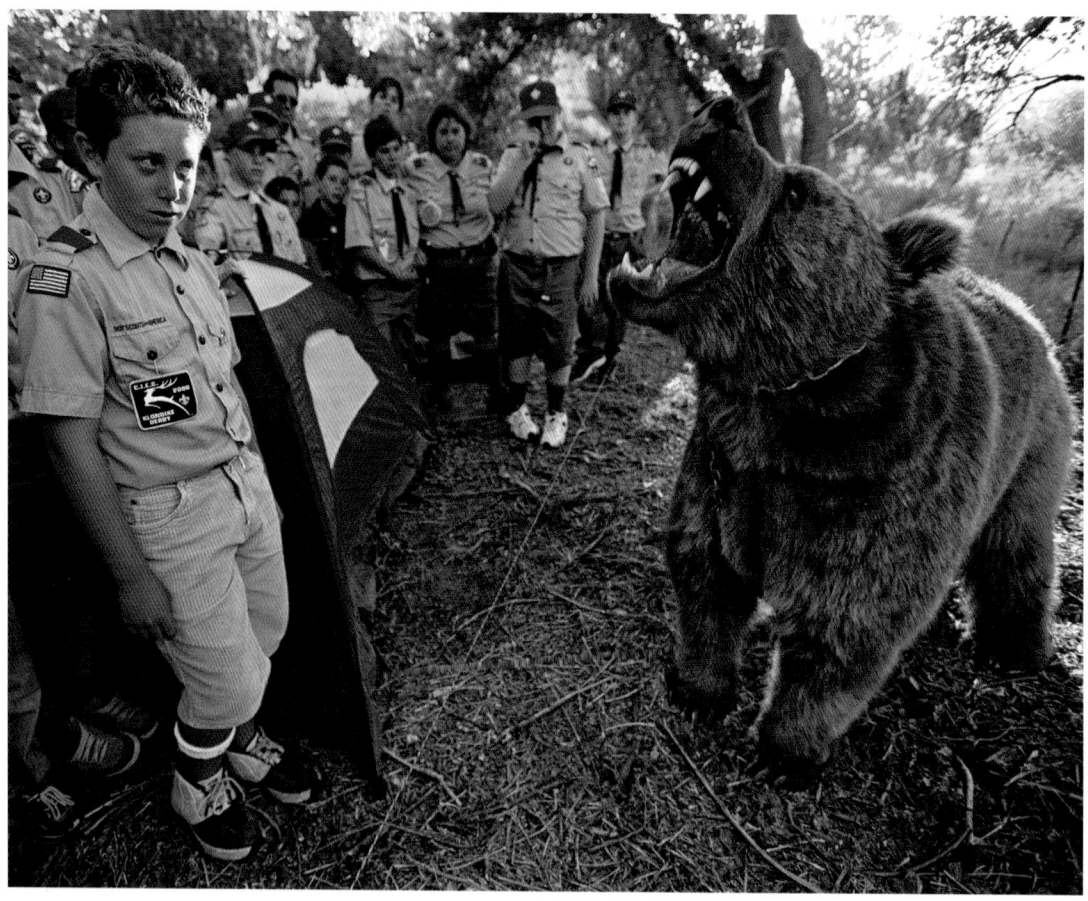

A trained bear is all roar and no bite, showing off for a group of Boy Scouts in southern California

But, more important, when you pick up a camera, the choices are infinite. Where will you go? When, and why? The dance of life is different each and every day. So is the light. And you can completely change everything in a photograph by simply turning around. It can all be so overwhelming, right?

We yearn to capture the great moments in life. They're literally everywhere, but so fleeting, so hard to trap forever inside that little box.

So let's take a deep breath and start right here: In this book, I'd like you to open your mind to the visual possibilities that abound in your daily life. You don't have to go to the other side of the world to make great photos. Indeed, the pictures you make at home should be among your best. This is because you really *know* this subject, and you have 24/7 access. With vision, patience, and practice, shooting at home can pay off in ways that will really satisfy.

And, by the way, you'll get far more credit from me when you find an ordinary scene in your own backyard and capture it in a way that's all your own.

The good news is that seeing well doesn't have to be tech-heavy or overly expensive. I really don't care much about the gear, or the latest bells and whistles. Just shoot what's interesting to you. If you love your subject, it'll eventually love you back.

And once you've honed your photographic skills, I ask you to take it a step further—do something truly good with your work.

The power of photography to tell stories well is amazing. A good photograph can literally change the world. Whether your thing is to help save dogs and cats down at the local animal shelter, or to celebrate a clean beach, there's nothing like putting your photos to work.

Knowing all this, I started the Photo Ark some 14 years ago. Today, we've done studio portraits of more than 10,000 animals, well on our way to photographing every species in human care around the world. Hopefully, these images will stand the test of time, and inspire future generations to protect our natural heritage.

But enough about me. Come on. Jump in. Right now. The water's fine.

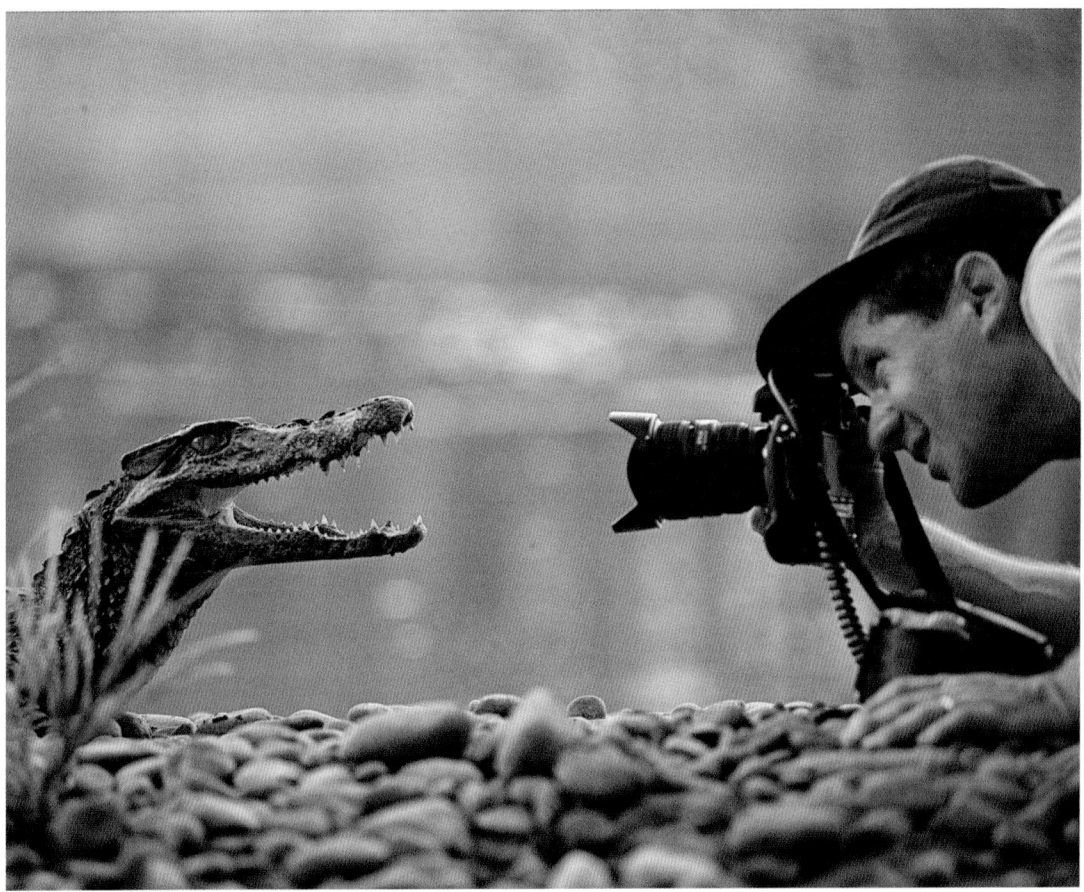

Sometimes you have to get up close and personal with animals, like I did with this juvenile caiman, to get an intimate portrait.

HOW TO USE THIS BOOK

In *National Geographic Photo Basics,* you'll find knowledge, advice, and useful tips for beginning photographers. With National Geographic photographer Joel Sartore as your guide, you'll learn the fundamentals of great photography and how to put them to work in your own photos. In Part One: The Basics, we'll go over the essential gear, techniques, and skills that you'll need as you learn your way around a camera.

In Part Two: Practicing the Basics, we'll put those skills to work in a number of different scenarios, from family portraits and food photography to traveling abroad and extreme sports.

LESSONS
The book is divided into two-page lessons, each focusing on a specific element of photography.

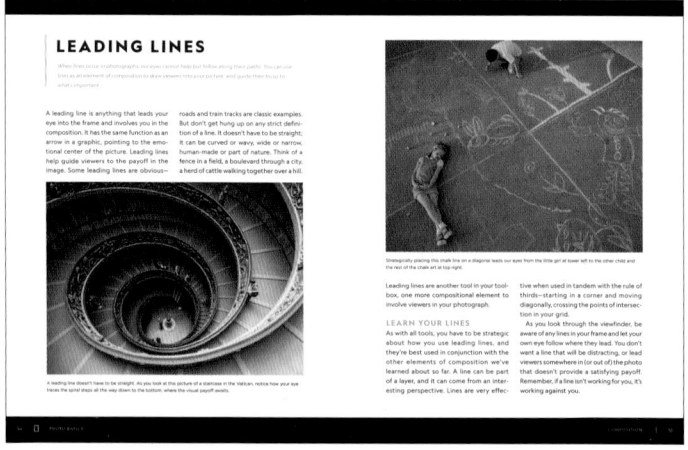

PRO TIPS
Beyond the basics, these pieces of advice will teach you how to take your photography to the next level.

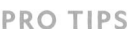

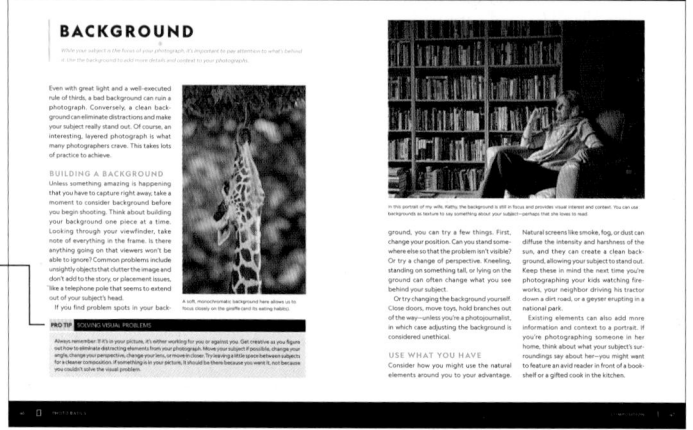

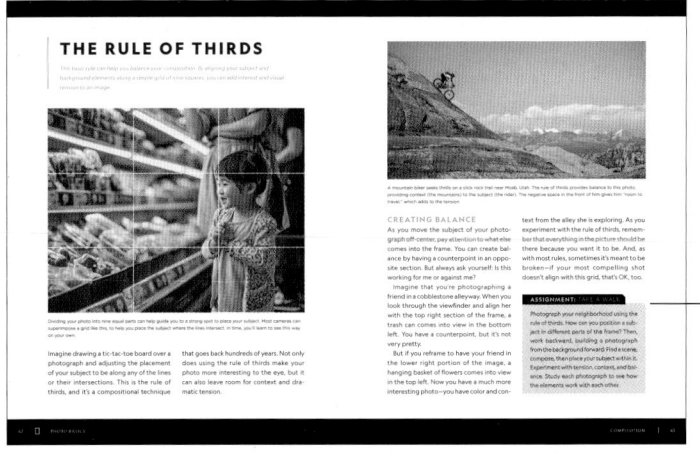

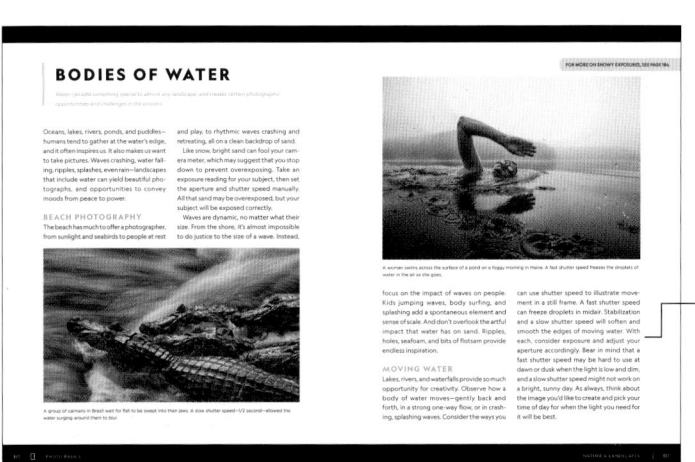

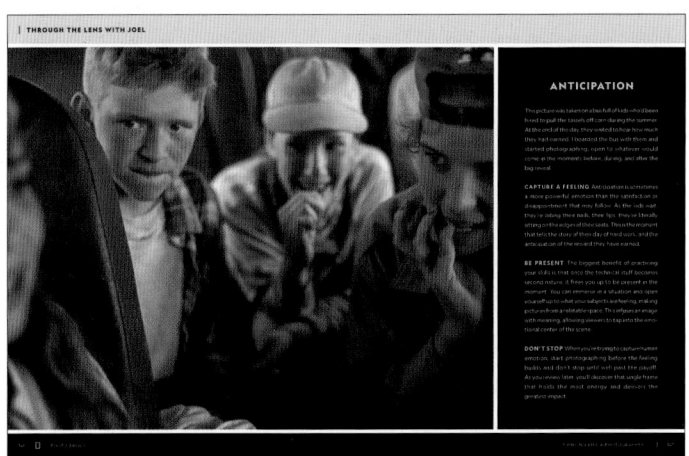

A WORD ABOUT TERMS A glossary, beginning on page 242, gives definitions of terms that might be unfamiliar to you.

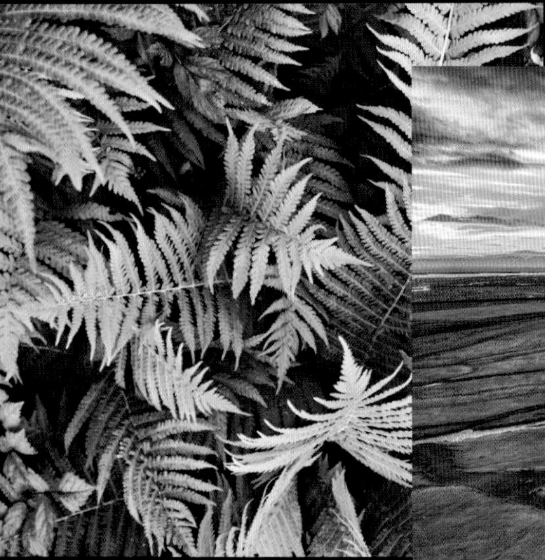

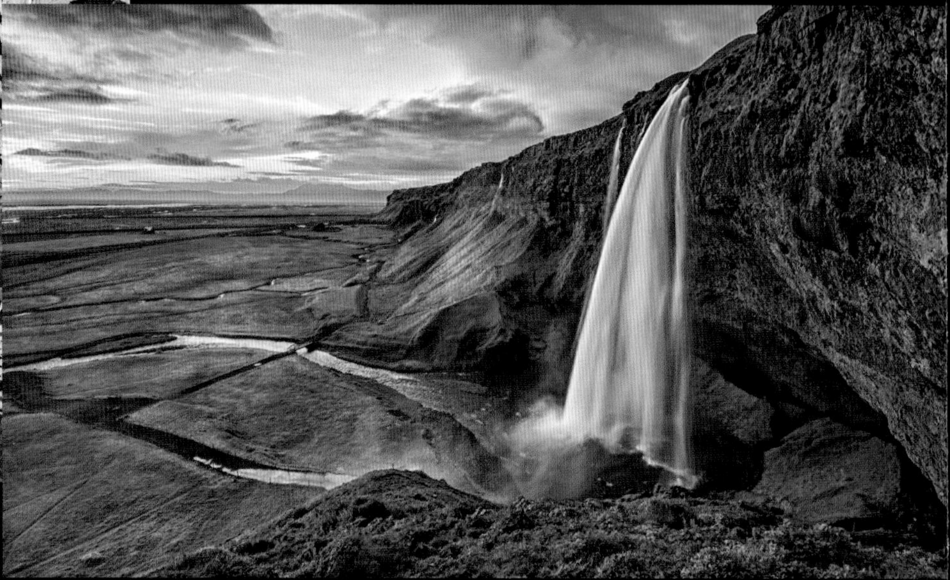

PART ONE: THE BASICS

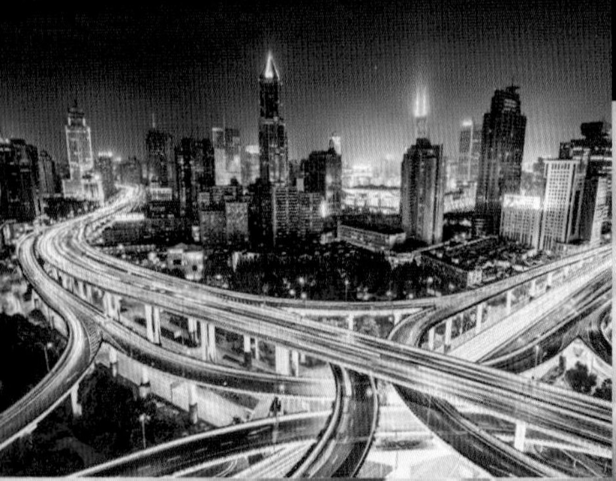

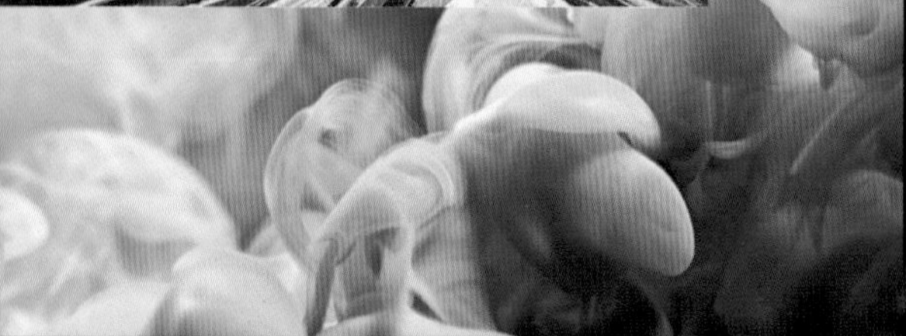

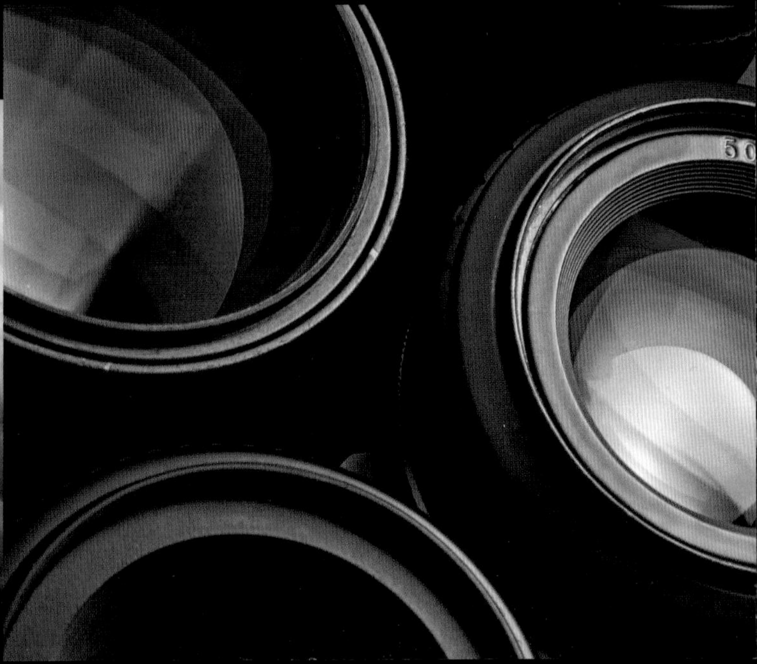

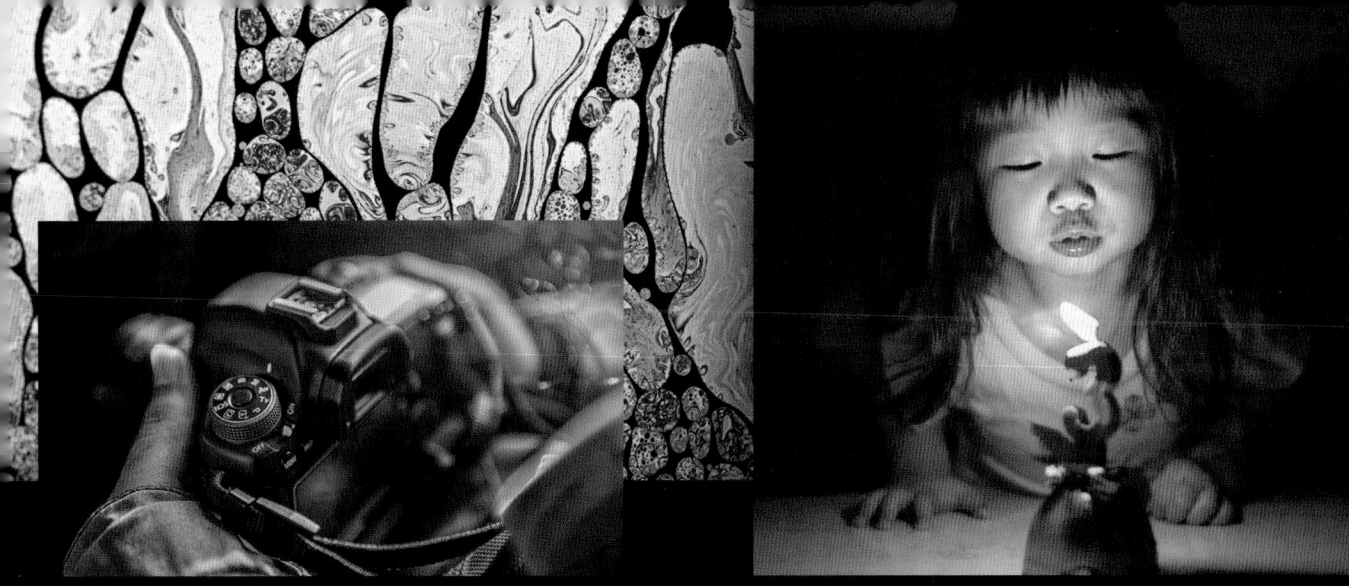

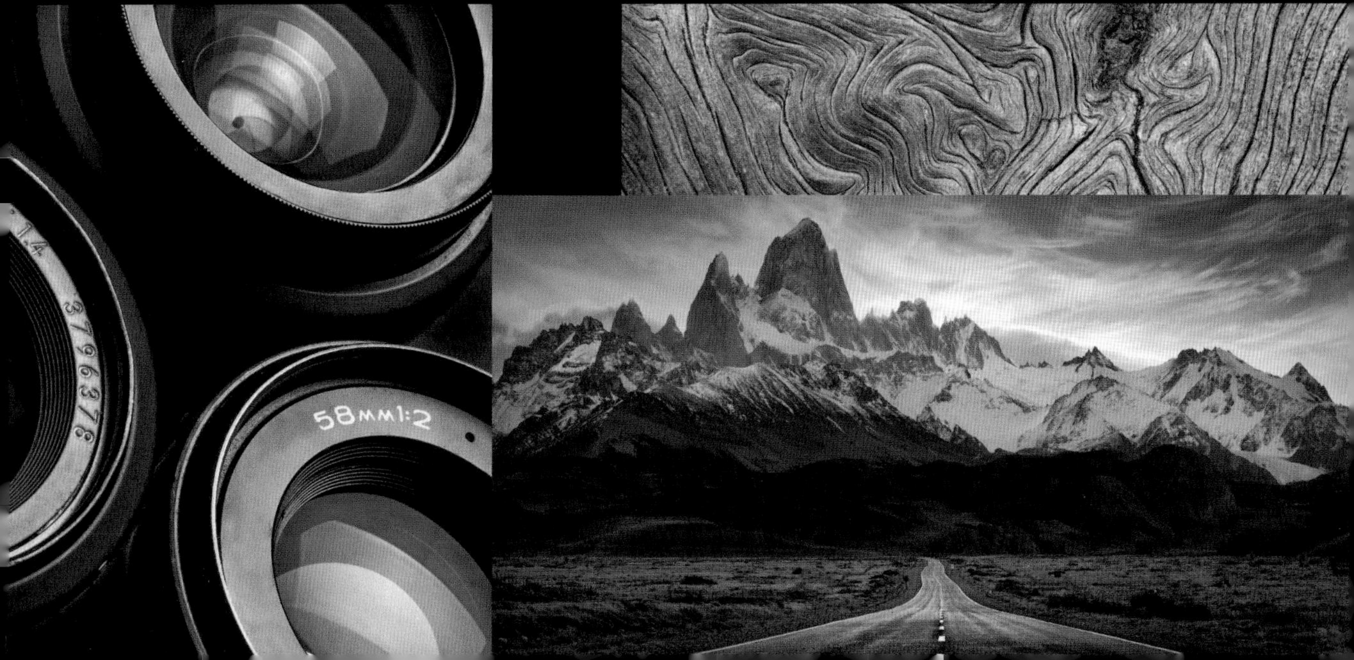

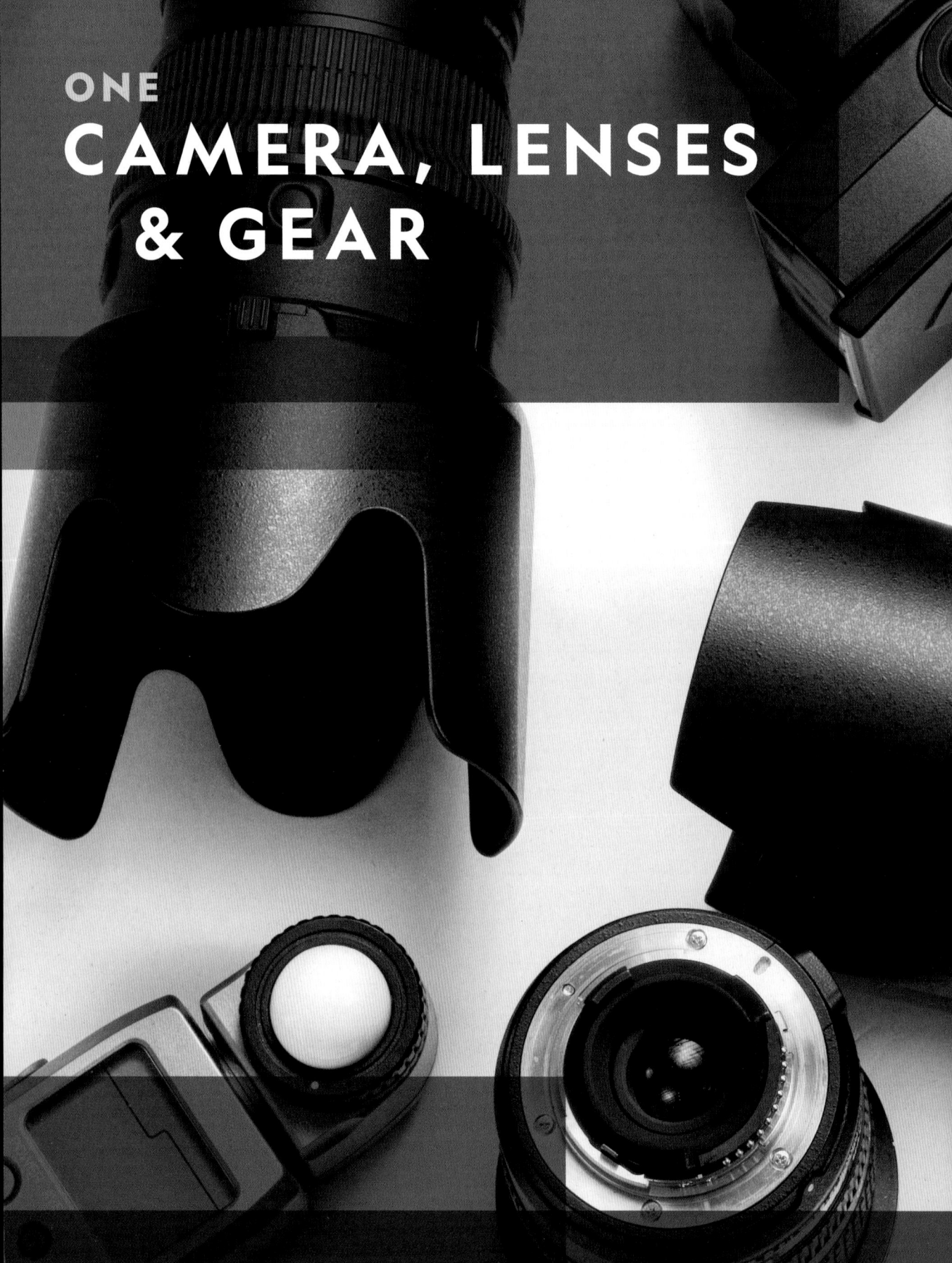

ONE
CAMERA, LENSES & GEAR

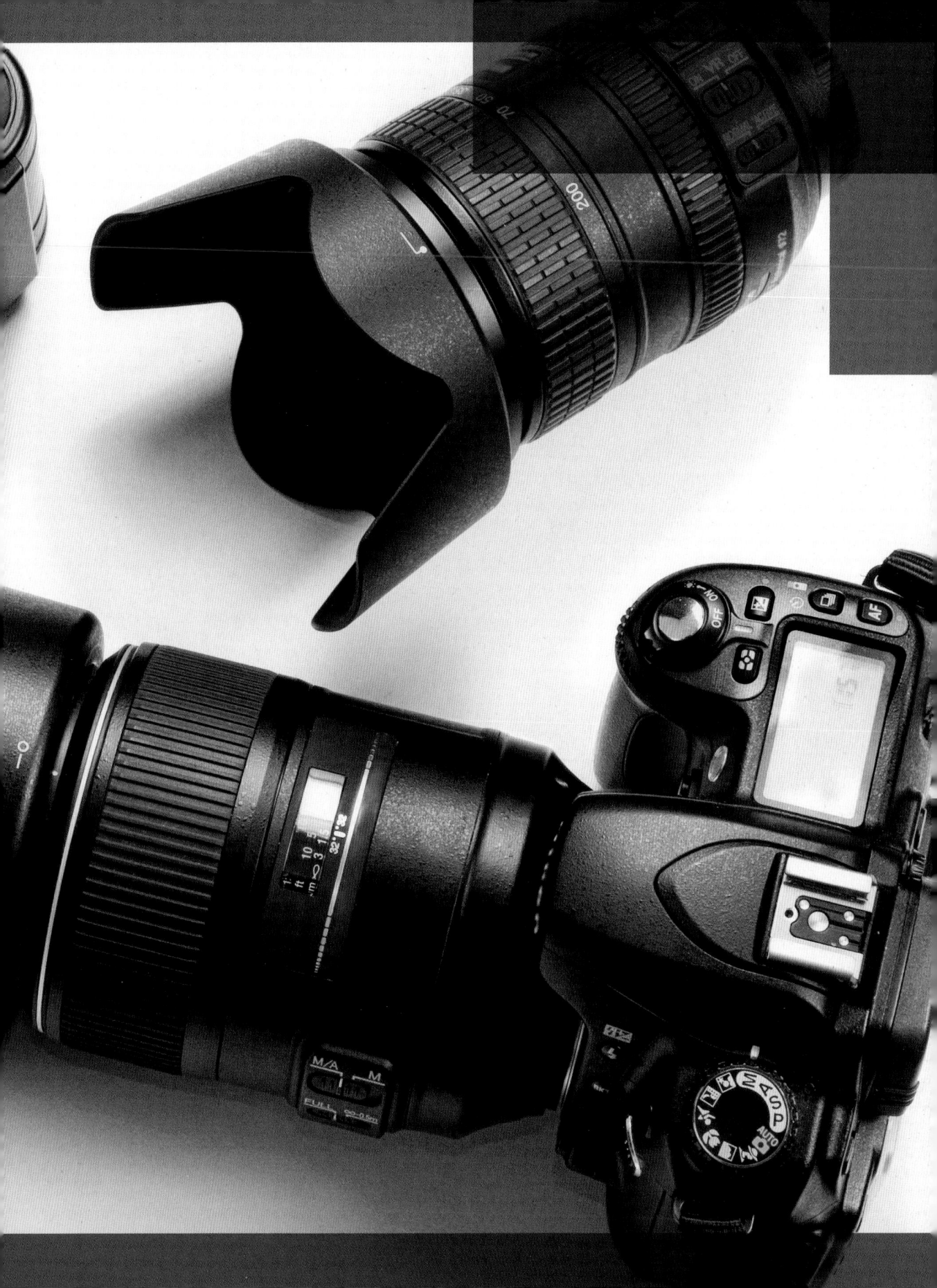

WHAT YOU NEED TO GET STARTED

Professional photographers often have elaborate gear in their kits, from scuba tanks to climbing ropes. In mine, I have everything from boots melted by lava in Volcanoes National Park to a box designed to contain venomous snakes while I photograph them. In this first chapter, we'll get outfitted for whatever photography adventures you plan to undertake.

For most people, everything you need to make great photographs can fit into a backpack. You'll always want to have the following: a camera you're familiar with, a lens or two, extra memory cards, batteries or a battery charger, and a lens cloth—but a clean T-shirt will do in a pinch! Depending on your goals for the shoot and your camera, you may also want an external flash.

We'll go over the options you have when choosing a camera and different pieces of equipment. In all of this, it's important for you to invest in the equipment that's right for you. Consider your goals, the amount of time you have to devote to photography, and what your budget will allow. You may want to find a local camera shop where you can get professional advice as well as the chance to try out different cameras in person. Ultimately, you've got to put together a kit that will go with your style—of work, of shooting, of storytelling. If you can tell the story with less, don't drag around extra gear just because a book tells you you should. As in life, you'll be most successful in photography if you're true to yourself.

On a warm spring day, a woman photographs flowers in a blossoming orchard.

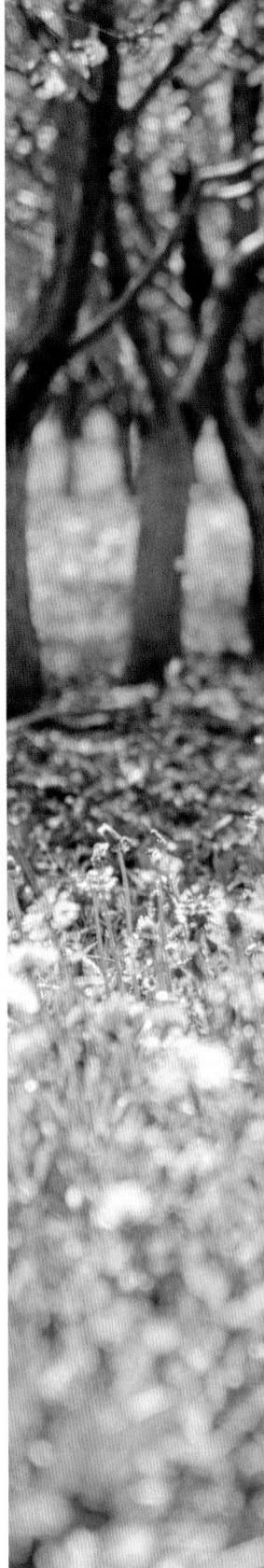

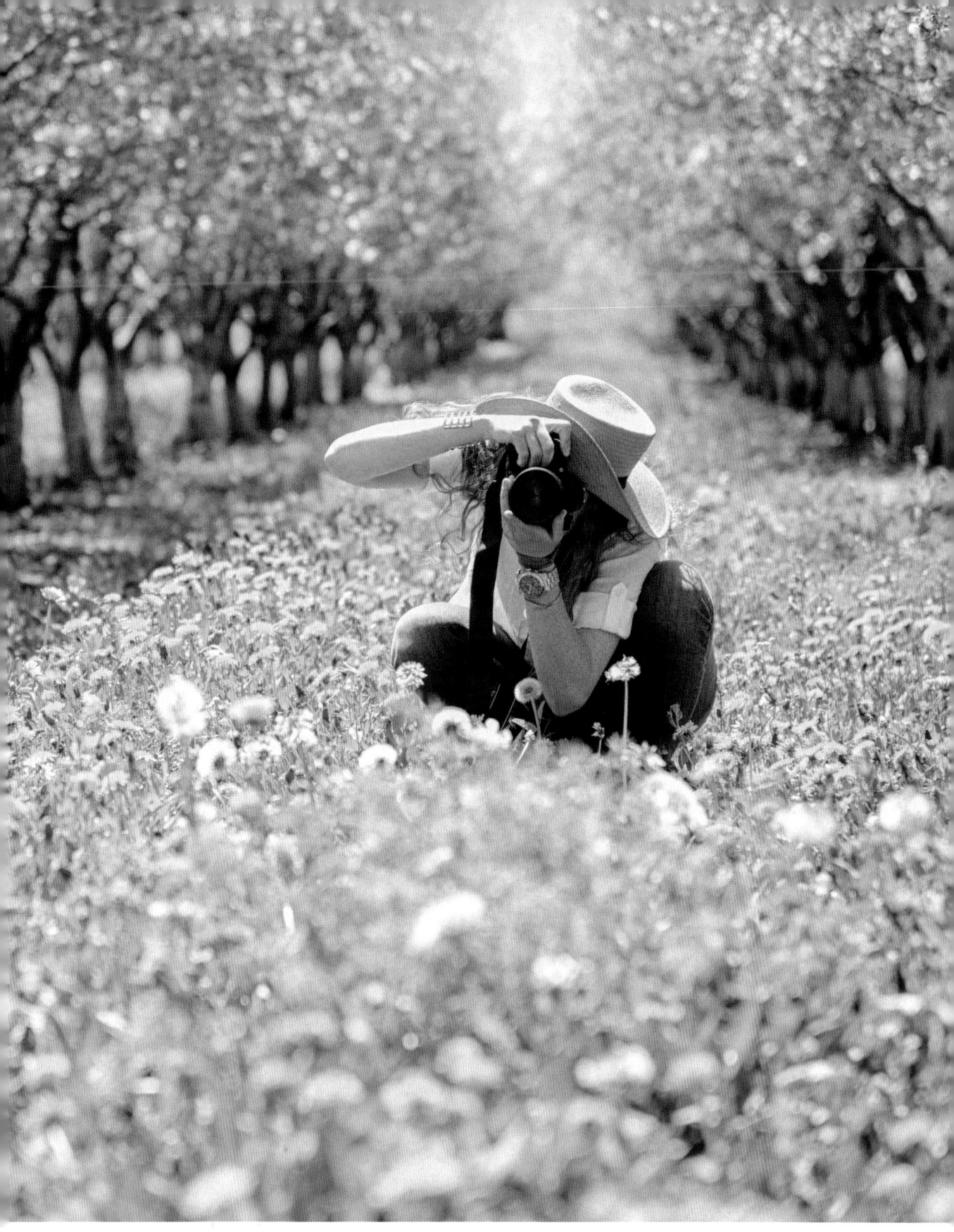

ANATOMY OF A DSLR CAMERA

No matter what type of camera you're using, understanding the mechanics of how an image is made will make you more comfortable with your equipment.

A digital single-lens reflex (DSLR) is probably the most common type of camera for those who take a serious interest in photography. Many of the DSLR components noted here appear on other types of cameras as well.

1 FLASH

A small, built-in flash comes with most DSLR and point-and-shoot cameras.

2 VIEWFINDER

This is where you'll get a preview of the image you're about to shoot. A DSLR has an optical viewfinder, which gives you a mirrored display of what the camera sees.

3 IMAGE SENSOR

Light passes through the lens and camera shutter to the image sensor, which converts it to digital data. That data becomes your picture. The resolution of the image is determined by the number of megapixels in the sensor.

4 REFLEX MIRROR

This is a small mirror that reflects the light entering the lens up into the viewfinder.

5 ZOOM RING

When using a zoom lens, turning this ring adjusts the focal length of the lens, changing how close or far away your subject appears to be.

6 LENS

This light-focusing device makes photography possible. At the base of the lens is the aperture—a small, circular opening that can be widened or narrowed to control the amount of light reaching the sensor.

7 MANUAL FOCUS RING

Turn this ring to change which elements of your image are in focus. Some photographers only use manual focus; others use the manual focus ring to fine-tune after autofocus makes the first move.

8 SHUTTER RELEASE

Inside the camera is a shutter—a door between the lens and the image sensor. When you press the shutter release button, this door opens to allow light to reach the sensor.

9 MODE DIAL

This dial shows different camera modes. Most cameras have a fully automatic mode, a fully manual mode, and a few options in between that let the camera do some of the work for you.

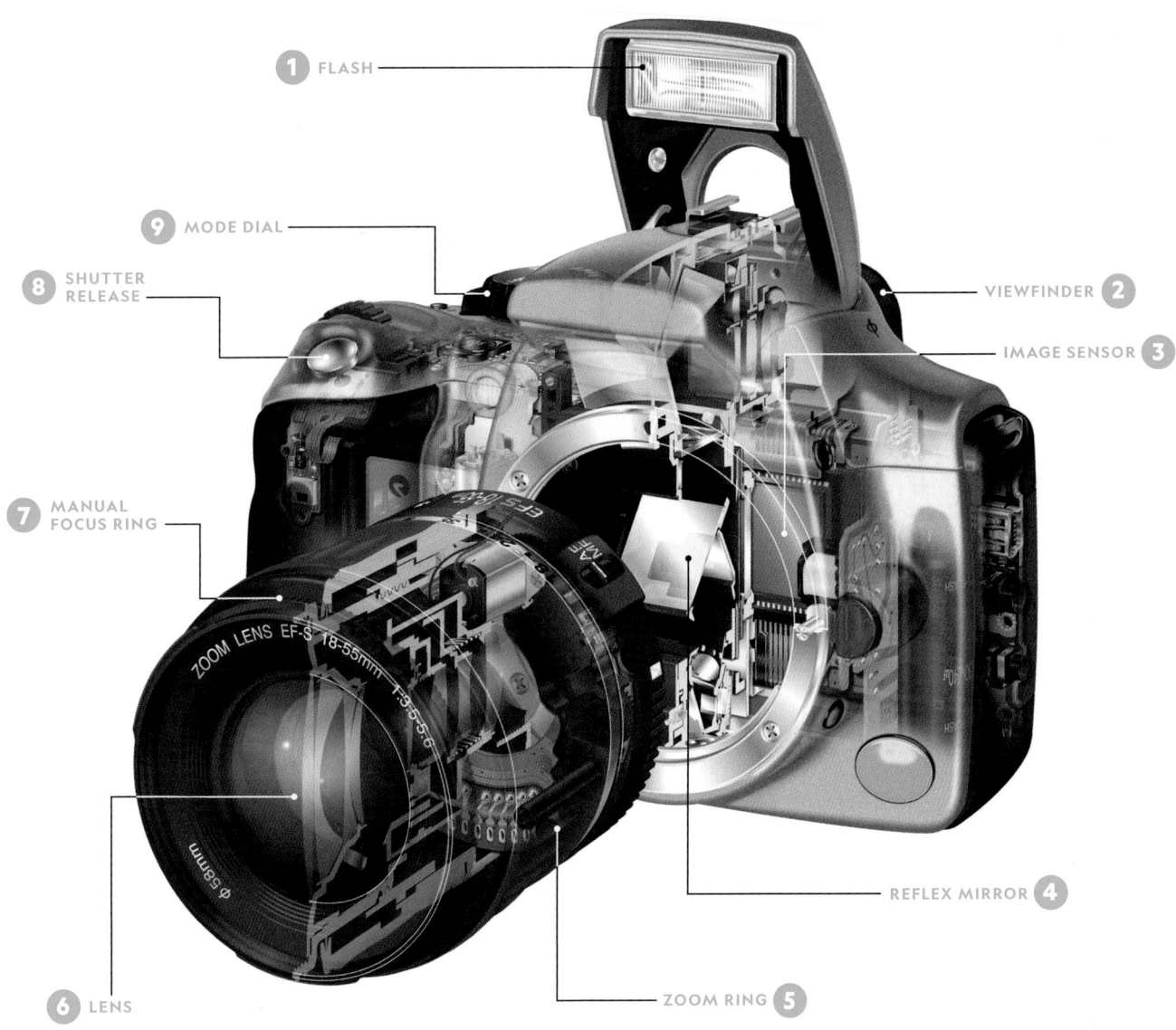

1 FLASH

9 MODE DIAL

8 SHUTTER RELEASE

7 MANUAL FOCUS RING

6 LENS

VIEWFINDER 2

IMAGE SENSOR 3

REFLEX MIRROR 4

ZOOM RING 5

BASIC CAMERA CONTROLS

There are three basic camera settings that you can control: aperture, shutter speed, and ISO. Preset modes can eliminate guesswork while you learn your way around a camera, but understanding how these settings work together will make you a better photographer.

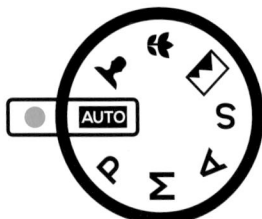

AUTO

Fully automatic, the camera decides your ISO, aperture, shutter speed, flash, everything. This setting is fine for quick snapshots, but most of the time you'll want more control.

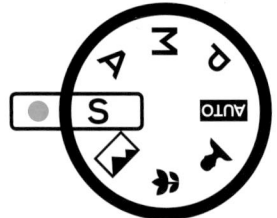

SHUTTER PRIORITY

This mode enables manual control of ISO and shutter speed, while the camera adjusts the aperture for proper exposure.

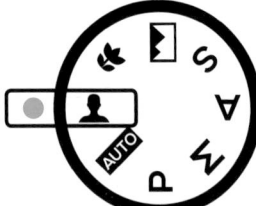

PORTRAIT

This preset mode usually widens the aperture to make a soft background for a portrait. Some cameras may have facial recognition technology in this mode.

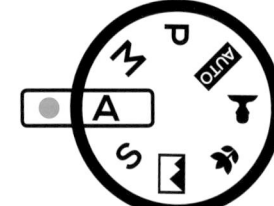

APERTURE PRIORITY

This mode enables manual control of ISO and aperture, while the camera adjusts the shutter speed for proper exposure.

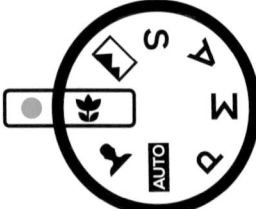

MACRO

This setting allows you to focus on subjects close to the camera lens, often used for photographing flowers, insects, or other subjects you'd like to magnify.

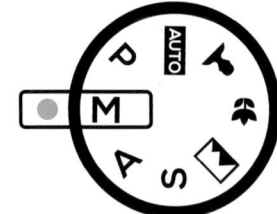

MANUAL

Fully manual, you will set each parameter to your preferred setting.

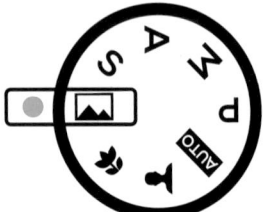

LANDSCAPE

This preset mode sets the camera up with a narrow aperture, putting more of the scene in focus—best for broad scenic views.

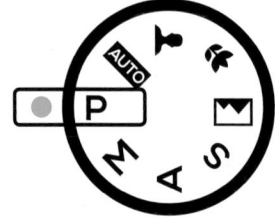

PROGRAM

The camera calculates shutter speed and aperture, while you choose other settings, such as ISO, white balance, and whether or not you'd like the flash.

APERTURE

The aperture is the opening in the camera's lens, and its size determines how much light is allowed in. Each setting is called an f-stop and it corresponds to a number. The higher the number, the smaller the hole and the less light will reach your camera's sensor. An aperture setting of f/22 is very small and lets in very little light. An aperture of f/2.8 is much bigger and lets in a lot of light.

FOR MORE ON METADATA, SEE PAGE 228.

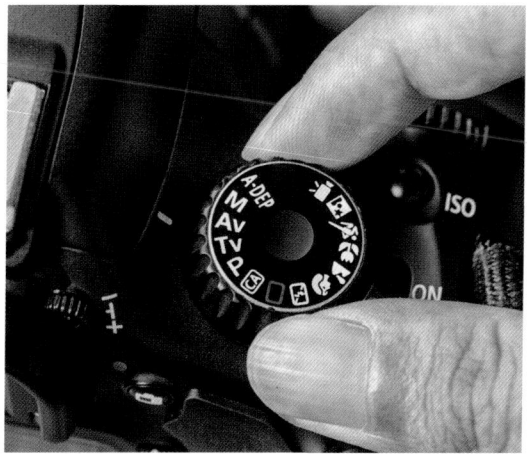

Preset modes can come in handy, but manual and priority modes will give you more control over your images.

In bright sun, a small aperture is sufficient to let enough light into your camera. But in a dimly lit room, you need a wider aperture to allow in as much light as possible. Keep in mind that your aperture will help determine how much of the image is in focus. More on that later.

SHUTTER SPEED

The shutter speed setting controls how long the shutter stays open to let light in. The number indicates seconds or fractions of a second. A shutter speed of 1 means the shutter stays open for a full second, which is quite slow. A slow shutter speed can cause blur in an image if the subject or camera moves while the shutter is open. Blur can be used for artistic effect, but if that's not your goal, consider using a faster shutter speed or a stabilizer. A shutter speed of 1/250 or faster is quick, and freezes the action.

Aperture and shutter speed work together like the faucet on your kitchen sink—the handle controls how much water comes out, and for how long. Set them together—a faster shutter speed often needs a wider aperture to let in more light, while a slower shutter speed often needs the opposite.

ISO

The ISO controls the camera's sensitivity to light. The higher the ISO number, the harder the camera works to gather available light. On a sunny day, the camera doesn't have to work all that hard, so an ISO of 100 is sufficient. But in a dim room, an ISO of 800 or higher will allow the camera to collect more light, for a better exposure in your final photo.

CAMERA MODES

Point-and-shoot cameras often control these settings automatically. On a DSLR, you have the choice of fully automatic, fully manual, or somewhere in between. Priority modes are perfect for when you want the camera to do some of the work, but not all of it.

ASSIGNMENT: MEET YOUR CAMERA

Choose a subject and photograph it many times, experimenting with different combinations of aperture, shutter speed, and ISO. Try creating a label for your photo by writing the settings on a card and placing it in the frame for future reference. Digital cameras also save the settings in the metadata of your photos, so you can review them later.

TYPES OF CAMERAS

There's an old saying among photographers: The best camera is the one you have with you. When figuring out what type of camera is right for you, think about what you'll carry, how much creative control you want, and what you're willing to spend. You can get decent pictures with an inexpensive point-and-shoot, but a DSLR will give you more control over what they look like.

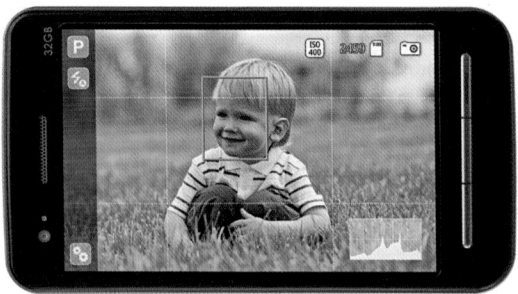

<< SMARTPHONE CAMERAS

Most smartphones have high-quality cameras built right in. These cameras are getting more advanced with every new model of phone, with better image quality and more photographer control. If it's always in your pocket, you won't miss a shot as long as your battery is charged.

POINT-AND-SHOOT CAMERAS >>

These small and lightweight cameras are usually about the size of a deck of cards. The lens and flash are built in, leaving you with fewer customization options. But they tend to have larger sensors and more storage capacity than phone cameras, making them a great option if you don't want to carry anything big or heavy.

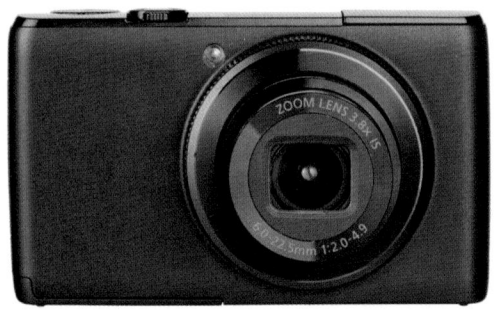

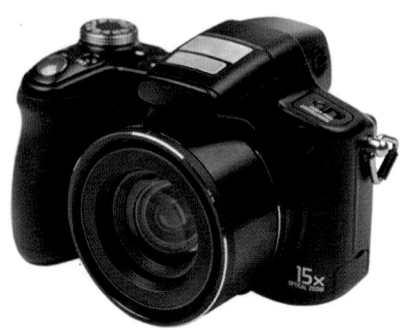

<< ADVANCED COMPACT CAMERAS

Still relatively small and lightweight, advanced compact cameras offer more stability and settings, which can help create higher-quality photos. Although the lens can't be changed in advanced compact cameras, their zoom capability can be quite powerful, so you can still travel light.

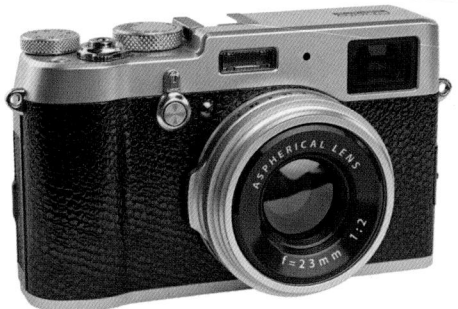

<< MIRRORLESS CAMERAS

A mirrorless camera is a digital camera without an internal mirror system. Many of these models have interchangeable lenses, but with a lighter and thinner camera body. Instead of the optical viewfinder, you'll have an electronic viewfinder to preview your image, where the camera projects what it sees onto an LCD screen on the back of the camera body. With fantastic image quality and nearly silent shooting, mirrorless cameras are on the rise with professional photographers, but at a higher price point, they remain a little beyond what most hobbyists will want to spend.

DSLR CAMERAS >>

A digital single-lens reflex camera, or DSLR, allows you total control over settings and lenses. You can often buy a starter kit that includes a camera body and a zoom lens that will work in a variety of situations, and gradually add more lenses to your kit over time.

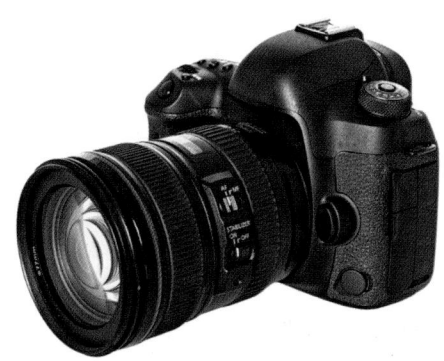

PRO TIP THE RIGHT CAMERA FOR YOU

Ultimately, you have to pick what works best for your needs. If you just want a point-and-shoot, don't buy a complicated and expensive system. But don't under-buy either. If you want to create fine-art photographs in your garden, or dramatic long-lens shots of grizzly bears in golden light, you're going to want the options and flexibility a DSLR provides. Find a good camera store so you can hold different cameras in your hands. Don't buy anything too heavy or you'll never want to carry it. Ask yourself: What do I really want to do with my camera? What am I willing to carry? And how much can I afford to spend?

FOCAL LENGTH

The focal length of your camera's lens influences everything from your angle of view, to how close your subject appears, to how much of the final image is in focus. It's one of the most important factors in determining the look and feel of your photos.

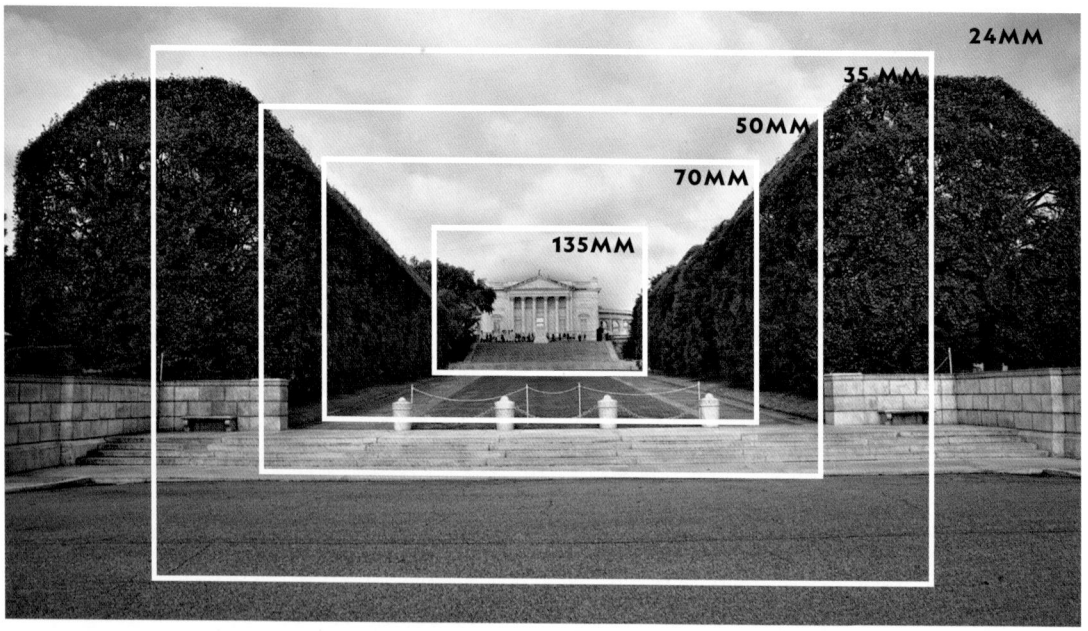

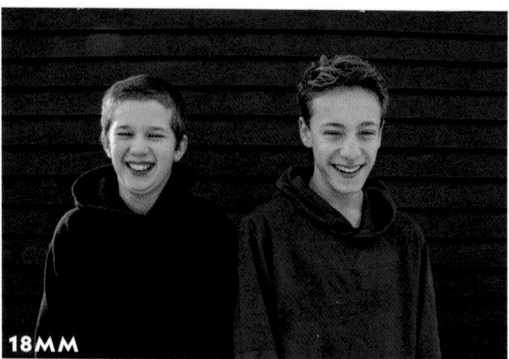

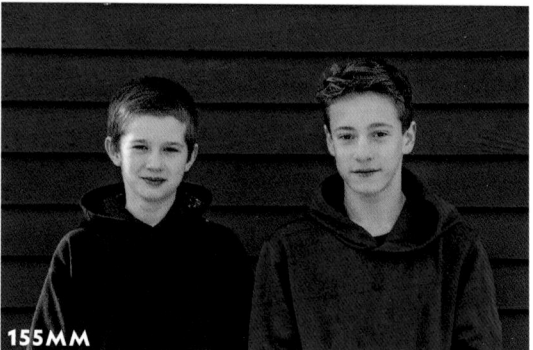

Each rectangle (top) represents the amount of the scene captured when you change the focal length of your lens, but not your camera-to-subject distance—meaning, you stay in the same spot. The shorter the focal length, the wider the angle of view. These two portraits (bottom) show how focal length changes the feel of an image. The shorter focal length (left) has a slightly distorted or bent look, with more of the background in view and largely in focus. The longer focal length (right) captures the boys' faces more naturally, and while the background is not distorted, it is cropped more tightly and is slightly out of focus.

FOR MORE ON DEPTH OF FIELD, SEE PAGE 70.
FOR MORE ON MACRO PHOTOGRAPHY, SEE PAGE 124.

Technically speaking, focal length is the distance in millimeters between the lens and the camera's image sensor when the subject is in focus. It's the measurement we use when we talk about different types of lenses—the greater the number, the longer the lens, the narrower the angle of view.

With a long lens, you're reaching out and grabbing a single point in the landscape, like birds sitting on a telephone wire.

With a shorter focal length, sometimes called a wide-angle lens, you're showing much more of the world, like the birds, the wire, the telephone poles, and the entire street scene beneath them. In addition, wide-angle lenses tend to have a greater depth of field, meaning more of your scene will be in focus.

When shopping for camera lenses, you'll see that some have one number, like a 35mm, and some have a range, like 70-200mm. The former is a fixed, or prime, lens, which only has one focal length, and the latter is a zoom lens, which has variable focal lengths.

FINDING FOCAL LENGTH

When deciding on a focal length, think about what kind of image you're trying to make. Lenses with a focal length between 35mm and 50mm are often called "normal" lenses, because they mimic what the human eye naturally sees. A 24-70mm zoom lens is a good starting option,

because it helps capture exactly what you see—and then some.

If you want to capture a closer look, whether of one flower in a field of many or of an owl in a tree, you'll want a longer lens to reach out and "touch" it. A longer focal length will help distant objects fill the frame.

If you want to photograph a majestic landscape, or a room in your house where you can't back up very far, you'll need a wide-angle lens, like a 24mm. Try to keep your subject near the center of the frame, as wide-angle lenses will warp the appearance of anything near the edges. They can also cause a mild distortion if the camera-to-subject distance is very short.

If you're photographing small subjects up close—insects, for example—you may want a macro lens, which can magnify tiny subjects and often reduces the camera-to-subject distance required to focus.

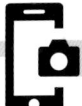 **PHONE SMARTS: FOCAL LENGTH**

The focal length of a smartphone camera tends to fall between 24mm and 30mm (though this varies from one brand and model to another). Because of the wider angle of view, phone cameras are often better suited to landscape shots than portraits or macro photography, though many phones have accessory macro adapters or special portrait modes.

LENSES

The two main categories of lenses are prime (fixed focal length) and zoom (variable focal length). Some lenses capture an image similar to how the human eye sees it, while others alter the perspective for a unique effect.

STANDARD

A standard, or normal, lens has a focal length between 35mm and 50mm. Lenses in this range are some of the most commonly used, because they work well for everything from portraits to landscapes. Many DSLRs come bundled with a zoom lens that covers this range of focal lengths.

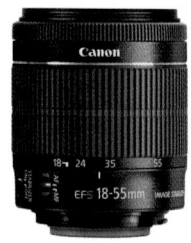

FISH-EYE

A fish-eye lens gives a picture a curvy effect—a product of the super-short focal length—often 12mm or lower. These lenses can be useful in situations where you want to capture a really wide angle, but be aware of the significant distortion.

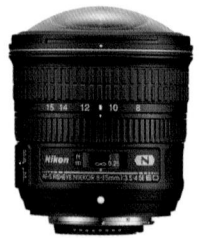

MACRO

A macro lens allows you to magnify tiny subjects, and focus at a closer distance than a normal lens. Most macros have a very limited depth of field, meaning very little in the image will be in focus.

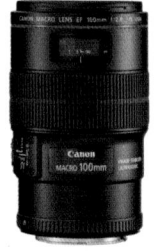

WIDE-ANGLE

A wide-angle lens has a short focal length (between 14mm and 24mm). These lenses show a wider angle of view than the human eye sees without moving, and are best used for landscape photography or tight locations where you cannot back up. They also tend to have more depth of field than longer lenses. Wide-angle lenses can cause distortion if you are very close to your subject or place your subject near the edges of the frame.

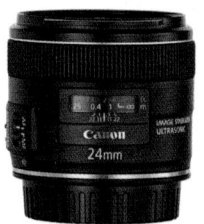

TELEPHOTO

A telephoto lens can have a focal length of 200mm or more—a great choice for most wildlife and sports photographers who can't be close to their subjects. With less depth of field, a telephoto lens may not include much detail around your subject and the background may appear soft (out of focus). This effect also makes a telephoto lens a nice choice for portraits, but be aware you will likely need some distance between you and your subject.

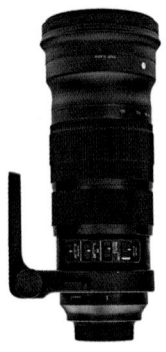

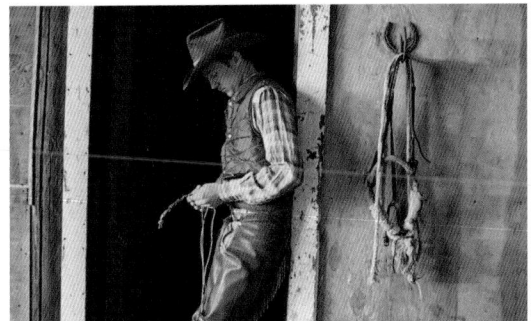

Standard lens

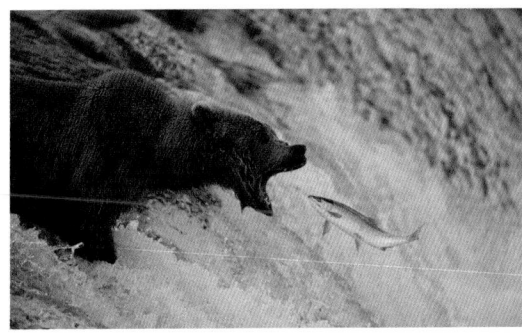

Telephoto lens

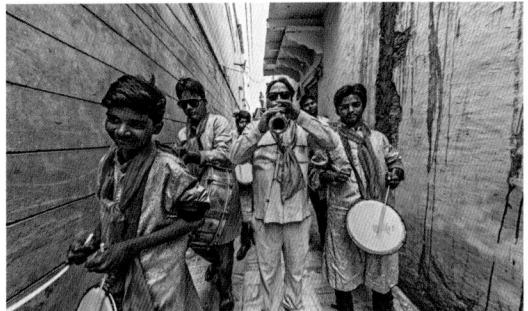

Wide-angle lens

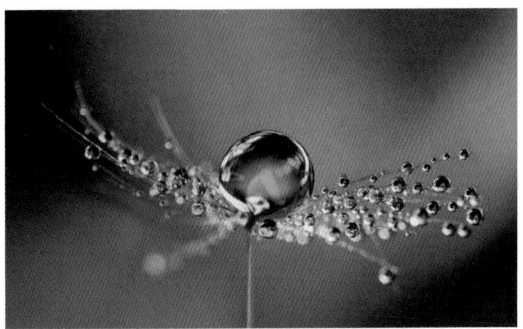

Macro lens

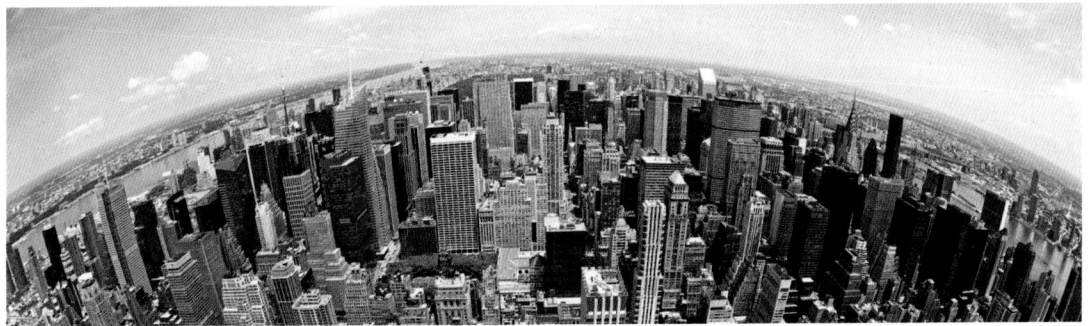

Fish-eye lens

PRO TIP — FIXED VS. ZOOM LENSES

A prime, or fixed, lens is one with a single focal length—meaning you won't be able to use the lens to zoom. Instead you'll have to "zoom with your feet," or move your body into a position that yields the result you want. A zoom lens has a range of focal lengths—meaning it's a bunch of lenses in one. A 24–70mm zoom is a good workhorse lens. This lens sees as much as the human eye, and then some. It's the lens you'll likely use the most. Keep in mind that, while fixed lenses are cheaper, zoom lenses are far more convenient, especially if you'd like to carry only one.

VIEWFINDER

On a digital camera, the viewfinder is where you frame your shot. It also provides a lot of information to consider as you compose.

The optical viewfinder and liquid-crystal display (LCD) on the back of your camera are useful tools, whether you're using them to compose, check your settings, or review your images. At first glance, the display may look confusing, but it's full of useful information. The display may vary from one camera brand to another, but a typical viewfinder or LCD screen might show you information like this:

1 METERING

Shows where the camera's exposure meter is reading light within the frame.

2 SHUTTER SPEED

Shows your current shutter speed. Here, 125 means 1/125 of a second, a midrange shutter speed.

3 APERTURE OR F-STOP NUMBER

Shows your current aperture setting. This viewfinder says f/5.6, a relatively large aperture.

4 EXPOSURE COMPENSATION SCALE

Reports the camera meter's reading of available light. Tick marks toward the plus side mean the camera thinks the image will be overexposed. Tick marks toward the minus side mean the camera thinks it will be underexposed.

5 NUMBER OF FRAMES

This is the number of photographs you have remaining before your memory card is full.

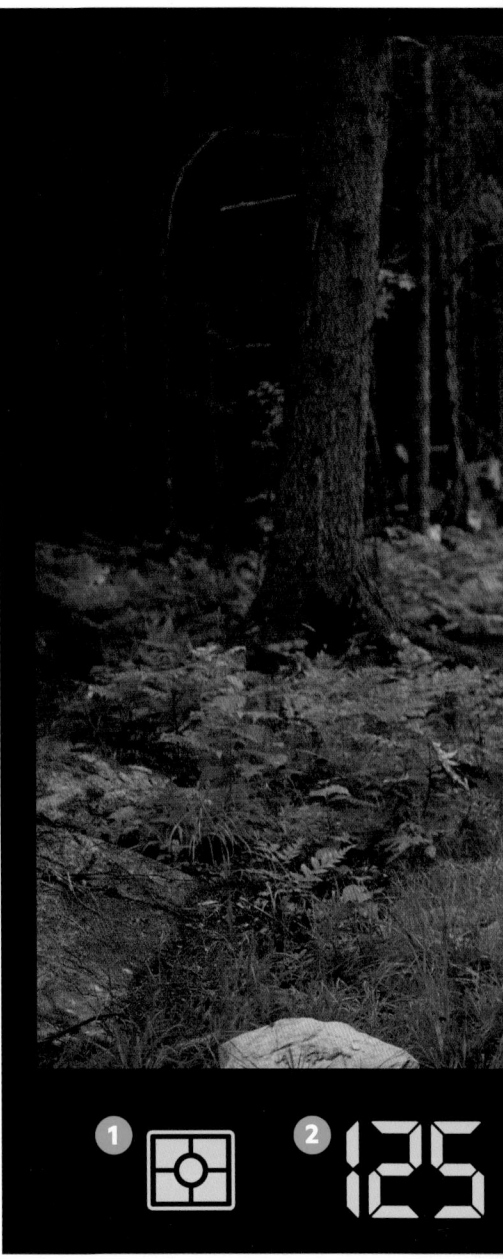

FOR MORE ON EXPOSURE, SEE PAGE 64.

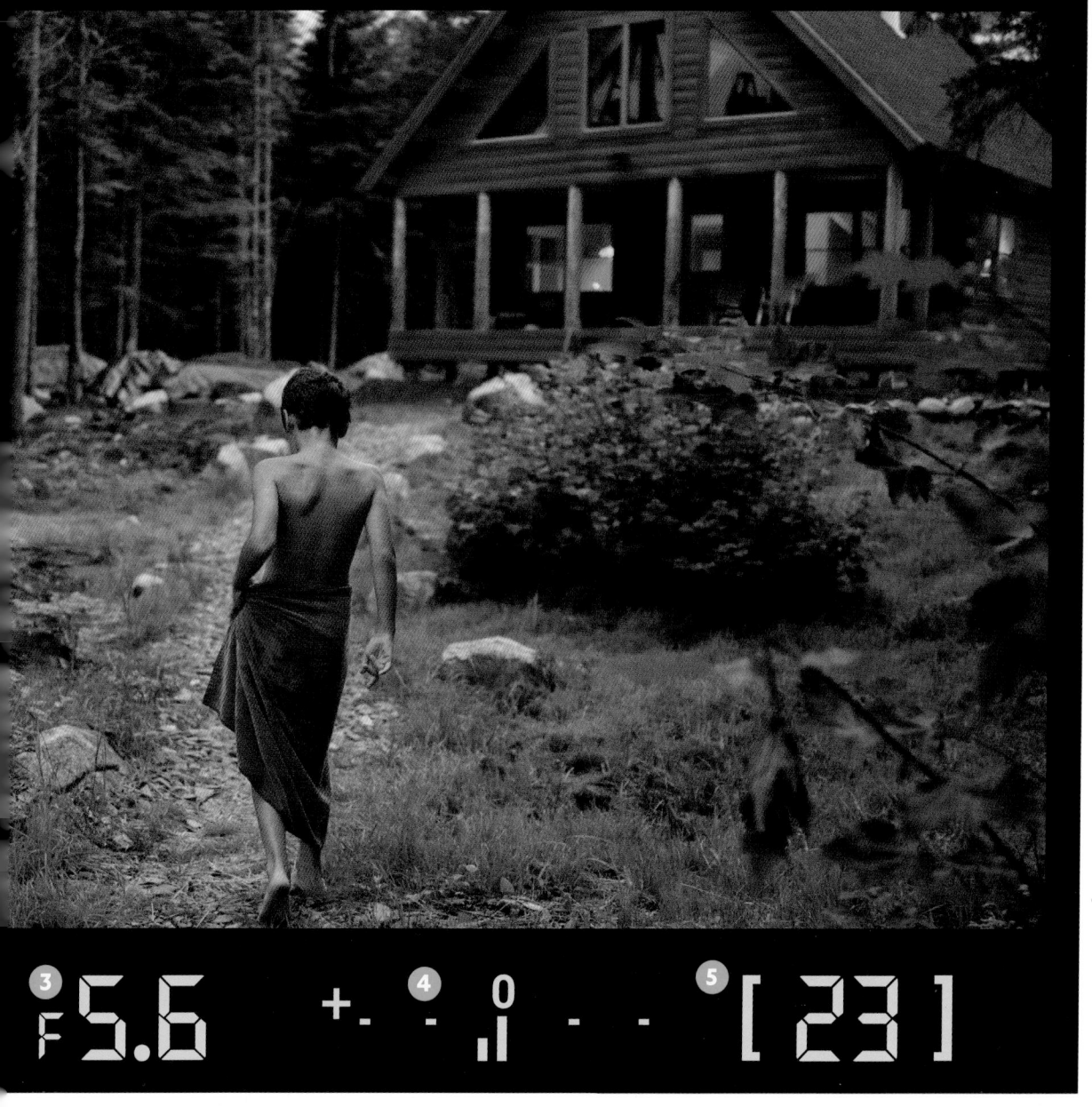

A boy walks up the path to a log cabin after a lake swim at dusk in northern Maine.

STABILIZATION TOOLS

Keeping your camera steady is critical when using a slow shutter speed. You can get creative with long exposures if you know how to keep your camera perfectly still.

You may notice that you cannot always hold the camera as steady as you'd like. There are all sorts of work-arounds to get a steady shot, like leaning against a doorway, finding protection from the wind, holding your breath while pressing the shutter, or using a beanbag to prop up the lens on a table. Some lenses have stabilization technology built in. A tripod is a simple tool that essentially bolts your camera to the ground—very useful, but also cumbersome to carry. Look around for stationary objects that can help you keep a steady hand without adding to your load.

WHEN YOU'LL NEED TO STABILIZE

Common situations in which you'll need a camera stabilizer are when shooting in low light, when you're focused tightly on a dis-tant subject, or when you're choosing to blur the action of moving subjects like water, traffic, or carnival rides.

In low light, your aperture will be a little wider, or your shutter speed will be a little slower. Without a stabilizing tool, you run the risk of unintentionally blurry photos.

If you're focused tightly on a subject with little depth of field from your telephoto or macro lens, even the smallest movement can result in a loss of sharpness in your final image. Stabilizing the camera lets you concentrate on getting just what you want in focus.

If you want to experiment with longer exposures, stabilization is essential. Keeping your camera totally still will help maintain sharpness in the background while allowing a moving subject—like a waterfall or a lit carnival ride at night—to appear blurred with movement.

PRO TIP WHEN YOU NEED SUPPORT

- You're on vacation in the mountains when you see a bighorn sheep on top of a faraway cliff. When you grab your telephoto lens, connect it to a tripod, or steady it atop a boulder so your shaking hands won't prevent you from focusing on the subject.

- Your friend asks you to photograph his Ultimate Frisbee game. By using a monopod, you're able to easily move up and down the sidelines and maintain a steady camera to capture the action shots.

- You're photographing your child in a running race. You'd like to illustrate her speed, while keeping the rest of the track in focus. Stabilize the camera with a tripod or by resting it on a railing of the stands. The scene will be in focus, but your fast-footed daughter will create a blur as she runs past.

TYPES OF TRIPODS

If you decide a tripod is for you, these are three common types, all handy at different times.

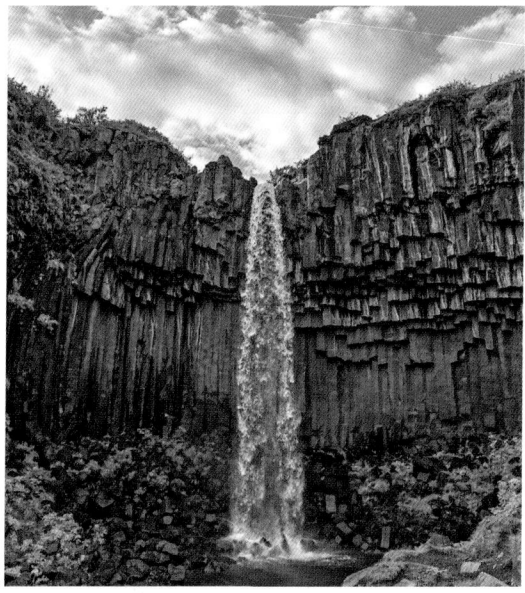

A fast shutter speed freezes the water in motion at Iceland's Svartifoss Waterfall.

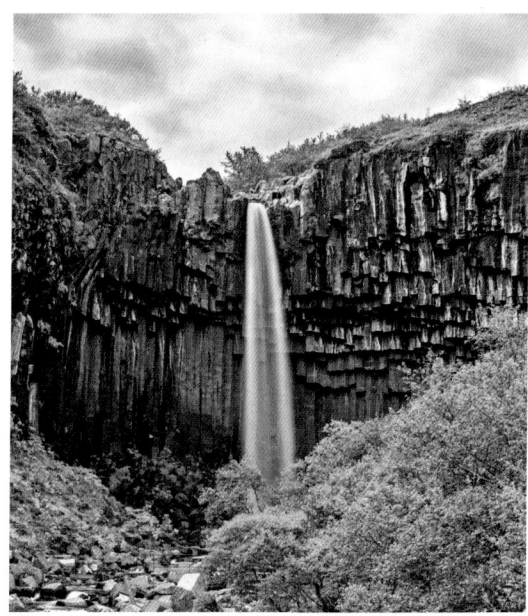

A slower shutter speed blurs the movement of the waterfall.

STANDARD TRIPOD

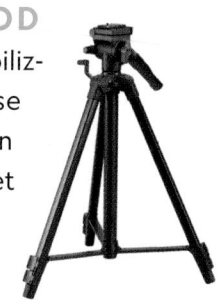

These three-legged stabilizers are really all-purpose tools. The legs are often adjustable, so you can set them based on the terrain. You'll want to purchase one sturdy enough to hold your heaviest camera and lens—but not one so heavy you won't want to carry it.

MINI-TRIPOD

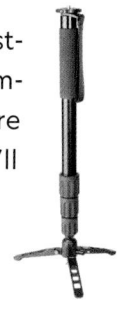

A small tripod can be useful to carry in your bag when you don't want to lug a regular tripod around. It can be great for macro photography, when you need to get really close to a small object, like a flower or an insect. Some have bendable legs, which make them more versatile for getting into tight spaces. Be sure to investigate the weight a mini can handle—not all of them can support a DSLR camera body with lens.

MONOPOD

A monopod has a single, adjustable leg. It helps steady the camera while also giving you more flexibility in movement. You'll often see sports photographers using monopods on the sidelines.

LIGHTING TOOLS

Light is one of the most important factors in photography, whether you're capturing natural light or introducing it yourself. These tools can help when the natural light isn't perfect, and can give your photographs an extra edge.

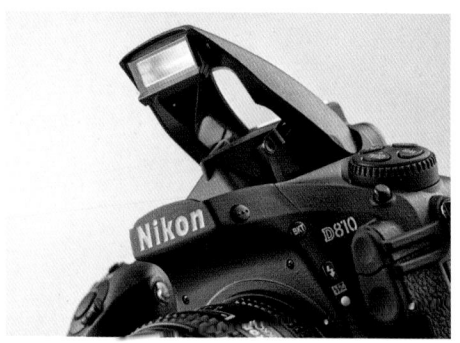

BUILT-IN FLASH >>

Most compact and DSLR cameras come with a built-in flash unit. These are small and relatively low-powered. In my opinion, this little flash will only cause you trouble, adding dreaded red-eye to your photographs, and making them look more like snapshots. I say, leave it off.

<< EXTERNAL FLASH

If you want more control over the power and direction of your light, you can use an external flash. These units have more power than a built-in flash, and you aren't limited to having the light right above your lens. Moving the flash off the camera avoids the red-eye effect, and can help soften the light, making it look more natural.

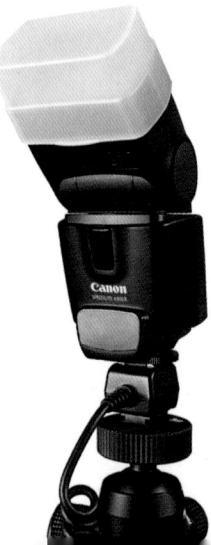

FLASH DIFFUSER >>

This is a simple light modifier that attaches to an external flash unit. It's designed to spread out the concentrated bursts of light that come from a powerful flash. With a modifier, you get softer, more even light, eliminating heavy shadows that can result from direct lighting. You can fashion a makeshift diffuser by wrapping a tissue around your flash, keeping it in place with a rubber band.

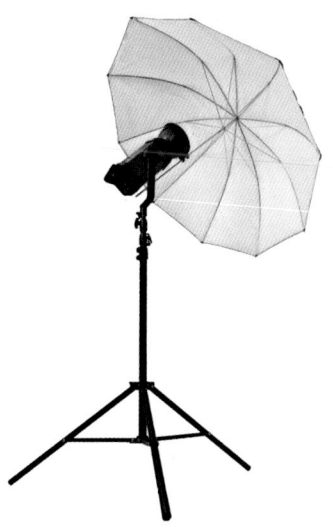

<< UMBRELLA

By bouncing the flash into an umbrella, you enlarge the size of your light source and produce much softer light on your subjects. This is ideal for portraits. You can get a similar effect by bouncing your flash off a reflector, white poster board, or even a white wall or ceiling. You can also use a translucent umbrella and have the light pass through it (rather than bounce off it). Both bouncing and diffusing work to soften the light in slightly different ways.

REFLECTOR >>

A reflector is an object used to reflect light onto a subject. Although you can buy a tool for this purpose, you can also use what's available to you, like a wall or even a T-shirt. Keep in mind that the color of the object will impact the reflected light. White reflectors bounce neutral light, while silver yields a cool tone and gold gives a warm tone.

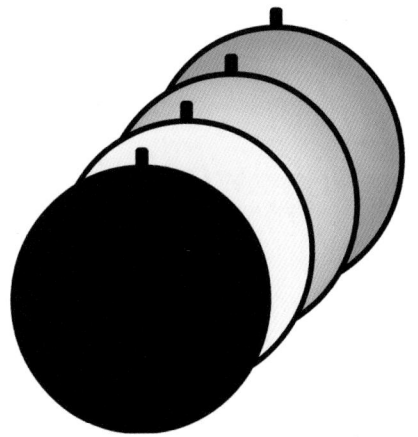

<< LENS FILTERS

In general, it's good practice to have a filter on your lens to protect it from dust and scratches. Filters can also impact the image. A polarizing filter will darken skies and reduce glare off of reflective surfaces like water. Filters may also impact your exposure, so choose wisely. These days, most filter effects can be applied relatively easily in your digital darkroom after the fact, so don't sweat it if a filter isn't in your budget. More on postproduction of your photos later.

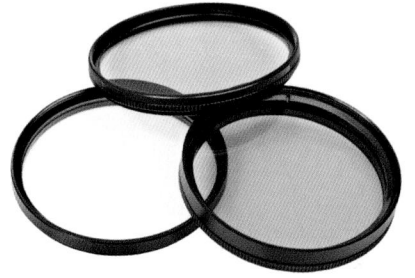

OTHER GEAR

Beyond the standard lenses and lights, some accessories can make your work easier. But don't get bogged down with so much gear that you don't want to go make pictures! These accessories are optional, and you should select only the ones that complement your style and goals.

EXTRA MEMORY CARDS >>

Few things are more frustrating than coming across a great scene and having no room on your card to make more pictures. Depending on your camera, you'll need CompactFlash (CF) or Secure Digital (SD) cards. Many cameras are using microSD and other kinds of media cards as well. Buy the right card for your camera, along with a compatible card reader for downloading your images to your computer. Always format the cards to your camera in advance, and keep them in a warm, dry place.

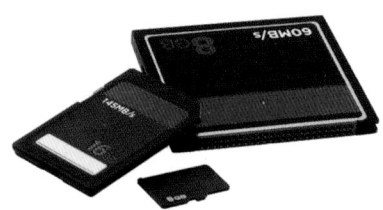

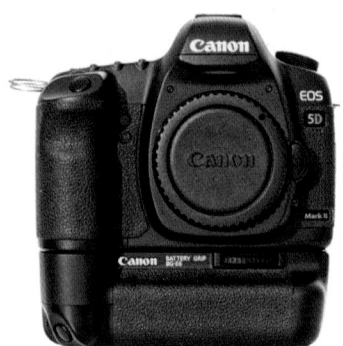

<< BATTERY GRIP

This attaches to the bottom of your DSLR camera. It provides space for more battery power so you can shoot longer, and has a secondary grip with a shutter release, giving you a more ergonomic feel when shooting vertical images. It also adds considerable size and weight to your camera, so consider your needs before you get one.

LENS HOOD >>

If you've ever seen a circular light flare in a photo, it was caused by light hitting the glass of your lens at an angle. Adding a lens hood can prevent this effect, but so will using your hand to block the sun, or adjusting your stance slightly. I misplaced my lens hood years ago and never replaced it. It's a useful tool, but you can get by without it.

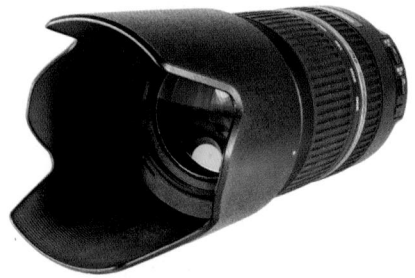

GEAR BAG >>

You'll want an efficient way to transport all your gear. There are lots of great options for carrying your equipment, from backpacks to side bags, harnesses, and photo vests. Go to a camera store to try out all the possibilities and see how they feel. Think about how and where you'll be shooting, and how accessible you need each item to be.

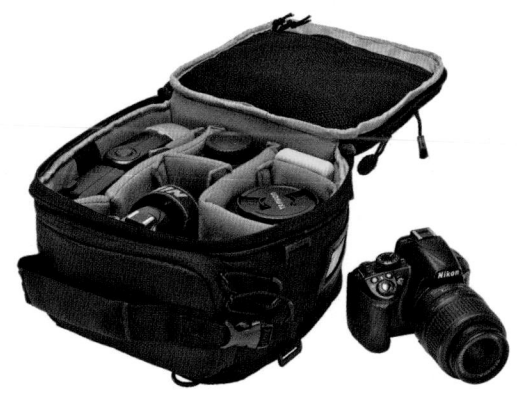

<< REMOTE SHUTTER RELEASE

This is a way to take a picture without actually touching the camera. It's especially useful with a tripod, when pressing the shutter release button might shake an otherwise steady camera, or if you can't be there to push the button at all, as in the case of self-portraits. Remote releases can attach to your camera with a cable, or they can be wireless, using radio, Wi-Fi, or Bluetooth signals. If you want to use a remote shutter release, make sure to find one that is compatible with your camera. Before making this investment, check out your camera's self-timer option. Propping it up on a table and setting the timer can often help you do the same job.

SPARE BATTERIES >>

You never want to run out of battery power while you're out shooting, so carry plenty of fresh batteries for your camera as well as for your external flash. If your camera battery is rechargeable, consider buying an extra so that at least one is always charged and ready to go.

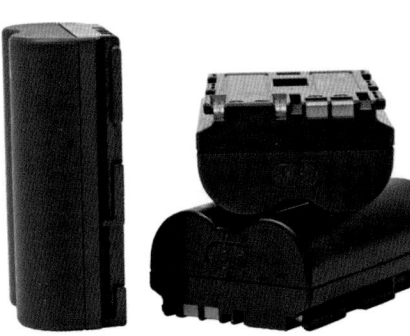

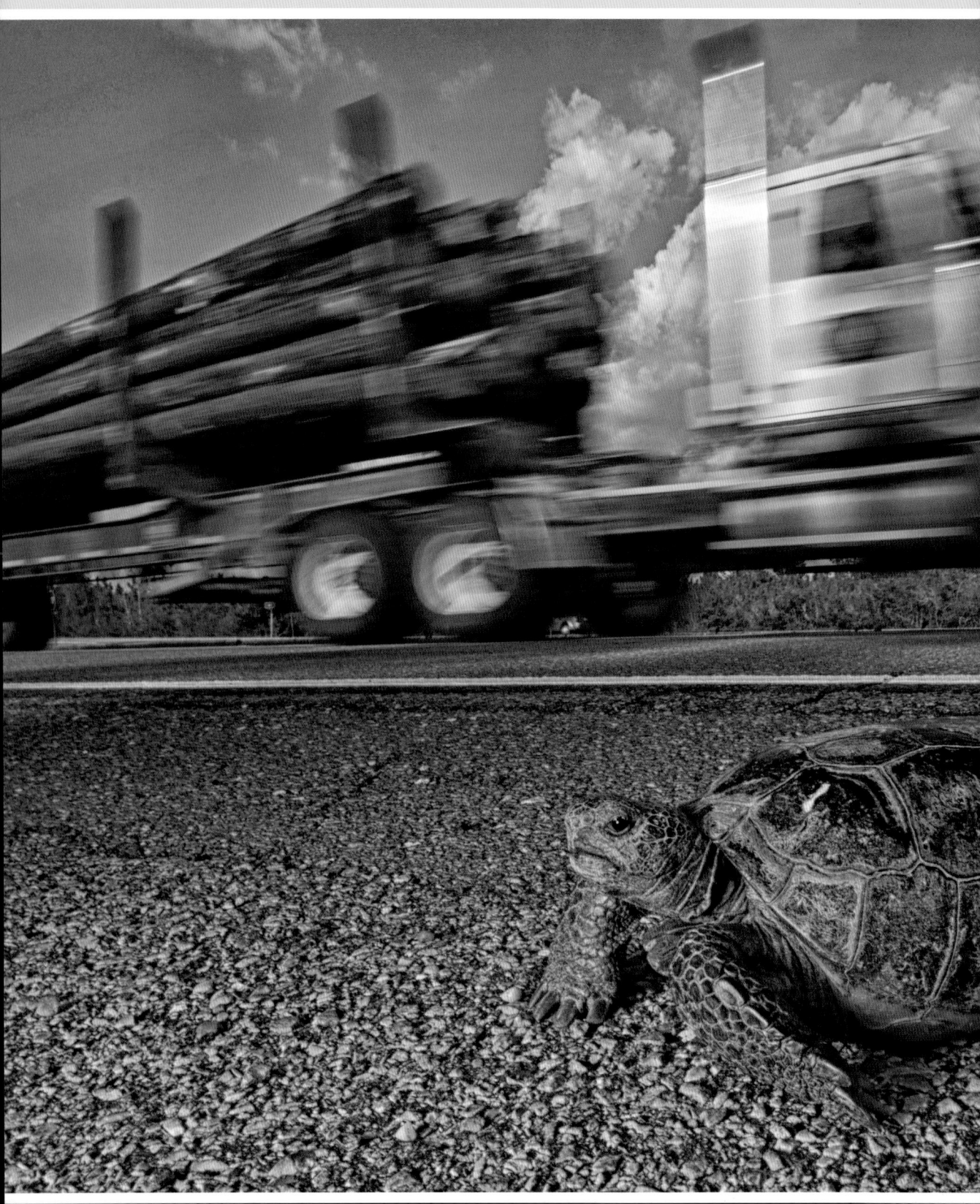

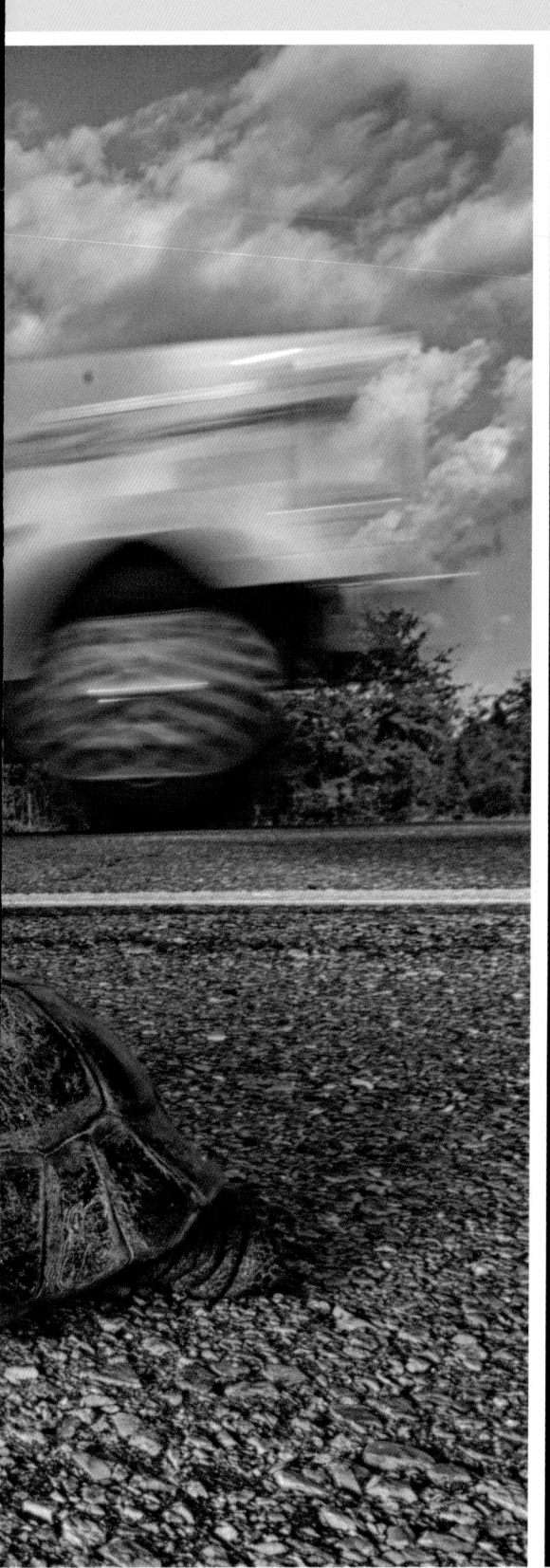

SLOW AND STEADY

I photographed this gopher tortoise along a four-lane highway near Wiggins, Mississippi. I wanted to illustrate the risk of the journey and have this image say something about the threats facing this species. Fortunately, he wasn't the fastest guy in the world, so I was able to wait until action came into the frame I'd envisioned. I took a number of photos as different cars drove by, but the best frame happened when a logging truck passed, which spoke to the fact that loss of forest habitat poses a serious threat to this species.

GETTING PERSPECTIVE I used a wide-angle lens because I knew I wanted to include the hectic road in the background and provide context for this tortoise's position. I got down low, on the tortoise's level, which made him larger in the frame and allows the viewer to see the threat of traffic from the tortoise's perspective.

IN MOTION Notice that the truck is blurred while the tortoise is still. To achieve that, I set my shutter speed slow enough so that anything fast-moving would blur. I also used a fill flash, which helped the tortoise stand out against the road, and, at the same time, froze his movement in the frame.

GIVE IT MEANING Traffic, logging, and development are all major contributing factors to the decline of the gopher tortoise population, so including those elements in a single photograph helps tell a more powerful story.

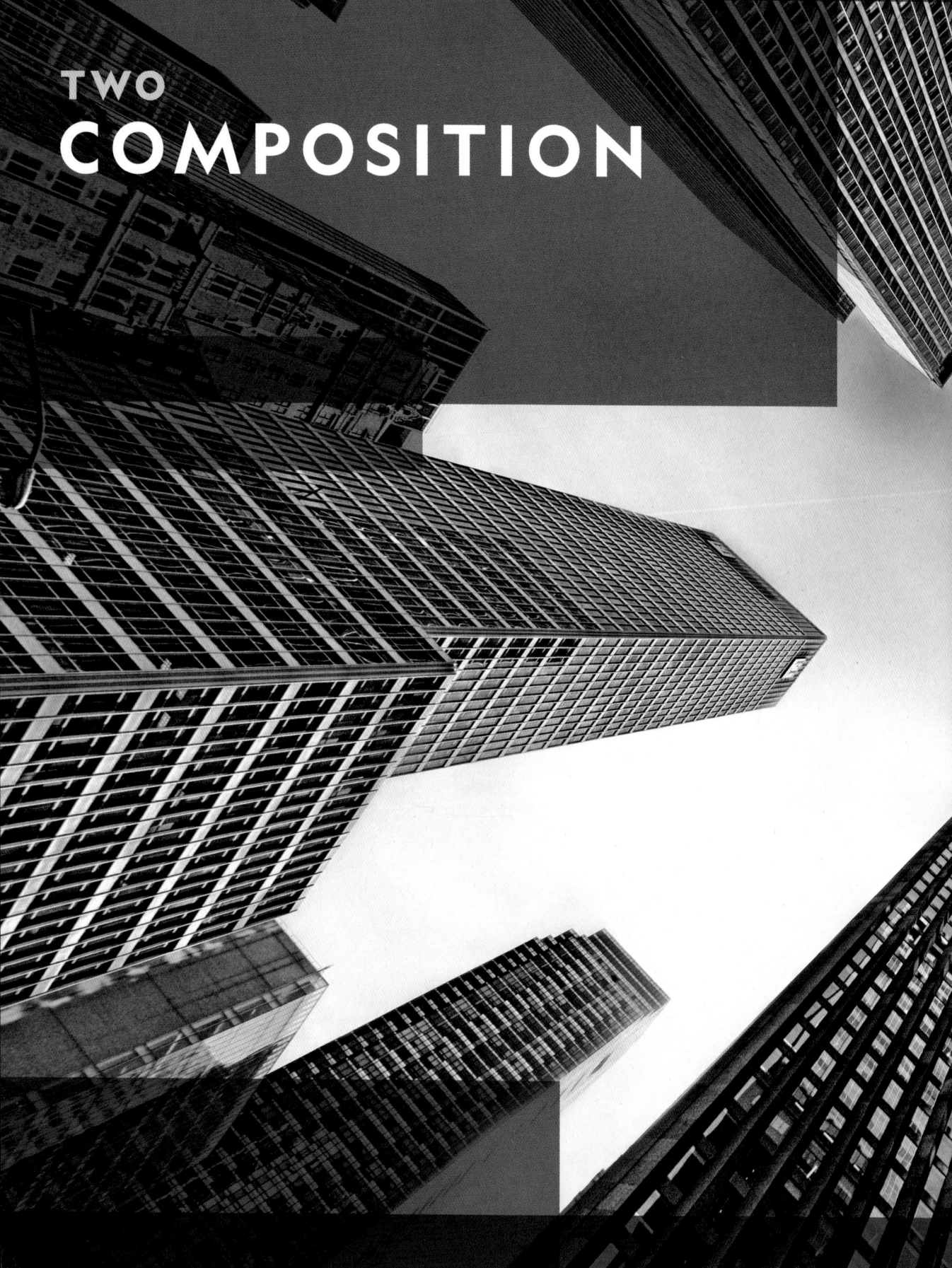

TWO
COMPOSITION

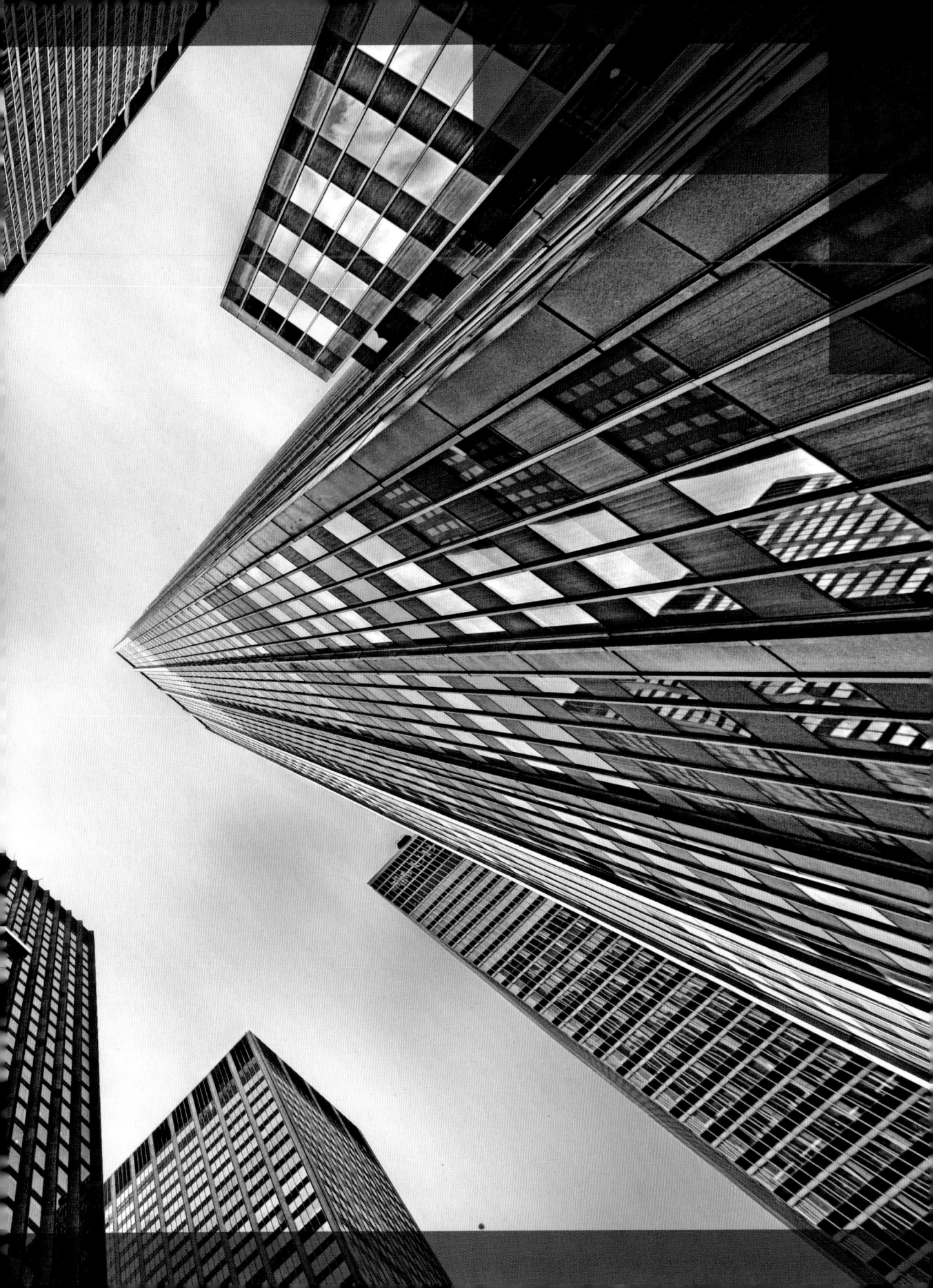

CONSIDERING COMPOSITION

Seeing well is the key to creating captivating images. If you master your camera's settings but don't learn how to see well, you won't make good photographs. Seeing well starts with the subject and moves out from there, with assessment of the light, the background, and the space around the subject. Each element works separately and in harmony with the others to create compelling imagery. This is the heart of composition.

Successful photographs bring order to chaos. Many elements—light, focus, and exposure—must come together to tell a story. It takes patience, thought, and honest self-critique to learn how to make well-composed photos.

Sometimes your subject matter will be so captivating, such as a baby panda bear or a cliff diver, that it will be almost impossible to mess up the composition. But more often, photographers are trying to make the everyday, the mundane, appear beautiful and compelling. That's when creative composition can make all the difference.

In this chapter, we'll go over techniques that can strengthen a photo's composition when employed correctly—everything from framing the shot to layering the subjects in it. As we go along, there's a helpful maxim to keep in mind: If it's in your photograph, it's either working for you or against you.

This foraging whooping crane is framed by the tall grass of its habitat in southern Wisconsin.

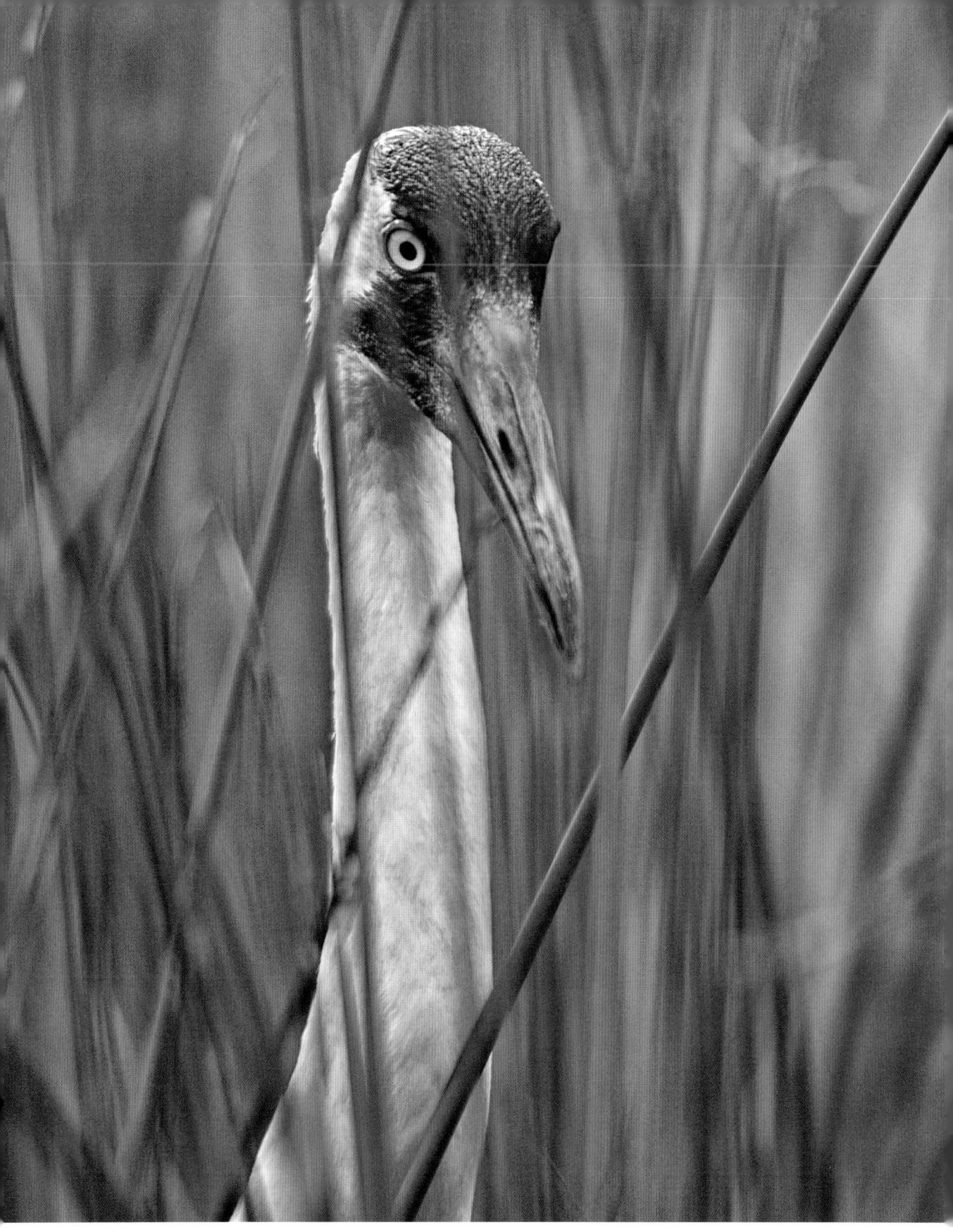

THE RULE OF THIRDS

This basic rule can help you balance your composition. By aligning your subject and background elements along a simple grid of nine squares, you can add interest and visual tension to an image.

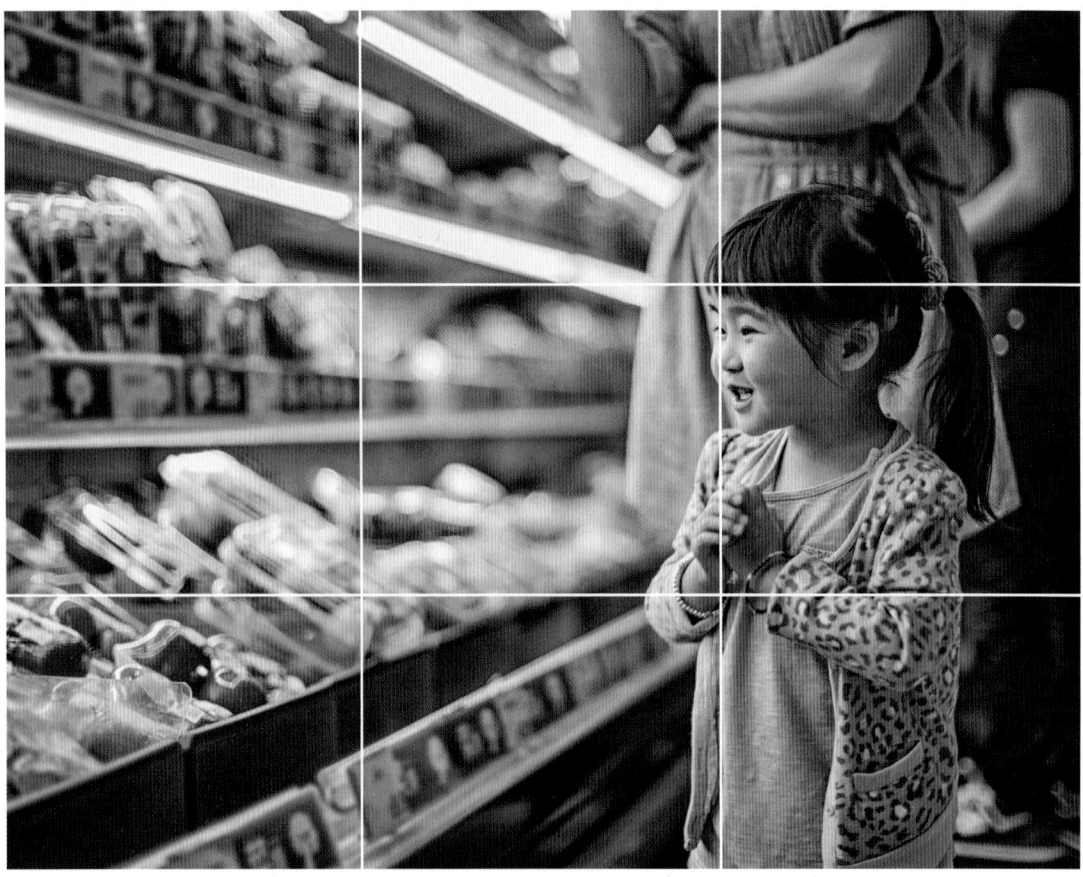

Dividing your photo into nine equal parts can help guide you to a strong spot to place your subject. Most cameras can superimpose a grid like this, to help you place the subject where the lines intersect. In time, you'll learn to see this way on your own.

Imagine drawing a tic-tac-toe board over a photograph and adjusting the placement of your subject to be along any of the lines or their intersections. This is the rule of thirds, and it's a compositional technique that goes back hundreds of years. Not only does using the rule of thirds make your photo more interesting to the eye, but it can also leave room for context and dramatic tension.

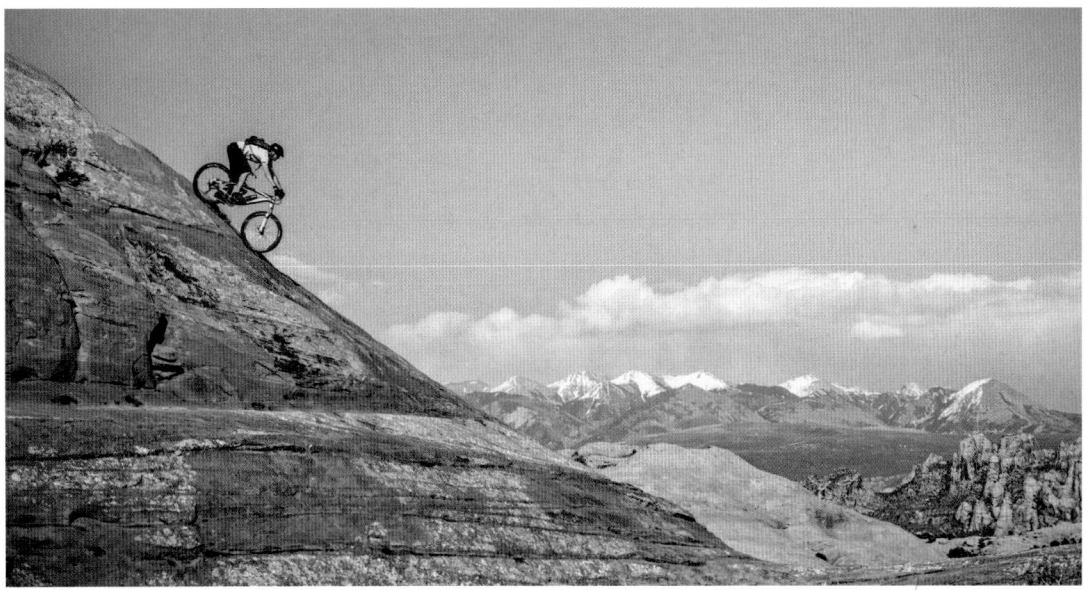

A mountain biker seeks thrills on a slick rock trail near Moab, Utah. The rule of thirds provides balance to this photo, providing context (the mountains) to the subject (the rider). The negative space in the front of him gives him "room to travel," which adds to the tension.

CREATING BALANCE

As you move the subject of your photograph off-center, pay attention to what else comes into the frame. You can create balance by having a counterpoint in an opposite section. But always ask yourself: Is this working for me or against me?

Imagine that you're photographing a friend in a cobblestone alleyway. When you look through the viewfinder and align her with the top right section of the frame, a trash can comes into view in the bottom left. You have a counterpoint, but it's not very pretty.

But if you reframe to have your friend in the lower right portion of the image, a hanging basket of flowers comes into view in the top left. Now you have a much more interesting photo—you have color and con-text from the alley she is exploring. As you experiment with the rule of thirds, remember that everything in the picture should be there because you want it to be. And, as with most rules, sometimes it's meant to be broken—if your most compelling shot doesn't align with this grid, that's OK, too.

ASSIGNMENT: TAKE A WALK

Photograph your neighborhood using the rule of thirds. How can you position a subject in different parts of the frame? Then, work backward, building a photograph from the background forward: Find a scene, compose, then place your subject within it. Experiment with tension, context, and balance. Study each photograph to see how the elements work with each other.

FOCAL POINTS

The focal point of your image is the heart of the story. Whether a single subject or a broader scene, what you choose to feature becomes the visual focus of your photograph.

A photograph should have an obvious point of interest. When our eyes roam around the frame directionless, the picture falls flat. Much like a written story, a photograph should have a starting point. Think about the information you want to include in the image and consider the rule of thirds. If you place your subject along the grid, how many other things can you include in the frame to tell your story? It is possible to include too much information in your photograph, though. If you suspect that your focal point is getting lost, ask yourself: What can I do to make the subject stand out?

KEEP IT SIMPLE

If your subject is lost in a busy scene, get closer. If you have a prime lens, zoom with your feet, physically moving your body closer to the subject. Or try a longer lens to grab your subject from a distance. Getting closer will help eliminate background ele-

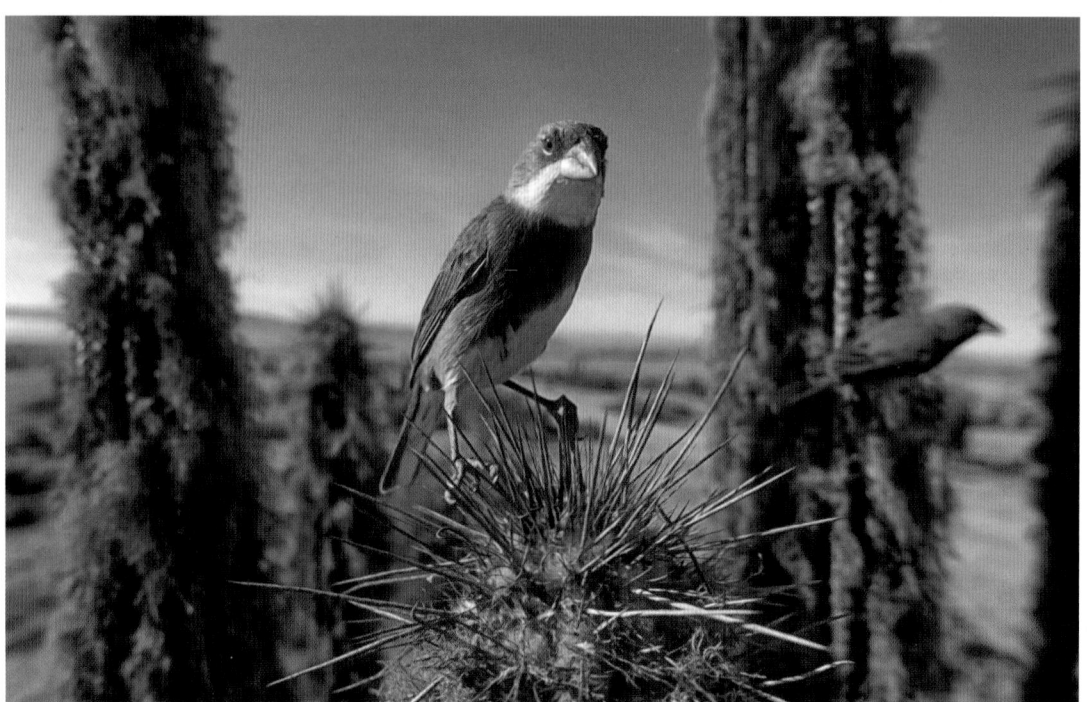

A diuca finch perches on the thorns of a cactus. Using a shallow depth of field to soften the background makes it clear that the focus of this photo is the bird. The cacti in the background frame it nicely, further defining it as our focal point.

FOR MORE ON FOCAL LENGTH, SEE PAGE 68.

ments from your field of view that may not contribute to the story of your image.

KEEP IT CLEAN

Another trick for ensuring that your subject is the focal point of the image is using negative (or empty) space. Scan the frame and be sure no elements overlap with the sub-ject in a way that confuses the eye. A simple adjustment of your position can often isolate your subject, allowing it to stand out.

As you play with focal points, keep asking yourself: Is it working for me or against me? Try a few different approaches to each image. You may be surprised by which version works best.

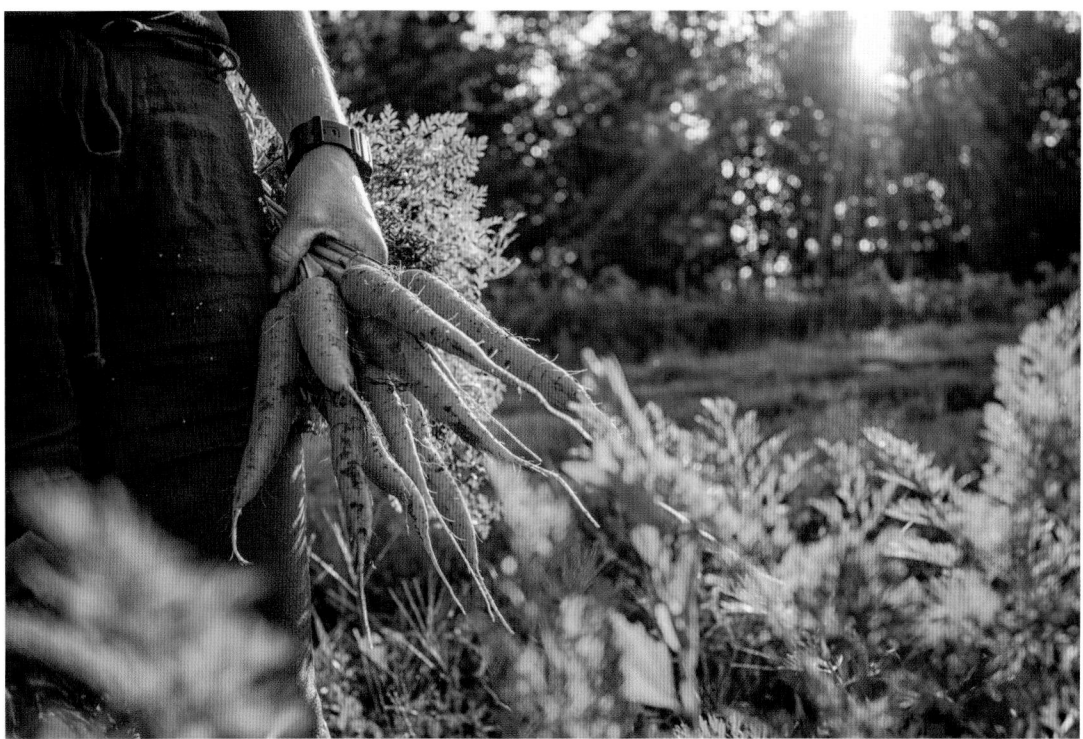

A farmer holds carrots she has just pulled from the ground. Their orange color makes them pop against a largely green frame, and negative space in the upper right corner keeps the image clean and simple.

PRO TIP | SHOOT MORE

The best way to improve your eye is to take a *lot* of photographs—many more than you think you need. With each shot, change something. Don't be afraid to take bad photos. Think of these as notes that will contribute to the making of an image with impact. When I shoot an assignment for *National Geographic*, only about a tenth of one percent of the photos I take end up published. A lot of what I shoot is experimental and exploratory in the moment. So if you shoot 1,000 photographs, and one turns out fantastic, you're on the right track.

BACKGROUND

While your subject is the focus of your photograph, it's important to pay attention to what's behind it. Use the background to add more details and context to your photographs.

Even with great light and a well-executed rule of thirds, a bad background can ruin a photograph. Conversely, a clean background can eliminate distractions and make your subject really stand out. Of course, an interesting, layered photograph is what many photographers crave. This takes lots of practice to achieve.

BUILDING A BACKGROUND

Unless something amazing is happening that you have to capture right away, take a moment to consider background before you begin shooting. Think about building your background one piece at a time. Looking through your viewfinder, take note of everything in the frame. Is there anything going on that viewers won't be able to ignore? Common problems include unsightly objects that clutter the image and don't add to the story, or placement issues, like a telephone pole that seems to extend out of your subject's head.

If you find problem spots in your back-

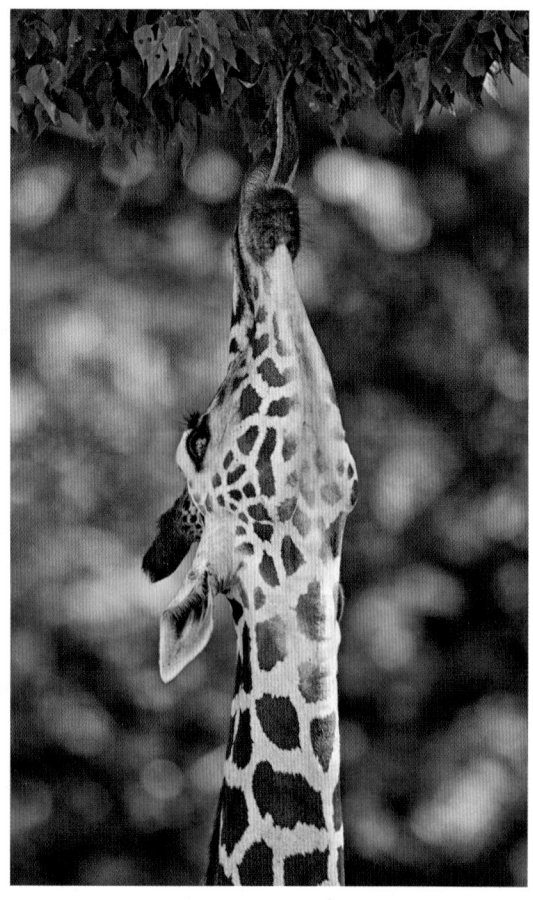

A soft, monochromatic background here allows us to focus closely on the giraffe (and its eating habits).

PRO TIP SOLVING VISUAL PROBLEMS

Always remember: If it's in your picture, it's either working for you or against you. Get creative as you figure out how to eliminate distracting elements from your photograph. Move your subject if possible, change your angle, change your perspective, change your lens, or move in closer. Try leaving a little space between subjects for a cleaner composition. If something is in your picture, it should be there because you want it, not because you couldn't solve the visual problem.

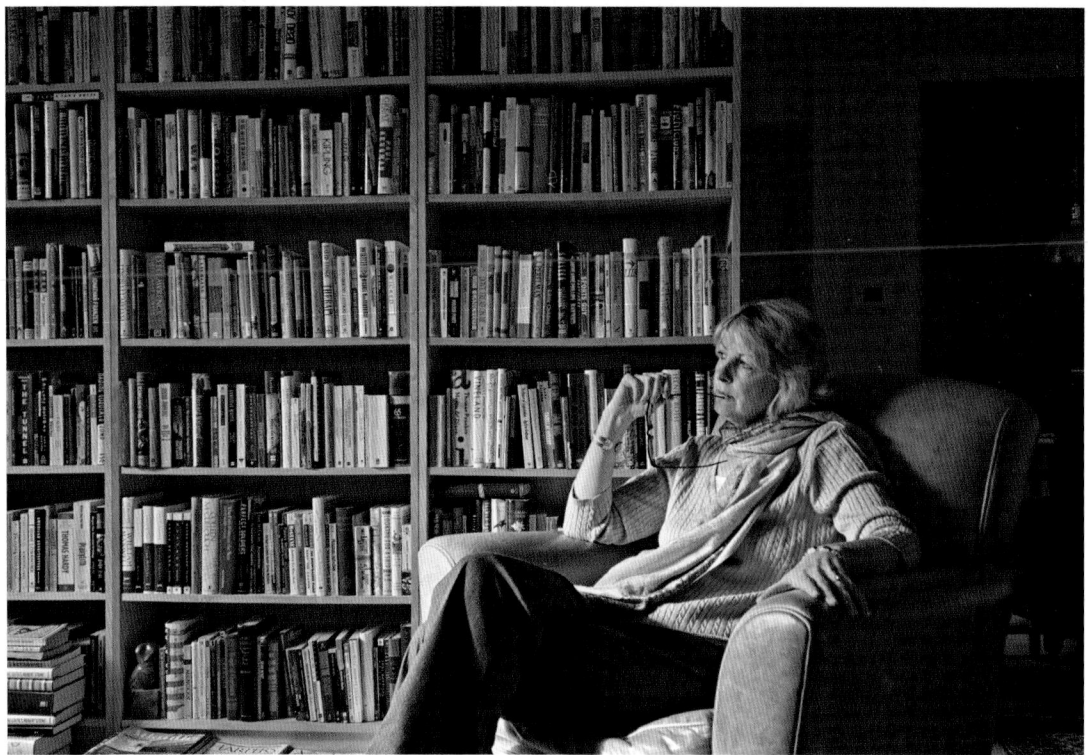

In this portrait of my wife, Kathy, the background is still in focus and provides visual interest and context. You can use backgrounds as texture to say something about your subject—perhaps that she loves to read.

ground, you can try a few things. First, change your position. Can you stand somewhere else so that the problem isn't visible? Or try a change of perspective. Kneeling, standing on something tall, or lying on the ground can often change what you see behind your subject.

Or try changing the background yourself. Close doors, move toys, hold branches out of the way—unless you're a photojournalist, in which case adjusting the background is considered unethical.

USE WHAT YOU HAVE

Consider how you might use the natural elements around you to your advantage.

Natural screens like smoke, fog, or dust can diffuse the intensity and harshness of the sun, and they can create a clean background, allowing your subject to stand out. Keep these in mind the next time you're photographing your kids watching fireworks, your neighbor driving his tractor down a dirt road, or a geyser erupting in a national park.

Existing elements can also add more information and context to a portrait. If you're photographing someone in her home, think about what your subject's surroundings say about her—you might want to feature an avid reader in front of a bookshelf or a gifted cook in the kitchen.

PERSPECTIVE

The angle of a photograph can say a lot about your subject and how you want to portray it. Think about what your perspective adds to an image, and don't be afraid to try out some unusual approaches to help tell the story more effectively.

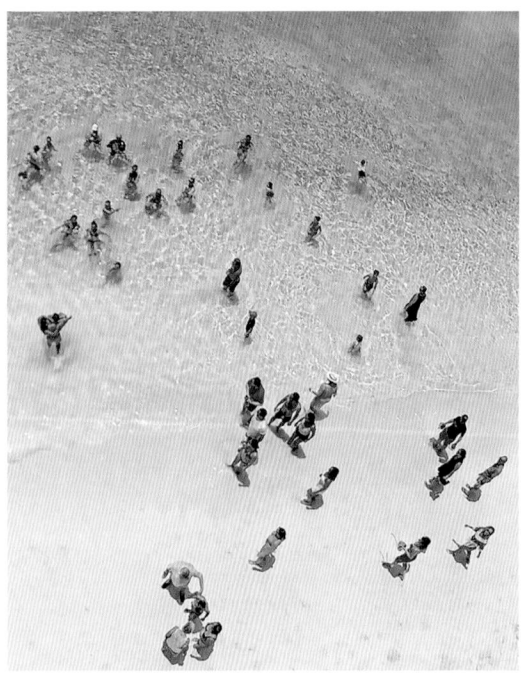 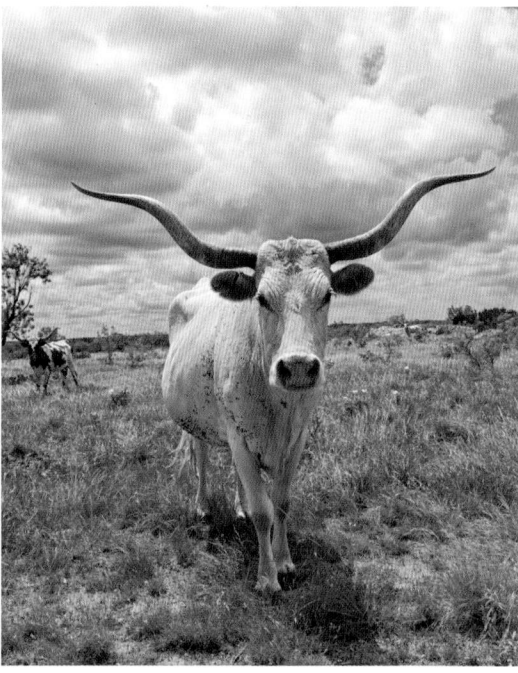

Looking down on a tropical beach from a high-rise hotel window makes the swimmers look like tiny creatures gathering at the water's edge in the Bahamas (left). Framing this Texas longhorn from just below eye level puts the head and horns above the horizon, giving it a powerful, imposing feel (right).

Ever been told that you need a little perspective? As in life, getting a new perspective in photography can really change how you see things. When we talk about perspective, two meanings come to mind. First is the technical definition: Perspective is how we present three-dimensional objects in a two-dimensional photograph. Second: Perspective is the way we look at things—the experiences in life that influence the way we view the world, and the pictures we make of it.

LOOK AROUND

Pay attention to the little things in your daily life during your commute or while you're out on a walk. What scenes capture your attention and imagination? It doesn't always have to be something special, like a brilliant sunset, a new baby, or a delicious

Set up a scene where you'll be able to photograph from different perspectives. Move all the way around, above, and below your subject, shooting from as many angles as possible. As you change position, how does it affect what's in the frame? How does the story in the photograph change?

meal. Try photographing anything that catches your eye, just for the sake of practice. You might be surprised by the beauty you find in ordinary things.

Finding interesting perspective is all about angles. How can you change your position relative to your subject? How does the picture feel different when you lie on your belly or stand on a chair? Pick a room in your house that has potential for a good background. Get a 360-degree look through your viewfinder. Where's the best light? What elements in the room add context to your image?

After establishing your vantage point, get a friend or family member to enter the frame. Practice shooting at eye level, from up above, and from down below. If you change your perspective, you may get some unique photographs out of the exercise.

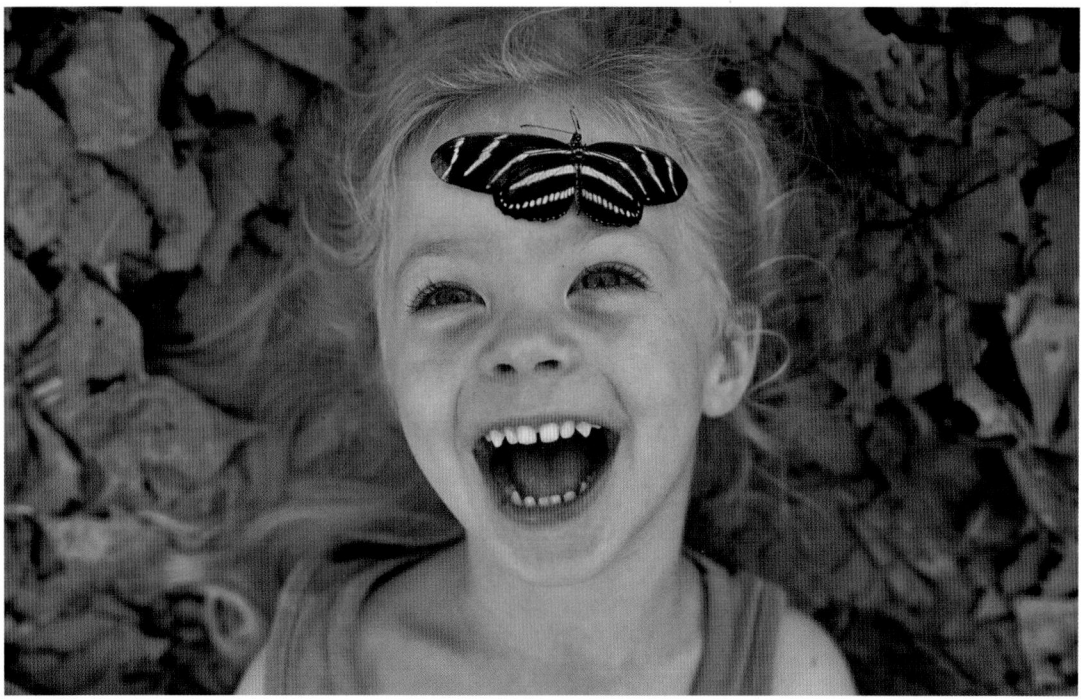

A butterfly alights on my daughter Ellen's face at the Lincoln Children's Zoo. The tight framing and vertical angle make for a simple but layered picture that feels intimate and personal. We'll talk about layering in the next section.

LAYERING

Layering elements in the foreground, middle ground, and background of your image can add depth, interest, and context.

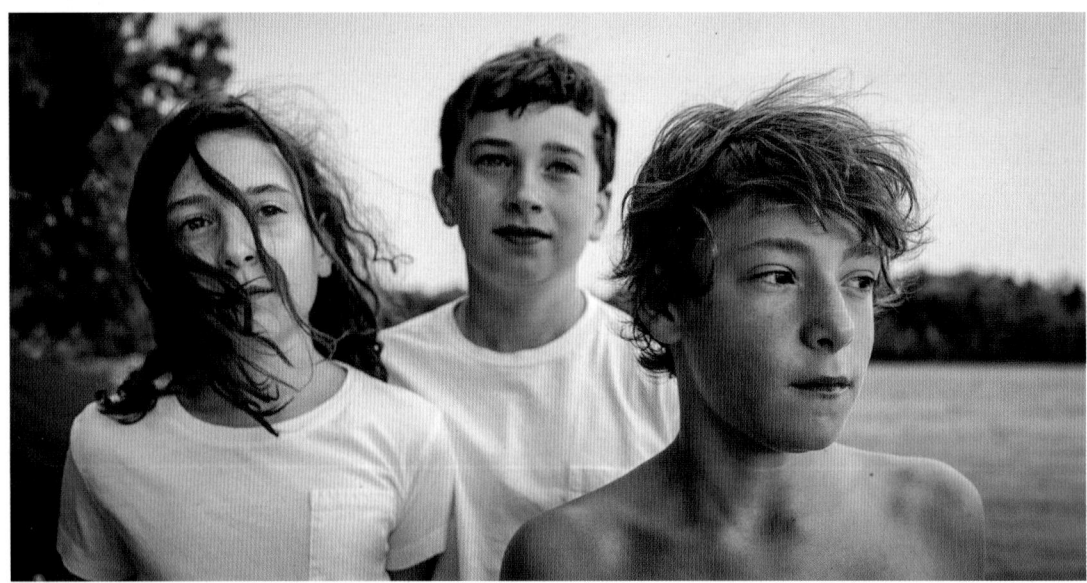

These three kids form natural layers in the image. Their eyes give us a strong focal point as they are looking to something beyond the frame. Starting in the back, the eyes lead us from one face to the next, and out into the world they see.

Once you've got the hang of backgrounds and perspective, you can start thinking about adding layers to your photographs. This means there are interesting elements in the foreground, middle ground, and background. Layering can add depth to your photograph and give context to the subject. As a result, the viewer lingers on the photo a little longer, absorbing the entire story.

MATCHING ELEMENTS

What makes layering so difficult is that all the techniques you've learned should be executed well for each layer. Just like building your background, you should craft each layer, deciding what gets included and what should be in focus.

Layering is a useful tool for landscape photographs. If you're in a place with a well-known landmark, like the Golden Gate Bridge in San Francisco or the opera house in Sydney, including it in the background will help set the scene, even if that landmark isn't the main focus of your image.

One way to set up layers is through framing, a technique we'll talk about in the next lesson.

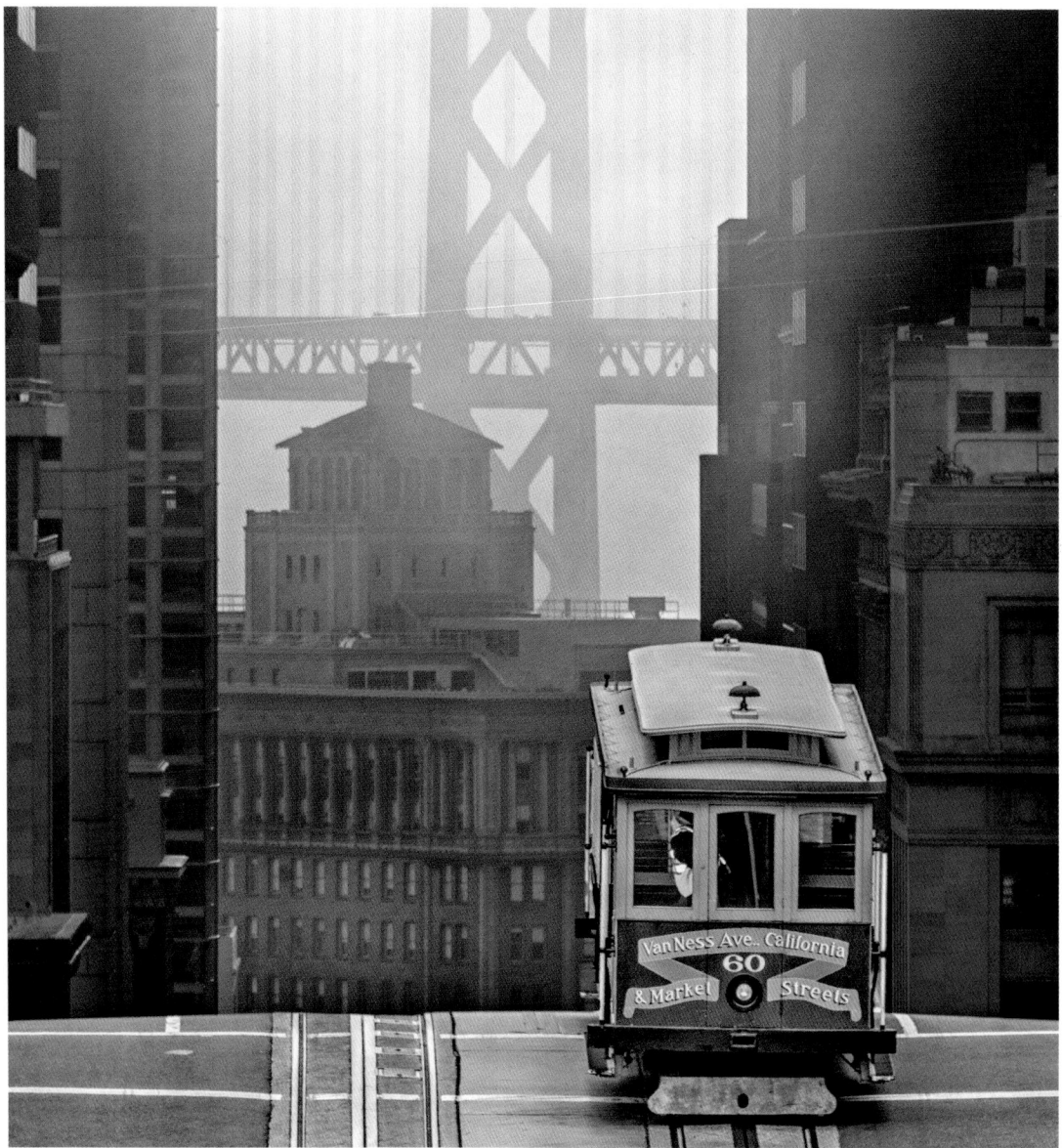

Beautifully crafted layers highlight a quintessential San Francisco scene: in the foreground, an iconic cable car; in the middle ground, the buildings of this city block; and looming in the background, the Bay Bridge.

PRACTICE

Good layering makes for complex, artful pictures, but it sure is tricky. If this all sounds intimidating, don't sweat it. These techniques take lots of practice to master. Don't be afraid to make mistakes. Review your work carefully, noting which images impact you most, and why. If you stick with it, you'll train your eye to note layers everywhere—a second nature way of seeing.

FRAMING

Creating a dynamic image within the frame of your photograph takes skillful use of the elements of good composition. Be sure that everything in your frame contributes to the image, and that there is balance between foreground and background components.

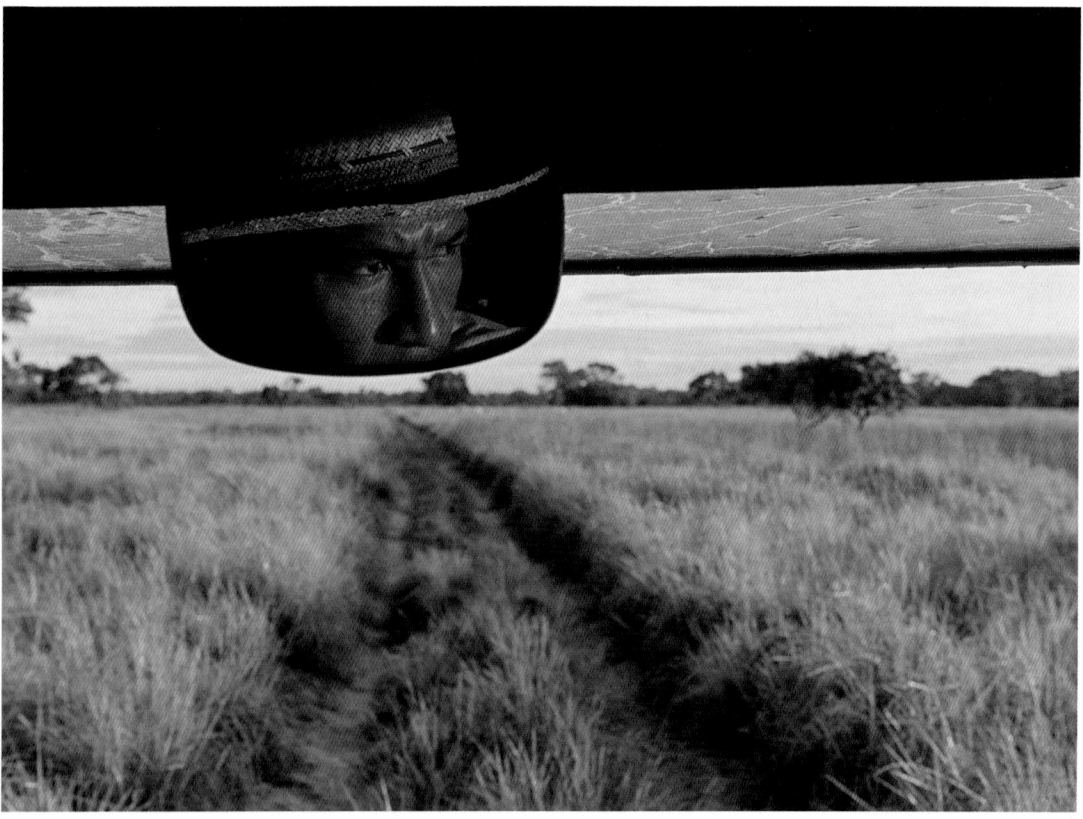

In this picture from Pantanal, Brazil, a wildlife spotter's face is framed in a rearview mirror. This technique allows us to see both forward and backward at the same time, framing the subject and the environment in which he works.

When you hear the word *frame* you probably think of a picture frame that displays art. But framing is also an element of compelling composition. Generally, framing refers to the scene within your shot—what you choose to include in a photo and what you choose to leave out. You want to fill your frame with interesting subject matter. Look to the edges to make sure that nothing is encroaching or being cut off in an unappealing way.

Most of us hang art inside frames, so it's an easy leap to start thinking about how to incorporate a frame *inside* your photograph. Within an image, a frame can be an object in the foreground that emphasizes the main subject. It's a layering technique that lends depth and focus to the picture.

FINDING FRAMES

Imagine that your kids are outside playing in the snow. As you photograph them through your window, step back and include the window in the foreground, as a frame to the scene. Think about what it adds to the story—the children are having fun outside, and you are watching, warm and dry inside. Will you suit up and join them, or whip up some hot chocolate for when they come back in? It's the story of a winter day in a frame. Isn't that cozy?

As you experiment, keep a few things in mind. First, the frame has to be part of the environment or setting, and it should add to the story. The frame should accentuate, not distract from, the subject. And consider focus: A frame should be sharp when it's part of the subject—the straight lines of architecture, for example, or a frame can be completely blurred when it's a suggestion of context—as in the case of our window on the winter day.

Some frames are obvious choices, like windows or doorways. But the world is full

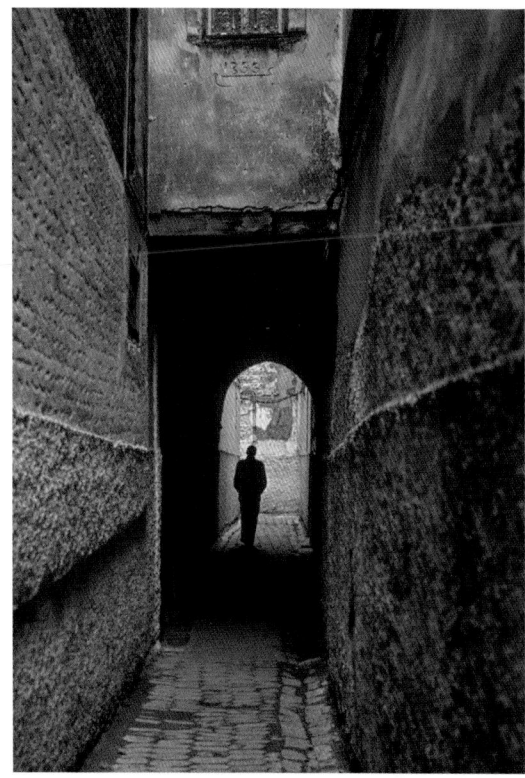

An easy way to practice framing is to place your subject in a doorframe or arch, like this shot from Fez, Morocco.

of frames if you start looking for them: trees, bridges, the mouth of a cave, the hole of a doughnut. Inside your car, you'll find that windshields and rearview mirrors make interesting framing devices, and they add a new layer through reflections, which let us look both forward and backward at the same time.

ASSIGNMENT: FRAME SOMETHING IN AN UNEXPECTED WAY

Frame a subject using something from your house or neighborhood. No doorways, though—that's too easy. Consider the unusual: You could frame someone sitting at a table, as reflected in a chrome napkin holder. Or set your camera's self-timer, place it in the fridge, and capture a picture of someone grabbing a bite to eat, framed by the jars and shelves.

LEADING LINES

When lines occur in photographs, our eyes cannot help but follow along their paths. You can use lines as an element of composition to draw viewers into your picture, and guide their focus to what's important.

A leading line is anything that leads your eye into the frame and involves you in the composition. It has the same function as an arrow in a graphic, pointing to the emotional center of the picture. Leading lines help guide viewers to the payoff in the image. Some leading lines are obvious— roads and train tracks are classic examples. But don't get hung up on any strict definition of a line. It doesn't have to be straight; it can be curved or wavy, wide or narrow, human-made or part of nature. Think of a fence in a field, a boulevard through a city, a herd of cattle walking together over a hill.

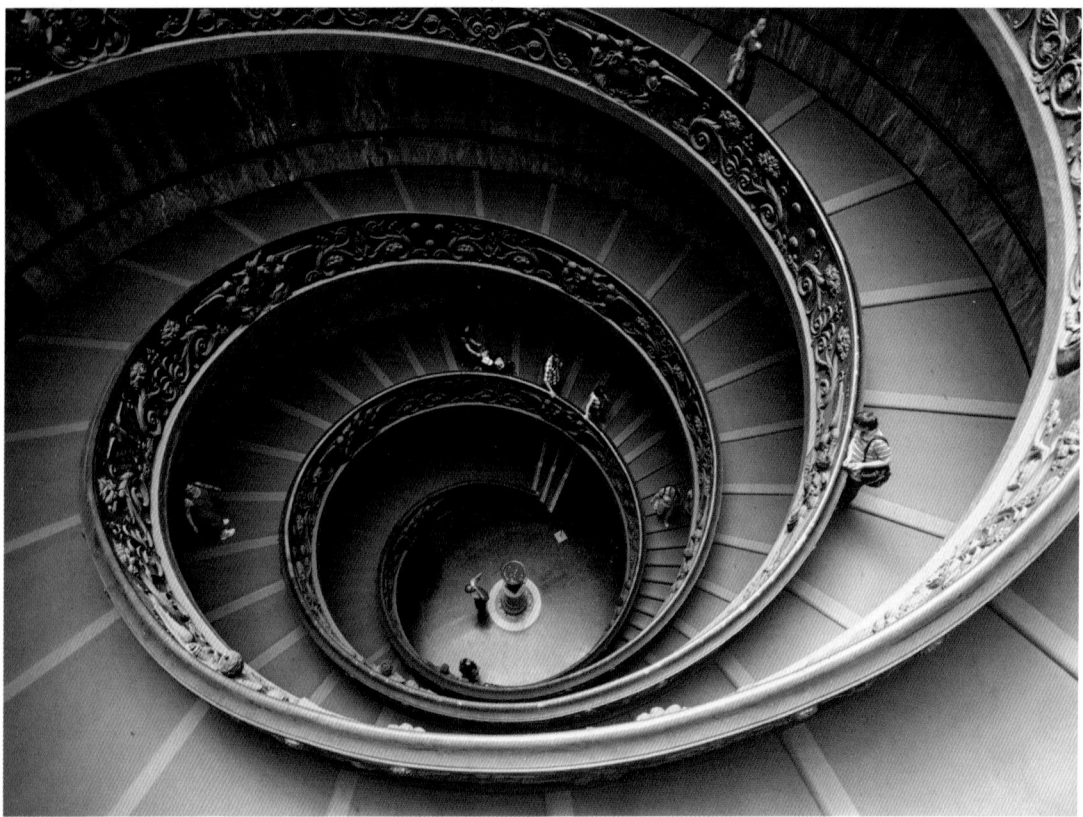

A leading line doesn't have to be straight. As you look at this picture of a staircase in the Vatican, notice how your eye traces the spiral steps all the way down to the bottom, where the visual payoff awaits.

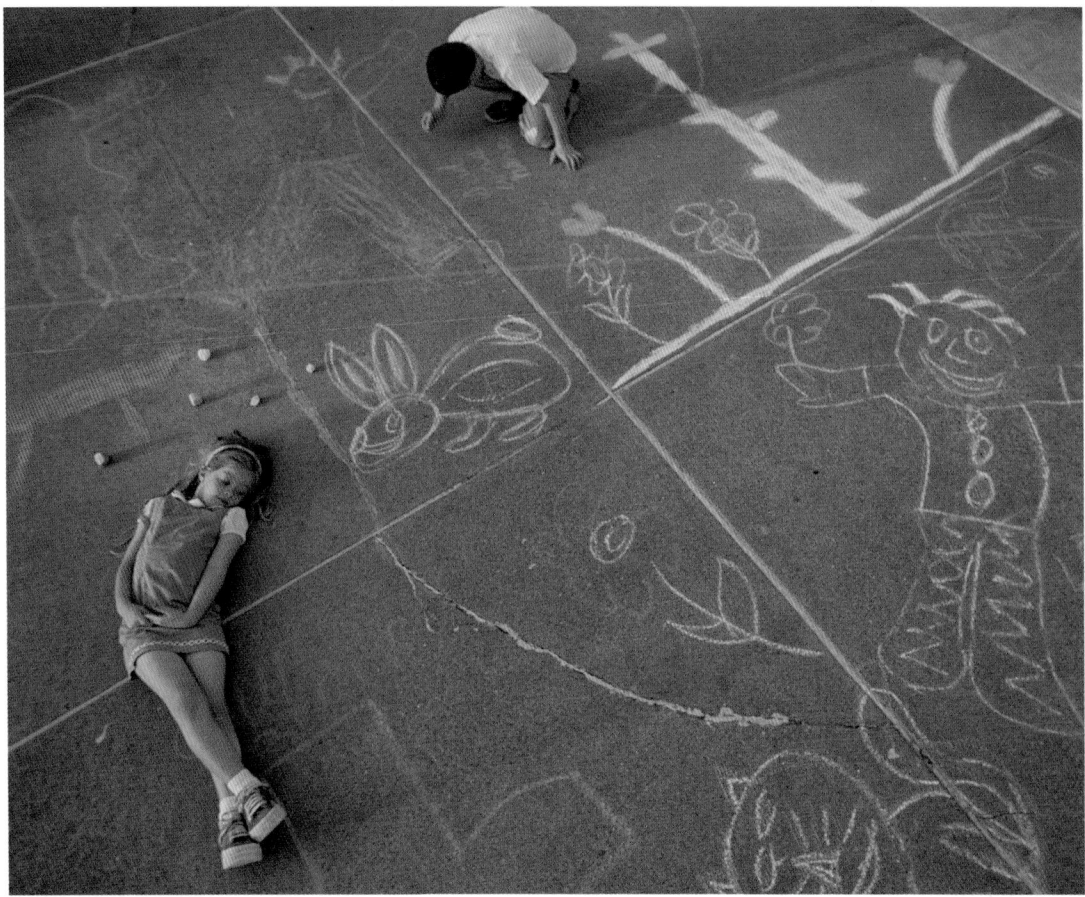

Strategically placing this chalk line on a diagonal leads our eyes from the little girl at lower left to the other child and the rest of the chalk art at top right.

Leading lines are another tool in your tool-box, one more compositional element to involve viewers in your photograph.

LEARN YOUR LINES

As with all tools, you have to be strategic about how you use leading lines, and they're best used in conjunction with the other elements of composition we've learned about so far. A line can be part of a layer, and it can come from an interesting perspective. Lines are very effec-tive when used in tandem with the rule of thirds—starting in a corner and moving diagonally, crossing the points of intersection in your grid.

As you look through the viewfinder, be aware of any lines in your frame and let your own eye follow where they lead. You don't want a line that will be distracting, or lead viewers somewhere in (or out of) the photo that doesn't provide a satisfying payoff. Remember, if a line isn't working for you, it's working against you.

THE HORIZON

Whenever you're shooting outside, pay attention to where the horizon line falls in your image, and think carefully about how it contributes to the scene.

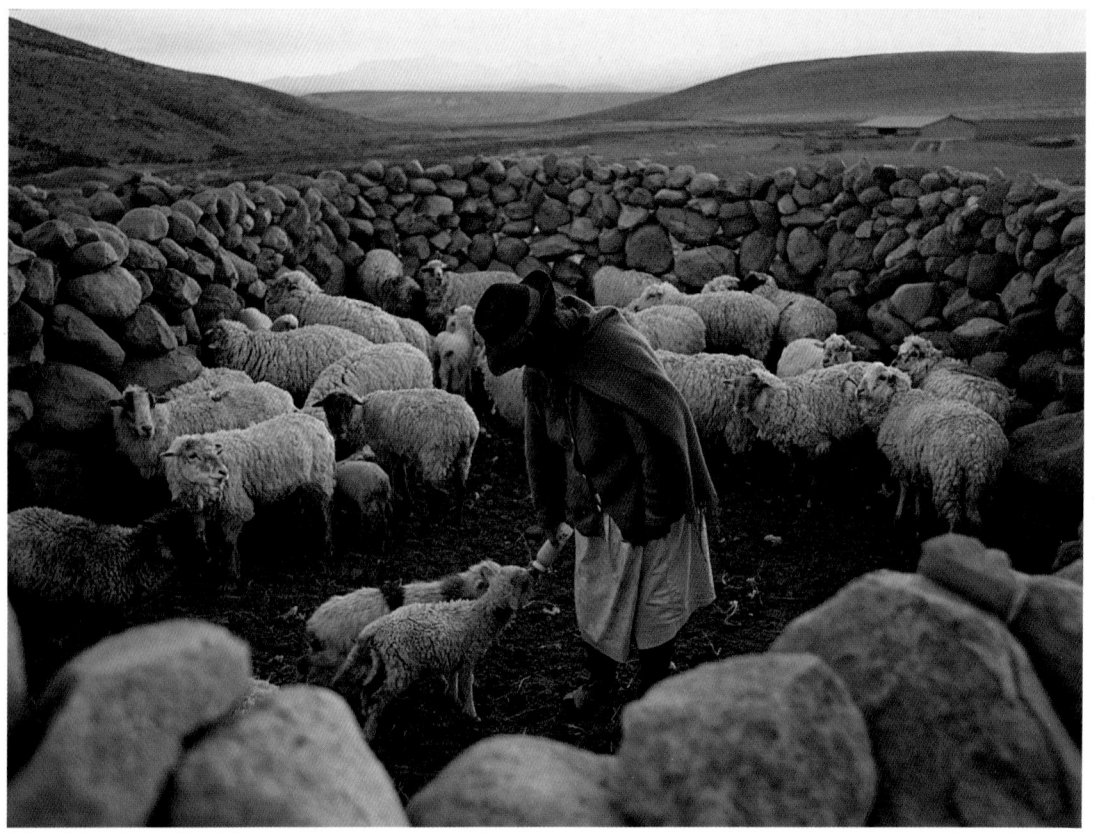

Taken from just above the subject, the horizon line is high in this picture of a shepherdess in the Andes, leaving very little sky in the photograph. But it's a stylistic choice that allows the woman to be more fully surrounded by the sheep—her livelihood—and shows the vastness of her environment.

As you compose a photo, make note of where the horizon line lands. When used creatively, your placement of the horizon can infuse a picture with emotion and meaning. Choosing where it appears in the image is a critical part of building a background and seeing all the layers that are part of it.

IT'S ALL RELATIVE

Whether it's a straight line where sky meets land, or a jagged city skyline of buildings, notice if your horizon is level in your frame. Unless it's very intentional, a slanted horizon usually detracts from the image and makes viewers feel off-balance.

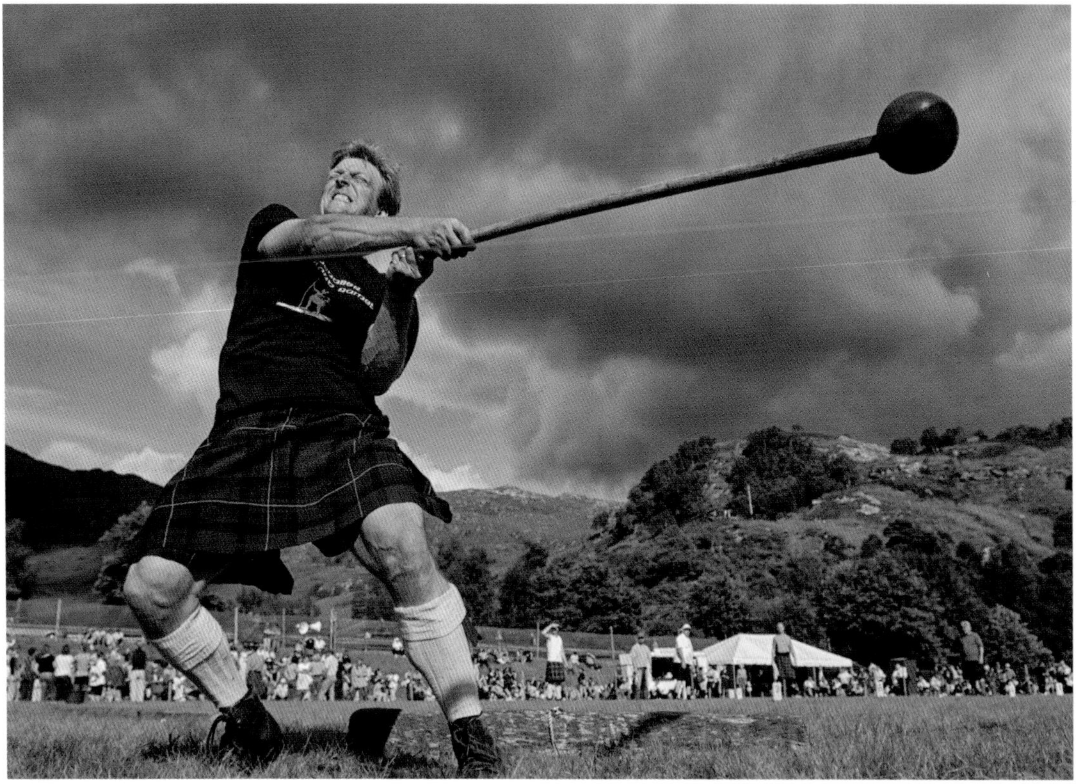

By getting below this Scottish athlete and keeping the horizon line beneath his shoulders, we've given him a powerful appearance, while also making the sky a clean background for the object he's throwing.

As a general rule, the horizon line shouldn't pull attention away from your subject. By moving it higher or lower in the frame, you can change the whole perspective of the picture. To make a subject look powerful or imposing, frame your picture so that the shoulders are above the horizon line. Or, to make a subject look small and meek, shift the horizon line so it's completely above the subject. You'll find that you may need to physically change your perspective to make these effects possible. Crouch down on the ground or stand on a chair—you're in charge of where the horizon crosses your frame.

Attention to horizon gives your image a solid foundation; it's an important part of building your photographs carefully.

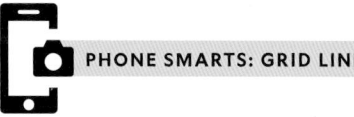

PHONE SMARTS: GRID LINES

Turn on the grid feature of your phone's camera for help in lining things up when you're shooting on the go. Most phones have at least a three-by-three grid setting that will guide you in the rule of thirds, and help you keep the horizon level.

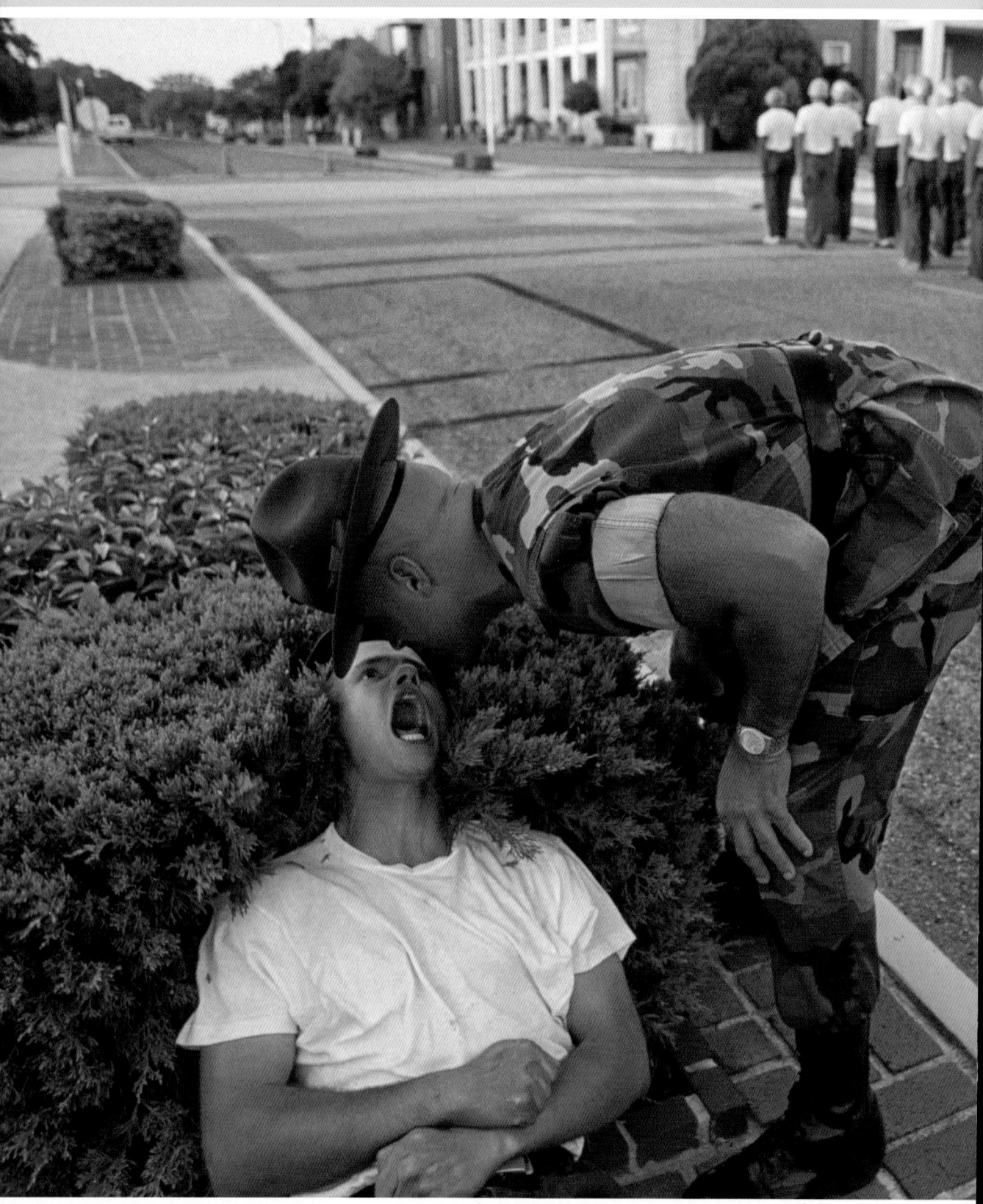

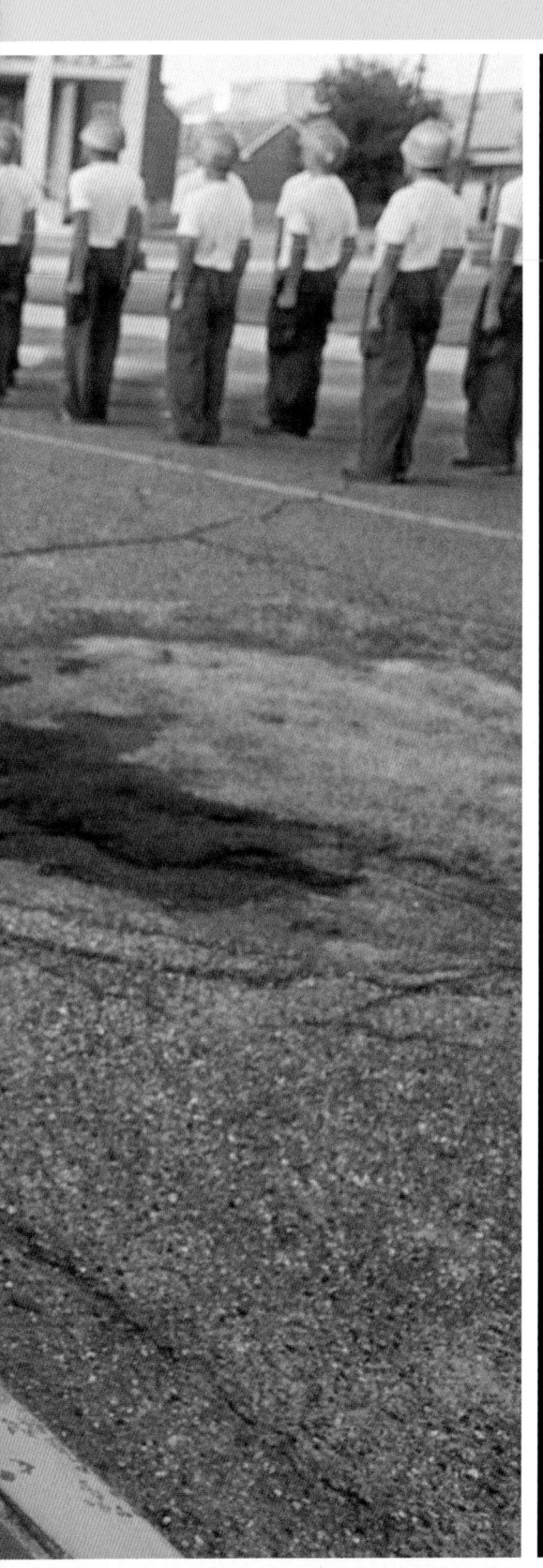

CAREFUL COMPOSITION

Your subject's position in the frame helps communicate a story. When you put somebody down low—as this drill sergeant literally did—it can make him look (and feel) small. The horizon line here is up high, making the road ahead look long. Look how the soldier's head is buried in that bush with the drill sergeant right in his face. You can see the rest of the platoon lined up and listening to the exchange, probably relieved that it's not them. These elements tell the story of a peculiar and uncomfortable moment, with a dash of humor.

TELL A STORY This photo features new recruits at Naval Air Station Pensacola, a military base in Florida. These first days are called "Hell Week," for good reason. Recruits get very little sleep and learn absolute discipline. My goal was to capture that intensity in a single photo.

FOLLOW THE RULES The rule of thirds is in play here, but at that moment I wasn't thinking about too much other than capturing what was going on in the foreground, while adding context by showing the whole scene. These elements help to fill the frame, balance each other out, and keep things interesting in two corners of the image.

ATTENTION TO DETAIL I made many frames as the sergeant berated this recruit. This one had a few quirks that put it above the rest: The young man is answering the sergeant's question with intensity. I love the way his hands are clenched into tight fists, and how close the drill instructor's face is. The line of recruits adds context and tension, as we wonder how and why this poor kid got singled out.

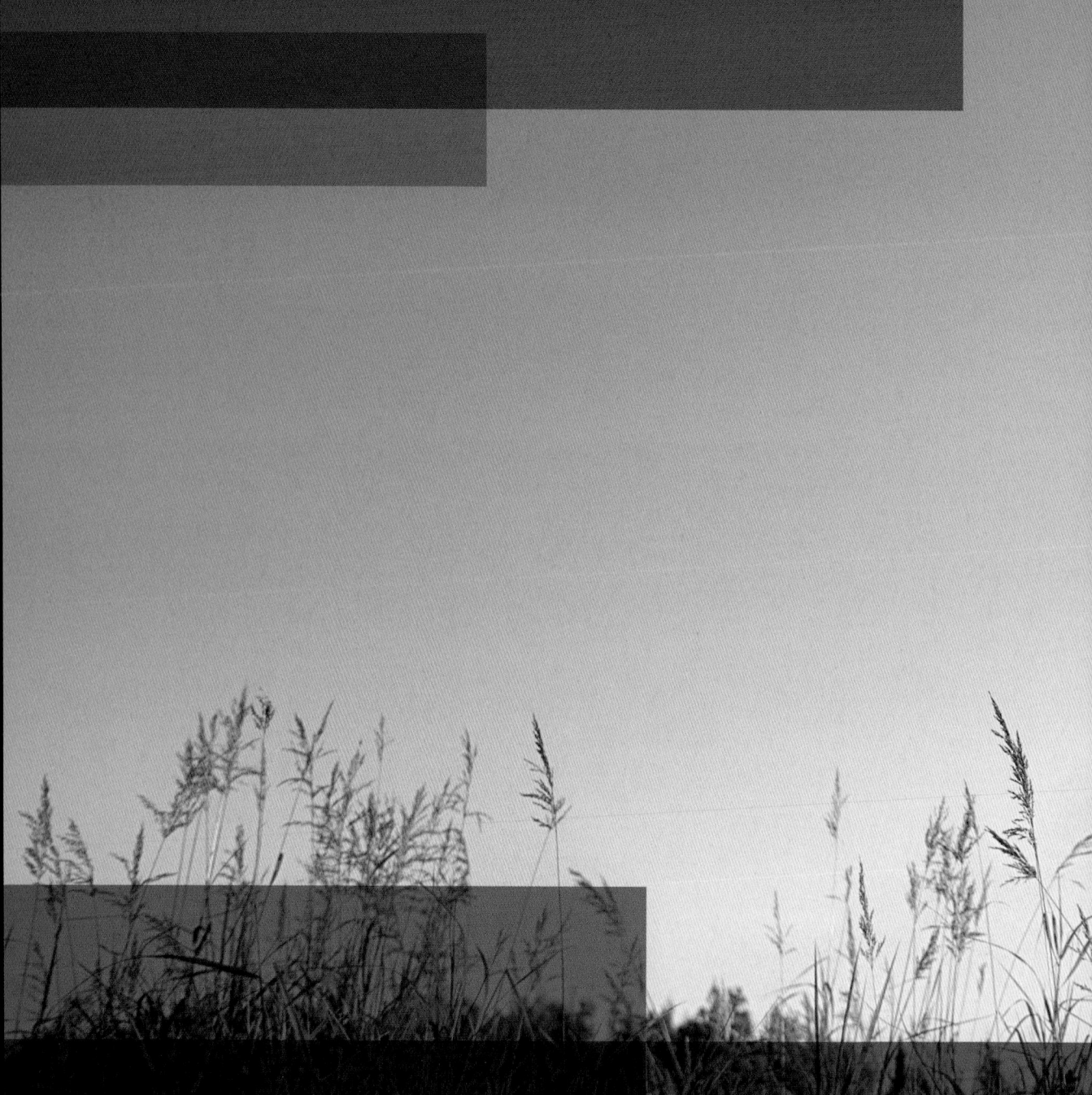

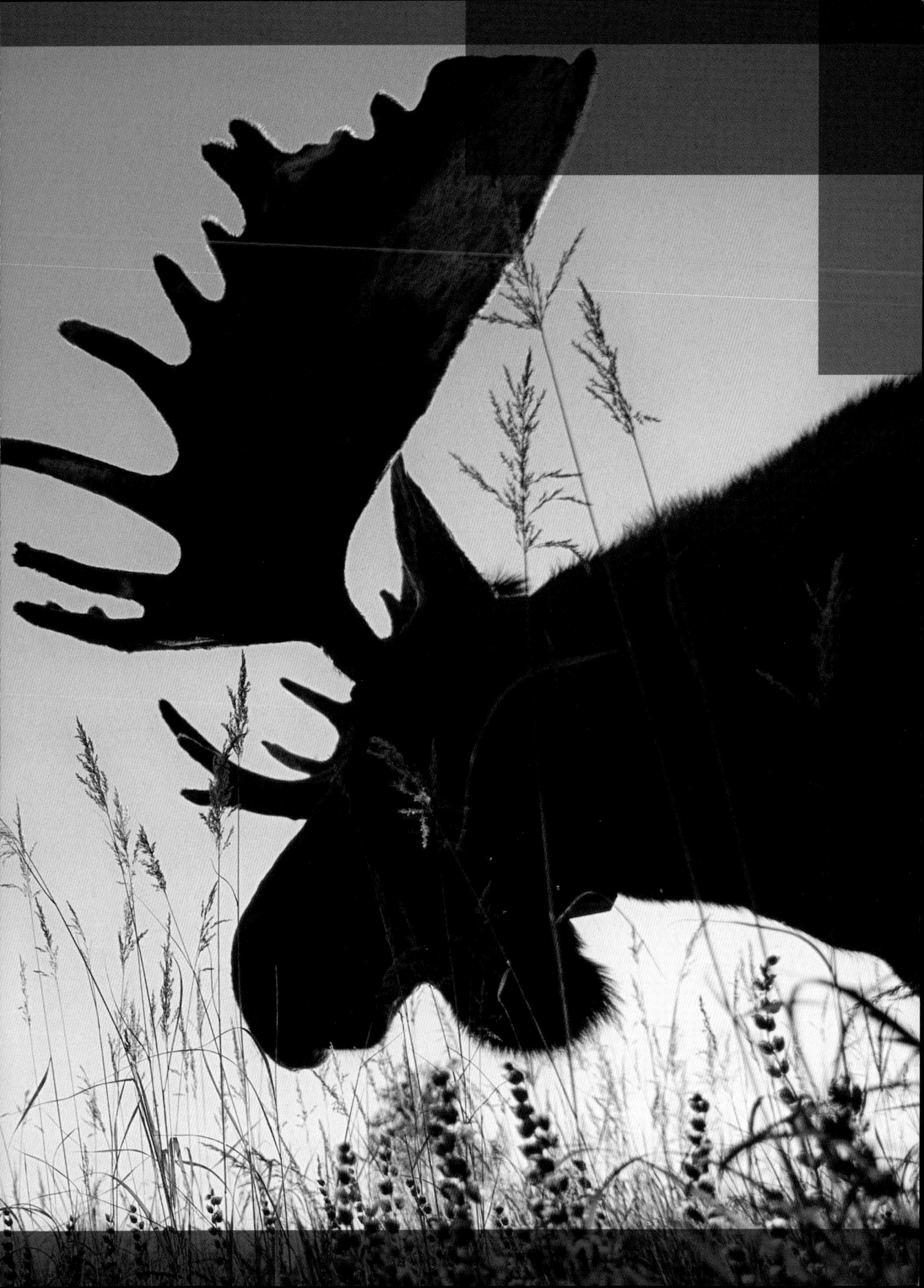

UNDERSTANDING
EXPOSURE

Exposure is one of the most important elements in any photograph. At the technical level, it is the amount of light to which the digital sensor is exposed. This is determined by two major factors: aperture and shutter speed. The aperture is the size of the opening that allows light through the lens, and the shutter speed is the length of time the shutter stays open to let light pass. These settings work together to yield the correct exposure.

Your camera works just like an eye. The aperture is like the pupil, contracting and expanding to control how much light gets in. And the shutter speed is like your eyelids, opening and closing in intervals. In photography, as in eyesight, your vision will suffer if either function isn't adjusted for the amount of light hitting your lens.

You can ask the camera to make these adjustments for you. But for more advanced, creative photography, you'll want to take control of the elements of exposure and customize your settings. In this chapter, we will discuss aperture, shutter speed, and a third factor called ISO, and how they all work together. We'll go over depth of field and focus, and what impacts these aspects of your photograph. And, of course, we'll talk about the ways you can use all these elements together to achieve certain results, whether that's a crisp action shot or a soft motion blur. As you read through these sections, remember that, as in life, balance is key in making a strong photograph.

A woman uses a flashlight to paint stone columns with light in a Nebraska park.

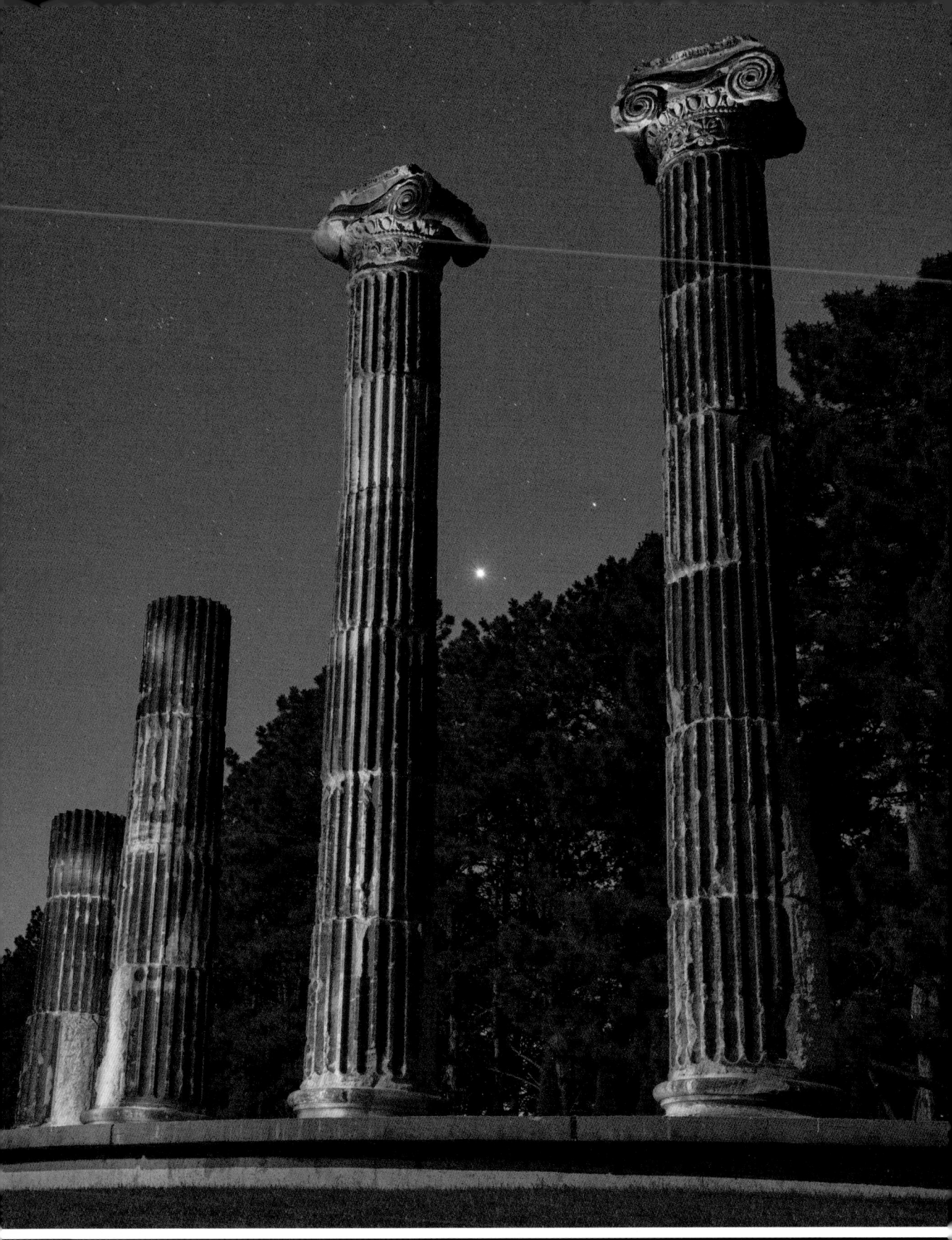

THE ELEMENTS OF EXPOSURE

Proper exposure comes from a delicate balance of factors. Understanding these elements—aperture, shutter speed, and ISO—is the first step to gaining the most creative control of your photographs.

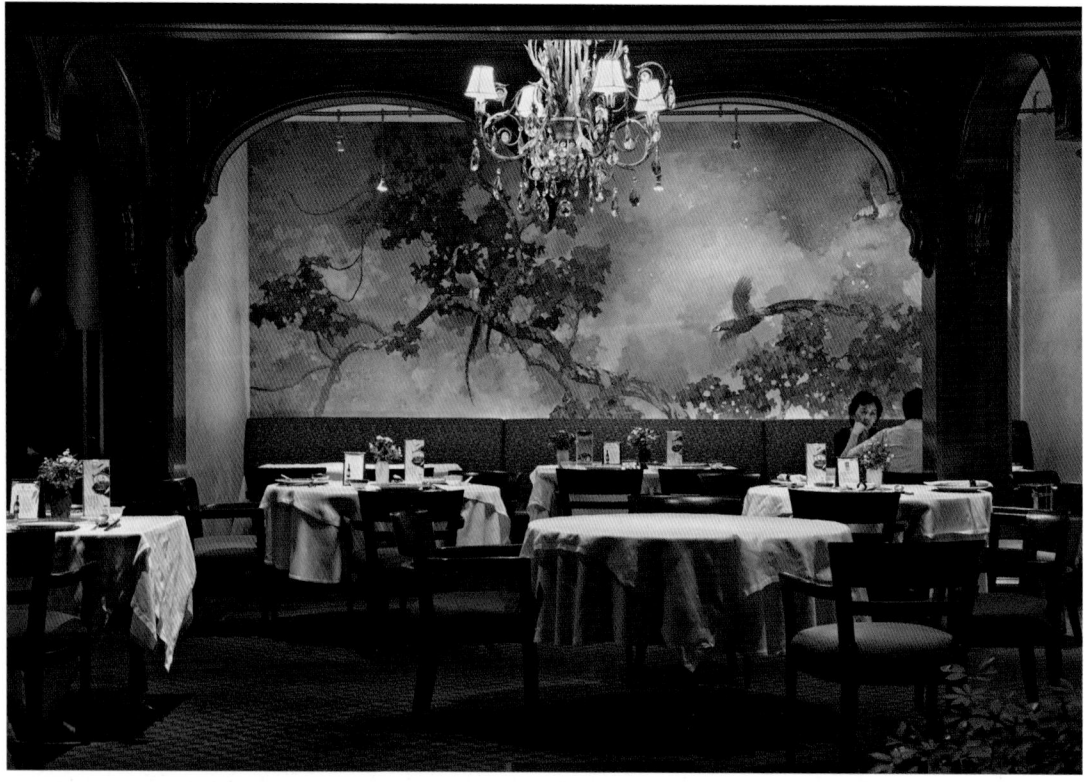

In this image of locals dining in a tiny restaurant, shadows are allowed to dominate the image, lending an aura of mystery and authenticity. Perhaps this is a place few people know about.

I often compare setting exposure to baking a cake. For a cake to turn out well, you have to bake it in the oven for the right amount of time at the right temperature. Setting your camera controls is just like setting your oven, but instead of balancing heat and time, you're balancing light and time. You should always set aperture and shutter speed together. A wide aperture lets in a lot of light, and a fast shutter speed keeps that light from hitting the sensor for too long. Conversely, a narrow aperture limits the amount of light coming in, and a slower shutter speed will allow it to hit the sensor a bit longer.

SETTING GOALS

Finding the "correct" exposure means choosing settings that accomplish the goal you want for the photograph. If you're shooting in a dim, moody nightclub, you might want shadows to dominate the image. And if you're shooting a wedding on a beach, you likely want more of your subjects to be bathed in light without harsh shadows. So there's room for preference in this discussion. But first, there are basic parameters: If you let in too much light, the photo will be washed out. This is called *overexposure*, and the whites will be "too white," meaning all the information in that part of the image will be lost. If you don't let in enough light, the image will be too dark. This is called *underexposure*, and the shadows will be too deep, also resulting in a loss of information. Getting it right is about understanding the look you want and how to create the balance to achieve it.

Understanding light is a process. Most digital cameras have an LCD screen on the back where you can review your image to see how the exposure came out. Experiment with combinations of settings to see how they impact the look of the image. Becoming familiar with the relationship among ISO, aperture, and shutter speed will give you the creative control to make the most of the light you are working with.

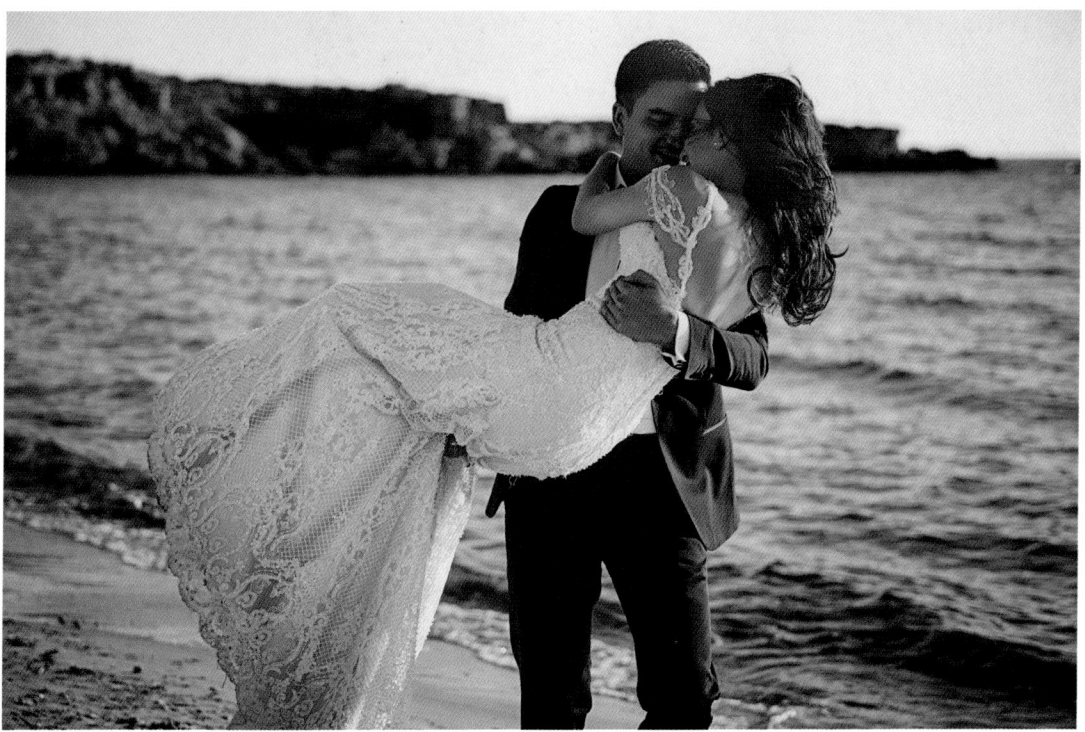

This happy couple appears bathed in light—appropriate to commemorate their wedding day on the beach.

APERTURE

The aperture is the opening in the camera's lens that determines how much light is allowed to reach the sensor. It's also a major determinant of depth of field—how much of the scene will appear in focus.

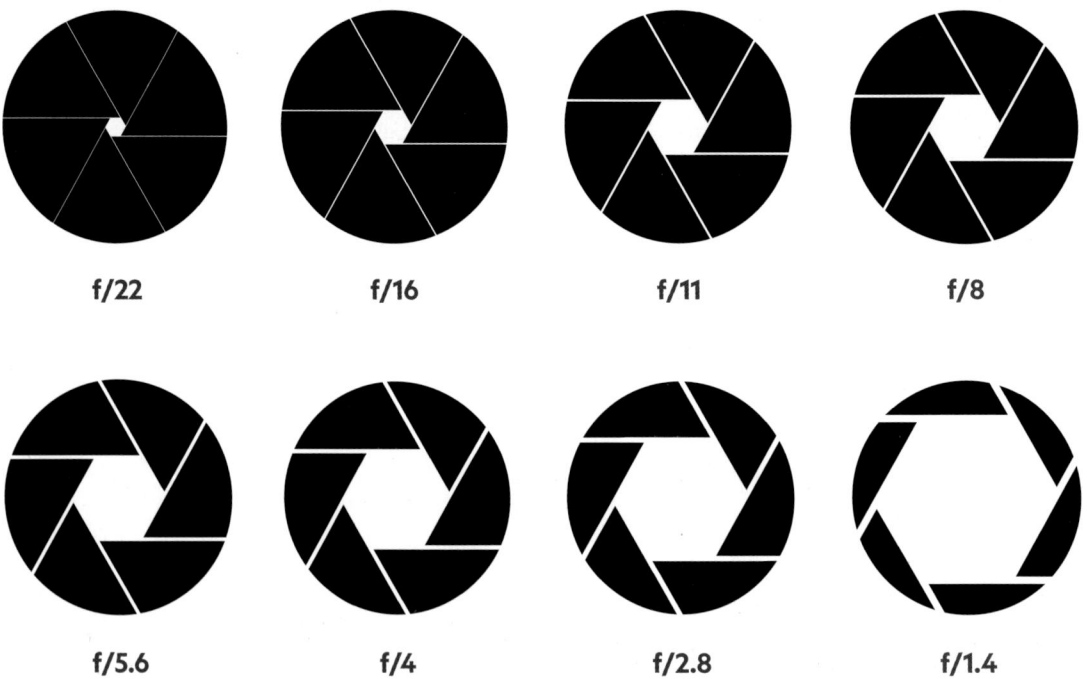

f/22   f/16   f/11   f/8

f/5.6   f/4   f/2.8   f/1.4

As we learned earlier, the aperture of a lens expands and contracts like the pupil of your eye to control the amount of light that passes through it. Aperture is measured in f-stops (also called stops), which correspond to a number. The higher the number, the smaller the opening. For example, an aperture setting of f/22 is a very small opening, and lets in very little light. An aperture of f/2.8 is relatively large, and lets in a lot more light.

CHOOSING APERTURE

On a bright, sunny day, you may opt for a small aperture—say f/11 or higher—as there is plenty of light available to properly expose the image. But in a dimly lit room, you'll want a larger aperture—maybe f/5.6 or lower—in order to allow in as much light as possible. So the aperture contributes to the exposure equation, but your selection of f-stop has another important impact on the image: It determines your depth of field—a concept we'll cover in detail in a later section.

For now, know that a wide aperture (low number) has a shallow depth of field, meaning that one shallow layer of the photograph will be in focus. This can be useful

FOR MORE ON PRIORITY MODES, SEE PAGE 80.

when you want your subject to be sharp and stand out in a chaotic scene.

For example, imagine that you're taking a portrait on a sidewalk in New York City. Rather than having the buildings, signs, and crowds in focus, using a wide aperture will allow you to focus exclusively on your subject, while artfully softening the background so that it doesn't distract from your focal point. If you want the opposite effect, perhaps while photographing a

PRO TIP   ONE STOP ABOVE

With many lenses, images tend to get a little soft, or slightly out of focus, at the widest aperture setting. Keeping your aperture set to at least one stop above the lowest f-stop will help ensure sharp, crisp images.

still life arrangement on your kitchen table, you'll want a smaller aperture (higher number) to keep more of the elements in focus.

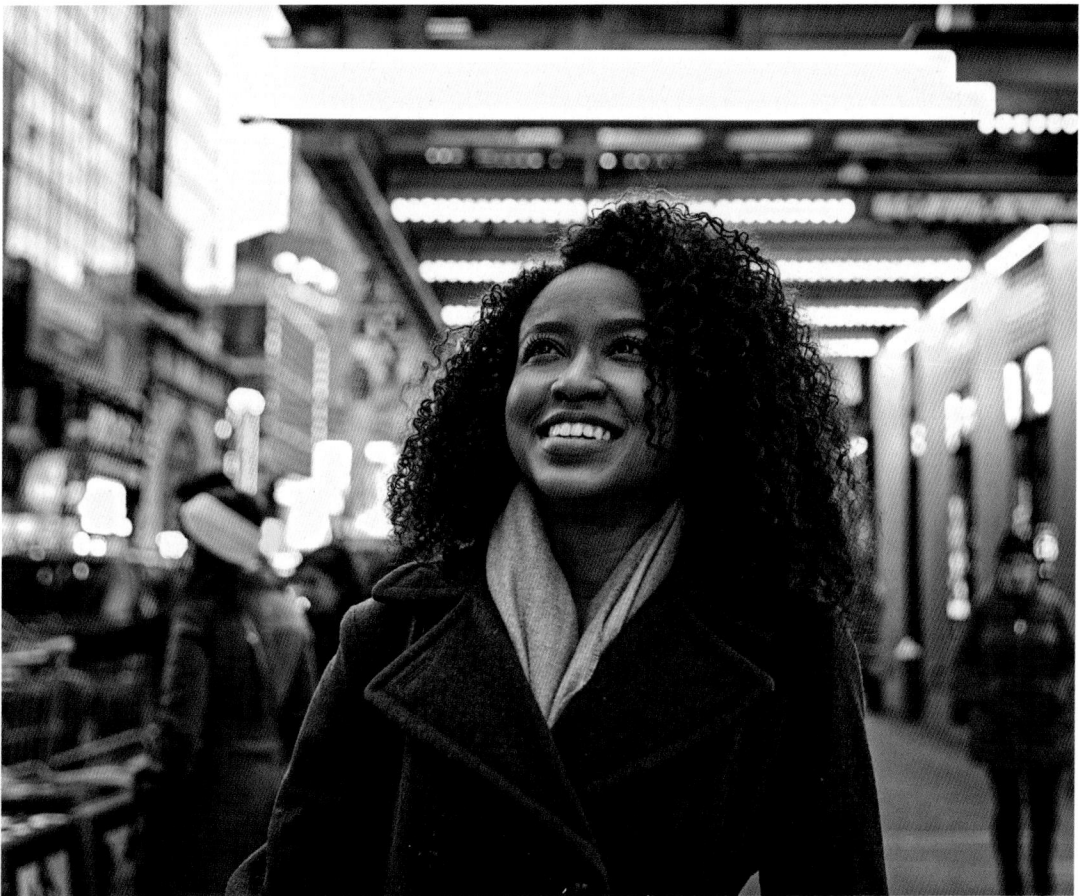

A relatively wide aperture of f/4 makes the subject sharp against the softened background of this city market. A shallow depth of field here helps the subject pop in an otherwise visually chaotic scene.

FOCUS

A strong photograph usually has an area of sharp focus somewhere in the frame. Aperture, shutter speed, and focal length contribute to focus in different ways. Understanding each is critical to creating and controlling focus in your photographs.

In an earlier lesson, we talked about focal length in terms of choosing a lens: the greater the number, the longer the lens. With a long lens, you're reaching out and grabbing a single point in the landscape. With a shorter focal length, usually called a wide-angle lens, you're showing much more of the world.

FOCAL LENGTH AND FOCUS

So what does focal length have to do with exposure and focus? A wider aperture on a long lens tends to have a shallower depth of field than that on a wider-angle lens, meaning less of the frame will be in focus. With a long lens, if you focus on a far-off subject, it will be sharp while the background may be

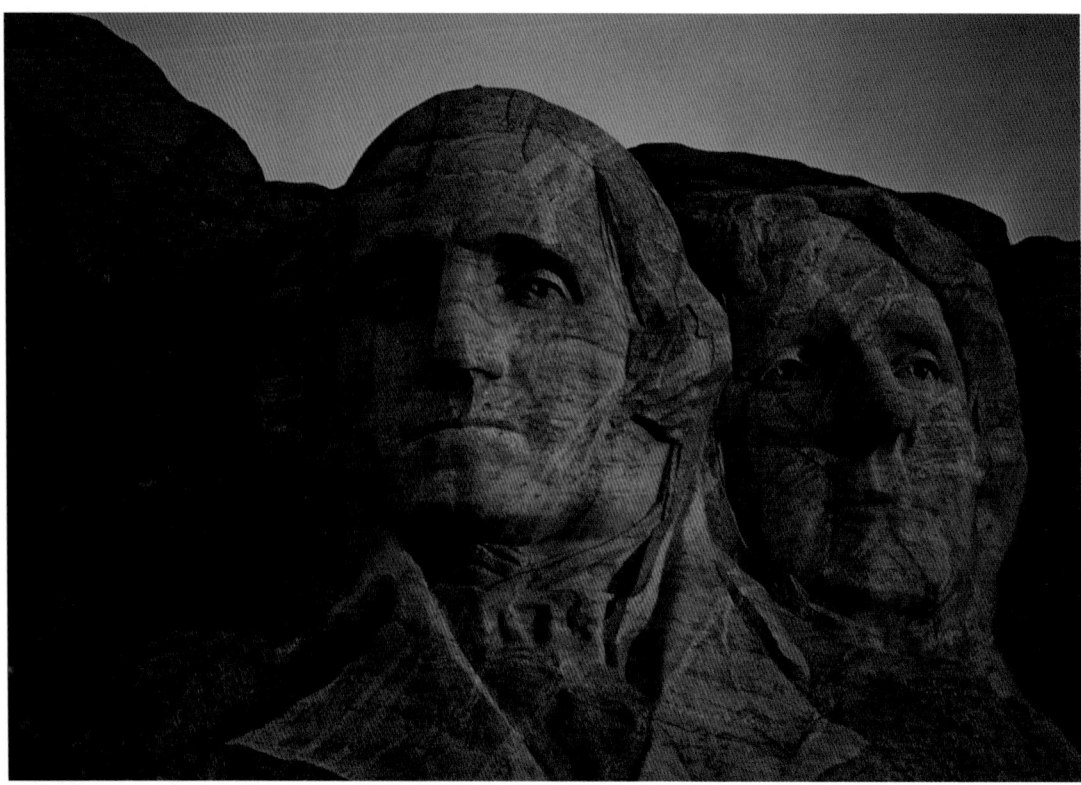

A long lens allows us to tightly frame the distant faces of Mount Rushmore, keeping their eyes in the sharpest focus. Lots of light is required to use a small aperture and maximize depth of field with a telephoto lens.

FOR MORE ON FOCAL LENGTH, SEE PAGE 24.
FOR MORE ON SHUTTER SPEED, SEE PAGE 72.

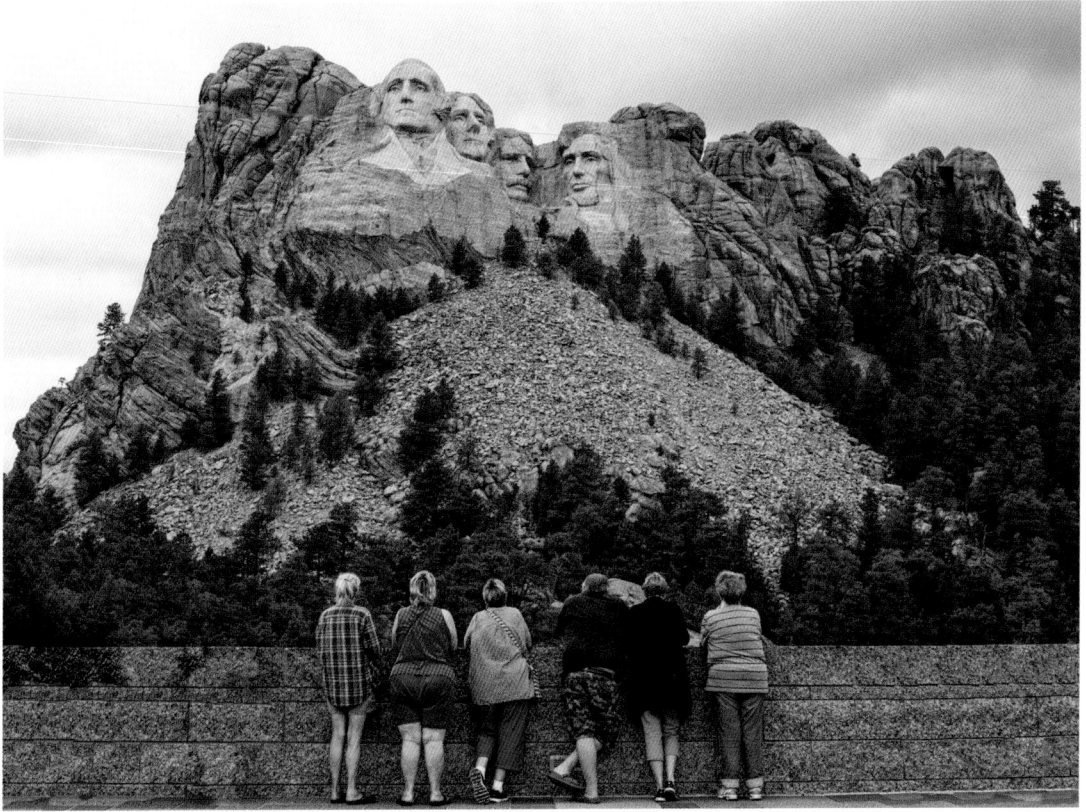

A wide-angle lens not only captures more of the scene at Mount Rushmore Memorial Park, but keeps everything, from the faces of the monument to the gawking visitors, in focus.

soft. On the other hand, wide-angle lenses not only capture more of the world, but they also keep more of it in focus.

No matter what type of lens you're using, your aperture should be balanced by shutter speed to produce proper exposure. Longer lenses tend to need more light than wide-angle lenses, so keep in mind that if you're using a long lens and choose f/22 for maximum depth of field, you'll likely have to slow the shutter speed way down to compensate. We'll explore shutter speed in more depth later.

For each image, you have to make a choice. Are you looking to focus on a single detail, making a shallow depth of field helpful to make your subject stand out? Do you have plenty of light? Then a long lens is for you. Or do you want to show more of the scene and have it be mostly in focus? Or is the light waning as the sun sets behind a mountain range? If so, a wide-angle lens might be a better choice. A zoom lens is often an excellent choice because it means you can have both on your camera at once.

DEPTH OF FIELD

Mastering depth of field will allow you to bring exactly what you want into focus. A shallow depth of field can make a small detail pop against a soft background, while greater depth of field will keep more of the scene in focus. Either way, aperture is your most powerful tool to define what stays sharp.

Focus allows you to emphasize what viewers see first in your picture. In general, we pay attention to what's in focus, and overlook anything that isn't. When we talk about depth of field, we are basically talking about a layer, or a plane of focus, within the image. With a shallow depth of field, that plane is very slim. With a wider depth of field, the plane of focus extends deeper into the image.

DETERMINING FACTORS

As we just learned, depth of field is influenced by the focal length of your lens: The longer your focal length, the less depth of field. The shorter the focal length, the more depth of field.

But the biggest impact on depth of field comes from the size of your aperture.

It's pretty simple: The smaller the aperture, the greater your depth of field; the wider the aperture, the narrower your depth of field.

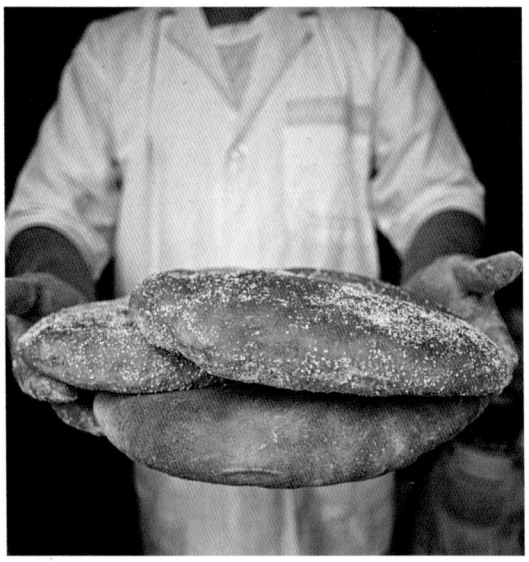

Freshly baked loaves of bread are the focus here, while the baker holding them is soft, beyond the depth of field.

You likely won't be able to see the depth of field you'll be capturing in your viewfinder or live view display *before* you take the photograph. Some cameras have a depth-of-field preview button, but it's difficult to tell where you'll end up. Your best

---

ASSIGNMENT: EXPERIMENT WITH DEPTH OF FIELD

Set up a still life and, without moving, photograph it multiple times, changing the aperture each time. Start wide open with an f-stop of 2.8, and make your aperture smaller with each photo, ending with f/22. As you review, you'll notice that the plane of focus extends deeper into each image, bringing more of the objects in your frame into focus.

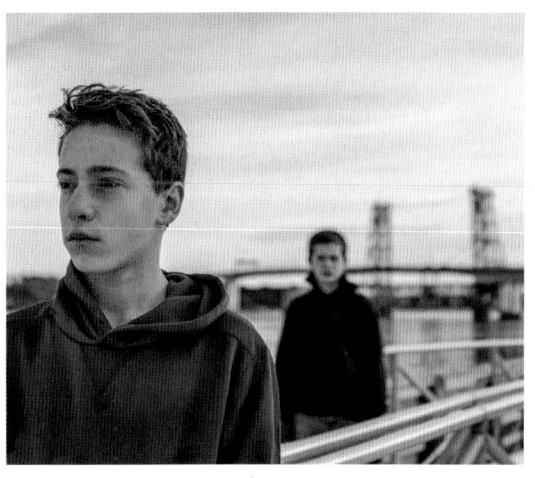

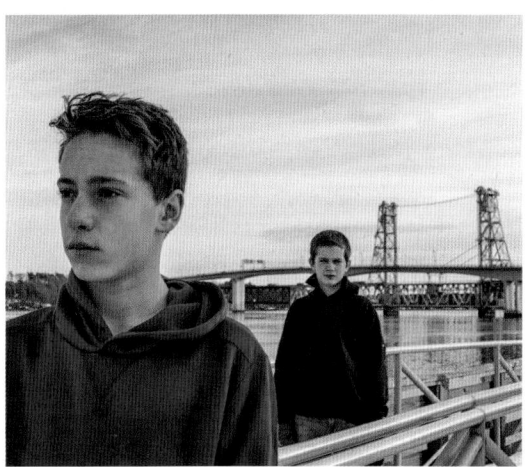

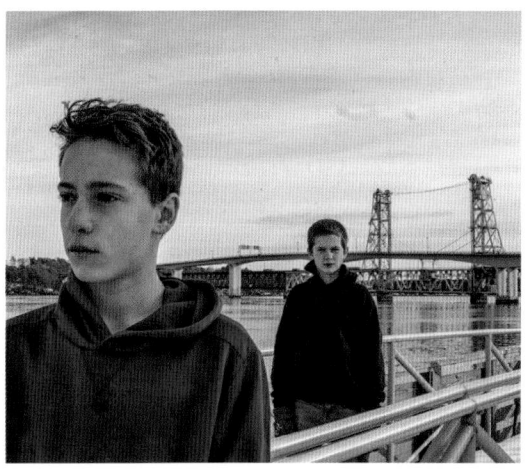

bet is to make many frames using different apertures (adjusting the shutter speed accordingly for exposure), and then review the results on your screen. Once you find what you're after, settle on your f-stop and make as many photographs as you can. With practice, you'll become familiar with what kind of depth of field you can expect from each f-stop, making your choice quick and easy when you begin to shoot.

PUTTING IT TOGETHER

As with exposure, it's the combination of factors that will allow you to use depth of field most creatively. With a wide-angle lens and a small aperture, nearly everything in the frame will be crisp, providing a lot of detailed information in a single photograph. With a long lens and a large aperture, you can isolate your subject, making it stand out while the rest of the image is soft.

Soft, out-of-focus objects still add information to the picture—remember our winter day photograph through the window? The inclusion in the foreground of a set of hands holding a teacup with steam rising, even if they are soft and out of focus, will help tell the story of how you spent a winter day, focused on the kids playing outside in the snow, while you're warm and cozy inside.

Notice how depth of field changes in these images as the aperture gets narrower. An aperture of f/2.8 (top) keeps the boy in front sharp, but focus quickly falls away. At f/8 (middle), both boys are in focus, but the background is still soft. At f/22 (bottom), the depth of field includes both boys and the bridge in the distance.

SHUTTER SPEED

The shutter is a door that opens to let light reach your camera's sensor. The length of time that door remains open is the shutter speed. Shutter speed needs to be balanced with aperture for proper exposure, but it can also be used for creative impact in your images.

Remember the kitchen sink comparison? You can open the tap wide to fill the sink up fast, or you can open the tap to just a trickle that fills the sink slowly. When it comes to photography, light is like the water filling the sink, and the shutter speed is how long you leave the faucet running.

Shutter speed is another creative tool you can use to make dynamic photos with impact. You might think there's not much difference between one second and 1/250 of a second, but that fraction can have a massive effect on an image. Getting the shutter speed just right can take a picture from being a mere snapshot to becoming something iconic, enhancing a memory of the original moment.

SPEEDING UP, SLOWING DOWN

In conjunction with your aperture, a fast shutter speed is helpful in bright light to avoid overexposure—it limits the amount of time light reaches the sensor. But a fast shutter speed can also be used when you want to freeze time—the spray of water from a garden hose, a dog catching a Frisbee in midair, the look on a bridesmaid's face the exact moment she catches the bouquet.

On the opposite end of the spectrum, a slow shutter speed is useful in low light to avoid underexposure—it gives the sensor more time to gather what little light is available. But you can also use a slow shutter speed to illustrate movement or the passage of time—kids writing their names with sparklers, car lights tracing paths down the interstate, stars moving across a night sky. A slow shutter speed will capture the path of an object in the extended time before the shutter closes.

In the next two lessons we'll dive more deeply into fast and slow shutter speeds. You'll want to practice and experiment. Grab a stabilizer and some patience—creative use of shutter speed takes time to master, but yields distinctive photos to those who wait.

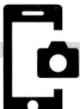 **PHONE SMARTS: SHUTTER SPEED**

A typical phone camera will automatically adjust the shutter speed based on the available light, and many don't yet have the option to take a long-exposure image. You can download apps that allow you to manually adjust shutter speed for your phone camera, effectively giving you a shutter priority option.

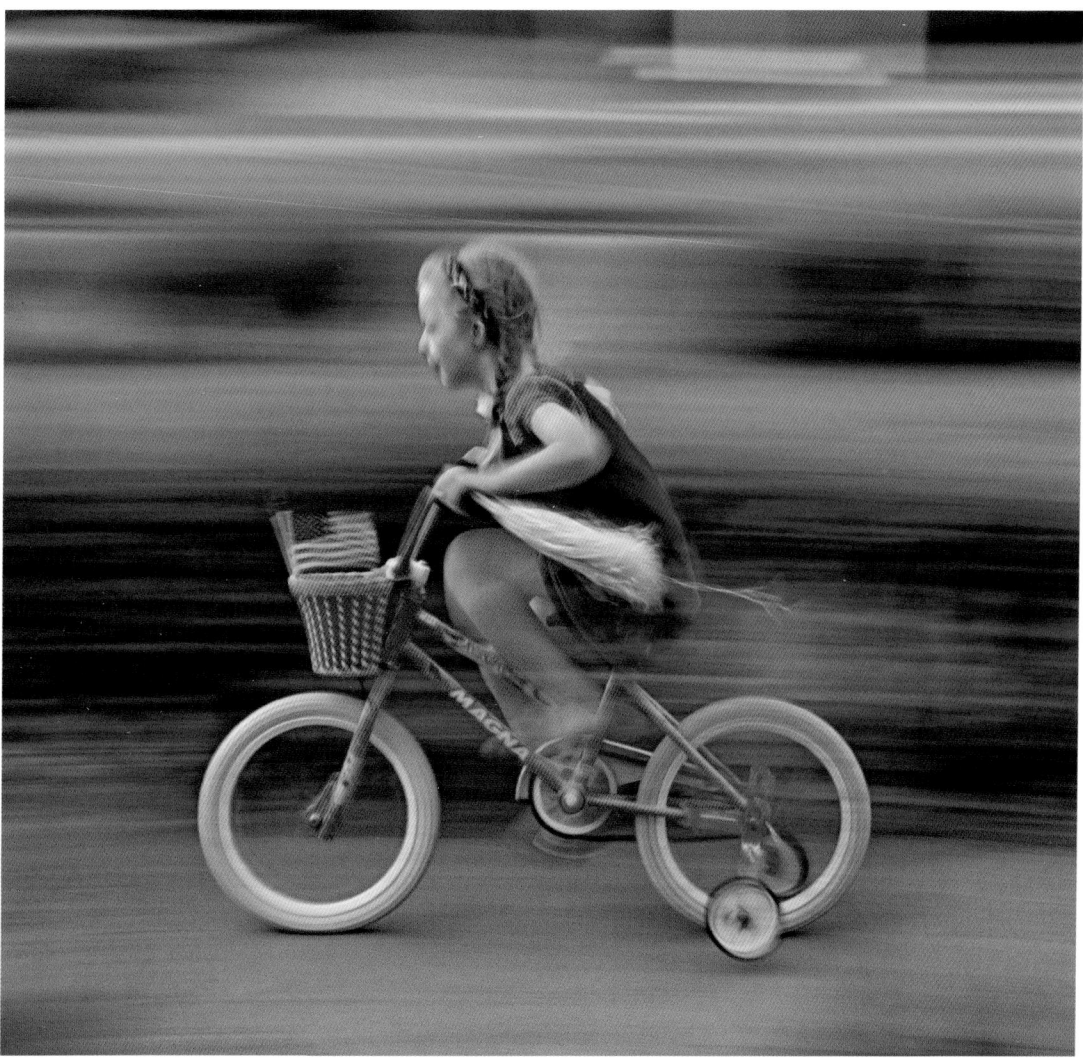

This young cyclist appears partially frozen against a blurred backdrop, using a technique called panning. A slow shutter speed is combined with moving the camera at roughly the same speed as the subject.

SHUTTER SPEED		
SLOW	AVERAGE	FAST
Use when light is very dim, or to intentionally blur a subject or background. Requires stabilization.	Use for subjects that don't move too fast, and in average, outdoor light.	Use to freeze fast-moving objects, and in very bright light.
1/4 second	1/125 second	1/800 second
1/8 second	1/250 second	1/1000 second
1/15 second	1/320 second	1/2000 second

FAST SHUTTER SPEEDS

Ramping up the shutter speed on your camera allows you to freeze fast action like a butterfly mid-flight or the first sprinter across the finish line. Freezing time effectively requires observation, anticipation, and lots of practice.

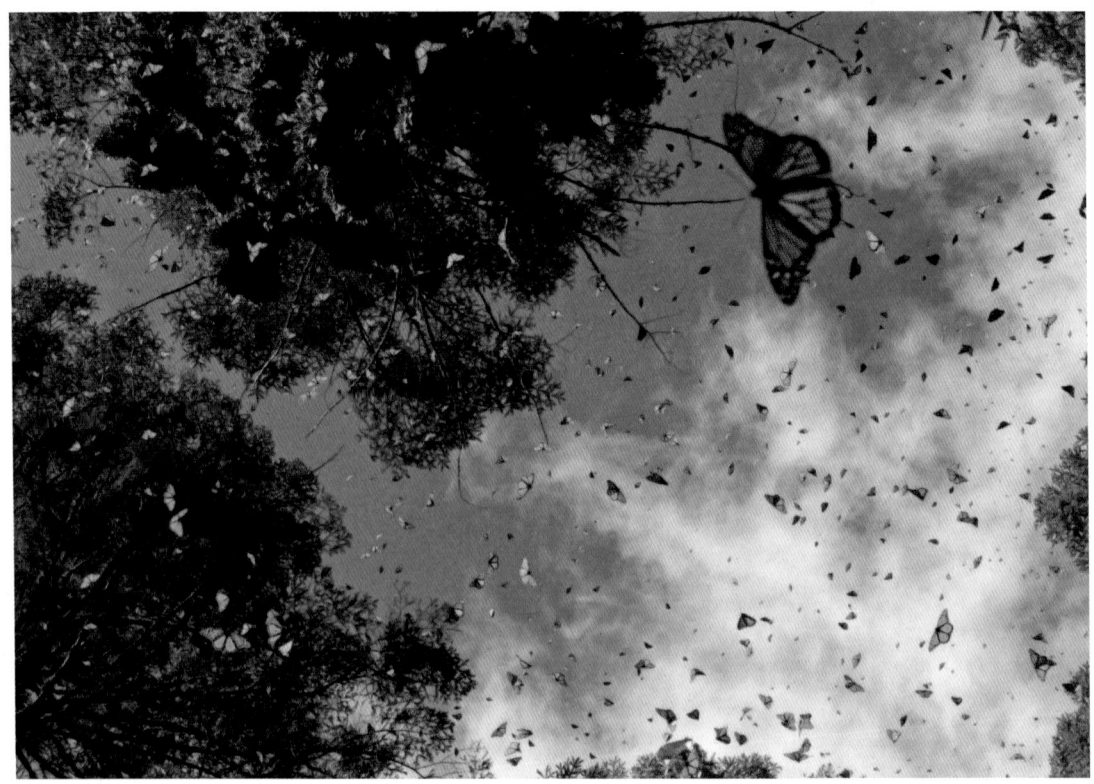

A fast shutter speed captures a single moment in the migration of these monarch butterflies. By freezing the action here, we crystallize the scene, getting a sense of the amazing number of butterflies on the move.

A fast shutter speed—generally 1/800 of a second or faster—means your shutter isn't open for very long. It's faster than you can blink, and perfect for freezing a moment in time. And, obviously, the faster your subject, the faster your shutter speed must be.

Fast-action photography can be tricky to master because you have to snap at exactly the right moment when the action you want to freeze is at its peak. Anticipating that moment is crucial to success. Generally speaking, if you *see* the fast-breaking moment, you've probably missed your chance at getting a picture of it. If you've got the luxury of repetition, say, watching pole-vaulters at a track meet or cresting

To practice with different shutter speeds, find a water source—it can be a river, a drinking fountain, or the faucet in your tub. Shoot the same scene over and over again, working your shutter speed from fast to slow, and see how it illustrates action in each photograph. An image shot at 1/500 of a second freezes individual water droplets in midair. In an image shot at 1/10 of a second, the water blurs together in a continuous stream. Remember, you will most likely need to stabilize your camera when using any shutter speed slower than about 1/60.

waves at the beach, just sit and observe for a while to get a sense of what will happen when and where.

LETTING IN LIGHT

Remember, the faster your shutter speed is, the wider your aperture should be to balance the exposure. As you experiment with shutter speed, try using shutter priority mode (usually "S" for shutter or "Tv" for time value on the mode dial). This will let you control shutter speed while the camera automatically sets the aperture based on the available light. This will free you up to anticipate and capture the fast-paced moments in front of you.

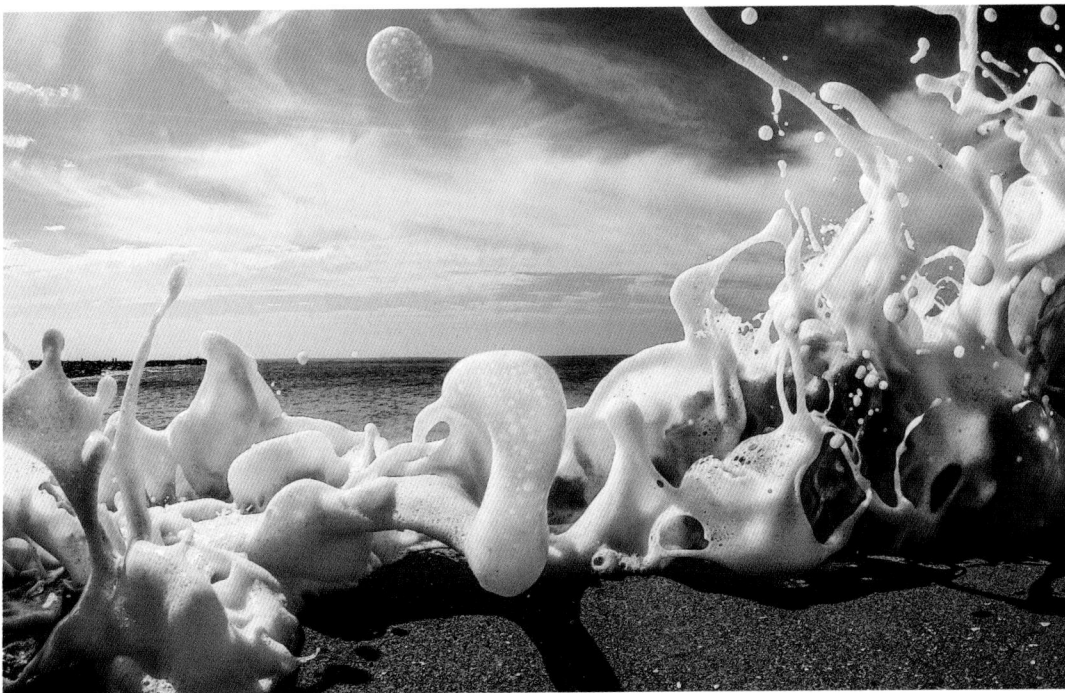

A super-fast shutter speed freezes the foam from a crashing wave in midair. Plenty of available light means the aperture can also be fairly small. The result is the crisp droplets popping against a background of sky and sea that is also in focus.

SLOW SHUTTER SPEEDS

A slow shutter speed helps you illustrate movement or show the passage of time, by leaving the shutter open long enough to blur motion or capture the path of light. Essential to success are stabilization, practice, and patience.

A world of creative possibilities opens up using slower shutter speeds, as you allow the shutter to stay open for larger fractions of a second, like 1/8, 1/4, 1/2, or even a full second. A slower shutter speed lengthens the amount of time light can reach the camera sensor. This longer exposure allows us to take full advantage of even fading light, making it possible to shoot late in the day as the sun is setting, or in dim indoor settings.

MOVEMENT

You'll find that most subjects move more than you think they would in a half second, creating a blur in your image. When used effectively, a slow shutter speed and the resulting blur can convey motion in a still frame—think of a dancer twirling in a skirt, or water cascading down a cliff face.

Slow shutter speeds are great for subjects that create a path of light, like traffic, carnival rides, lightning, fireworks, and stars.

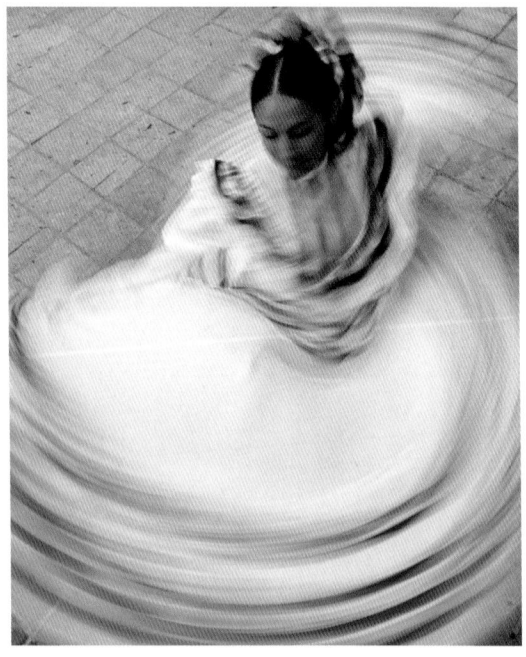

A slow shutter speed lets the skirt of this twirling dancer blur in the frame, nicely illustrating movement. To keep the background sharp, the camera must be stable.

These types of images are the opposite of capturing a single moment. Instead, they show the passage of time.

PRO TIP | PANNING

With a technique called panning, you can follow a moving subject to capture it in partial focus, while the background is totally blurred, conveying speed. To be effective, the camera must be moving at almost exactly the same speed as your subject while the shutter is open. Think of following the trajectory of a soccer ball, or a racehorse as it passes by. The result is a dynamic image that lets viewers feel as if they're hurtling along with your subject.

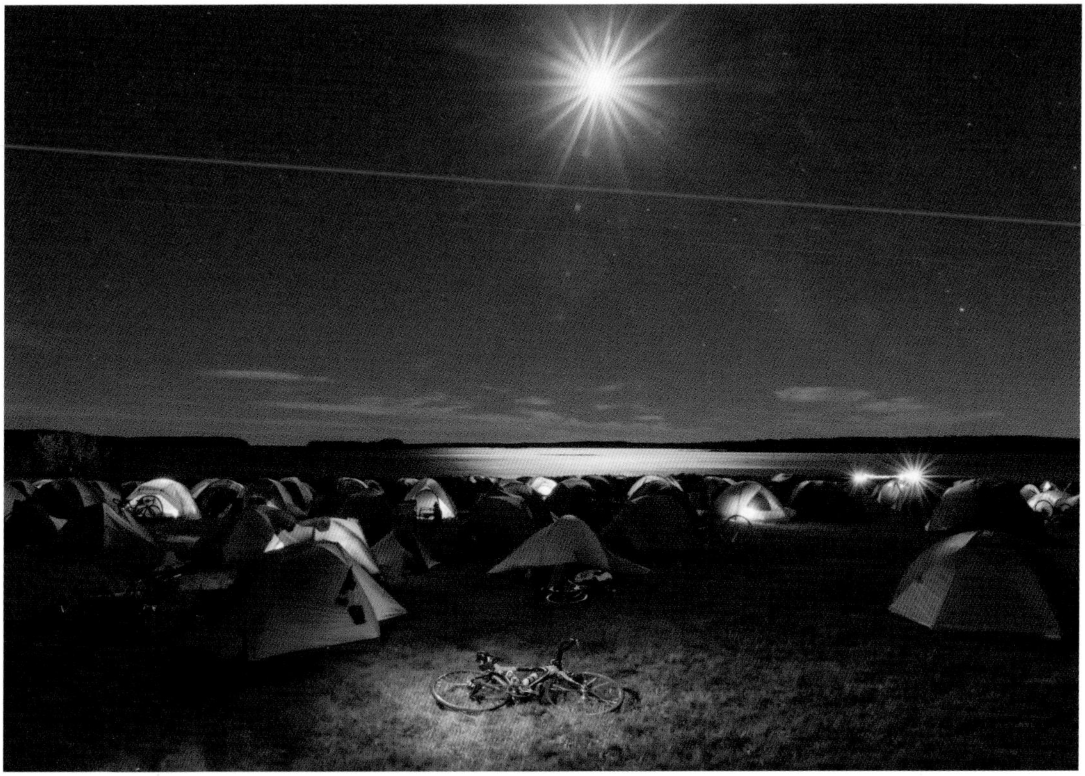

![Photograph of a campsite at night with tents, a bicycle lit in the foreground, a bright star burst in the sky, and water on the horizon.](full-page-image)

This image was created with a shutter speed of about 20 seconds, which required a tripod. A highlight here is a technique called light painting—a flashlight briefly lit up the bicycle in the foreground, giving it this spotlight effect.

STAYING STILL

It's nearly impossible to hand-hold a camera perfectly still for even 1/20 of a second, so you will need some stability in order to keep some portion of the frame sharp. Lean against a wall, put the camera on a flat surface, or break out your tripod once the shutter speed drops below 1/60.

As always, consider exposure. Adjusting the aperture to balance your slow shutter speed is critical in making sure you don't let *too much* light hit the sensor. As a result, slow-shutter photography is tricky on bright sunny days, when you can't make the aperture small enough to prevent overexposure. You may choose to add a filter to your lens, which can block some of the light, or wait until later in the day when the light naturally fades.

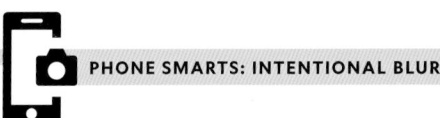

PHONE SMARTS: INTENTIONAL BLUR

When the shutter speed on your phone cannot keep up with the scenes around you, make it a creative choice. Be intentional about including motion blur in your photos, and you can create some dynamic images of busy, bustling spaces.

ISO

The third factor in the exposure formula is ISO, which controls how sensitive your camera is to light. Learning to read the available light around you will help you determine the best ISO setting for your situation.

The ISO is the designation of a camera's sensitivity to light. The higher the number, the harder the camera works to gather available light. On a bright, sunny day, your camera won't have to work very hard, so a low ISO of 100 or 200 is fine. Indoors or after sunset, you'll need a higher ISO to make the most of the available light—start around 800 and go up from there.

BUYING LIGHT

I like to think of ISO as a way of "buying" light so that I can use the aperture and shutter speeds I'd like in a given setting. Say you're at a late-afternoon soccer game. You want to freeze the action, and you want most of the players in focus. You set your shutter speed to 1/350 and aperture to f/11, but find that you don't have enough light to expose the frame adequately. Never fear—ISO is here! Try bumping it up to 400, 600, or 800. As you do, the aperture and shutter speeds you want will become more usable.

BALANCING ACT

As you practice, you'll get familiar with your camera's limitations in different levels of light. Once you reach that point, it helps to set your ISO based on your assessment of the light, and go from there. It might be tempting to use a high ISO all the time so you don't have to worry about aperture being too large or shutter speed being too slow, but picture quality can diminish as the ISO climbs to the highest numbers. While bumping up the ISO buys you some wiggle room for your other settings, it comes at a cost. As usual, making a great image means striking the right balance with the circumstances and the tools available.

HIGH ISO

If you're working with really low light, such as a dark concert venue or outside on a moonless night, you may have no choice but to crank up your ISO. Higher ISOs tend to yield grainy images—the higher you go, the more grain. Camera sensors are always improving, making many camera models better in low light, but it's something to pay attention to.

Some post-processing filters and techniques can help reduce grain or "noise" after the fact, but they should be used with caution, as they can reduce sharpness in your final image. Another choice is to just lean into the grainy effect you may be stuck with in low light, and consider it a stylistic choice. Work with what you have, and use the low light and the grain to create a mood that fits your story.

FOR MORE ON POSTPROCESSING, SEE PAGE 236.

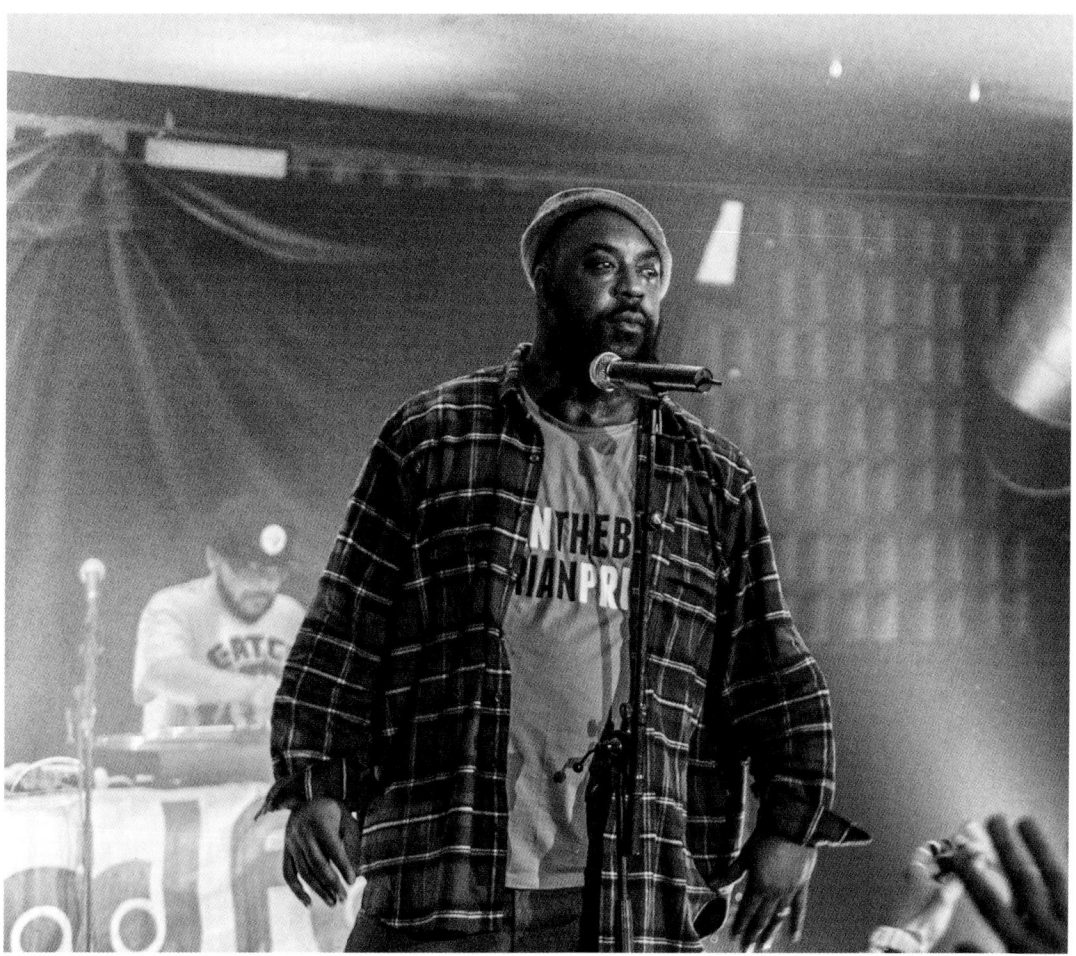

The late American rapper Sean Price performs at Carpe Noctem in Munster, Germany. A high ISO allows the camera to gather light in a dark room, but adds a grainy look, called "noise," visible here in the background. Generally, you want to avoid noisy images, but including it can be an interesting stylistic choice.

ISO SETTINGS		
LOW ISO	MEDIUM ISO	HIGH ISO
When light is abundant, on a sunny day or in a very brightly lit room Pros: Great image quality, low noise. Cons: Requires a lot of light.	On a cloudy day or in solid shade Pros: Image quality still good, buys you room for fast shutter speeds or small apertures.	After sunset or in dimly lit rooms Pros: Buys you room for midrange shutter speeds or apertures. Cons: More grain or noise in the image.
100	400	800
200	500	1000
300	600	1200+

PRIORITY MODES

Priority modes give you the advantage of selecting the ISO and aperture or shutter speed you'd like, given your circumstances, while letting the camera do the rest. Use these modes not as a crutch, but as an image saver in situations where light can change quickly.

Most digital cameras have settings that can help you learn to assess light. The fully automatic setting will establish ISO, aperture, and shutter speed for you, producing an exposure the camera's meter deems correct.

With priority modes, you decide which element you want to control, and the camera will respond, helping keep consistent exposure.

APERTURE PRIORITY

In this mode, usually marked by an "A" or "Av" on the mode dial, you choose the ISO and aperture, and the camera responds with the appropriate shutter speed. It's useful when depth of field is the most important factor. Say you're making a portrait outside: You want a shallow depth of field so your subject's face will be sharp but the background will be soft. There's plenty of light, so you

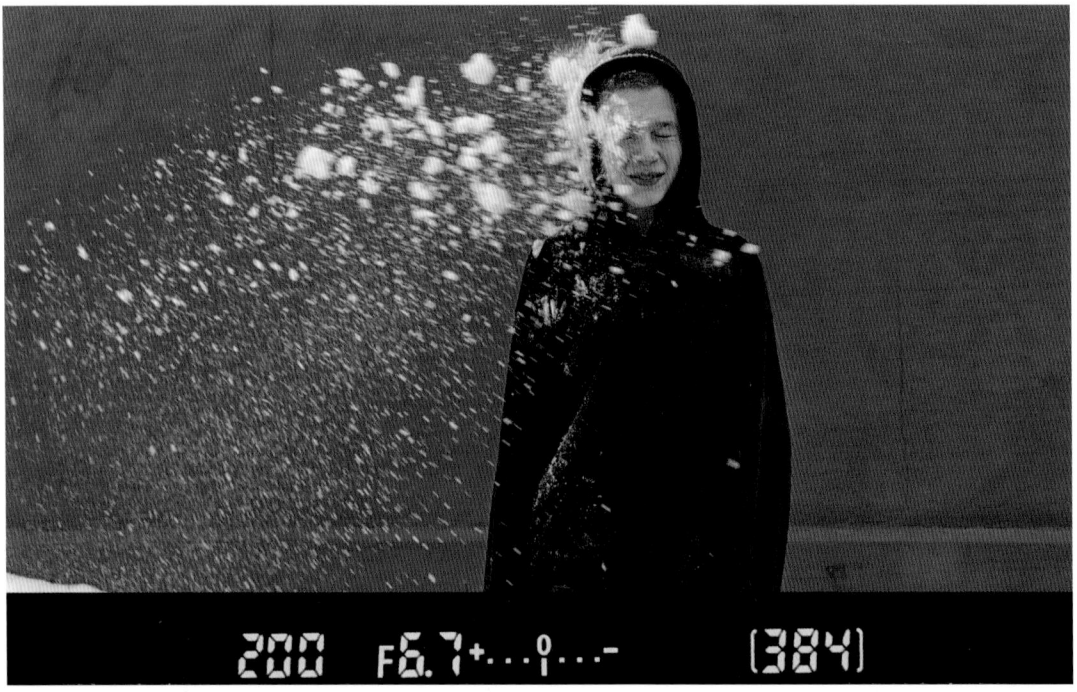

In both of these photographs, the camera is set on aperture priority with an f-stop of 6.7. In this frame, the sky was overcast and the camera set a shutter speed of 1/200 to make a balanced exposure.

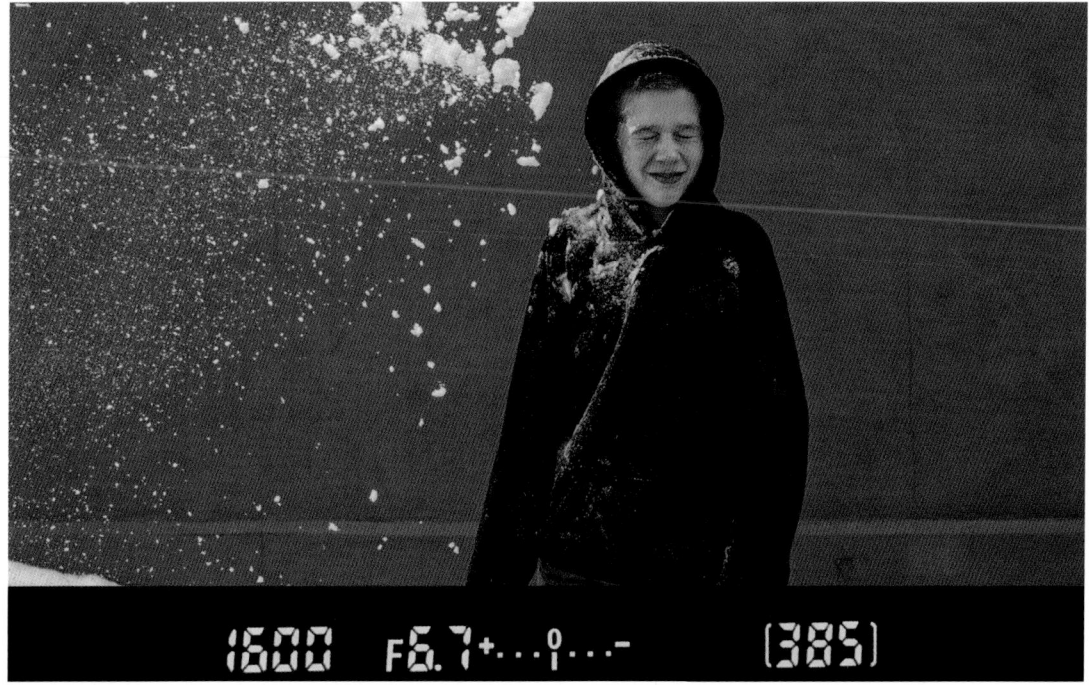

1600 F6.7+···º···–   (385)

A few minutes after the first shot, the sun came out, adding significantly to the available light. The camera set the shutter speed to 1/1600 to make a balanced exposure. The change is also noticeable in the crispness of the moving snowball.

start with an ISO of 200 and an aperture of f/4. Given this, the camera sets a shutter speed of 1/350. Then, a cloud passes overhead, reducing the available light. The camera determines that a slower shutter speed, maybe 1/125 or 1/60, is better, and adjusts automatically. If the light changes so much that the shutter speeds start to get a little *too* slow, you can always bump up the ISO to buy a little more speed. But with the camera adjusting shutter speed, you can pay attention to the portrait without worrying about underexposing when that cloud passes by.

SHUTTER SPEED PRIORITY

Usually an "S" or "Tv" (for time value) on the mode dial, this setting lets you choose the ISO and shutter speed, and the camera sets the appropriate aperture. Shutter priority is best when your subject is active and you want to freeze or blur motion. Having the camera adjust the aperture as the light changes is critical to avoid missing a shot. If the aperture gets too wide, you still have ISO to buy more light.

MANUAL MODE

Usually an "M" on the dial, this mode gives you total control over ISO, aperture, and shutter speed. The meter is there to guide you, but it can be tricky when you're thinking about all the other elements of your photograph. If you want to learn to read light, manual mode will be your best teacher.

PUTTING IT ALL TOGETHER

Exposure is the foundation of photographic expression. To some extent, exposure is an aesthetic: Some photographers prefer shadows and contrasts; others prefer bright whites and washes of light. Find your tone and discover the formula that helps you create photographs you love.

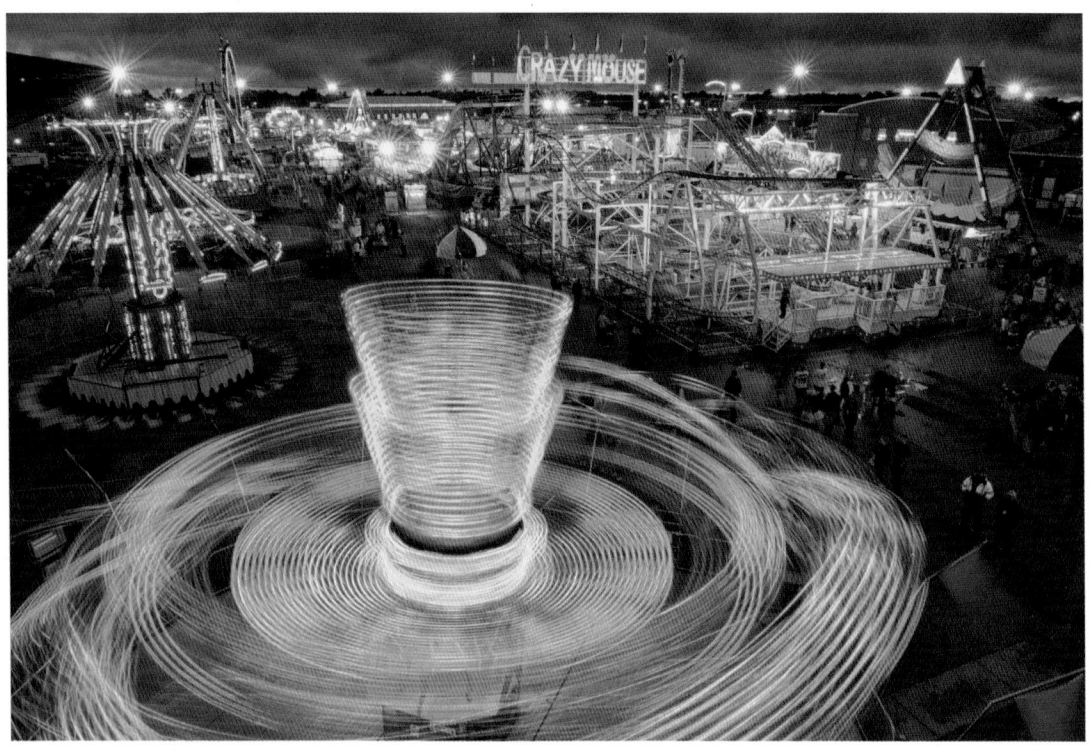

This image from the Kansas State Fair demonstrates a slow shutter speed with almost nothing in focus. The result is a movement-driven image that communicates the energy and whimsy of the carnival.

As in life, your best moments in photography will come when you've struck the right balance between your goals and the conditions you're given. F-stops, shutter speeds, ISO numbers, depth of field, and focal planes—it's a lot to understand, never mind balance. Like learning a language, the best way to become fluent is through immersion. Understanding the concepts is important in your journey as a photographer, but it's not nearly as important as getting out and making pictures.

DECISION-MAKING

Aside from learning the language of exposure, you have tools you can and should use. Remember your camera's built-in light meter. Even in manual mode, you should use the meter as a guide when selecting your settings. Priority modes can help make some of those selections quickly in rapidly changing conditions. But before you let the camera do too much work, remember that it can't make *creative* decisions. Your vision should determine the tone and mood you set for each photograph—sometimes you'll want to overrule the camera's suggestions. A camera can't define your voice as a photographer; it's merely a tool for you to express yourself.

LOOK AT PICTURES TO MAKE PICTURES

The best way to understand what you'd like to create as a photographer is to look at lots of photographs. It's never been easier—most of us have access to the internet, which places millions of photographs in the palm of our hand. Make note of the images you like. With your new understanding of composition and exposure, try to dissect and pull them apart. Ask yourself: How was this photograph made? Where is the light? What kind of depth of field is there and how was that achieved? What does the picture tell you about time? What works for you in the image, and what doesn't?

PICK UP THE CAMERA

If this doesn't all come naturally to you, don't panic. Experiment and play and allow mistakes to happen—you might even decide you like some of them! Become fluent in the language of exposure so that choosing your settings becomes second nature. Then look with eyes and heart and make choices that will help you express yourself in the most powerful way.

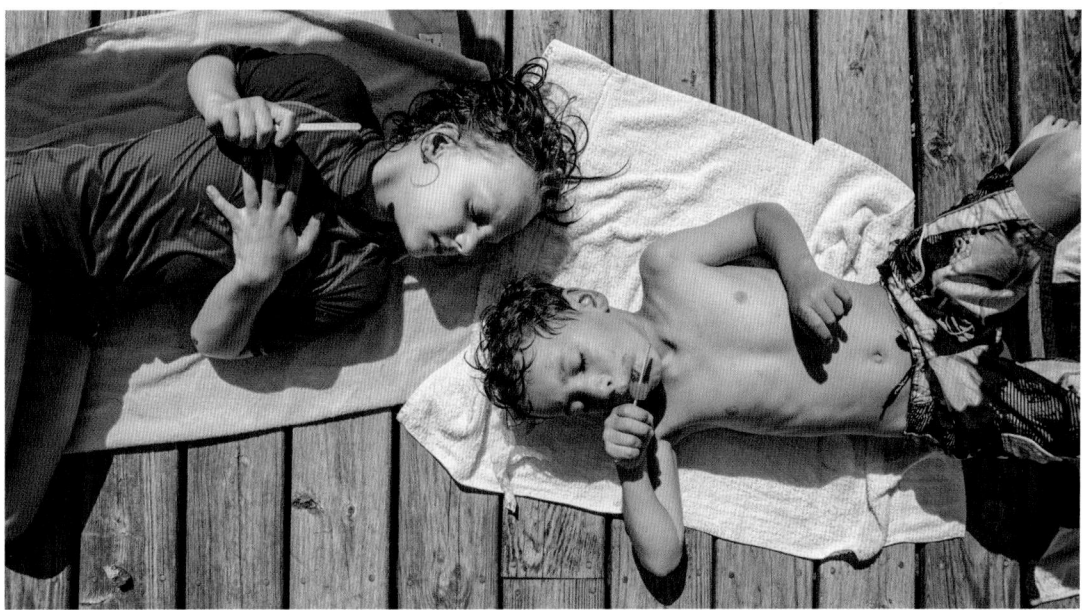

In between sprinkler runs, two neighborhood kids are lost in the moment with an ice-cold treat on a hot summer day.

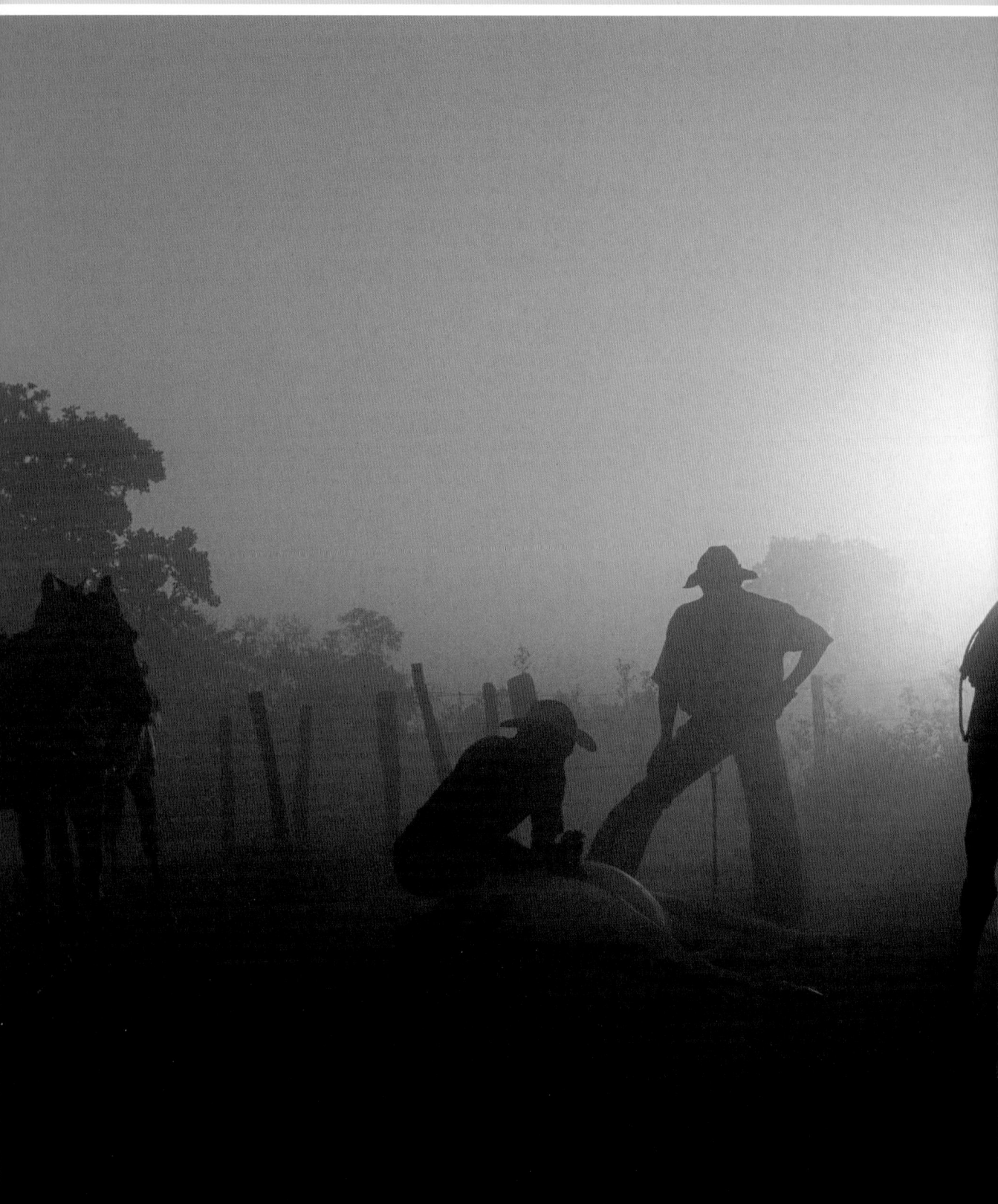

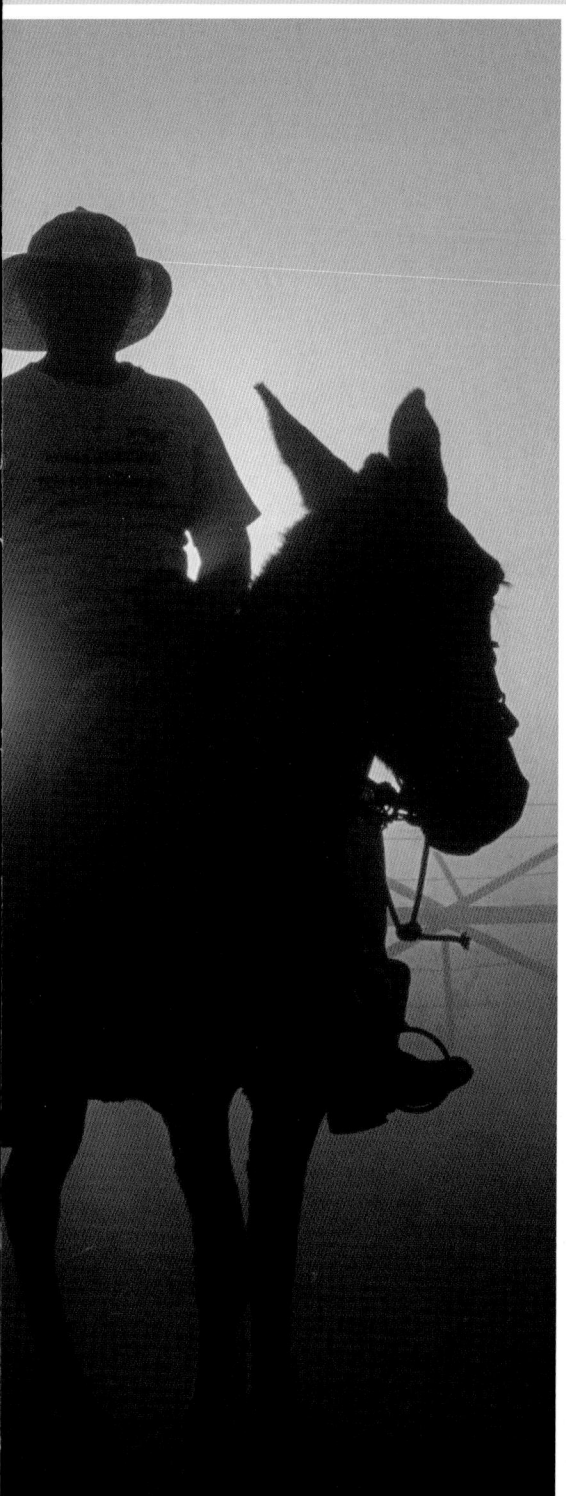

MEN AT WORK

As the sun sets in the Pantanal of Brazil, cowboys end their day by working on one last cow before dark. This seasonally flooded marshland goes from wet and impassable to bone-dry every year, with opportunities for great shots in any season.

DUST AS DIFFUSER The name of the game here is the dust; it's everywhere. Not fun to breathe in, but great to shoot in. All those suspended particles in the air soften the light, creating a surreal scene that's right out of a movie. It's hard to make a bad picture, provided that you've got a strong subject and composition to anchor your image. That's where cowboys come in, whether on horseback or working throughout the scene. If you can't make a good frame here, you just ain't tryin'.

BACKLIGHTING In the dust, everything is silhouetted. The key to enhancing that look is to shoot right into the sun, but positioning the camera so that a cowboy is always in front of the light. I kept moving as the cowboys moved to keep blocking the sun, producing the effect you see here.

APERTURE AND SHUTTER SPEED All that light meant I could choose a small aperture, say f/11, giving the image lots of depth of field and having all layers in focus. I chose my shutter speed to expose for the pastel sky, which helped keep the cowboys sharp and in total silhouette. As the scene was unfolding, I worked quickly, knowing it wouldn't last long. Nothing that good ever does.

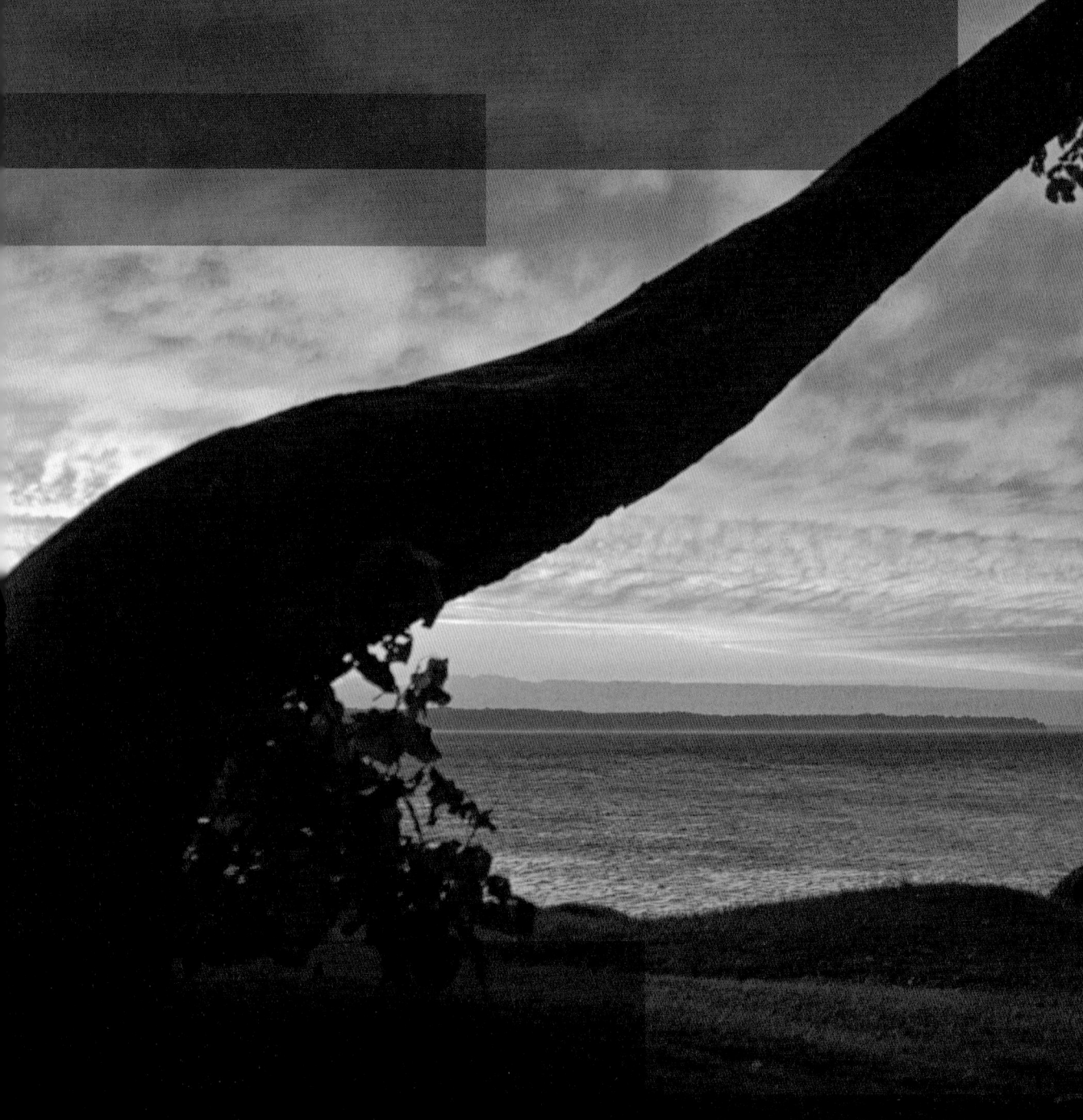

FOUR
LIGHT

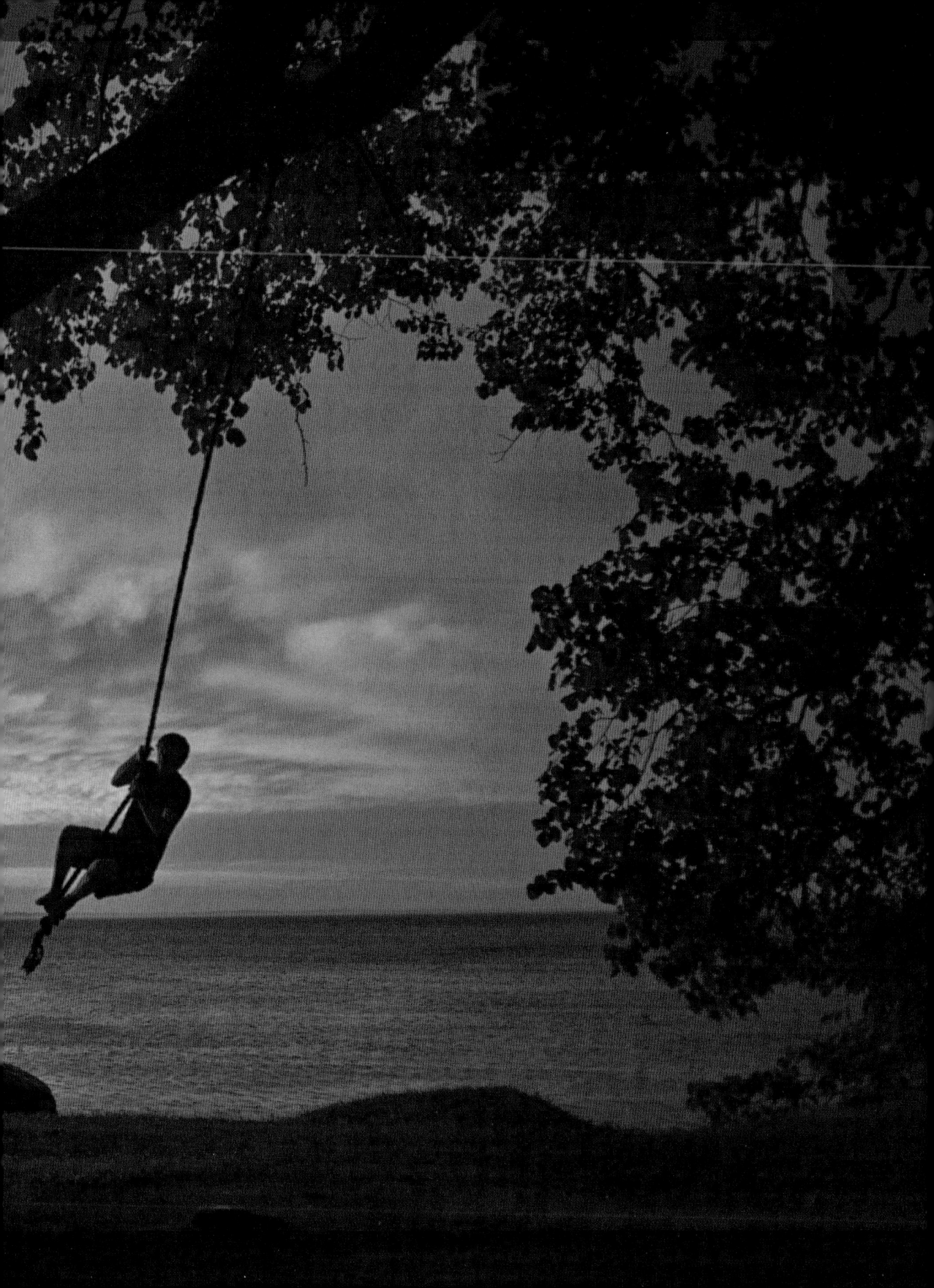

CHASING
THE LIGHT

Light is the key element in all photography. Quite liter-ally—if light didn't reach a camera's sensor, we wouldn't have anything. Jim Stanfield is a veteran photographer who gave me my break at *National Geographic* magazine. He always says, "It's not the light, but where you are in it."

In this chapter, we'll talk about the different kinds of light and how to take advantage of them. We'll start with the quality of light, and what it means when light is "hard" or "soft." Then we'll learn about ambient light—the light in a scene that you don't create—and how to identify great light indoors and out. We'll also discuss the color of light, and how warm and cool lighting can influence your pictures.

Sometimes it can feel like light is an element you cannot control, so we'll look at introducing light in the form of flash. Throughout, we'll talk about how to make light work for you, and how to find your place in it. And, of course, we'll learn a little more about camera functions, while keeping in mind the basics of ISO, aperture, and shutter speed.

The good news is that there are few completely unac-ceptable light conditions. Some light is more challenging to work with than others. Regardless, light can make or break a photograph, and how we face the challenge of mastering it is what shapes us as photographers.

In Howes, South Dakota, a horse pauses by a fence at sunset.

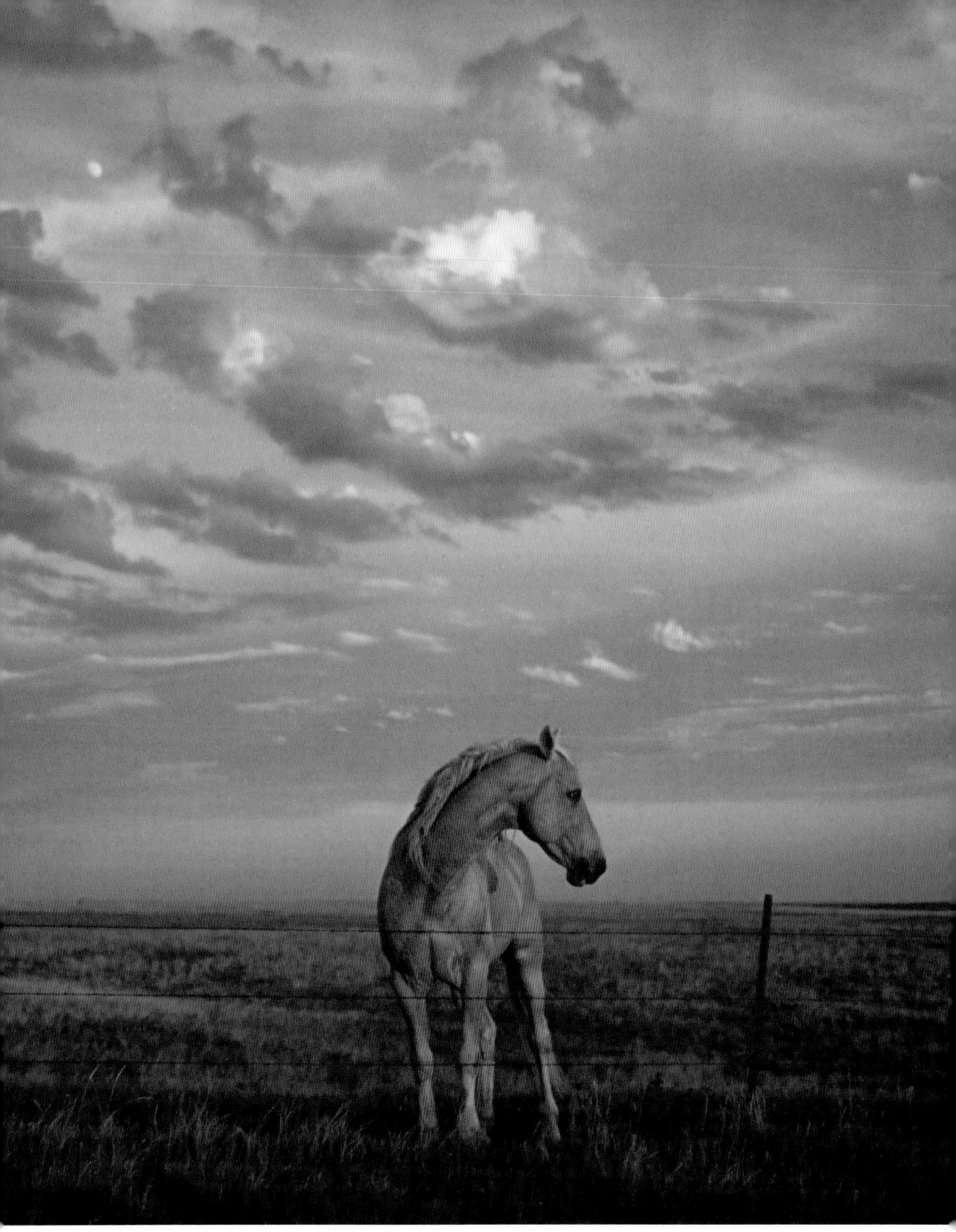

QUALITY OF LIGHT

The quality of light available to us is constantly changing—each geographical region, season, day, and even hour has its own specific light.

Light seems like a simple thing, but once you start paying attention to it you'll notice that it can behave in a million different ways. Capturing the light in a location or season accurately can help tell the story of a place and time, so learning to identify and work with the quality of light is an incredibly useful skill. We use the terms *hard* and *soft* light, but what exactly do they mean?

HARD LIGHT

Hard lighting comes from a single source, usually a bright one, like the sun, a spotlight, or a bare light bulb. In addition to creating a bright spot of glare on your subject, hard light results in high contrast: The brights are really bright, and the darks are really dark. Think about the sun at high noon on a cloudless day: You see incredibly deep shadows

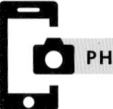

PHONE SMARTS: LIGHT METERING

Your smartphone will meter the light wherever you've placed the focus. Keep this in mind when you're shooting in harsh light, and tap a zone of your frame with mid-tones (in between highlights and shadows) to help the meter balance out the exposure.

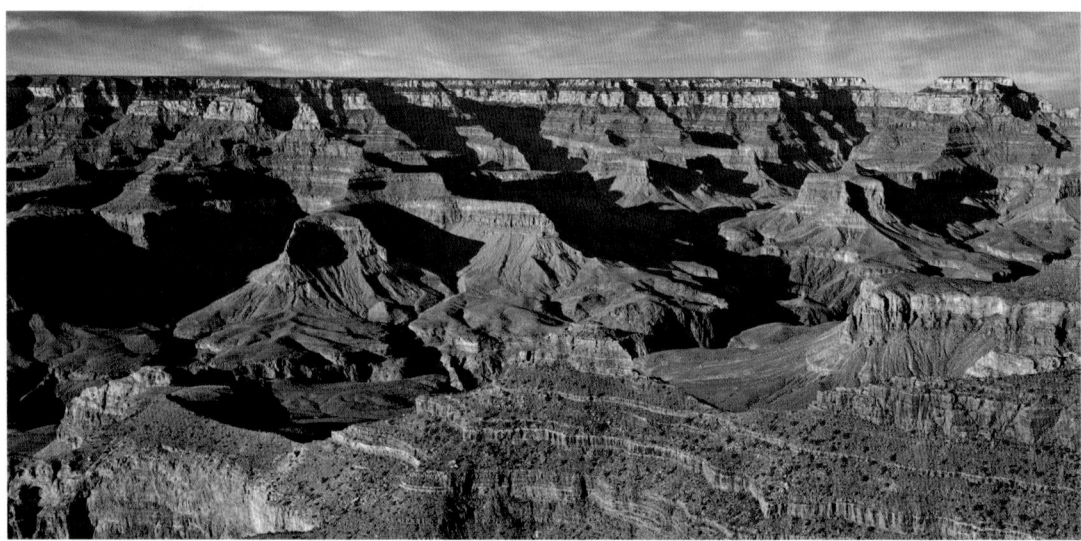

An unobstructed, late-morning light shines brightly on the Grand Canyon. From the direction of the shadows, you can tell that the light comes from a single source: the sun, which is high, coming from camera left, and creating harsh contrast.

with sharp edges where they meet brightly lit surfaces.

Sometimes you'll want this kind of effect—it can create drama and intrigue in a photo, or make a subject pop against the background. But when contrast is too severe, details get lost in both the dark and light areas. When shooting in very hard light, you'll usually want to either modify it somehow, or be strategic about the direction of the lighting, which we'll discuss later in this chapter.

SOFT LIGHT

Soft lighting seems more ubiquitous—it doesn't obviously come from any one source in particular, and it almost wraps around the subject. It doesn't produce extreme highlights or shadows; instead, things blend into each other more seamlessly. Without a sharp glare, colors often appear richer and more true to life.

Although many photographers prefer shooting in soft light, there's no single quality of light that works for every situation. Consider the light that fits your subject and creates the appropriate mood. Soft light can be gentle, and hard light can be dramatic—it's all about the story you're trying to tell.

TURNING HARD LIGHT TO SOFT

If you feel the light you are working with is too harsh, try diffusing or bouncing it. You can diffuse by introducing some kind of filter for the light to pass through before hitting your subject. You can buy large, flexible diffusers to hold between a light source and your subject, or you can use sheer fabric for the same result. To redirect or bounce light, use a reflective surface, or even something bright, like a white T-shirt, to fill harsh shadows on your subject.

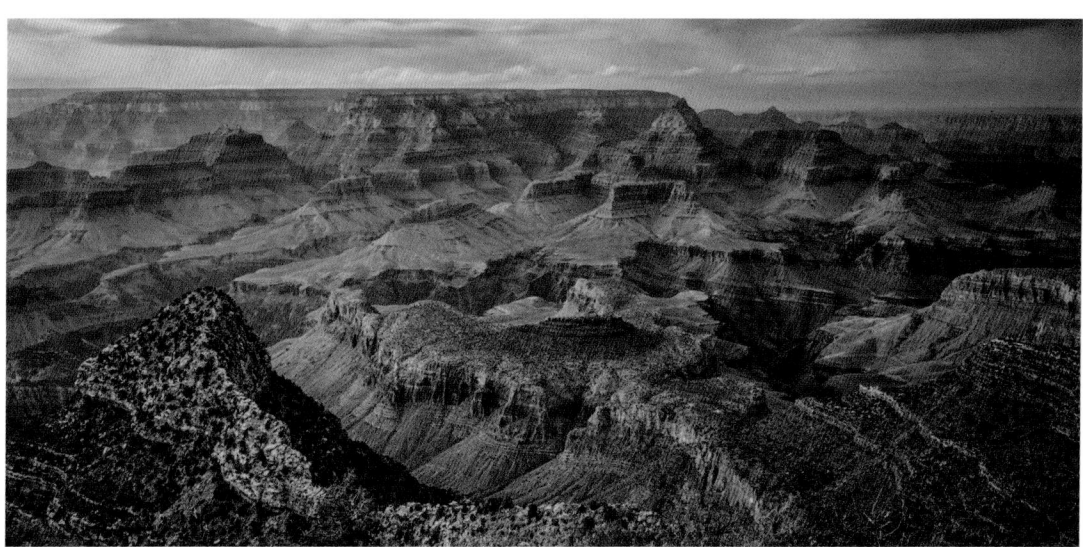

Here is the Grand Canyon on a cloudy day, just before a rainstorm rolls in. Clouds diffuse the sunlight, making it softer and less direct, eliminating harsh shadows and giving the canyon a more ethereal glow.

AMBIENT LIGHT

Outdoors or indoors, during day or night, you'll nearly always have some light already around you.
This is called "ambient light." Using what's already in your scene can help set the tone of your image.

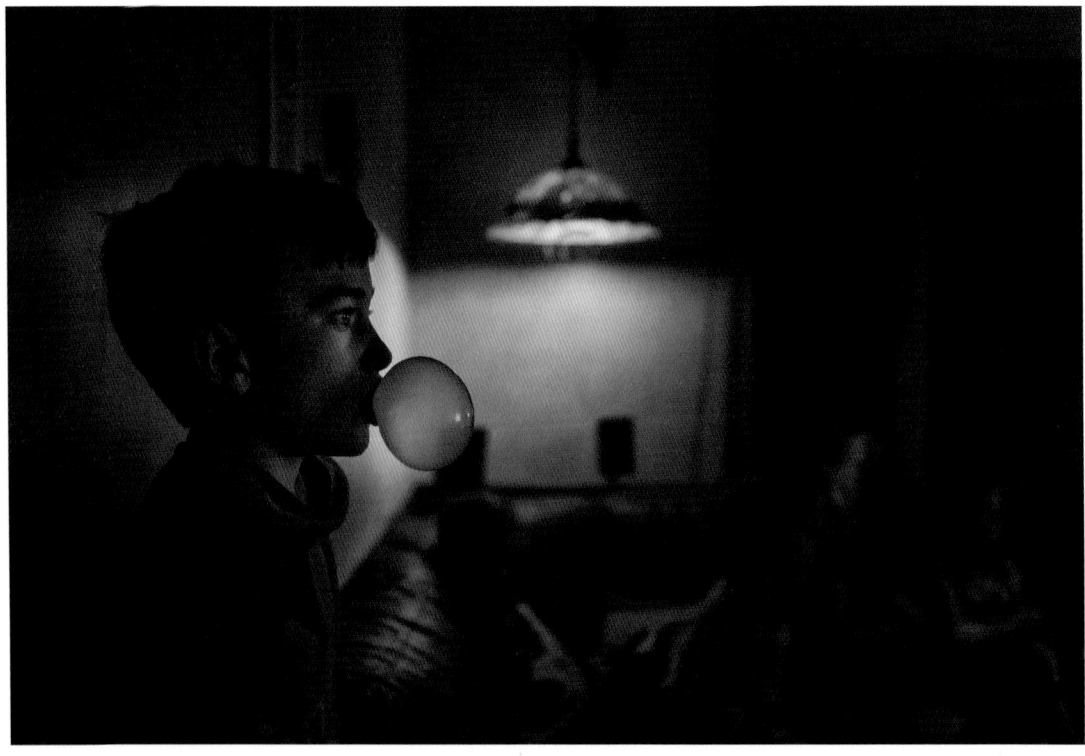

The shade of the hanging lamp in this room mostly blocks the bare bulb within it, but the soft light it emits comes through this boy's chewing gum bubble when photographed at this angle. His face is lit softly by the television screen on the other side of the room.

Ambient light (also called "available light") could be anything from a light bulb in your attic to sunlight in your backyard. Many photographers prefer to use ambient light because it means less equipment, and less time spent creating decent artificial lighting. While you don't control ambient light yourself, it has opportunities and challenges of its own.

WORK WITH WHAT YOU'VE GOT

Remember: Soft light is nearly always more pleasing to the eye than hard light. This can make shooting at noon on a sunny day a challenging task. If you don't like the light you have, look for ways to modify it by moving yourself, moving your subject within the scene, or modifying the light source. For example, look for shade to avoid bright sun, or hang some sheer fabric between your subject and a harsh light source for a softening effect.

If possible, walk all the way around your subject to find where the light works best in the frame, considering the tone and mood of your image as you go. Be patient and open-minded—sometimes the light will vary and solve problems for you.

TAKE IT OUTSIDE

An overcast day makes for the loveliest kind of light when shooting outdoors. A sky full of clouds diffuses sunlight, often bathing your scene in soft, even light. But a bright, white sky can confuse your camera. Your camera may suggest reducing aperture or increasing shutter speed to keep from overexposing a white sky, which might result in your subject appearing dark.

If you run into this, you can utilize a few tricks for getting rid of some of that confusion: Change your angle to shoot down on the scene, eliminating some sky, or fill the frame with your subject. Alternatively, you could try bouncing light onto your subject with a reflective surface to achieve a more balanced exposure. Or, just make an artistic choice to have an all-white sky in your frame.

Another great time to shoot outside is during the warm glow that often occurs right before the sun sets. This light will give your subjects a gold or rosy cast that most of us find calming. This "golden hour," as it is often called, can be fleeting, so be ready

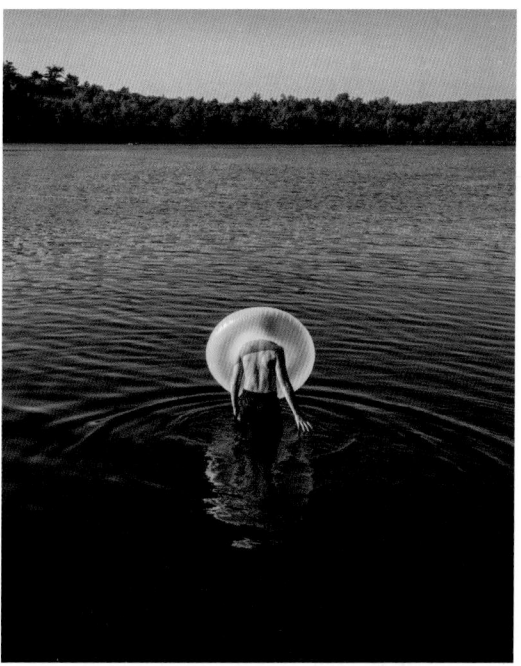

A bright green inner tube is illuminated by the afternoon sun as a boy wades into a lake in Maine. Keeping the image slightly underexposed allows the glow of the inner tube to pop in the frame.

for it. We'll explore the golden hour later in the chapter.

THE LIGHT WITHIN

It's not just the great outdoors that can yield beautiful light. Be on the lookout for interesting ambient light that occurs indoors. Shaded lamps can cast a soft and moody glow, and sheer curtains can softly filter sunlight streaming through a window.

Keep in mind that indoor scenes often have less light available overall, so to ensure a sharp image you'll likely need to choose a higher ISO or use a stabilizing technique to keep your camera still.

RANGE OF LIGHT

The camera's sensor picks up varying amounts of detail across a range of light. At one end of the range is black; at the other, white. In general, our target is a broad area in between—this is where we capture the most details of our image.

We talked about the extremes of exposure in chapter 3—if too little light hits the sensor, areas of the image will appear dark or black. Too much light, and areas of the image will "blow out" and appear white. Our eyes can see a broader range of light than a camera, so we can pick out details while the sensor sees simply black or white. To understand how your camera interprets information, two functions will come in handy: the light meter and the histogram.

LIGHT METER

No matter what mode you're in, your camera's light meter is always at work. It appears as a scale with little vertical lines, usually located at the bottom of your viewfinder. In the middle is a zero; one side goes toward a minus sign, the other toward a plus sign. When the lens is pointed at the scene, tick marks toward the minus indicate that your image will be underexposed. Tick marks

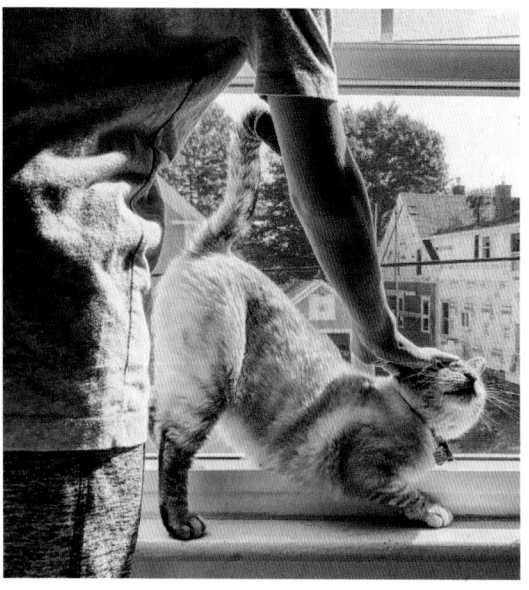

This photograph of a boy petting his cat in a window represents a wide range of light, with distinct shadows and highlights. The cat—the star of the frame—is exposed just right, balancing the image.

toward the plus indicate that your image will be overexposed. In general, you want to hover around zero. If you're creeping toward

---

PRO TIP   CHOOSING INFORMATION: INTENTIONAL OVER- OR UNDEREXPOSING

You may find that "correct" exposure is not your preferred exposure, depending on which details are most important to you. Exposing for what you want may mean other information is pushed into shadows or highlights. This can happen with areas of high contrast, like a dark object on a bright background or vice versa. For example, if a child is playing on the beach on a sunny day, the camera might expose for the bright sand, leaving his face dark. To capture his face, you might open up your aperture, intentionally overexposing the sand to compensate.

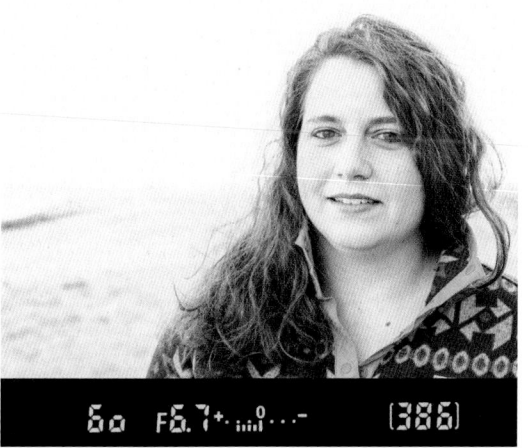

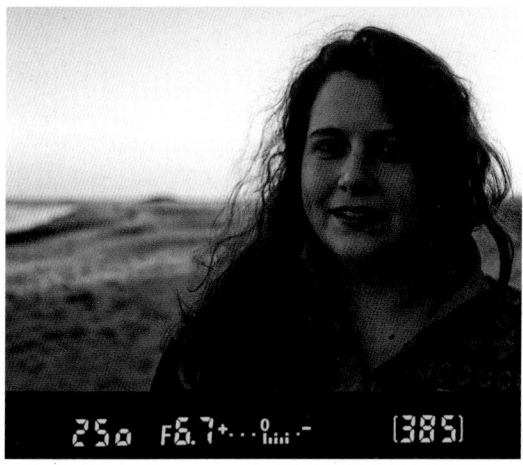

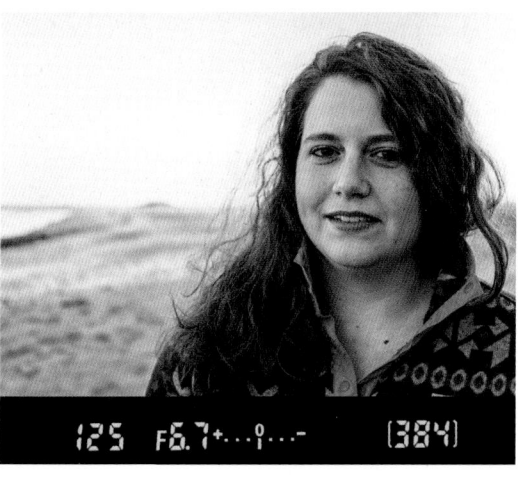

one end, adjust your aperture or shutter speed. Most meters have different modes for reading light—they can take the average of an entire scene (matrix metering) or concentrate on a specific point (spot metering).

HISTOGRAM

A histogram is a graph representing the dynamic range of the scene—the range of tones your camera detects across the frame. The left side represents black or shadows and the right represents white or highlights. A sharp peak on either end means your image is reading a lot of black or white (likely under- or overexposed areas), which are the places where you lose detail. As you adjust exposure, you'll see the peaks approach the center of the histogram, meaning that the bulk of information exists in the mid-tones, and within the range your sensor can record. Typically, a bell-shaped curve near the center of the graph represents a balanced exposure.

Regardless of what your eyes *see*, your camera's histogram will give you an accurate representation of the detail in your image. On most DSLR cameras, you will be able to pull up a histogram on your LCD screen while you have a scene framed in live view. Point your camera at light and dark areas and you'll be able to see how your histogram changes in real time.

As the shutter speed changes in these three portraits, the exposure goes from over at 1/60, to under at 1/250, to balanced at 1/125. The meter scale illustrates these readings.

INTRODUCING LIGHT

When ambient light isn't enough, you can add your own. Introducing light is full of both pitfalls and potential, making practice and patience key.

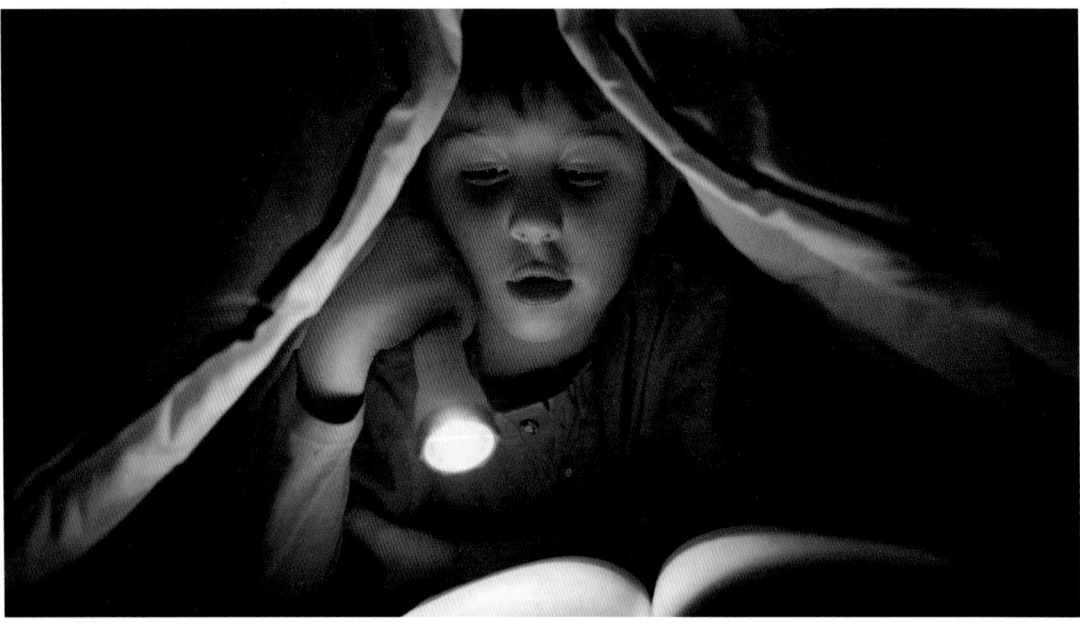

A boy reads under his covers while using a flashlight. The book's pages conveniently bounce softened light back to his face. This photo is a good reminder that you don't need professional lighting equipment to introduce light into a scene.

Sometimes you'll realize that the available light isn't enough for what you want to do with your camera. When you can't solve the problem by moving out of shade or opening curtains, you may need to introduce your own light. This could mean moving some existing lamps, buying an inexpensive floodlight, or using a photographic flash.

CONTINUOUS LIGHT

Light that stays on as you photograph is called continuous light. This can be a lamp, a floodlight, even the taillights on a car—get

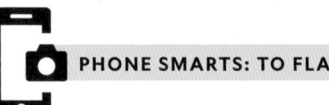

PHONE SMARTS: TO FLASH OR NOT

The flashes on most camera phones are very close to the lens, and seem to have one setting: bright. This makes for fairly unappealing photographs. The good news is that phone cameras tend to work pretty well in low light. It's generally best to keep the flash on a phone camera turned off. Once it gets too dark to photograph without it, put the phone away and enjoy your night!

Flash is almost always best when modified and shaped, and preferably coming from somewhere other than just above your lens—meaning the pop-up flash on top of your camera isn't ideal, and it's best to ignore it. If it's within your budget, try adding an off-camera flash to your kit for more natural-looking light. To make the most of any flash, try these techniques:

- A softbox is a tool that is mounted to the flash. It diffuses light from the flash to make it softer. The closer a diffused light is to the subject, the softer it is. Save money and simulate this effect by wrapping a tissue or sheer fabric around your flash and securing it with a rubber band.

- Bounce the light off a wall, ceiling, or even your shirt (but know that the camera will register the color of whatever you use to reflect that light).

- When choosing camera settings, keep in mind that most flashes won't sync with shutter speeds faster than 1/250.

creative with light sources. With continuous light, you can see what you're getting from it in real time. You are, in a sense, creating your own ambient light, and it will stay on your subject as long as you want it to.

As when working with ambient light, a reflector is a simple but powerful tool when you're introducing light. You can bounce and redirect light where you need it to go. You can get a reflector online or at any camera store. In a pinch, you can use a piece of white foam board or another reflective surface.

FLASH

Another way to introduce light is with a flash. This is a powerful tool that can be tricky to work with. As the name suggests, a flash is *not* continuous—its light lasts only an instant. And it needs to be close to your subject—output generally doesn't travel more than about 10 feet. When experimenting with flash, you'll want to regularly review the images on the back of your camera to see how the light hits your subject.

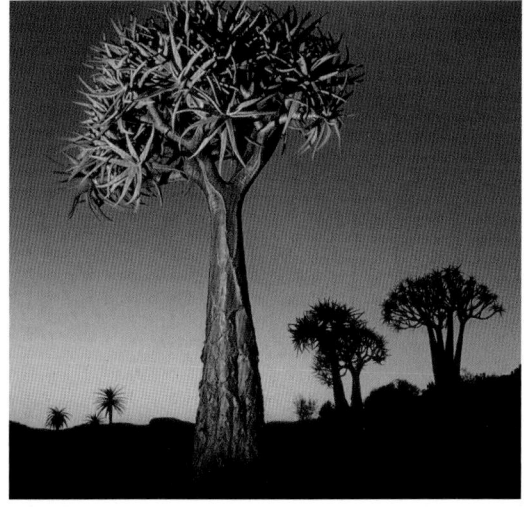

A flash lights up a quiver tree in South Africa, while the aperture and shutter speed are set to properly expose the dim pastel sky at sunset.

Flashes vary in power and the way they are triggered. We'll talk about flash more in the next lesson, but know that there are entire books dedicated to flash photography, and it can take a long time to master. Don't let early results rattle you—patience and practice will pay off in photographs that reach a new, sophisticated level.

FLASH PHOTOGRAPHY

Using a flash can enhance your photography indoors or outdoors. Subtlety and balance are key and take practice to achieve.

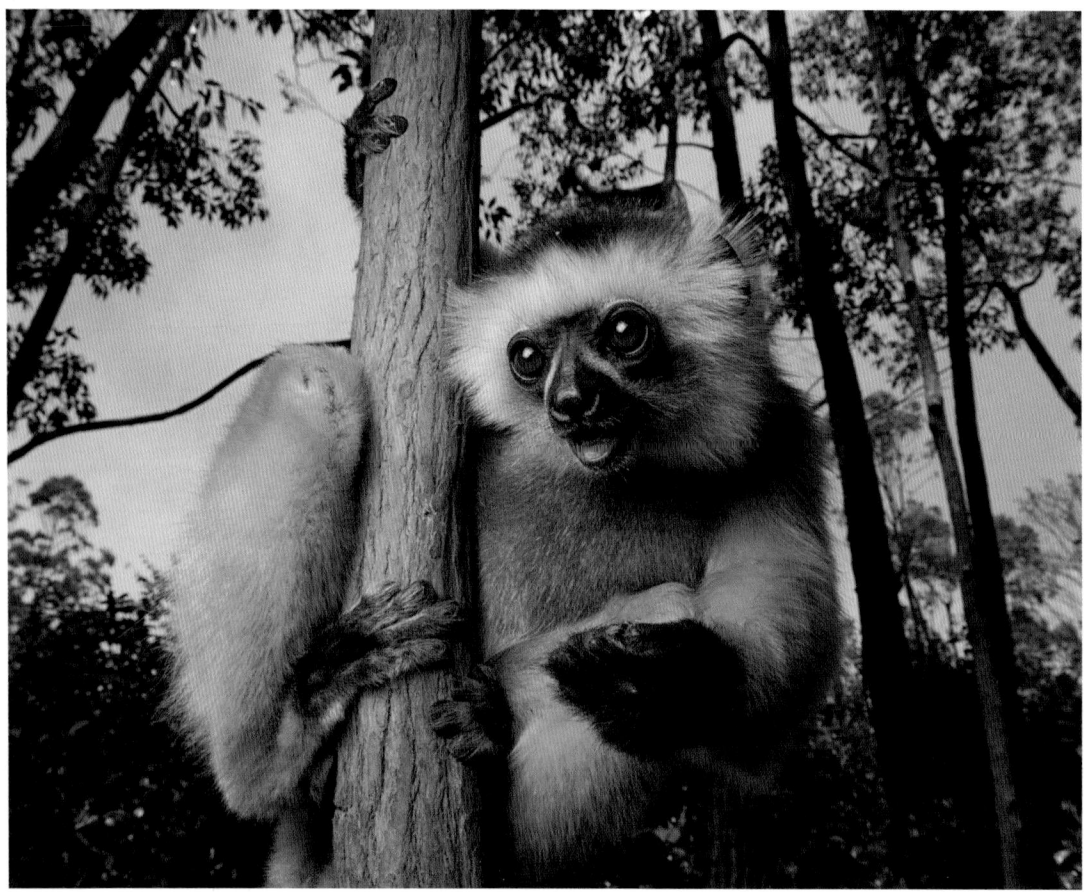

Although this picture was taken in Madagascar during the daytime, using a flash for fill lighting helped this diademed sifaka, a species of lemur, stand out from the forest in the background.

The biggest challenge in using flash is incorporating it into a successful exposure equation. To get the balance right, you need to decide what role you want flash to play. Is it an accenting light source, there to fill in shadows and make your subject pop? Or is it your only light source, responsible for the entire exposure?

FILL FLASH

The most common use of flash is to fill in shadows and illuminate details in your subject. To do this, you should choose your aperture and shutter speed to expose for the ambient light, then add flash for accent. Generally, your shutter speed will be responsible for letting in enough ambient light to expose the majority of the scene, while your flash highlights your subject. One thing to keep in mind is that most strobes won't sync with a shutter speed faster than 1/250 of a second—if your shutter speed is higher than that, you'll need to drop it down, then stop down (reduce aperture) to compensate. Your aperture will dictate the power and distance of your flash to add fill light on your subject.

FLASH ONLY

In a formal photo studio, most light is controlled, so the final image usually depends heavily on flash. In this case, I typically leave my shutter at 1/250, which is the sync speed of my flash. The exposure is a balance between the aperture and flash power. How much of the scene is illuminated depends on the distance of the subject from the background, and the tools used to soften and shape the light.

THROUGH THE LENS

Many off-camera flashes have a Through The Lens (TTL) metering function that will make choices for you about the amount of light emitted by your flash. If adding one more element to your exposure equation feels overwhelming, don't hesitate to leave your flash on TTL. You'll still have the free-

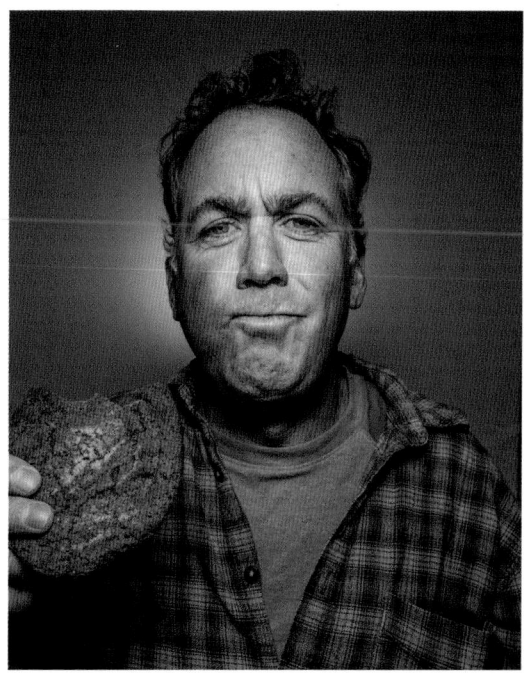

This portrait was made in a formal photo studio, where all the light in the image came from flash, and was under the photographer's control.

dom to adjust your shutter speed and aperture settings for the scene.

GAUGING RESULTS

We know bad flash when we see it—red eyes, harsh reflections, dark shadows, and too much contrast. Good flash should be subtle, perhaps barely noticeable. Light from a flash should almost always be shaped or softened, and you have a great many modifiers to choose from: reflectors, umbrellas, softboxes, sheer pieces of fabric. The biggest hurdle in flash photography is that there's no way to preview what the result will look like. Be prepared to slow down, experiment, check your work often, and adjust accordingly.

DIRECTION

When you set out to light your subject, consider the direction of the light. Simply adjusting the location of your light source can dramatically change the tone of an image and the appearance of your subject.

We're used to photographing with the sun at our backs—that seems like a no-brainer to light a subject. But this angle, also called "front lighting" or "direct lighting," can feel boring. When the sun is low on the horizon it can make tones richer and warmer, with longer shadows. But if it's harsh or too high, front lighting will flatten out the photo, yielding fewer shadows and less depth. So how can we play the lighting angles to get more creative?

- OVERHEAD LIGHTING means the light comes from above. When shooting portraits, this can be effective. Try having your subject look up toward the light to avoid shadows being cast down on the face. A reflective source beneath your subject can also help fill in unwanted shadows from the chin, nose, and brow.
- GHOST LIGHTING is just like when you held a flashlight under your chin to tell a scary story as a kid. The light coming up from below can be unflattering and creepy, a good choice if you're aiming for an eerie effect.
- REMBRANDT LIGHTING, named for the painter, is a three-quarter angle on the subject—on the side, and a little bit in front. This positioning means the side of the face closest to the light source is well lit, while the other side has a balance of soft shadows and "spill" light. The distinctly shaped shadows created by this type of light lend subtle drama to a portrait.
- HATCHET LIGHTING, or side lighting, is when the light is bright and harsh on one side of the subject, while the other side is in shadow. In portraiture, this effect may be moody and dramatic.
- BACKLIGHTING is when the light source is directly behind the subject. With transparent or translucent subjects, this can illuminate details that might otherwise be obscured in different light, like the delicate hairs on a baby's head. This is also called "silhouette lighting," because if you expose for the light source and your subject is opaque, it will look completely black with a halo of light around the edges.

These angles are easiest to experiment with when you are lighting your subject with an introduced light source, such as a flash, since you can move it wherever you'd like in relation to your subject. In order to change the angle of an ambient light source, such as the sun, you'll have to move your subject and the camera.

To explore the impact of light from different directions, photograph a person beside a bright window, a lamp, or using your flash. Take a few different frames, moving the light source or your subject around so the light comes from different angles. How does the look of the portrait change with the direction of light?

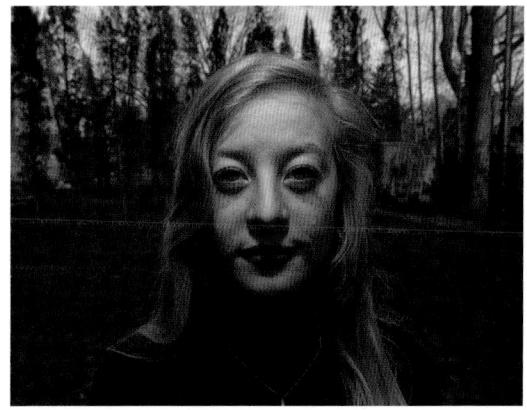

top lighting

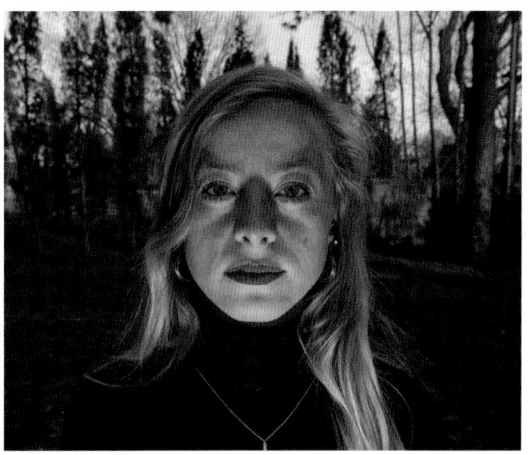

ghost lighting

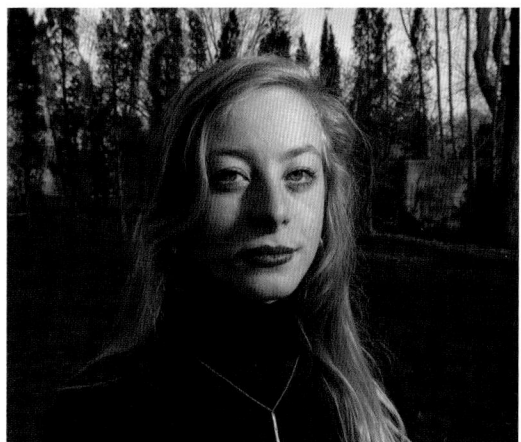

Rembrandt lighting

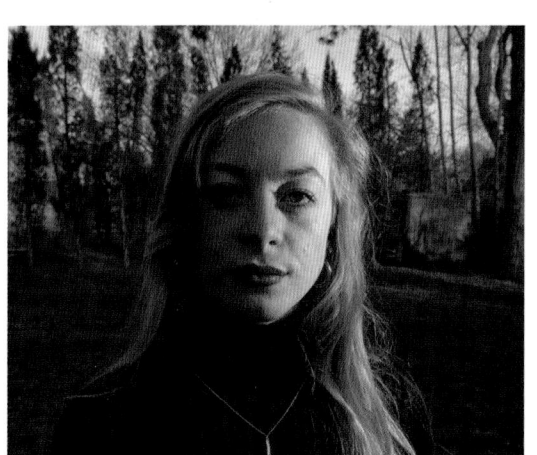

hatchet/side lighting

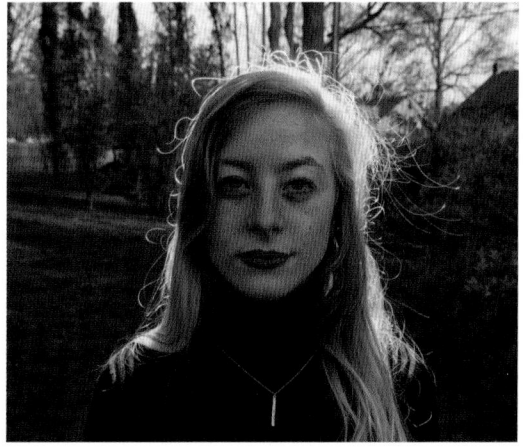

rim or backlit

COLOR TEMPERATURE

Light comes in different colors that we describe on a temperature spectrum from warm (red- and yellow-toned light) to cool (blue- and purple-toned light). The color of your light and your subjects interact to create a color palette, and set a mood for your photographs.

When you're observing the world with a photographic eye, a bright pop of color will often grab your attention. But evoking a mood or feeling in your images means going beyond the palette created by your subjects alone. Along with quality of light, learning to recognize and take advantage of the color temperature of light will make your photographs more impactful.

YOUR EYE VS. THE CAMERA

Recognizing the color of light can be tricky because our brains are working against us. Have you ever taken a picture on a day where the world seems to be blanketed in pure, white snow, only to find that the photo turns out blue? Or when you shoot indoors by lamplight, and everything turns out yellow? The camera captures true colors, while our brains correct what we see to the color we *think* it should be. Our brains think all light should be white, just like the sun—the ultimate source of white light. So when our eyes come across a colored light source, our

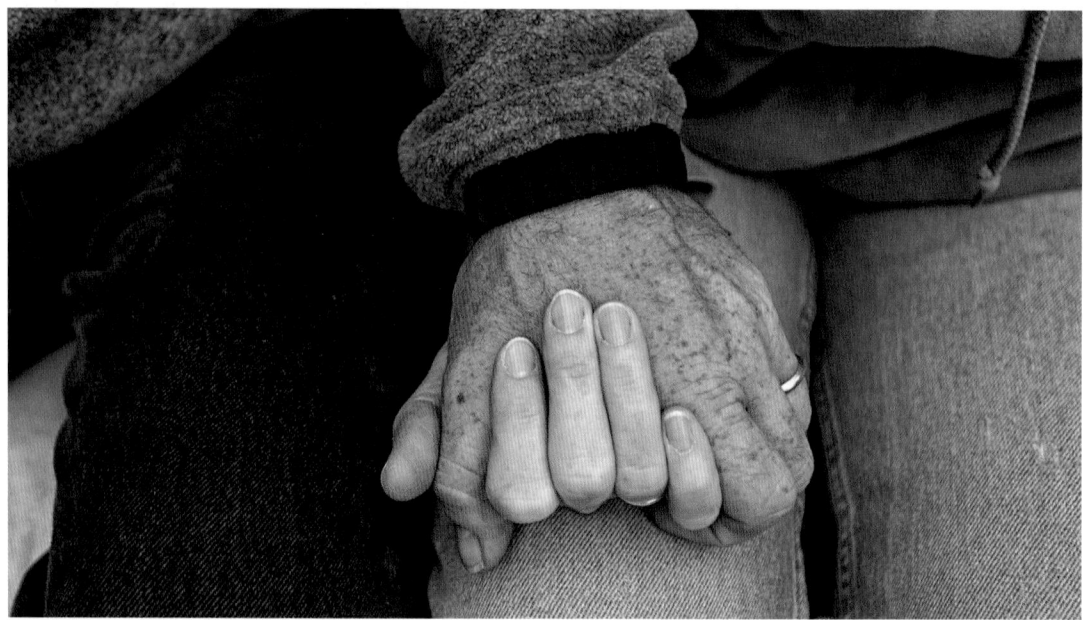

Here's a picture of my wife, Kathy, and me holding hands. The camera read the late-evening light around us as blue, which adds a nice, calm mood to the frame—perfect for a quiet moment between husband and wife.

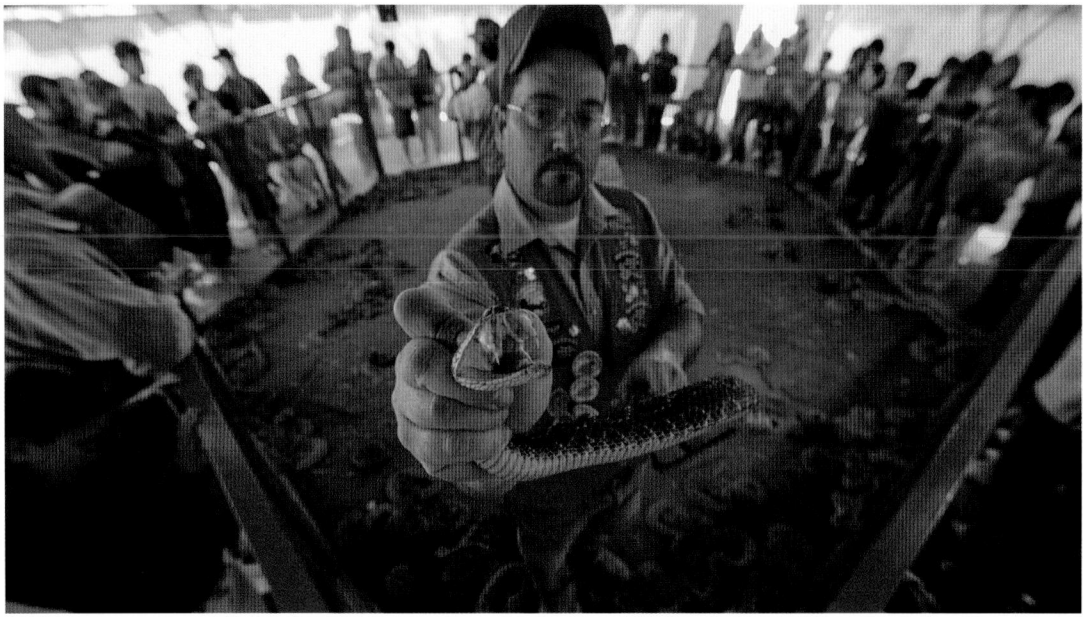

The red light in this photo adds energy, warmth, and a slightly mysterious tone to this picture from the Rattlesnake Derby in Mangum, Oklahoma.

brains autocorrect. The best way to understand how your camera sees the color of the light is to take pictures and look at the results. In time, you'll learn to predict the color cast your image will take on in many different scenarios.

COMBINING COLOR AND CONTENT

Pay attention to how the color of the light works with your subject to affect the mood of your picture. A blue-toned picture of a couple on our porch feels calm and peaceful. But an image of someone bathed in the blue light of a computer screen feels ominous. Similarly, red light behind a couple slow dancing feels romantic, but red light bouncing off a pit of rattlesnakes feels dangerous. In this way, the color temperature of light becomes one more tool we can use in making an impactful image that tells a story.

PRO TIP | THE TRUTH ABOUT COLOR TEMPERATURE

We often use the words *cool* and *warm* as descriptors of light. This can be confusing, because although we think of cool as blue and warm as red, a technical photographer could be referring to the *actual* temperature of the light—which is the opposite. The temperature of light is measured in degrees kelvin. When a light source is really "hot," it gives off white light—like the sun, which on a clear day may register around 20,000K. When a light source is cooler, it glows red—like the coals of a dying fire. The waning light at sunset may register around 2000K.

WHITE BALANCE

Sunlight at noon is considered neutral or "white" and is the standard to which the color temperatures of all other light sources are compared. White balance is the mechanism by which we correct an image to make any white in the frame look neutral.

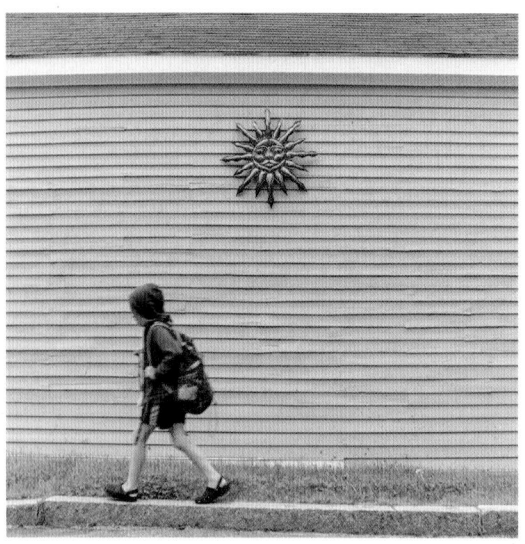
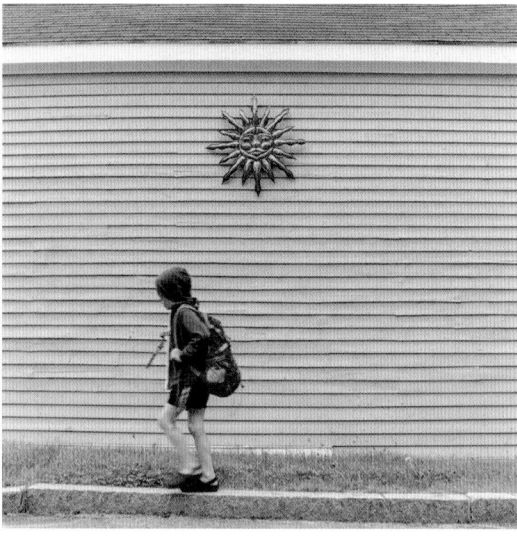
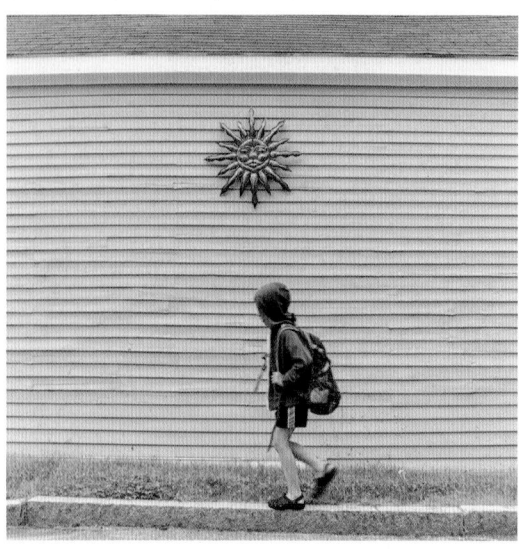
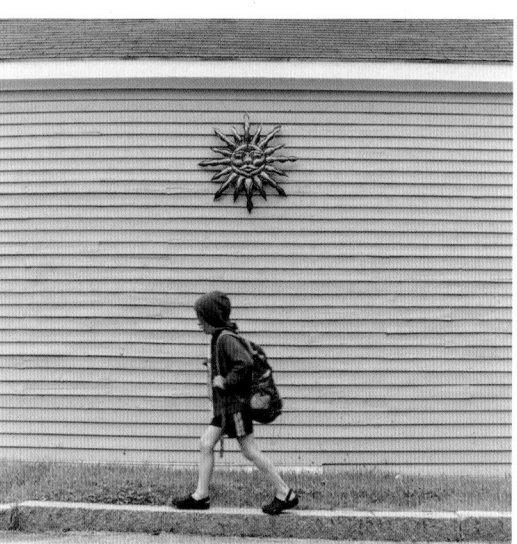

A camera's white balance settings produce different results based on the light they are designed for. Daylight (top left) gives a natural-looking tone to this image shot outdoors. Fluorescent (top right) adds a magenta cast, Shade (lower left) adds some warmth, and Tungsten (lower right) adds a cool tone.

In the last lesson, we talked about the color temperature of light. Different light sources have different hues, and while our brains tend to autocorrect for those differences, the camera doesn't.

For example: If you hold a white piece of paper under a lamp, an incandescent bulb will cast a yellow hue onto it. Your brain still registers the paper as white, but your camera captures the *true* color of the paper as lit by the lamp. The other colors in your scene are relative to the "white" recorded by the camera; therefore, they will all have a warm, yellow cast.

The same holds true for other types of lighting, such as fluorescent bulbs, which give off a blue hue that gives a photograph a cool cast. In addition to artificial light sources, factors like the time of day and the amount of cloud cover can impact the color of light in a photo. If you find that a particular color cast isn't working for your image, you have a tool to correct it.

AUTOCORRECTING

White balance is the mechanism by which the camera can autocorrect the way our brains do. Use it to indicate which color should register as white, and all the other colors in the image will be corrected accordingly. With the help of this tool, the colors that your camera sees will look more like the colors that you perceived. White balance can be done in the camera itself, or corrected later during postproduction editing—more on that in chapter 10.

IN-CAMERA WHITE BALANCE

Your camera may have preprogrammed white balance settings that can adjust for color temperature in shade, fluorescent lighting, incandescent or tungsten lighting, and more. Fluorescent bulbs emit blue light, so that setting will add a slight magenta cast, while a typical tungsten bulb emits yellow light, so the camera will add a cool tone to the image.

Depending on the model, your camera may also have an automatic white balance (AWB) setting, which sets the white balance, depending on what type of light the camera detects. This isn't foolproof, so you'll want to regularly check your results on playback to make sure that you're getting the colors you want. If your light source is consistent, it's good practice to set your white balance before you select your other settings.

| PRO TIP | DEFAULT WHITE BALANCE SETTING |

Over my years with DSLR cameras, I have found that presetting my white balance to "Daylight" gives me the widest array of colors in a photograph, no matter what my lighting source is. That, combined with shooting in RAW format, means I have the most to work with later in postproduction. We'll talk more about RAW and other capture formats, and postproduction editing later in this book.

THE GOLDEN HOUR

Two times of day produce soft, warm, beautiful light fairly reliably—the first and last hour of sun in the sky. Both are called the golden hour, and your thirst for great light will have you out making the most of it.

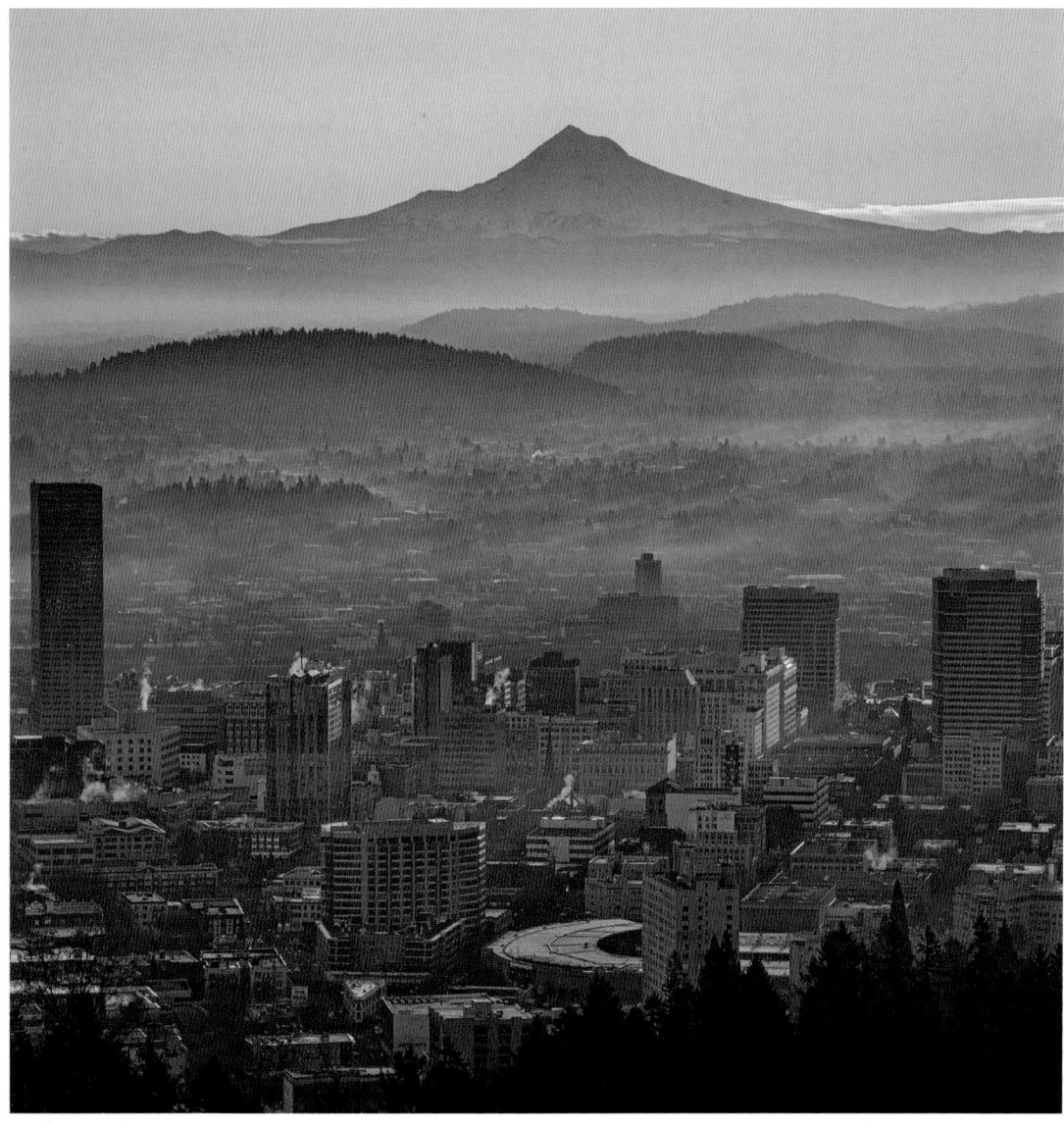

At the golden hour, the sun is low and its light diffuse as warm colors wash over this cityscape. The distant mountains look purple in the waning light.

In general, try to avoid shooting outside in the middle of a sunny day. The sun is high, the light is harsh, and photographs made midday are most often flat and uninteresting. The best hours are when the sun is low in the sky—usually just before sunrise to midmorning, and late afternoon to just after sunset. Bookending these optimal photographic hours are two brief but special periods—what photographers call the golden hour. This is a fleeting time when shadows are long, and the world is bathed in a warm glow.

THE MECHANICS OF THE GOLDEN HOUR

When the sun is low, just barely above the horizon, light must pass its greatest distance through the Earth's atmosphere. As a result, the light is less direct, yielding less contrast. In the absence of harsh glare, colors look deep and rich. The blue end of the spectrum is scattered more as light takes this long and filtered path, giving everything a reddish-yellow cast. Some photographers call this "magic light," and it can make for beautiful photographs.

And be ready with your camera—the word *hour* in the name is used figuratively. When we're lucky, the golden hour can linger, but often the most magical light lasts only a few minutes. As Robert Frost said, nothing gold can stay (unless, of course, you make a beautiful photograph of it).

MAGIC LIGHT IS JUST ONE TOOL

I hate going to a restaurant with a great view and bad food. It's not enough to let the view do all the work—I'm here to eat! Just because the golden hour yields great light doesn't mean you can throw all the other elements of good photography out the window. Consider exposure—warm, soft light probably needs a slower shutter speed or a wider aperture. Pay attention to composition and focus. A subject bathed in the fading sun's glow may be more interesting than the sunset itself. Think about the story you're trying to tell.

Making the most out of the golden hour might take some advance planning. You can search online for golden hour calculators to determine the exact times the golden hour occurs in your location. Think of some things you'd like to try, and head out just before the magic happens. Put together all you've learned so far to take the most advantage of this fleeting, fantastic light.

PRO TIP SPARKLING CITIES

Dawn and dusk are some of the best times to photograph city lights. You might think they'd shine best late at night, but the contrast between dark sky and bright lights can leave your cityscape photos looking flat. Lights from skyscrapers and monuments glow against the pastel colors of a sunrise or sunset, letting you capture more details with less contrast.

WORKING IN LOW LIGHT

Sometimes there are moments you'd like to capture after the sun has gone down, or in total shadow, or when the lights inside are dim. Understanding the parameters of your camera can help you extend your hours and bounds of photography, even when the light is low.

With each generation, digital cameras get better at working well in low light. More advanced sensors mean better image quality at very high ISOs, and improved in-camera stabilization means we can use slower shutter speeds with more ease. Nonetheless, shooting in low light requires technical know-how for good results.

REMEMBERING THE BASICS

Successful low-light photography means making the most of what's available to you. Start by setting ISO. Remember that you can "buy" light by pumping up the ISO. But, as we discussed in chapter 3, high ISO comes at a cost—the higher the ISO, the more noise in the photograph.

Next, we tap into our understanding of aperture and shutter speed. It helps to use a wide-angle lens with a very wide aperture. An f-stop of 4 is great, but f/2.8 is even better. In low light, a slower shutter speed is necessary for capturing as much light as possible, so use stabilization to avoid unwanted blur.

BALANCE LIGHT SOURCES

Once your camera is set up to make the most of the low available light, you may want to experiment with using flash to freeze your subject during a slow shutter period. You'll need an understanding of the flash you have available—how to adjust its power for aperture and the distance to your subject. Experimentation and patience are key here.

Take advantage of your tools for understanding light. Your in-camera meter wants everything to read as daylight, so in low light it may warn you about underexposure. This is where the histogram is helpful. If you want a photograph that uses every ounce of light in a more even tonal distribution, such as the moon against a soft pastel sky, look for a histogram with a curve toward the middle of the graph. If you're trying to preserve the darkness in a scene, such as exposing for a face lit by campfire, aim for a histogram peak at the left side of the graph, indicating predominantly dark tones.

KNOW WHEN TO SAY WHEN

Most important, remember that, as a beginner, your quest for a photograph should be an *enhancement* to your experience, and not something that causes you to stress and miss the experience altogether! If you're struggling to work with the tools you have to make something you like, consider putting the camera away and simply living the moment instead—no technical know-how required.

FOR MORE ON SLOW SHUTTER SPEED, SEE PAGE 76.
FOR MORE ON HIGH ISO, SEE PAGE 78.

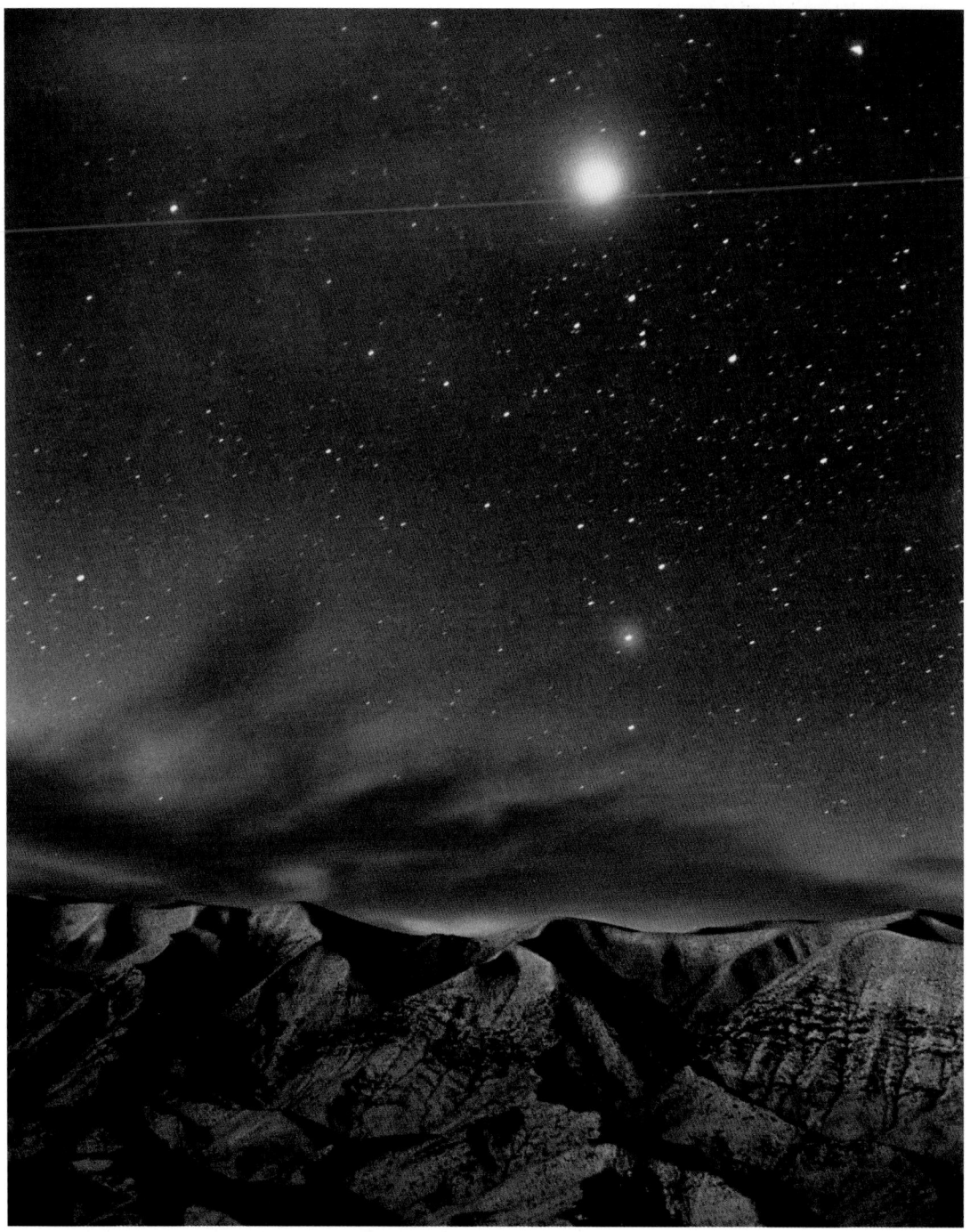

A long exposure captures the details of these mountaintops painted by dim moonlight. Using a tripod keeps the details crisp while the shutter remains open to gather as much available light as possible.

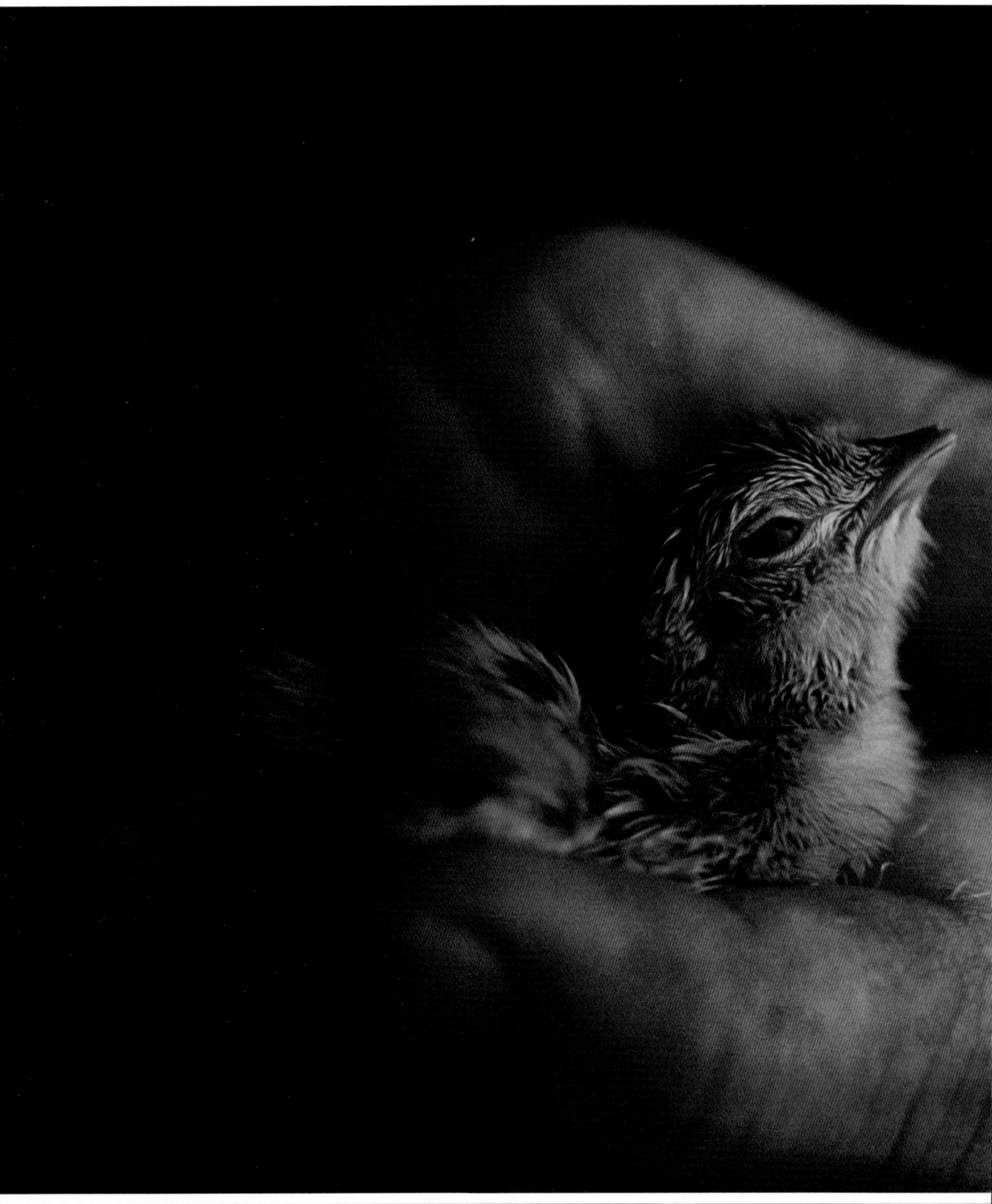

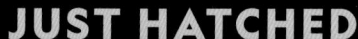

JUST HATCHED

This is a simple photograph of a rare bird called an Attwater's prairie-chicken. I took it while visiting the Fossil Rim Wildlife Center in Glen Rose, Texas, which was breeding these birds to restore their population. I had spent the night on the floor of the incubator room, hoping to photograph one of the eggs hatching. This is a minutes-old chick, just out of its egg. It's a delicate little thing, so I didn't want to blast it by using a bright flash. I wanted something very subtle, tender, warm, and caring.

COLOR They had a little heat lamp turned on in the corner of the incubator room, throwing off a faint, warm-colored light. I thought the warm, red glow matched the delicate feel of the subject, and illustrated the importance of human care to this species.

ADDITIONAL LIGHT I added a bit more light and dimension to this photo by bringing in a single tungsten bulb from a reading lamp. This helped by adding a touch of illumination to the chick's face from just outside the frame.

REPOSITION I asked the caregiver holding the baby bird to move closer to the light until we got just the right shot. When working on posed portraits, take advantage of the conditions around you, and nicely ask for what you want, to get the perfect picture.

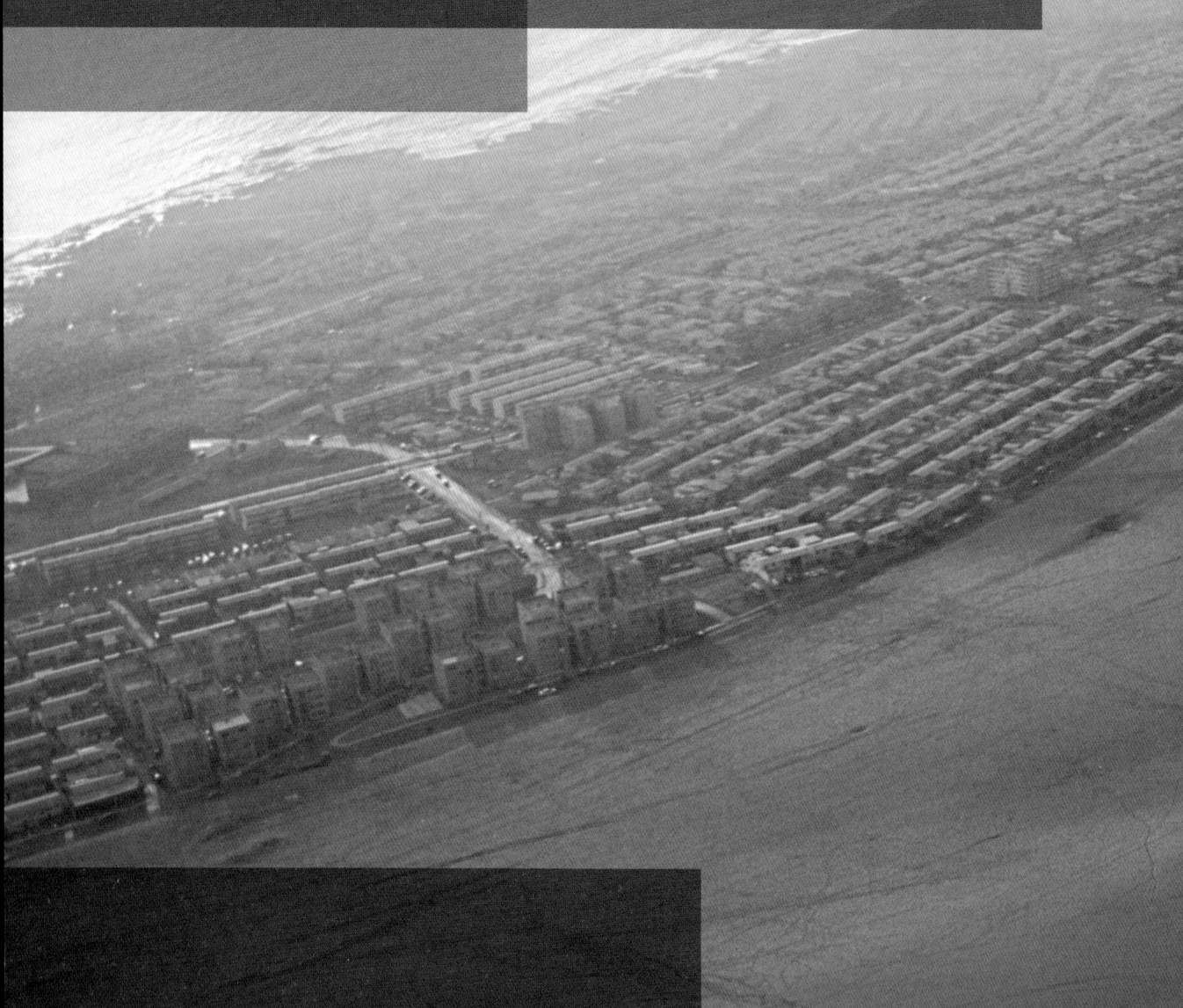

FIVE

COLOR & TEXTURE

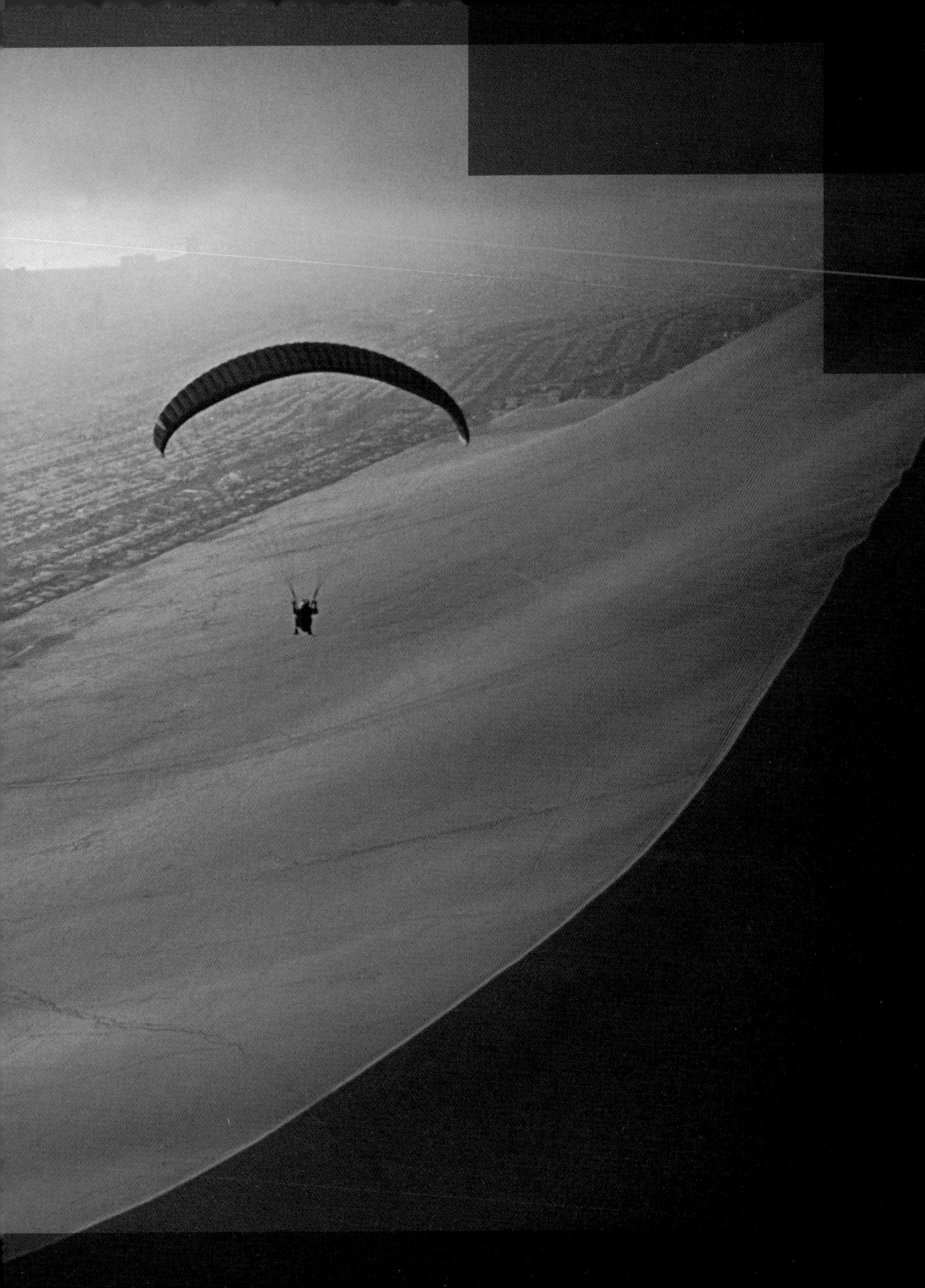

CONCERNING COLOR

There's a reason "What's your favorite color?" is such a popular question for kids and adults alike. Color rules our world, and it holds enormous power in photography. In this chapter, we'll discuss how to make the most of color in your photographs, whether you choose a single color palette for a picture or forgo color altogether for a black-and-white image. When it comes to color (or the absence thereof), your choices require careful thought and planning. Paying attention to your circumstances will guide you in the right direction.

We'll also explore the use of texture and patterns in your pictures. Have you ever seen a photo that you want to reach into and touch? Not only are patterns and textures pleasing to our brains, they can also evoke energy or calm, and can give photographs a feel exceeding two dimensions, creating a deeper experience for the viewer.

Finally, we'll look into macro photography. You can make a big impression by going small—as long as you have the right gear, light, and mind-set. By mastering just a few tricks, you can create compelling pictures of the tiny in the world around us.

A Cope's gray tree frog rests in a peony bush near Crosslake, Minnesota.

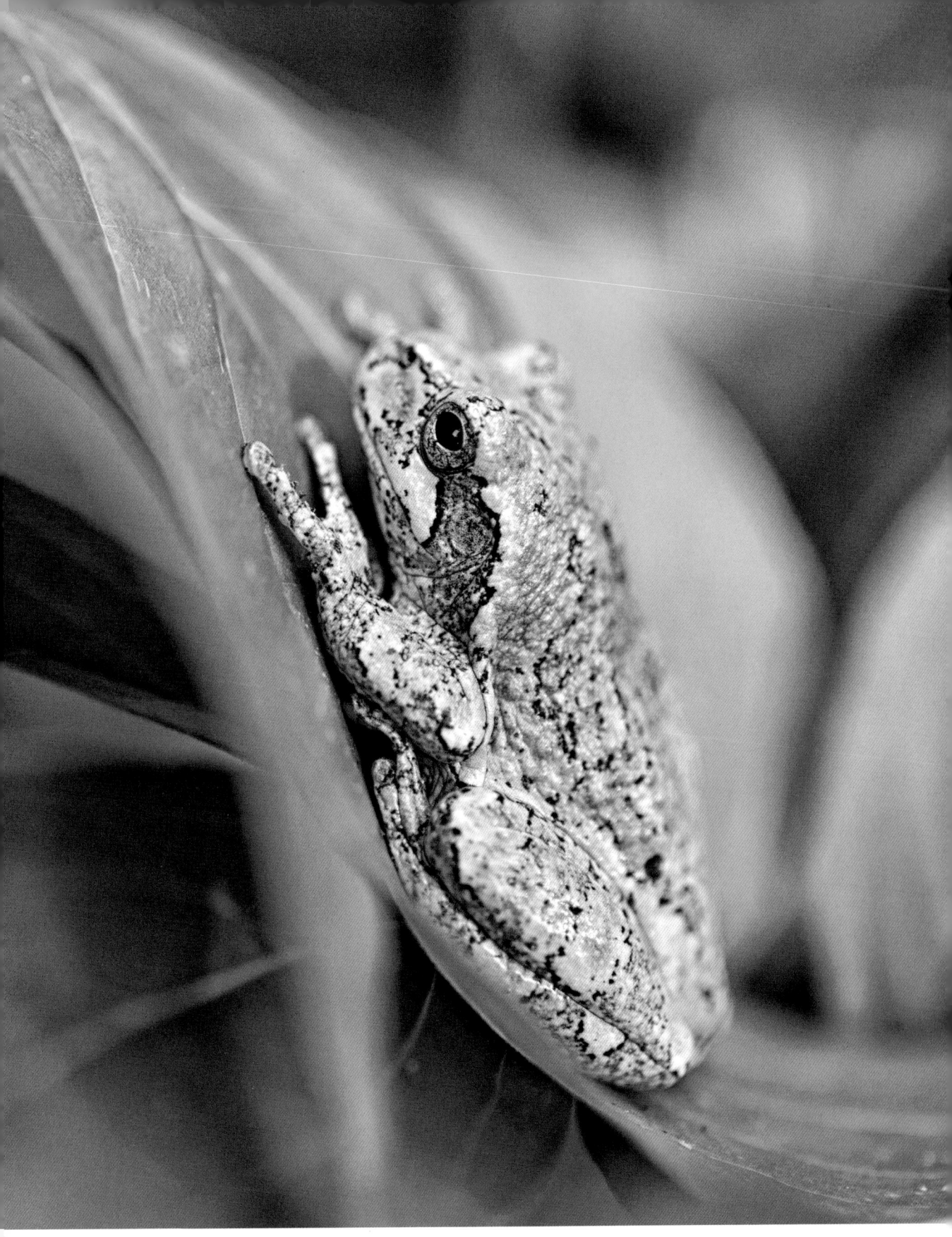

COLOR PALETTES

The color palette of any image carries weight. Which colors you choose, how many, and how vibrant they are all affect the mood and tone of your image.

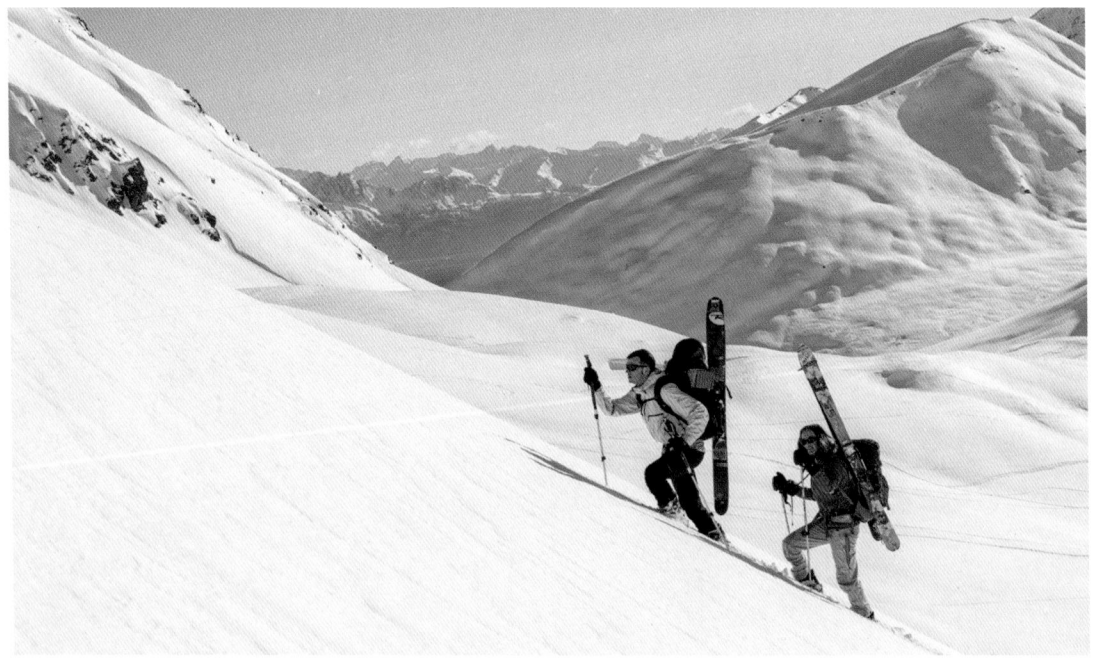

A couple carries ski gear through the backcountry of Alaska's Talkeetna Mountains. The blue sky and white snow help convey the climate, while the bright colors of their jackets add warmth and energy to the snowy scene.

As we've seen, there are many elements to keep in mind when creating a photograph—composition, exposure, focus, and light are the building blocks of any image. But the element that may transport a viewer the most is color. As we discussed in the previous chapter, most light has color, which can influence the mood of your photograph. A beach in yellow or orange light feels warm, and blue light with overcast skies can make a snowy landscape feel even colder.

You should also consider the color of objects in your picture—backgrounds, people, and things. The combination of the colors of light and the objects in focus work together to form a color palette, a tool we use to help the viewer feel something about the scene.

THE POWER OF COLOR

A bright color, even in a small amount, has visual weight, meaning it will attract the eye even more than a large object in a

Look around your house or yard with color in mind. Are there scenes of mostly one color? Are there scenes with too many colors? Frame an image and try adding and subtracting colored objects in different ways. Experiment with the ways color changes the frame, for better or for worse.

neutral or dull hue. Think about that snowy landscape again. Adding a person in a bright red coat adds a dynamic pop of interest with a contrasting warm feel. And on the beach, adding a blue or white umbrella adds a cool element to a warm scene. These are transformative elements in a frame.

Alternatively, choosing to use a single color in various shades, or repeating a color throughout the frame can create rhythm and harmony in an image—a visual constant that might evoke a feeling of calm.

Color can and should work hand in hand with other compositional techniques. If you have one brightly colored object in an otherwise muted scene, think carefully about where you place it, perhaps letting the rule of thirds guide your choice. Similarly, avoid an unintentional bit of color that disrupts an otherwise rhythmic field. Remember—if it's in your picture, it's either working for you or against you.

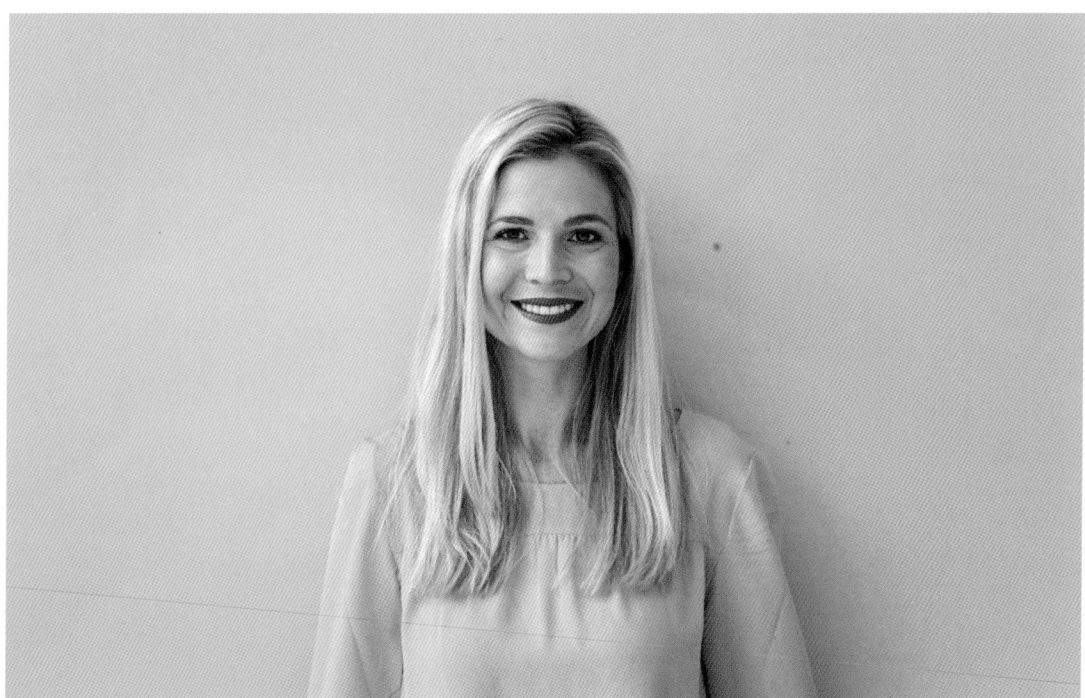

This portrait of a smiling woman in a yellow blouse against a yellow wall has a sense of warmth and happiness. The bright pop of her red lipstick is fun, and its placement in the middle centers us in this bright frame.

SATURATION

Like light, color comes in a range of intensities, from vibrant to muted, pure to nearly gray. As each color shifts down the range of intensity and saturation, it evokes different feelings along the way.

Each color carries its own set of emotional connotations, from energetic reds to warm yellows to soothing blues and greens. Vibrant colors often convey a high-energy, exciting scene, whereas muted tones can add a feeling of calm or tranquility. When considering color in your images, think about saturation—the vividness of a color—in addition to the color itself.

VIBRANT SHADES

Bold, fully saturated colors carry a lot of impact. We often associate busy, energetic, even chaotic scenes with vivid, bright colors. Take the brightly colored powders used during the Holi festival in India, or the neon lights of Times Square. Even if you've never been to these places, an image full of their vibrant hues gives you a clear sense of the

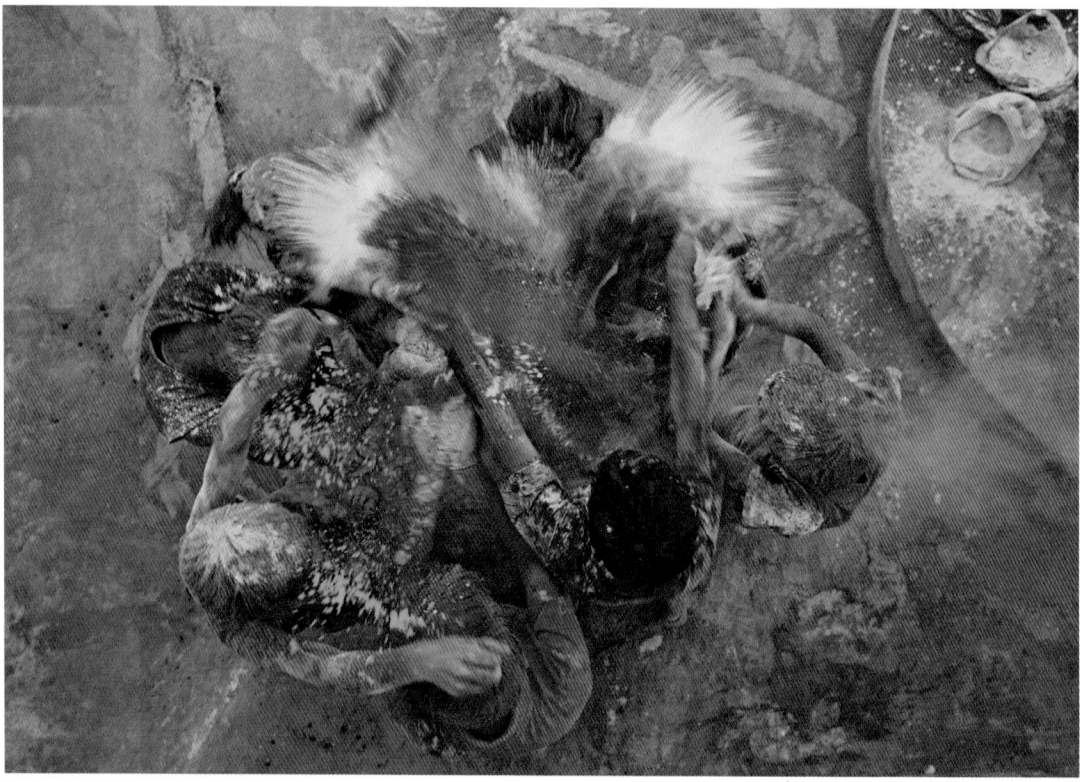

Children play with brightly colored powders at a Holi festival in Jodhpur, India. Color plays an obvious role in the energy of this photo, but composition and perspective are just as important to maximize their impact.

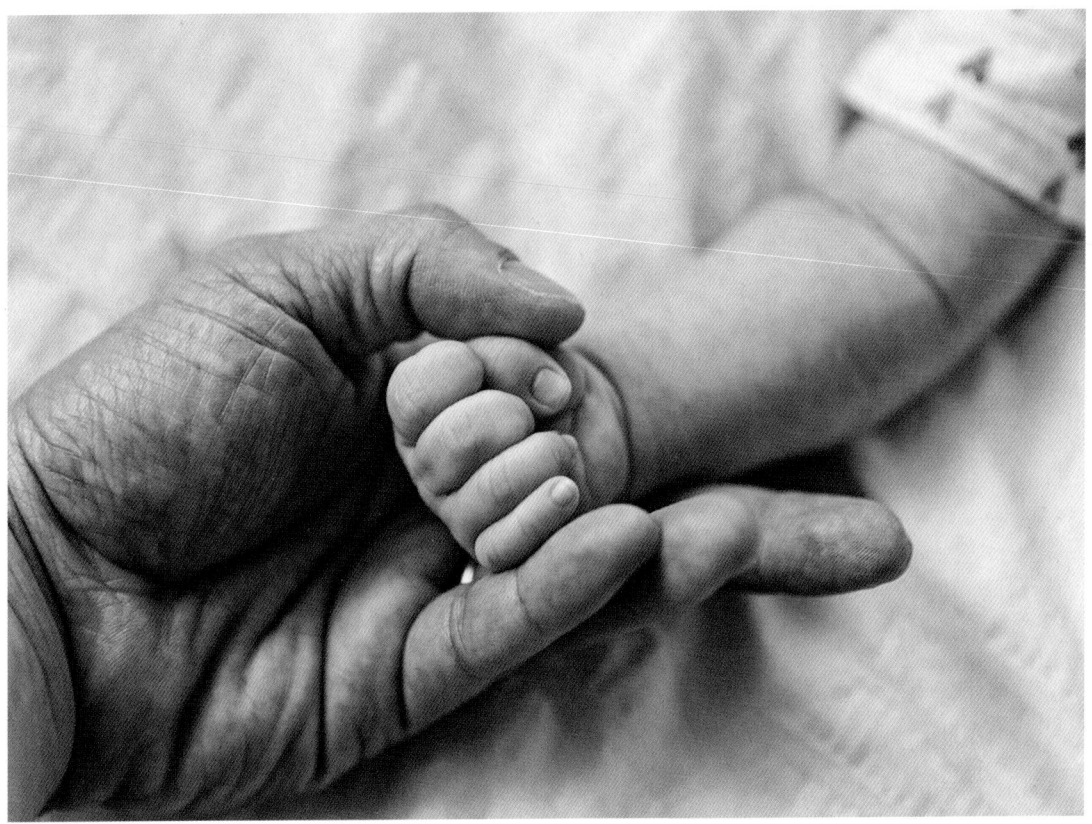

A father holds the hand of his newborn baby. The palette of this image is of muted, soft flesh tones, helping to convey the gentle, calm mood of a quiet moment between father and child.

scene. When combined with good composition and the right exposure, you can *feel* the energy. Bright colors can be tricky to balance; they make the mind feel busy, so it helps if they are set against a simple backdrop to avoid too much chaos. Move around and fill the frame so that your colors aren't competing with a lot of other noise.

You also can pull the viewer's focus with a single bright element in an otherwise quiet scene. The flash of a matador's red cape against the otherwise neutral tones of a bullfighting ring draws the eye straight to it.

MUTED TONES

Sometimes you want to convey a softer mood or a quiet scene. Neutral colors and muted, low-intensity hues set the tone in these situations. Soft, white light and less saturated color palettes are well suited to tranquil scenes, like parents with a new baby or a poignant moment at a wedding.

Muted tones aren't just for soft, happy scenes. With moody light, muted tones can add an element of mystery or foreboding—someone walking through a dimly lit forest or a ship barely visible in the fog.

BLACK & WHITE

Taking color out of the equation can add drama to your photos, give them a timeless feel, or put the focus directly on your subject. But creating powerful black-and-white photographs involves much more than just removing color from your final image.

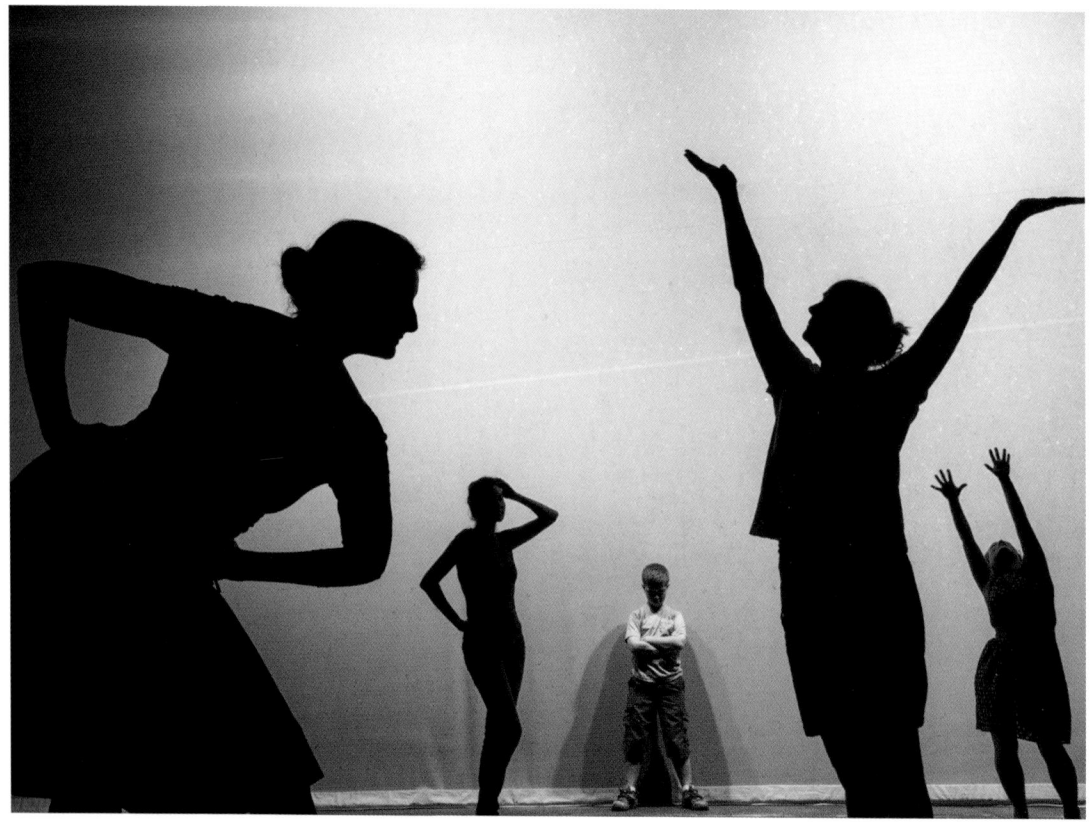

Shooting in black-and-white mode can simplify and add mystery to a scene, as in the case of this dance rehearsal. The elimination of color and the featureless background really enhance the patterns of the dancers' movements.

Back in the days of film, making a monochrome photograph meant loading black-and-white film into the camera. It was a choice we made before taking a picture. Today, we aren't limited by which type of film we put in the camera, and each image can have a different vision. But when it comes to black-and-white photography, intention and vision still set a good frame apart.

CHOOSING BLACK AND WHITE

Most digital cameras can be set to capture in black and white, but shooting in color and

- Commit: Set your camera to capture in black and white. This makes your choice totally intentional, and teaches you to see the way shapes and textures impact an image on their own. The results may surprise you.

- Or, consider shooting in color, and then converting to black and white on your computer. You'll be able to keep both a color and a monochrome version of your photo. You'll also have more control over the conversion process—pushing contrast, highlights, and shadows—in postproduction if you decide to delve into black-and-white editing techniques.

- White balance still matters when you're removing color from the image, as it will impact shades of gray. Try to get an appropriate white balance when the image is in color—you'll often end up with more distinct and relative tones in the final monochrome image.

converting to black and white later is also common practice. We'll discuss useful conversion techniques in a later chapter.

When should you choose to create or finish an image in black and white? Before you decide, consider the role color plays in your photo. Is it providing a point of interest, or a visual weight that balances the picture? Is color important to the story? Black and white works best when the *lack* of color accentuates contrast, texture, tone, or pattern in an image. When used skillfully, it can calm a distracting background and draw a poignant focus to your subject. Black and white should do an intentional service to your subject matter—it's not just a filter to slap over your photo.

SHADES AND SHAPES

Try to envision what the scene will look like in monochrome before you shoot. Busy scenes can be tricky to execute well without color. Our brains use color to help define elements like people, objects, and places in the scene. Changes in color help distinguish different objects. Simple backgrounds tend to work best for black and white, though contrast can help a subject stand out from a crowd. Pay close attention to your subject—if possible, change your position until negative space surrounds your focal point. This will prevent one element from running into another when both are in shades of gray.

A shallow depth of field can also help. Focus on shape and structure by looking for places where highlights and shadows intersect with your subject—these will become more important once you remove color.

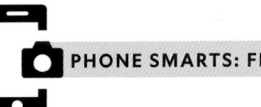 **PHONE SMARTS: FILTERS**

Editing apps handle black-and-white filters differently. If you don't like how the default filter has converted your image, don't settle for it! Using manual editing tools, remove all the saturation from your image and play around with contrast, highlights, shadows, and clarity until you get the black-and-white image you want.

PATTERN & TEXTURE

Our brains seek patterns as a way to make order out of chaos, and textures give us more information about an object. In a two-dimensional image, patterns and textures often make the viewer feel something, and see the scene in a more compelling way.

Patterns give our brains something to latch onto, by providing order and often context that lend a deeper meaning to an image. Likewise, textures—even when seen and not physically experienced—can fill in gaps for your audience, and can actually evoke the sense of touch in an image.

PLAYING WITH PATTERNS

A pattern can be a source of context—tiles on a subway wall, for example, or something abstract but rhythmic, like peaks and valleys of sand dunes. A pattern can add energy to an image, or a sense of calm predictability.

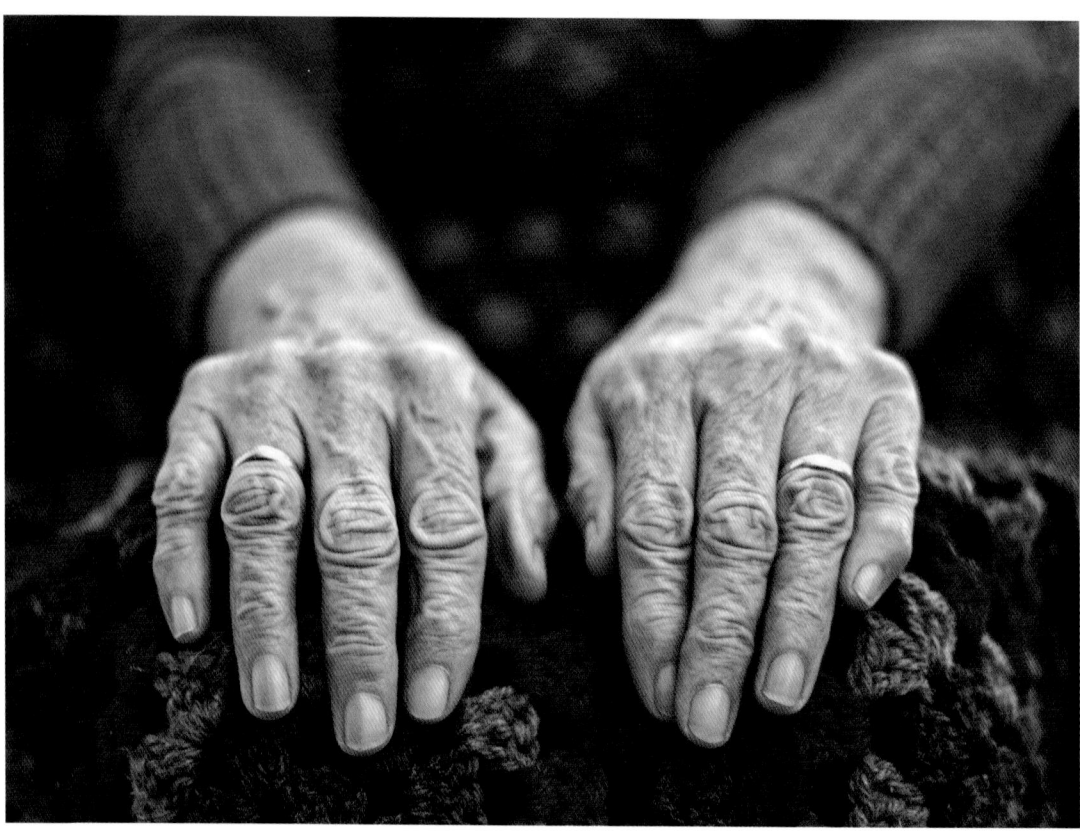

This woman's hands are the focal point of this image, atop a patterned afghan. The sharp focus allows her hands to become ours, so we can almost feel the texture of the crocheted blanket beneath them.

Grab your camera and take a walk around your neighborhood, keeping your eyes open for interesting patterns and textures. When you see one, make an abstract photo of it. How can you take a fresh look at the familiar?

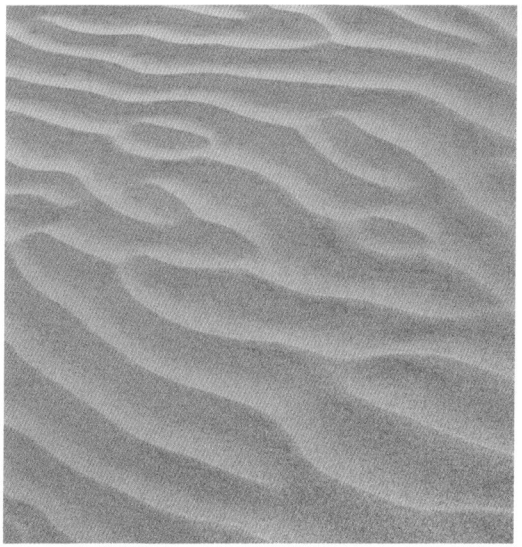 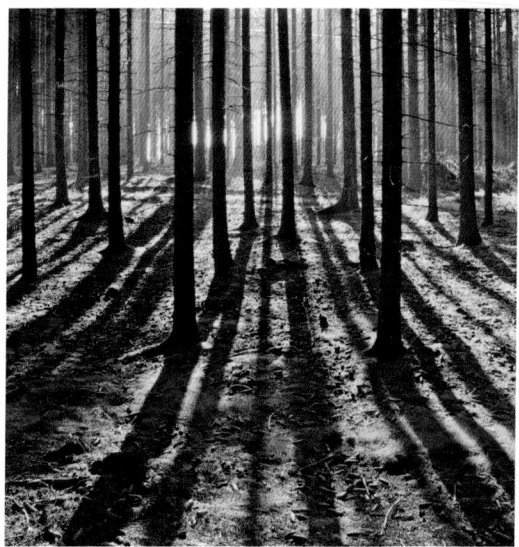

This picture of sand dunes in the Great Thar Desert (left) features the gritty texture of sand and the wavy pattern caused by wind. The absence of context here lets the pattern evoke a calming, rhythmic effect. Spruce tree trunks (right) do double duty: the straight lines of the trees and the diagonal lines of their shadows add both context and abstract pattern.

Pay attention to patterns in the world around you—bricks in a sidewalk, stripes on a shop awning, gaps in a picket fence. How can you compose your photo to include a pattern, and what does it add to the story of your image? How does it make a viewer respond?

FEELING TEXTURE

Textures make an image multisensory. You're not just seeing the stubble on a man's cheek or sand on bare feet—you're feeling it in your imagination, too. And when you examine a texture up close, you often see a pattern emerge.

Get creative with your composition and exposures when you have the opportunity. Note how a photograph of a desert sand dune against the clear sky is a much different viewer experience than a photograph of the meandering stripes the wind has blown into the sand. A photo of a forest has a different feel than a photo of the shadows the trees cast on the ground.

Being conscious of pattern and texture will force you to pay attention to the details. When you start looking more deeply within your pictures, you'll find elements that can transport the viewer.

MACRO PHOTOGRAPHY

There's a world of intrigue to be found in the tiniest details. With macro photography, you can make these details the stars of an image.

Our eyes do not normally see the reflection in a single drop of dew, or the threads that make up a piece of fabric. Macro photography lets us capture the normally unseen elements of plants, insects, and more. To make good macro photographs, carefully consider your light and depth of field, and choose the right gear.

TUNNEL VISION

To focus tightly on a small subject, consider investing in a macro lens, which will allow you to focus at a short distance. When you're filling the frame by being really close to your subject, you'll have a shallow depth of field. Consider which element to focus on, keeping in mind that everything else will be quite soft. When done well, the dramatic contrast in focus will make your tiny point of interest stand out beautifully.

Filling your frame with a small detail means any movement will rock your image like an earthquake, so stabilization is critical. Use a tripod and possibly a cable release (or a remote electronic release) for your camera. If you're photographing subjects that move, like small animals or insects, be sure to choose autofocus, and bring plenty of patience.

LIGHTING A MACRO PHOTO

If you'd like more depth of field in your

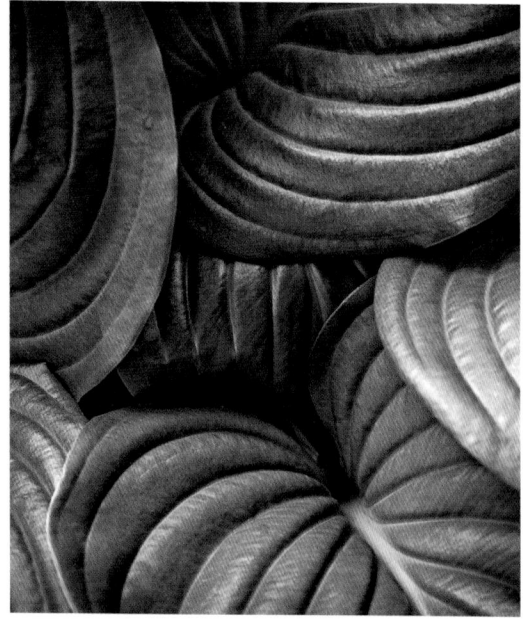

These leaves take on an abstract quality when framed and photographed tightly and up close with a macro lens. The texture of the leaves stands out, as does the rich but subtle contrast of light, shadows, and color.

macro photograph, you'll need to get as much light as you can on your subject in order to make your aperture as small as possible. Your light can come from anything, from a professional-grade flash with softbox to an expertly placed index card acting as a reflector. No matter what the source, you need plenty of light.

And consider lighting your subject from an angle, as you would when shooting a portrait. This allows you to retain some

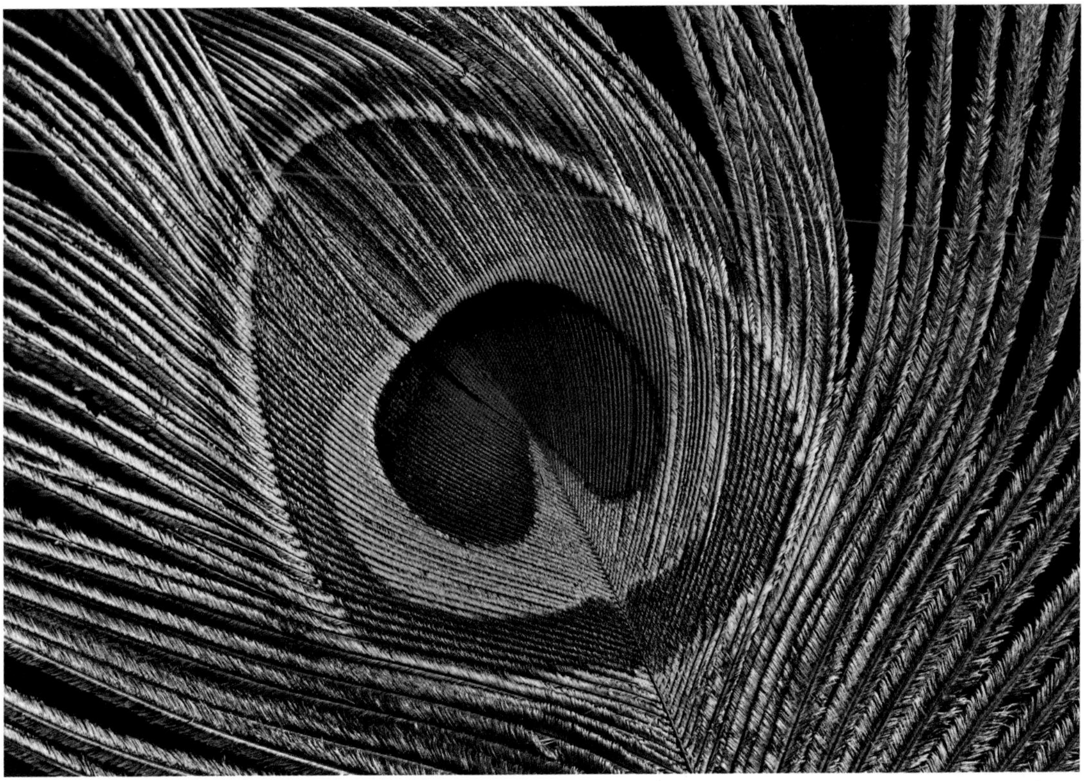

![Peacock feather macro photograph]

Macro photography is a great tool for taking a fresh approach to the natural world. When examined up close, this peacock feather becomes a detailed work of art, and we can see every tiny barbule that makes up its stunning pattern.

shadows on your subject, which will best mimic lighting from a natural source and add depth and dimension. Remember that good light is usually soft and subtle, so diffuse and bounce wherever possible.

SMALL SUBJECTS

You've probably been thinking about macro photography for flowers, bugs, or small animals. But just about anything has the potential for interesting close-up work—eyes, jewelry, or coins, for example. Working in macro allows you to show common things from a new, intimate perspective.

Even in the world of macro, the rules of composition still apply. Keep your backgrounds clean and look for interesting layers or frames.

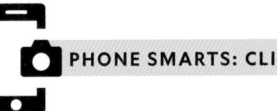

PHONE SMARTS: CLIP-ON LENSES

If you find yourself drawn to close-up images on the go, a clip-on macro lens for your smartphone is a good investment. It will help you get close enough to catch the texture of a flower petal or a drop of dew on a spiderweb, with a depth of field shallow enough to make features pop.

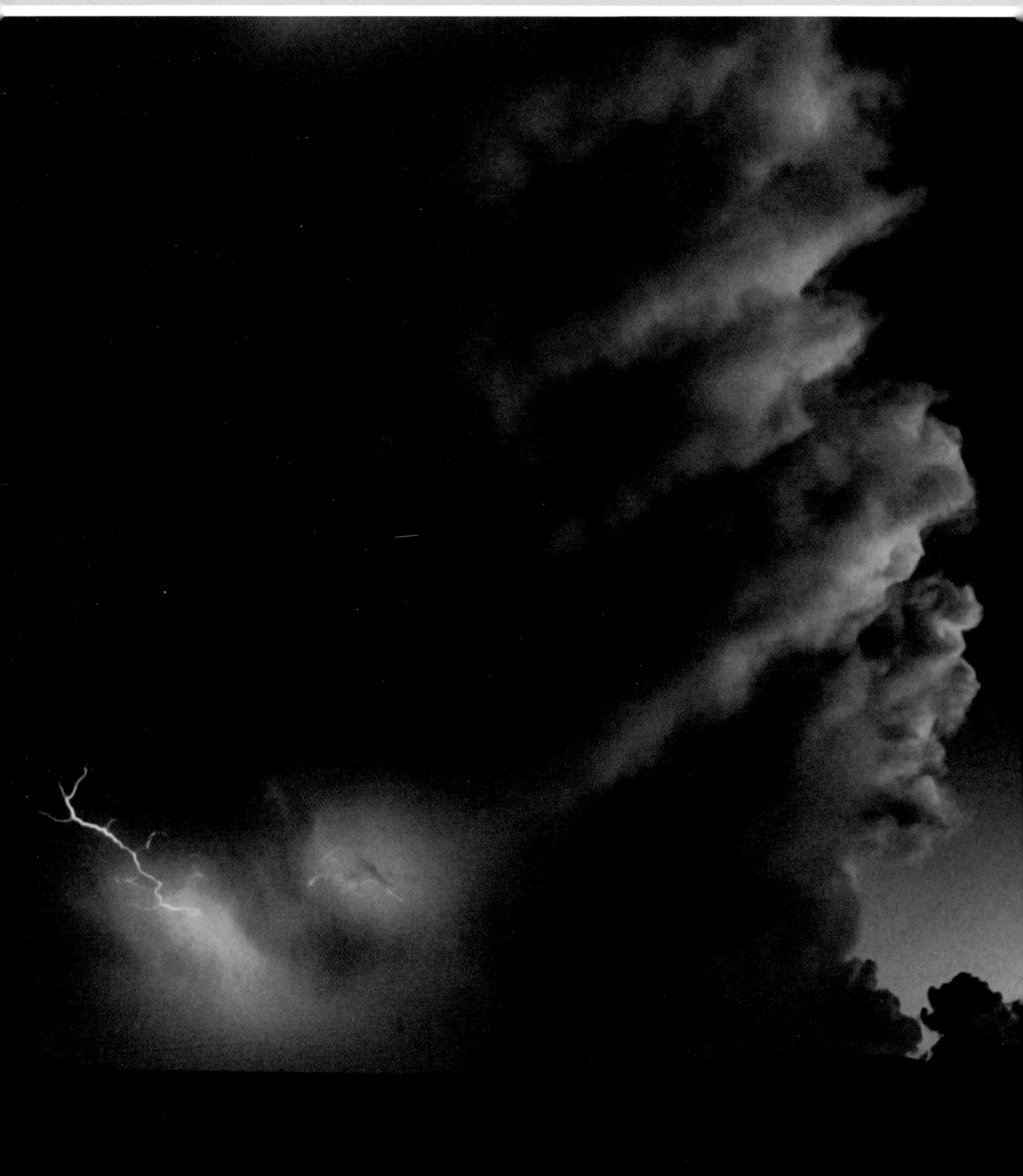

PERFECT TIMING

I was fishing in the Kansas Flint hills and had lost what I thought was the catch of a lifetime—a six-pound bass that had spit out my topwater lure. But when I turned around, I forgot all about it. Behind me the sky was begging to be photographed—a line of clouds on the leading edge of a storm spanning the entire southern horizon, lit by the setting sun. To top it off, an evening star and a crescent moon were framed in the developing scene. I had my camera and tripod with me, and quickly set up. I used a cable release and the "bulb" setting, shooting one long exposure after another, hoping to catch the lightning. I got only one, but sometimes that's all you need.

FLEETING MOMENTS Moments like this occur in nature, but they don't last. The key is to be ready to make the most of the world around you. You'll find that when you're open to it, colors and patterns are more prominent and amazing than you realized.

BALANCE This photo demonstrates the rule of thirds, with the lightning in the bottom left, and the moon and star in the upper right, balancing the frame. There are dynamic elements throughout the image, which keeps the viewer engaged.

TEXTURE You can almost feel the storm coming, and the change it brings through the contrast of heavy, soft clouds encroaching on clear, pastel sky. To this day I wonder what would have happened if I'd landed that fish. That storm moved quickly. Would I have turned around in time to even notice?

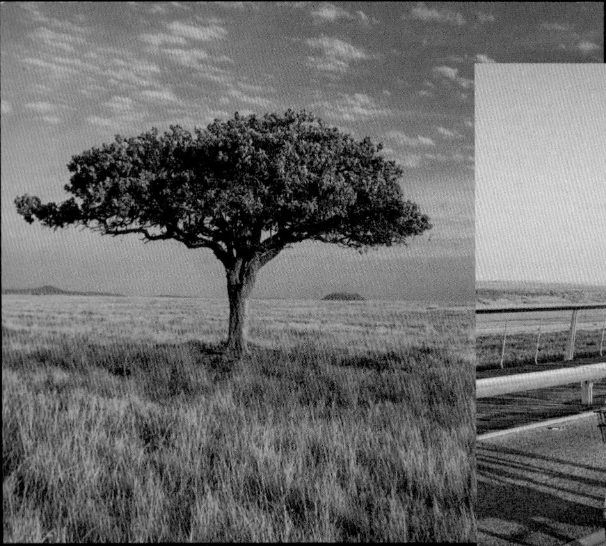

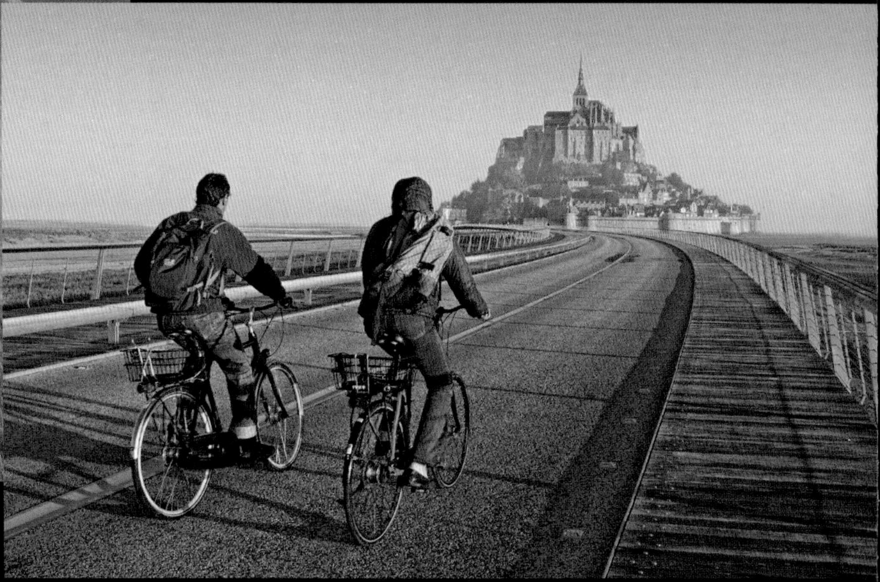

PART TWO: PRACTICING THE BASICS

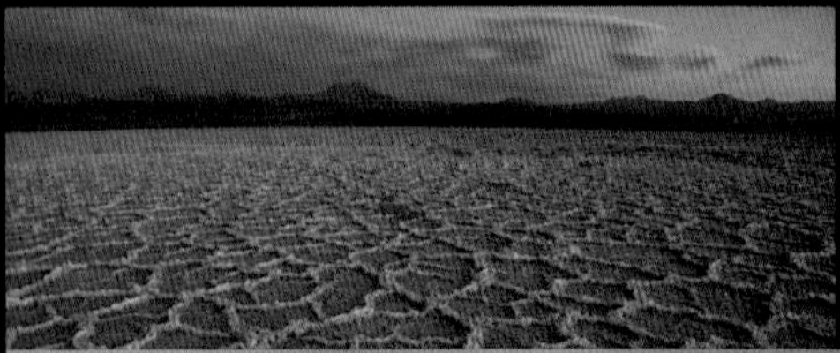

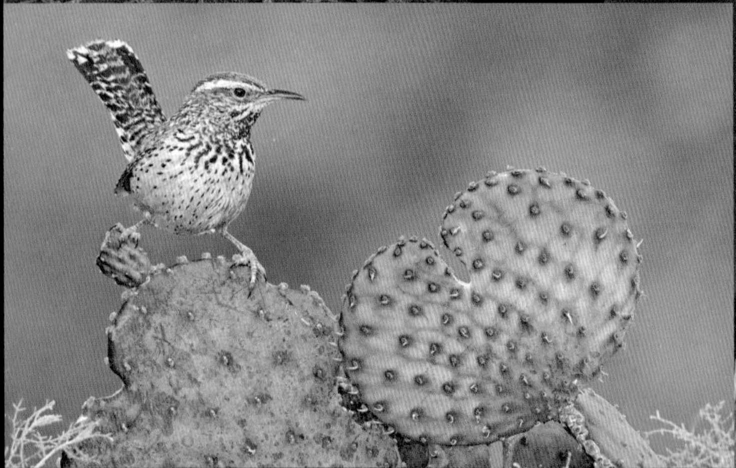

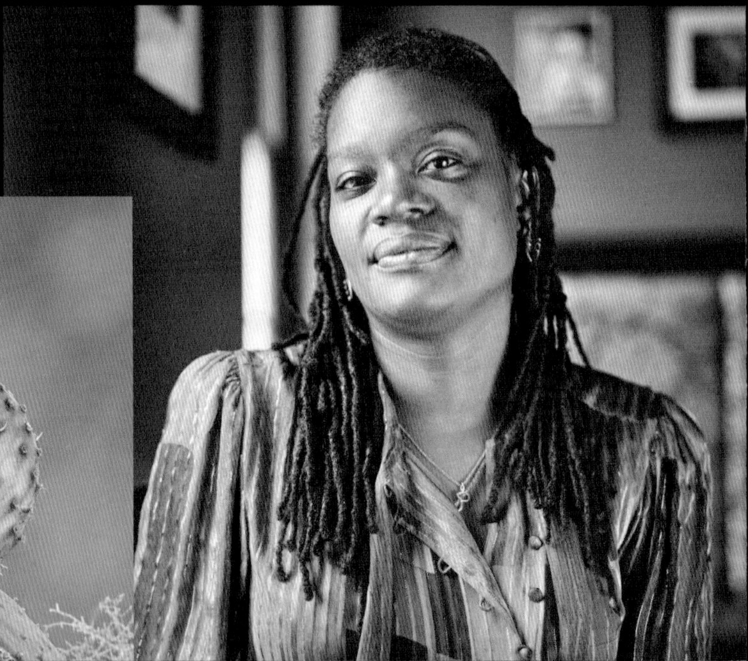

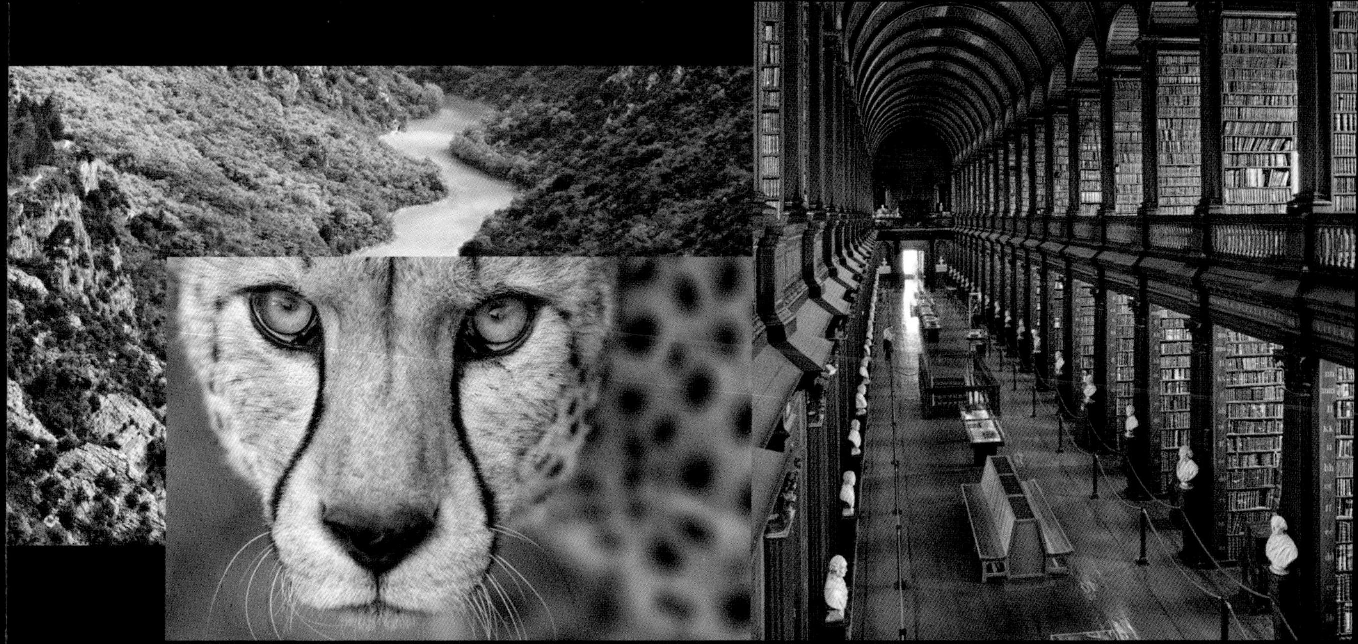

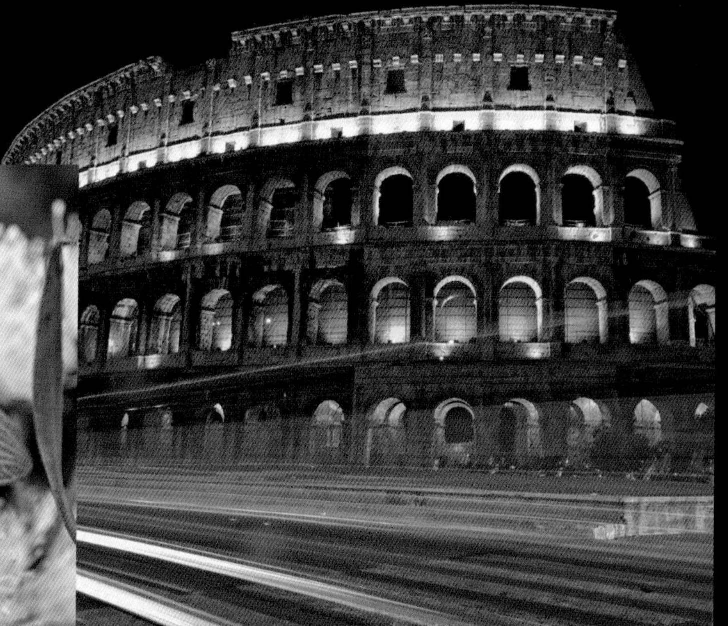
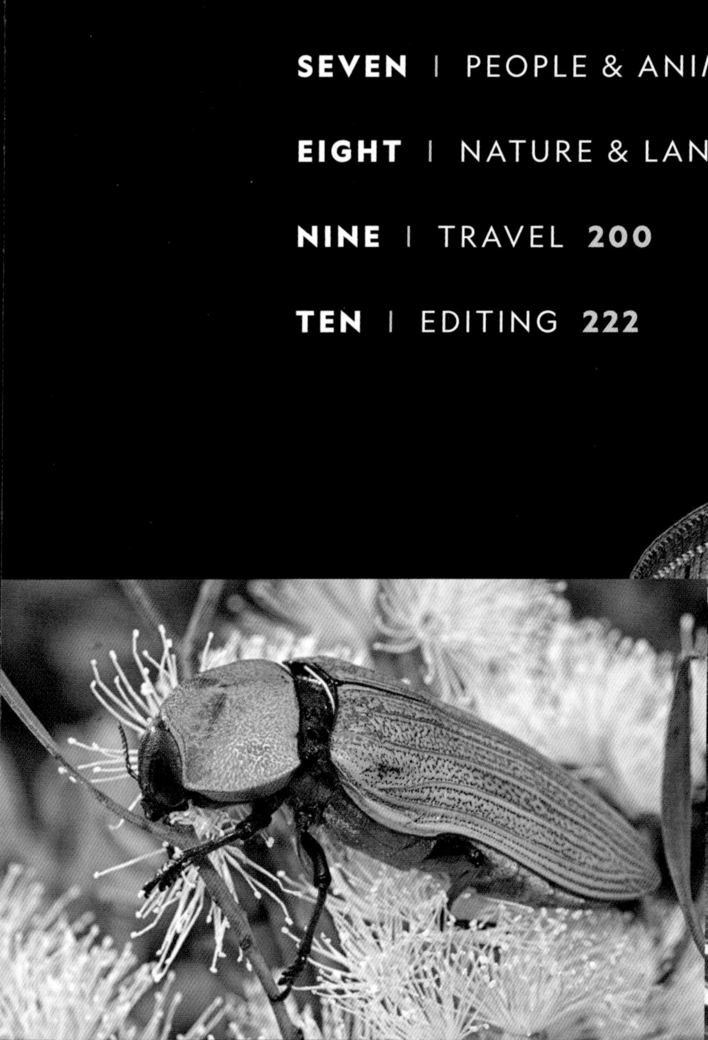

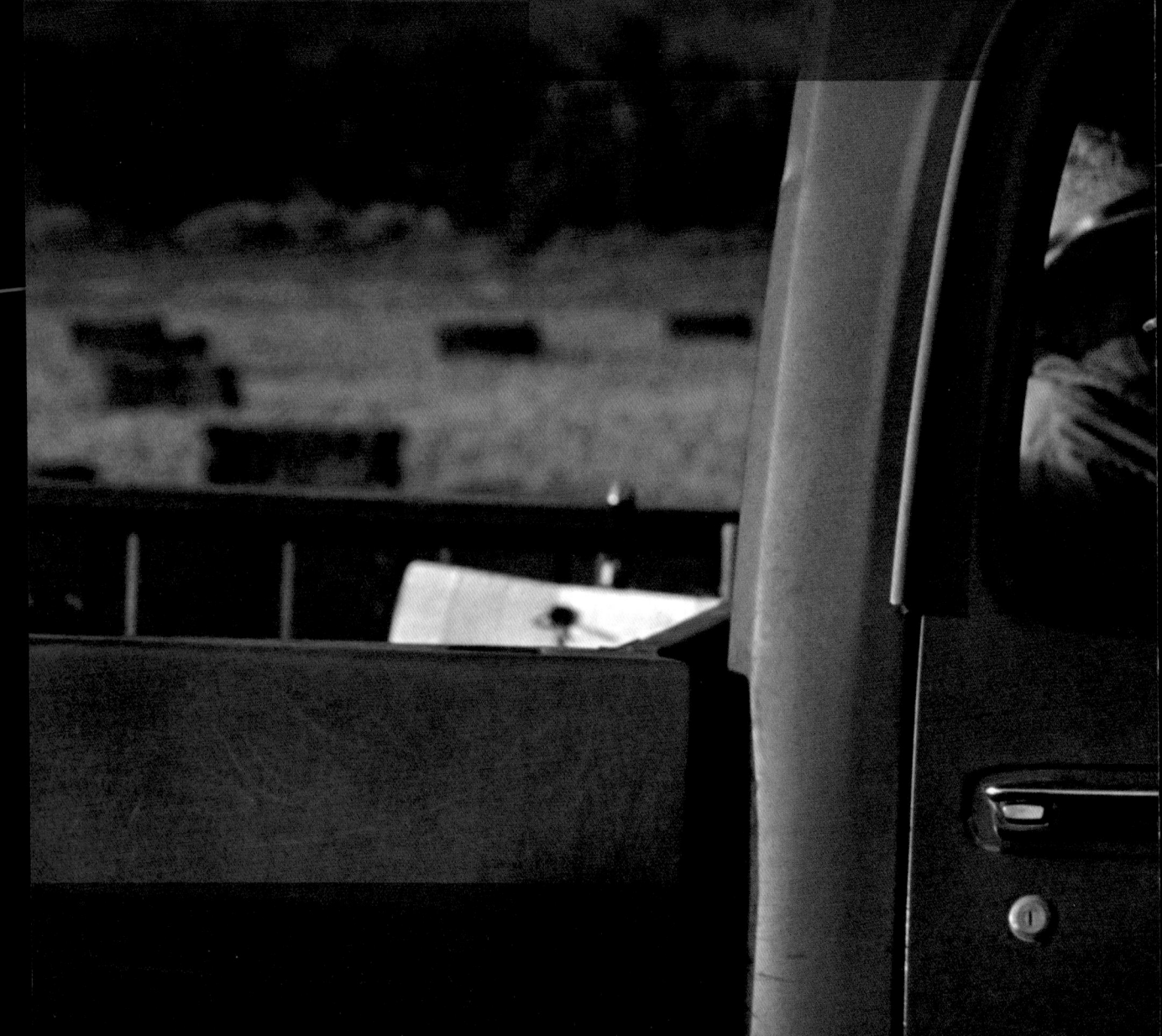

SIX

THINKING LIKE A
PHOTOGRAPHER

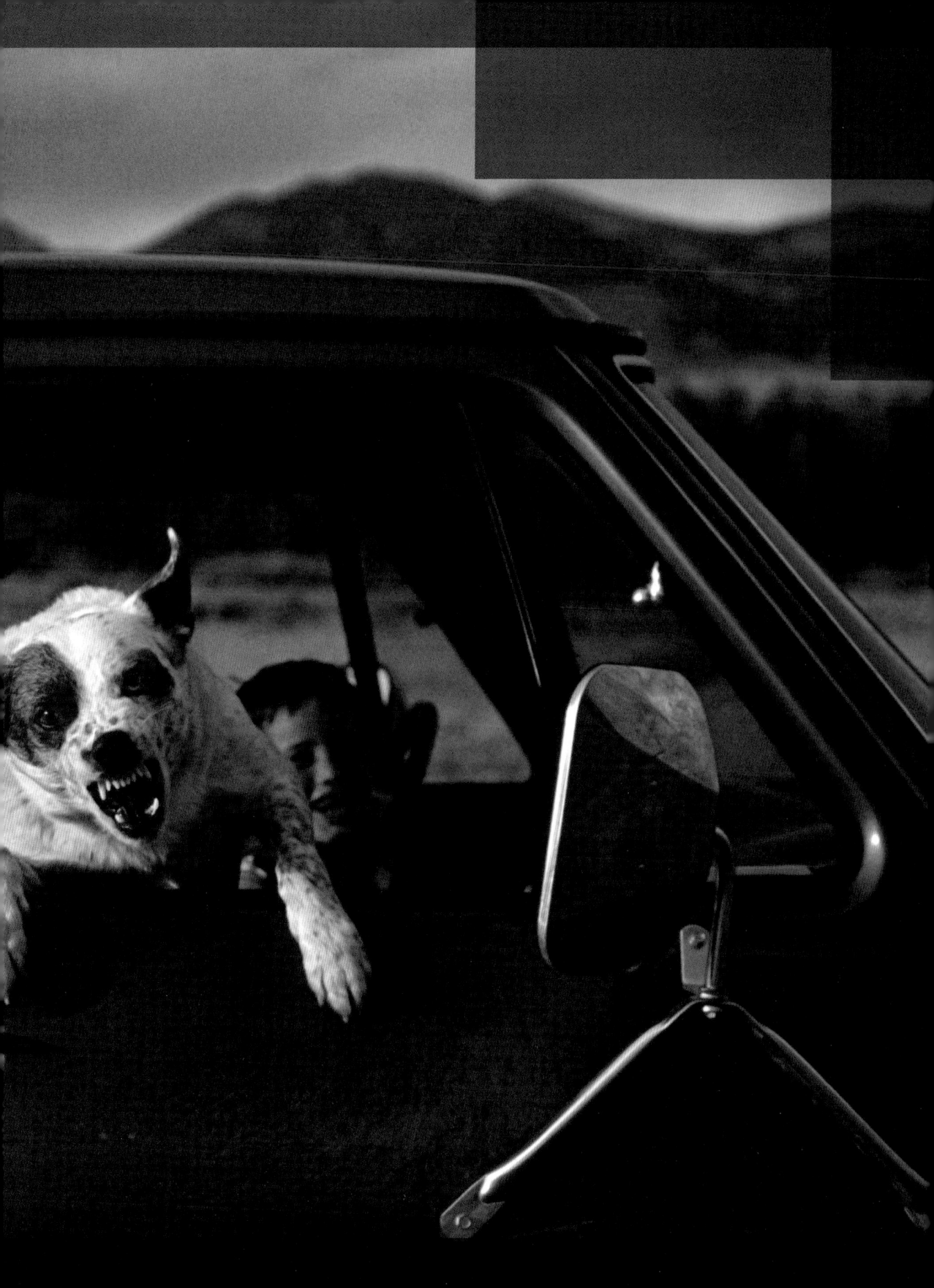

GET INTO THE MIND-SET

The goal of this book is to help you make pictures that capture a moment, convey an emotion, or mean something to you and those you love. You spend a lot of time with your family and friends, at all times of day and in all types of light. There's a saying among photographers that the best camera is the one you have with you.

Making good photographs means more than knowing how to work the controls on your camera. Thinking like a photographer means having a good eye for moments that could yield iconic images, but also developing patience and persistence, doing your research, and always showing up prepared.

Thinking like a photographer is also knowing that sometimes, you *shouldn't* take a picture. Years ago, I was in Laguna San Ignacio in Mexico, working on a *National Geographic* story about the Endangered Species Act. We were in a lagoon where gray whales that have no memory of being hunted come right up to the boat. You can reach out your hand and pet them, and they stick out their tongues to be scratched. It was incredible. But there were people on the boat who never stopped recording the encounter to actually pet the whales. Can you imagine? They were on vacation, and they never stopped to pet the whales!

There are going to be times in your life where you have to put down the camera and pet the proverbial whale. Don't get so caught up in making pictures that you forget to live the experience.

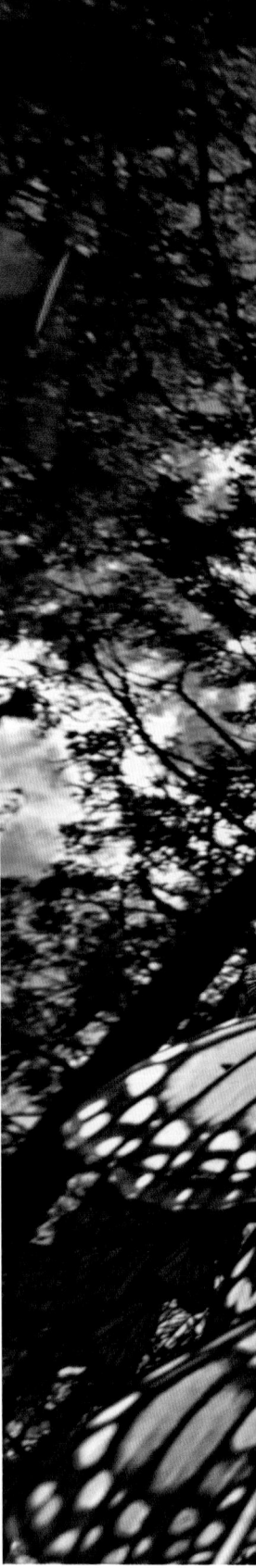

Sierra Chincua, Mexico, is a wintering roost for millions of monarch butterflies every year.

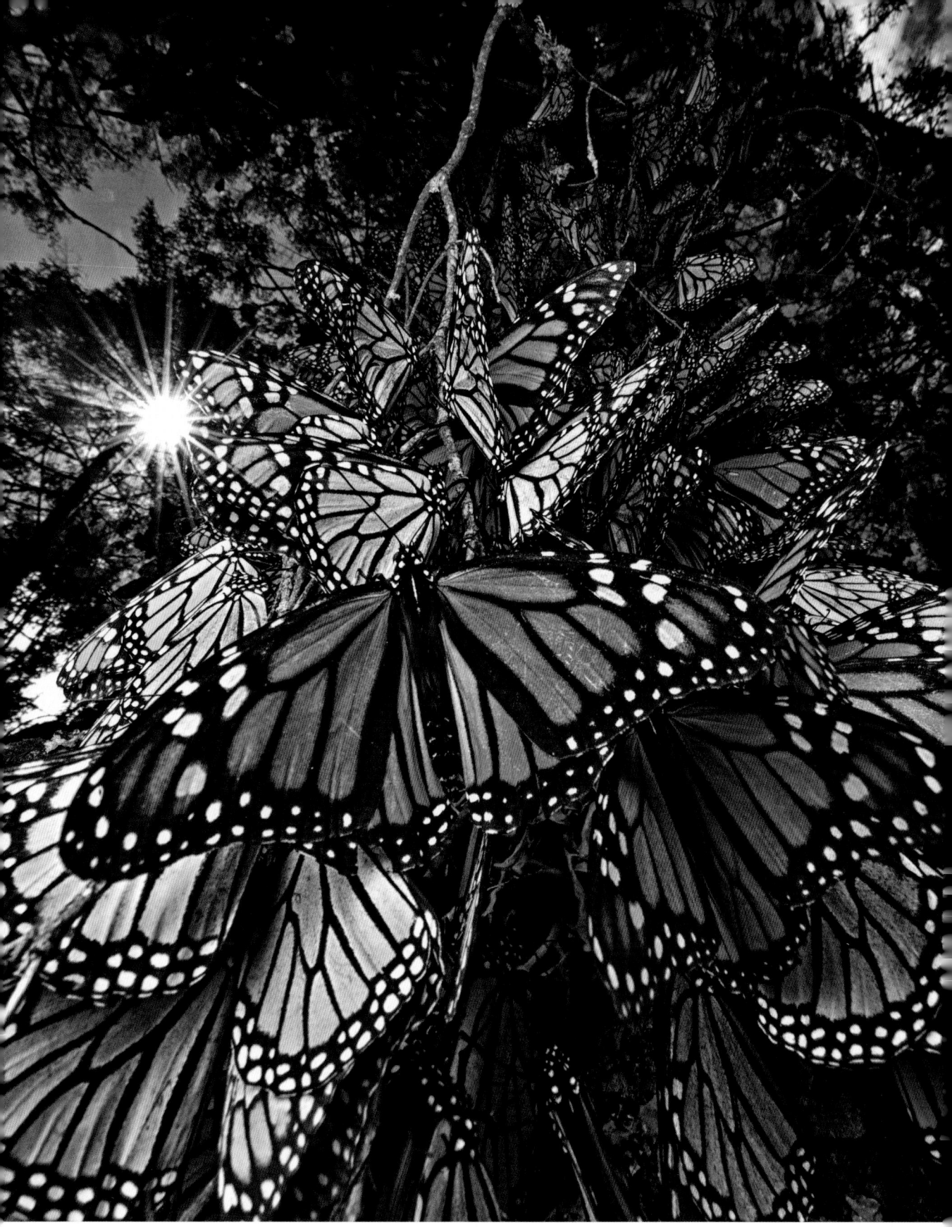

TELLING A STORY

One of the most important things you can learn as a photographer is how to tell a story in one image. The details you include—and the ones you leave out—are the keys to good storytelling.

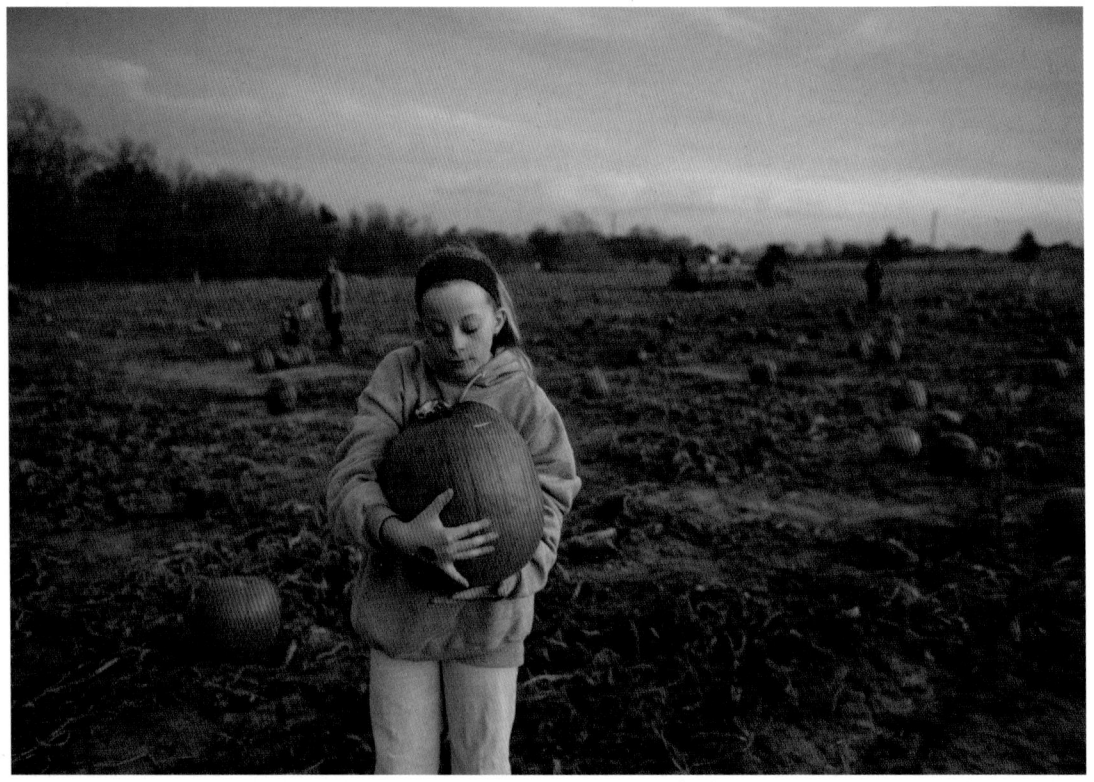

Quiet moments are often well worth recording and can be found anywhere, even in the local pumpkin patch. You don't have to travel far from home to capture meaningful images.

Photography is a storytelling medium. Each individual frame tells a story—about yourself, your loved ones, a situation, or a moment. We've said it throughout this book: If it's in your photograph, it's either working for you or against you. As you compose your photo, using all the techniques we've practiced, always ask, "What story does this tell?"

CLOSE TO HOME

It's important to remember that great pictures aren't exclusive to exotic locations—they can be in your city, neighborhood, or home. As you learn to think like a photographer, you'll see stories unfold before you. Think about the tone of each story: Is it energetic? Quiet? Tense? Hopeful? Look at the visual cues. Assess your resources—

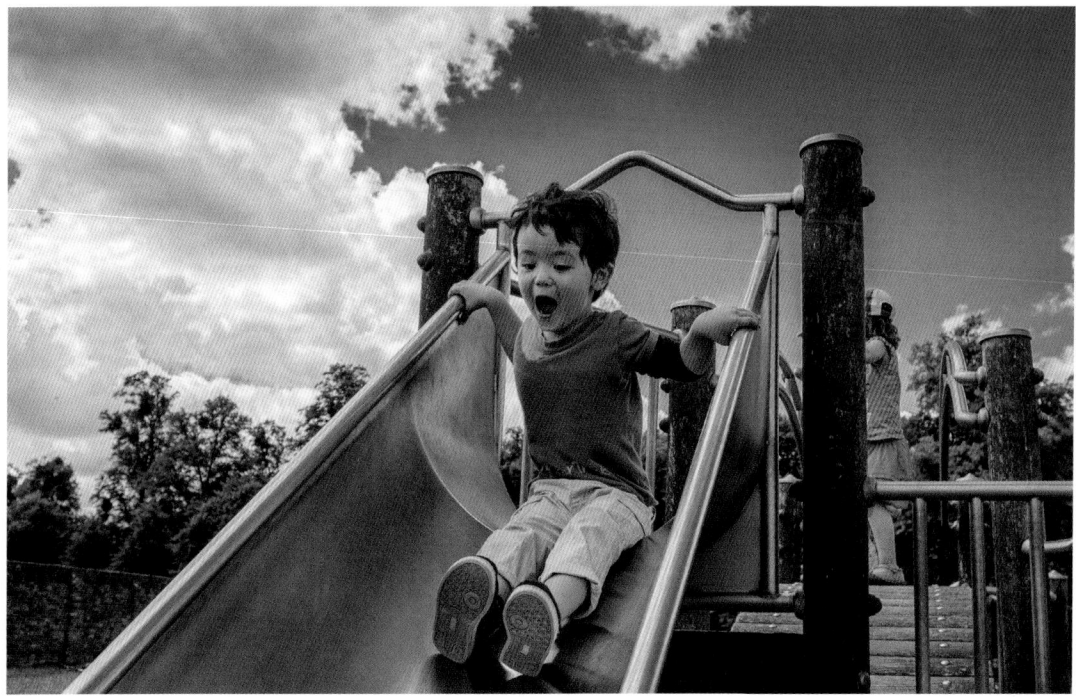

This little boy is experiencing his first ride down the slide. In his expression, we sense his excitement and surprise, perhaps even his first taste of independence—a significant moment for both parent and child.

light, color, subjects, and scene. Be open, put it all together, and your camera will become an instrument for these stories to move through.

Getting extraordinary photographs out of ordinary situations is about thinking ahead, going deeper, and uncovering the surprising things about a given moment.

Most of all, it helps if you enjoy the process, even when it's challenging. No matter where you live, there are stories worth telling and pictures worth making, from people in your town to the wildlife in your backyard. When you can get a great frame out of an ordinary situation, you know you're onto something.

ASSIGNMENT: PHOTOGRAPH AN ORDINARY PLACE

Go to the most visually uninteresting place you can think of—a hotel room, your office, a field, even your driveway—and make an interesting picture. Take a friend or a pet with you so you have a subject, and see what arises. I like to think of an "ordinary" place as a stage on which anything can happen, and anything can be interesting if we look at it the right way. It's easy to make great frames in exciting situations, but the mark of a real photographer is to make an image that tells the story of even a mundane moment in a compelling way.

PRESENCE & PATIENCE

Sometimes capturing a single moment requires hours of waiting, planning, and more waiting. Thought and patience are your greatest allies when you want to tell compelling stories.

Great pictures don't just happen. They're usually the result of many attempts and many failures. Preparation and patience are some of your most important tools. Even if you don't know anything about the situation you're headed into, you can gain a lot of insight just by showing up early and observing before touching your camera.

BE PRESENT

Never underestimate the power of sitting and watching, camera down, just being in the moment. What is the energy like? What people, objects, patterns, and activities tell a story? Absorb the vibe of the scene, become part of it, and then pick up the camera. Look for opportunities to capture the most telling moments from different perspectives. When you're lucky, you might find repeating patterns that you can latch onto, form a vision for photographing, and have more than one chance to make your own.

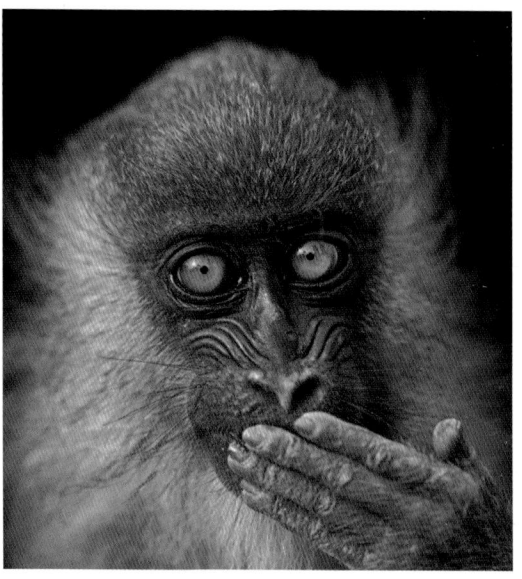

I made many frames before I got lucky with a human-like expression on this young mandrill. My camera settings were ready, and I was observing every movement so when he looked at me this way, I was able to capture it.

MASTER SKILLS

It can be difficult to fully immerse yourself in a situation and not stop thinking about technical considerations. By getting to a

ASSIGNMENT: SPECIAL ACCESS

Plan a shoot of an event or a site that requires special timing or access. Think sunrise at a remote location, backstage at a concert, or a rooftop view of Main Street in your town. This will take creativity, good social skills, and patience to plan and execute. Depending on the situation, you may need to consider the weather forecast, plan for extra time to set up your equipment, or get special permission.

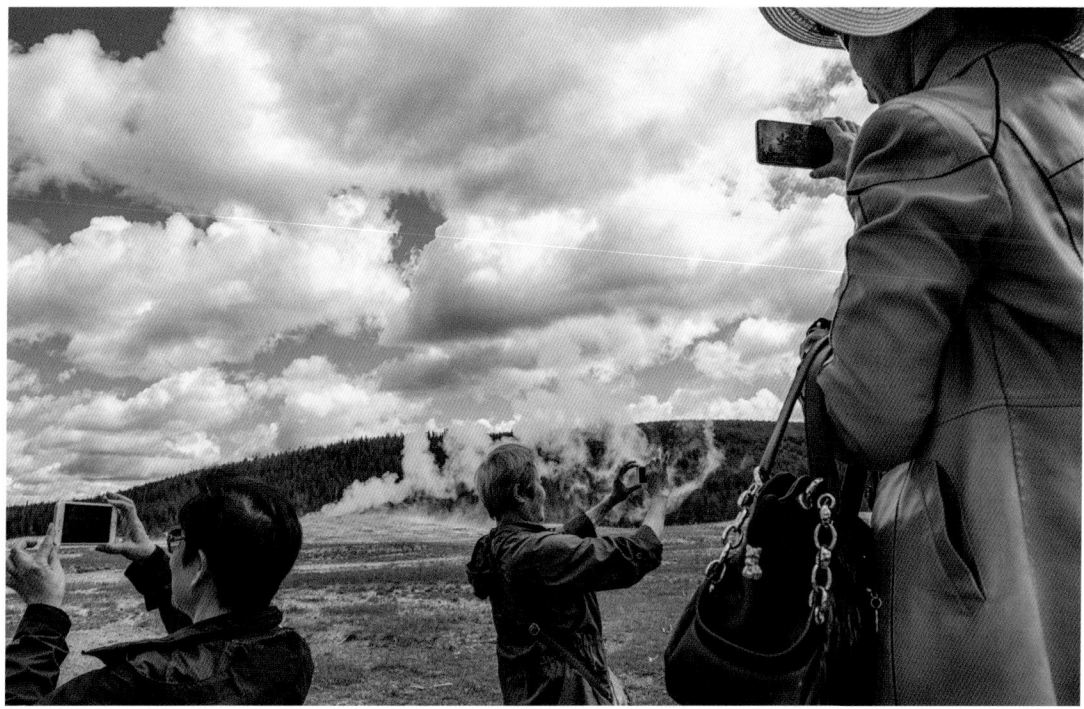

These tourists traveled a long way to see the eruption of Old Faithful at Yellowstone National Park. Even after the main event ended, these ladies were capturing everything they could see. This image tells a more interesting and complete story of visiting Old Faithful than another photo of the geyser alone.

place where your camera skills and your approach to light, color, and composition become second nature, you can feel prepared to make the most of the moment. As you enter a scene, note the light: Where is it coming from and how is the quality? Can you work with the ambient light, or do you need to add something? What settings will you need to set the tone? Are you capturing something fast-moving, and what do you need for depth of field? Are there lines you can take advantage of to lead your viewer through the image? Mastery means you can answer these questions for yourself without losing your connection to the scene.

STAY FLEXIBLE

You may make technical decisions before you start shooting, but check your results often and be ready to make adjustments. Try not to get frustrated when circumstances change—either in the action or the conditions. Be creative in solving problems and don't be afraid of mistakes! Most important, stay open to what arises in the scene—be ready to pivot and tell a different story if that's what presents itself. Patience—with the situation, with yourself, and with the process—is your greatest ally. Great photographs are not usually made impulsively or in a hurry. Perseverance plays a significant role in determining the end results.

RESEARCH

Often, the difference between a good picture and a great picture is the amount of time you put into it. Do your homework beforehand and notice the difference in your results.

A lot of the great photographs you'll make will come from spontaneous, everyday moments. By having your camera on hand, you'll be prepared to capture these moments. But when you set out with the intention of documenting a particular place or event, research is essential. A good rule of thumb is to spend one day on research for each day you'll be shooting on location.

MAKING PLANS

Think about where you're headed and your goals for the shoot. If it's possible to scout it out in advance, do it. Try to imagine what circumstances could affect your photographs, from traffic and road closures to the weather forecast. Double-check opening and closing times and secure any necessary permits. Be ready to adjust your plans,

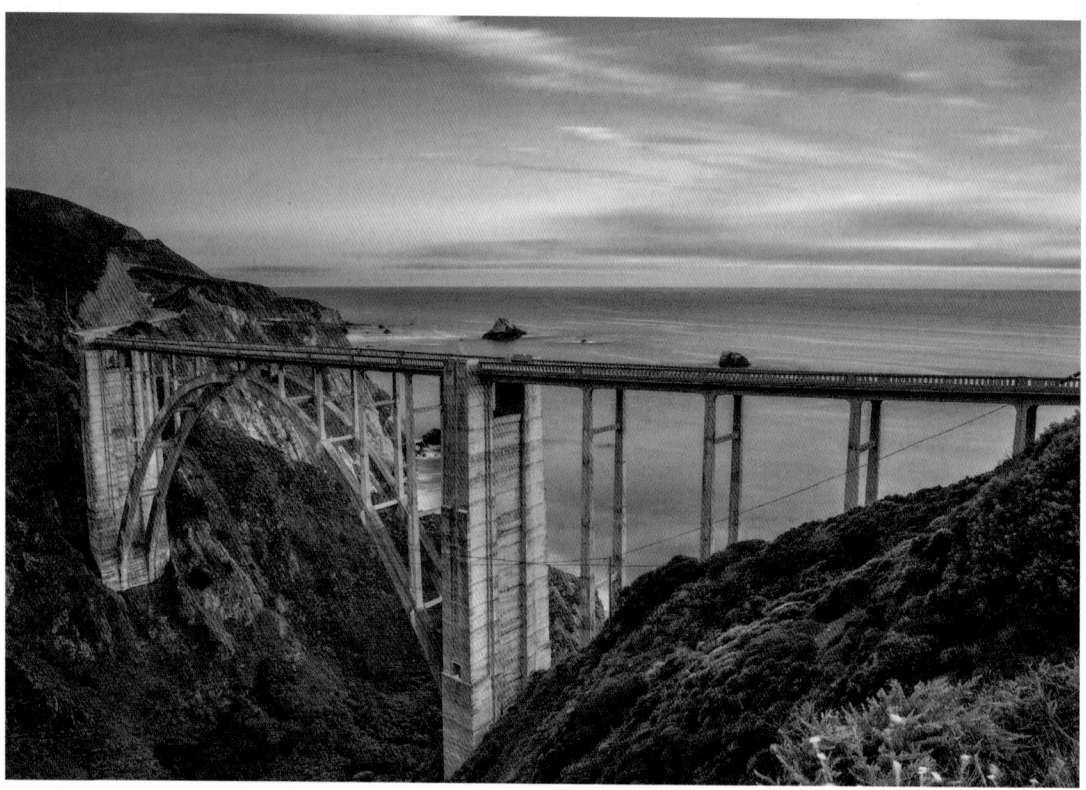

If you want to capture the magical light and color of sunrise, you'll need to plan ahead. Research local sunrise times, map routes, and show up in advance to scout a vantage point. Get set up so you'll be ready when the light gets good.

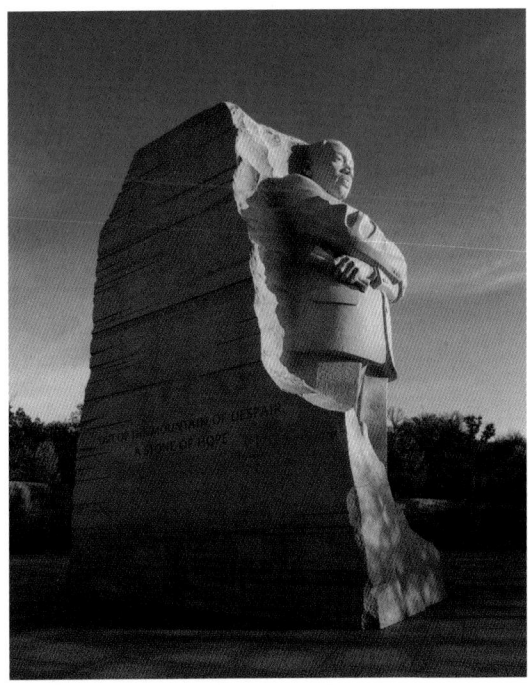

When photographing special locations, such as the Martin Luther King, Jr., Memorial in Washington, D.C., make sure you know where you're allowed to be and at what times. If necessary, seek out special permits in advance.

ury is to have someone along to assist you. Consider offering a favor in return to someone you can really rely on. Most important, be prepared to be surprised.

KNOW BEFORE YOU GO

The internet is one of your greatest assets. What used to require weeks of library research, mailing off requests for brochures, and making cold calls can now be accomplished in a few hours or days of online research and information gathering.

Reach out to all kinds of experts, from professors to tradesworkers to locals who have lived in the area their whole lives. Leave ample time for the information-gathering part of your project and know that this is every bit as important as pushing the button. The more you know, the more invested you will be, and the less likely you are to be derailed if (when) something doesn't go according to plan. You'll also be best prepared to take advantage of an unexpected opportunity.

reschedule if the conditions won't be right, or, better yet, solve a weather problem creatively (and with the right gear!). A lux-

PRO TIP GO BEYOND

- **Check times.** Research timing and activity patterns. Make up your schedule, then be prepared to show up early and stay late.

- **Get on the phone.** Email is a great way to make an introduction, but don't stop there. Make phone calls and politely request meetings to discuss your plans with experts and officials.

- **Seek permission.** Determine in advance who needs to approve your presence and any equipment you'll be using. Confirm the day before, and be sure to have on hand the contact info for the person who's approved your request.

- **Be persistent.** Remember that people in the scenario you are investigating may not know you and may not be readily willing to cooperate with you. Be courteous, and consider ways they might benefit from the project. What can you offer in return to the organization or community best suited to help you? Be respectful, sincere, and convincing, and don't give up.

PROBLEM SOLVING

As in life, hurdles to success in photography exist in spite of thorough planning and preparation. Creative problem solving might mean the difference between a set of great, hard-won images and going home with an empty memory card.

Only so many factors are under your control on a given day—equipment, skill, preparedness, and your attitude among them. Weather, animal behavior, timing, and your subject's demeanor are just a few things that may be out of your control. Always assume that something won't go as planned. It's important to yield to what you can't change and be creative in finding alternatives. Go with the flow and don't give up on making a good photograph, even if that means letting go of how you expected it to look.

SOLVING VISUAL PROBLEMS

You'll have to work in less than ideal conditions sometimes. If you have harsh light, can you find shade? Can you diffuse it? Can you overexpose part of the picture for a distinctive look? In a chaotic setting, can you obscure a busy background with shallow

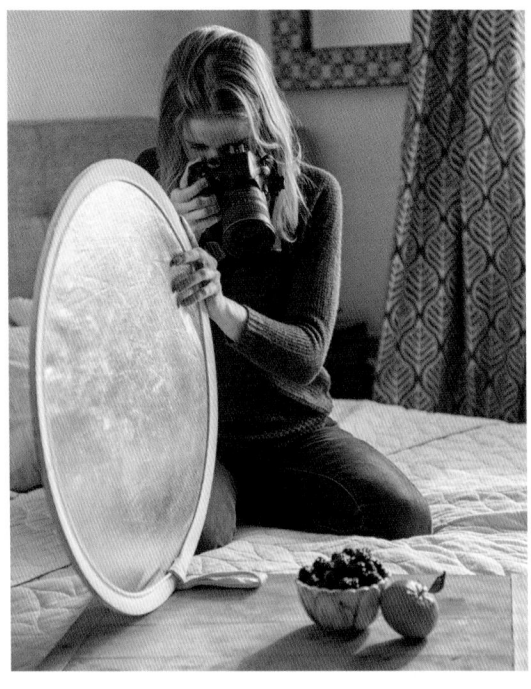

This photographer has solved a few visual problems rather than settling for a mediocre picture: She's made a clean background for her still life; she's positioned near a window; and she's using a reflector to bounce light back onto the subject.

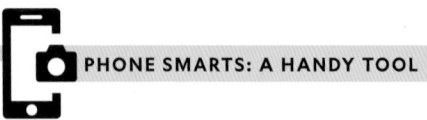

PHONE SMARTS: A HANDY TOOL

Your phone can be a handy tool, even when you have a bigger camera with you. Use the flashlight for a little extra light, or take a few test shots to play with perspective and composition.

depth of field or by zooming in on your subject? Can you change your perspective? Could you even use it to your advantage somehow? Composition and exposure are almost always under your control. Use them to make a good image in any circumstance.

Think on your feet and trust your skills. Try something out, even if it seems crazy, then review, adjust, and try again. Don't give up until you see results you like.

BUILD SUPPORT

Be invested in the photos you want to make. Share your ideas, plans, and enthusiasm with the people or communities that could make a difference in your access or opportunity. Most people will appreciate your paying attention to them or their cause. A respectful introduction about who you are and why you'd like to photograph them will often pay off. Try to build relationships in the place or community you're interested in. Making friends through your photography will result in having support as you plan and solve logistical problems, and will likely add to your life in the long run.

GOING WITH THE FLOW

One important note about problem solving: Don't compromise your integrity or the integrity of your subject by forcing a photograph. If your subject is unhappy with you or the situation, it will show in the photograph and leave you feeling lousy. Put your social skills and persistence to work. Embrace the circumstances that challenge you. You may be surprised by the results.

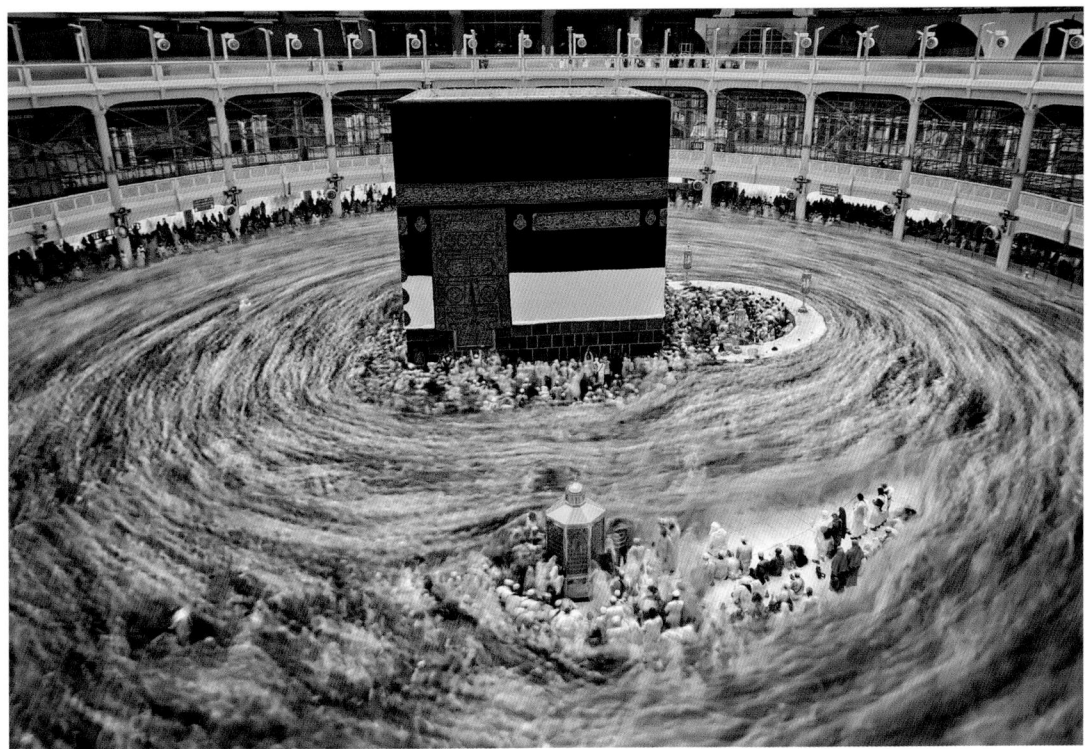

Pilgrims circle around the Kaaba in Mecca as part of the Muslim tradition of hajj. A long exposure shows the circular flow of the crowd, making for a more descriptive picture than a fast shutter speed might have. This photograph uses the movement to creatively tell a story.

BREAKING THE RULES

Rules are an important place to start, and great photographers master them before experimenting. But to develop your own style and create truly surprising images, you'll have to be willing to break the rules sometimes.

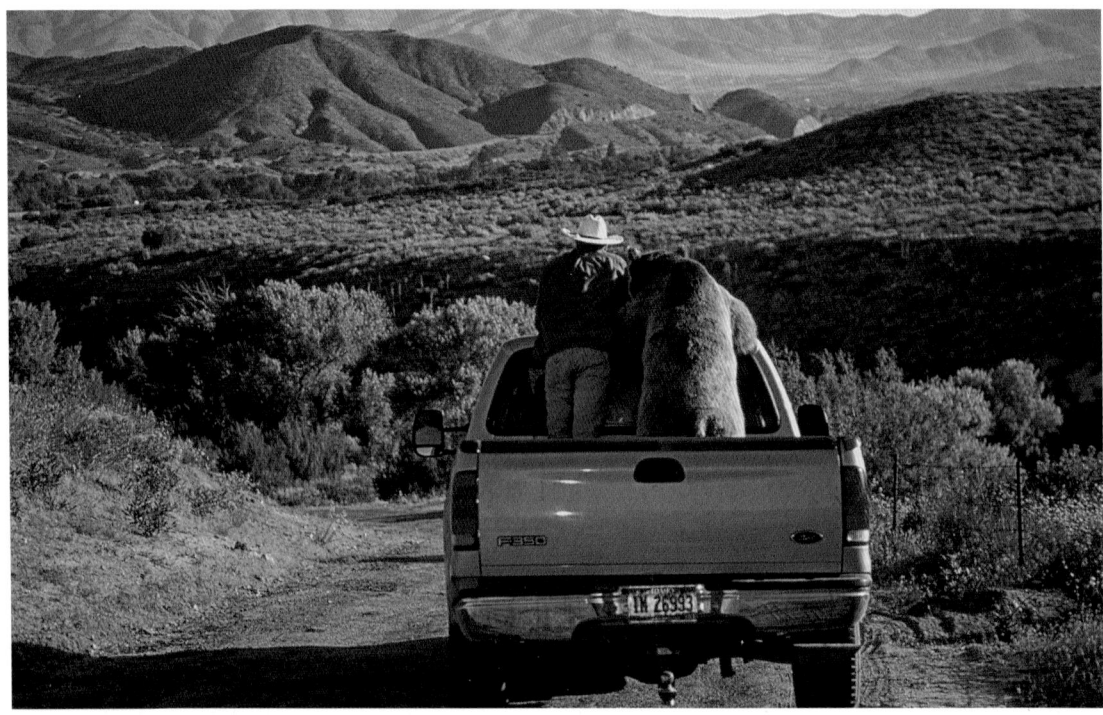

This is a picture of trainer Scott Handley and trained brown bear Baloo. It's not a typical picture of a trainer and animal—it doesn't even show their faces. But it's a lighthearted moment from a unique perspective that illustrates the special bond between these two.

We've talked about a lot of rules when it comes to photography: the rule of thirds, stabilizing your camera with slow shutter speeds, avoiding harsh lighting. But sometimes your best option is to do something that you've been told is a bad idea. Most photographers break the rules sometimes. As a professional photographer, you have to capture certain images for the story to be successful.

But it's important to make photographs that are just for *you*. The results can be magical, and they might only happen because you let go of convention and did what felt right, rather than following the rules.

MAKE YOUR OWN RULES

If you follow a formula all the time, you run the risk of never developing your own unique the entire focus of the image, staring you right in the eyes. Get out and shoot in harsh light. Test the parameters of your camera and your preference. Let a picture be a little blurry with movement—maybe it creates an abstract softness or energy that contributes to your story.

Look at the work of other photographers and note when they break the rules. What speaks to you and why? Try out their techniques and see what dovetails with your vision.

The rules we've discussed are an important foundation for your photography practice, but don't be afraid to put them aside every now and then. As you develop your own style, you'll find yourself making your own rules.

style. So stretch and play with boundaries and see how the results look—and how they make you feel.

Put a subject dead center in the frame, rather than using the rule of thirds—let it be

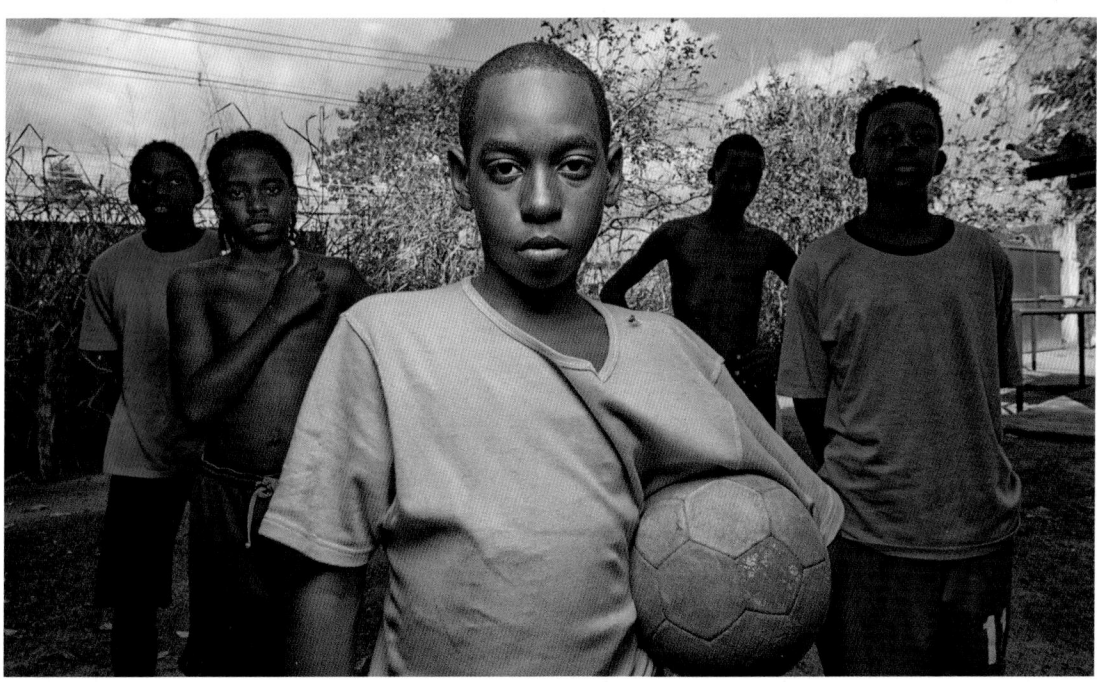

Lots of things about this picture of soccer-loving kids in Brazil break the rules. The kids in the back are in dark shadow, and the main subject is dead center in the frame. The background is well exposed but a little busy. But the boy's expression, combined with the way the light falls on his face, is so arresting that it still works.

PREPARATION

Thinking like a photographer means being prepared mentally, physically and logisitically. Whether you're headed out into your neighborhood for a couple hours or taking a three-week photography vacation, there are some things you can't leave home without.

You've done your research, checked on logistics, and planned your approach to your next photo shoot. To capitalize on all that hard work, set aside some time the day before to take care of some really important details.

PREP YOUR BAG

Start by emptying out your gear bag and tossing any detritus—you don't need the clutter or weight. Lay out the gear you'll need, then pack it in an organized way, with the things you use most often or will need in a hurry in a convenient place.

Pack extra batteries (already charged) for any gear that needs them. If you have room, it's a good idea to throw a charger in, too, just in case. Have a memory card in the camera, formatted and ready to go, along with a few extras, also formatted. Not since the days of film should we ever run out of frames!

Other items worth having on hand: a clean cloth for lenses, gaffer's tape—great for

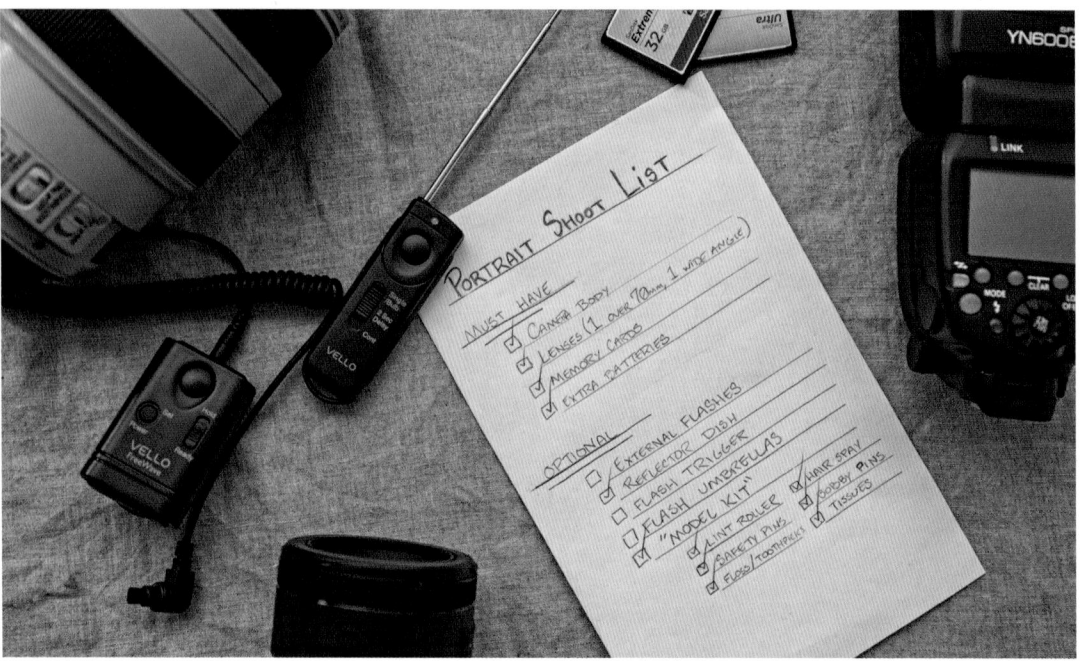

Make yourself a comprehensive checklist a day or two before your shoot. Clean out your bag and repack it so you know you've got everything you need on hand.

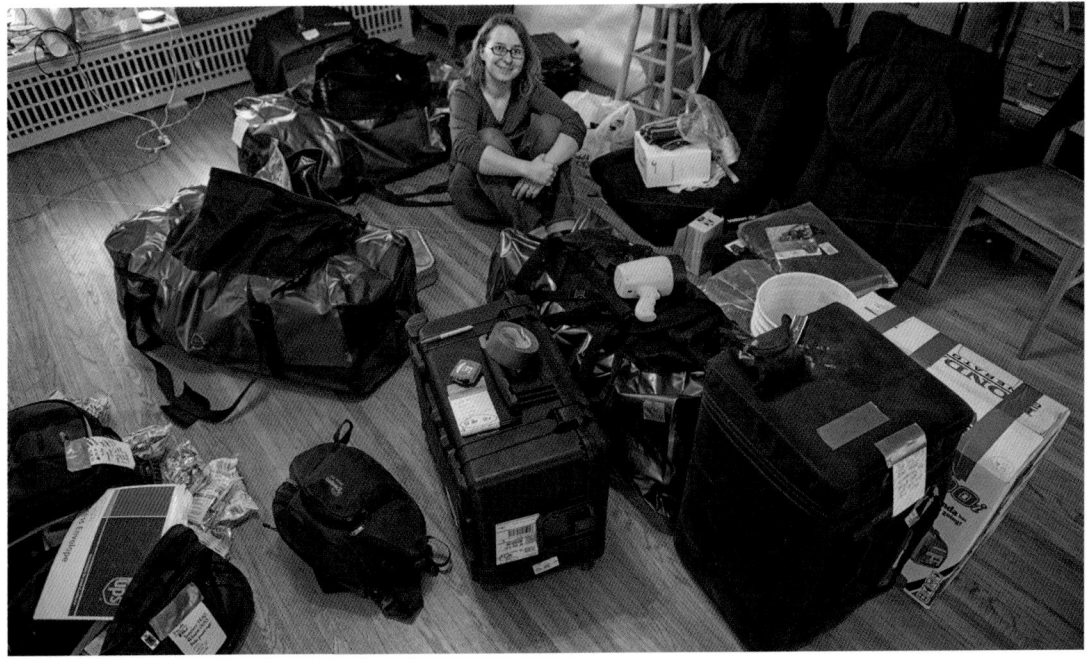

When photography is your bread and butter, your equipment needs can get pretty crazy. The average person won't need to pack quite this much gear, but it's important to know what you need and how you'll transport it before you go.

securing things—and a multitool to make small repairs.

SPECIALTY NEEDS

If you're shooting portraits, consider a small kit with hair spray, shine control powder, a lint roller, and a compact mirror. Clamps, clothespins, and safety pins can also come in handy for securing backdrops and clothes. If you're headed into the woods, bring a small first aid kit, bug spray, and a flashlight.

Wherever you're headed, assess your needs and balance them with the load you can manage. Prioritize extras—don't get caught without something you need, but don't weigh yourself down so much that your flexibility and comfort are compro-

mised. You won't be able to avoid mishaps 100 percent of the time, but if you make yourself a checklist (and use it!), you can save yourself a headache and focus on your goals.

PRO TIP PHOTO SHOOT CHECKLIST

- Spare batteries, charged
- Spare memory cards, formatted
- Camera with fresh battery and formatted memory card
- File type selected (more on this in chapter 10)
- Extra lenses
- Light-shaping tools—reflector, diffuser, flash, and the like
- Comfortable shoes or boots
- Water, snacks, any other personal gear you need for safety and comfort

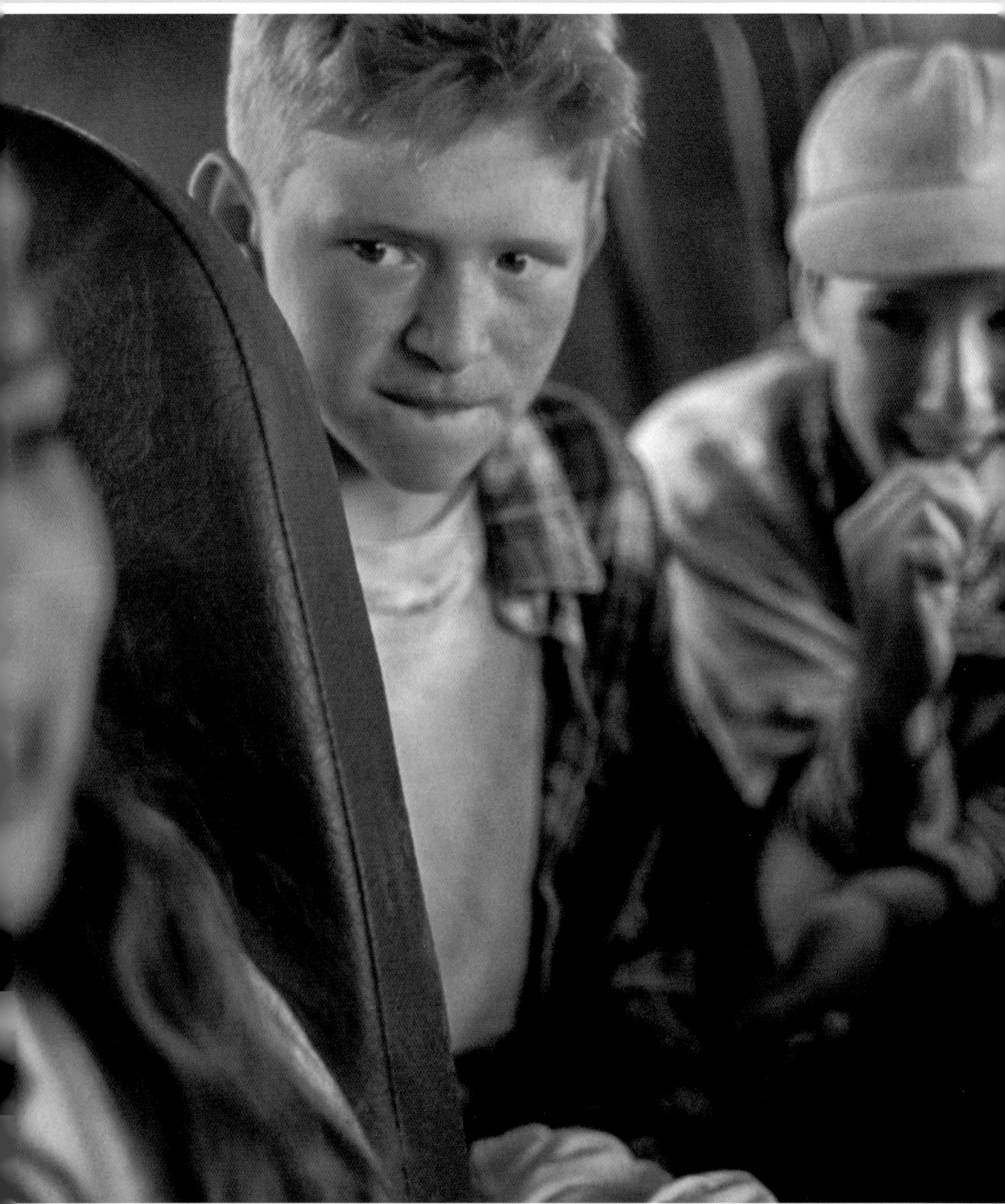

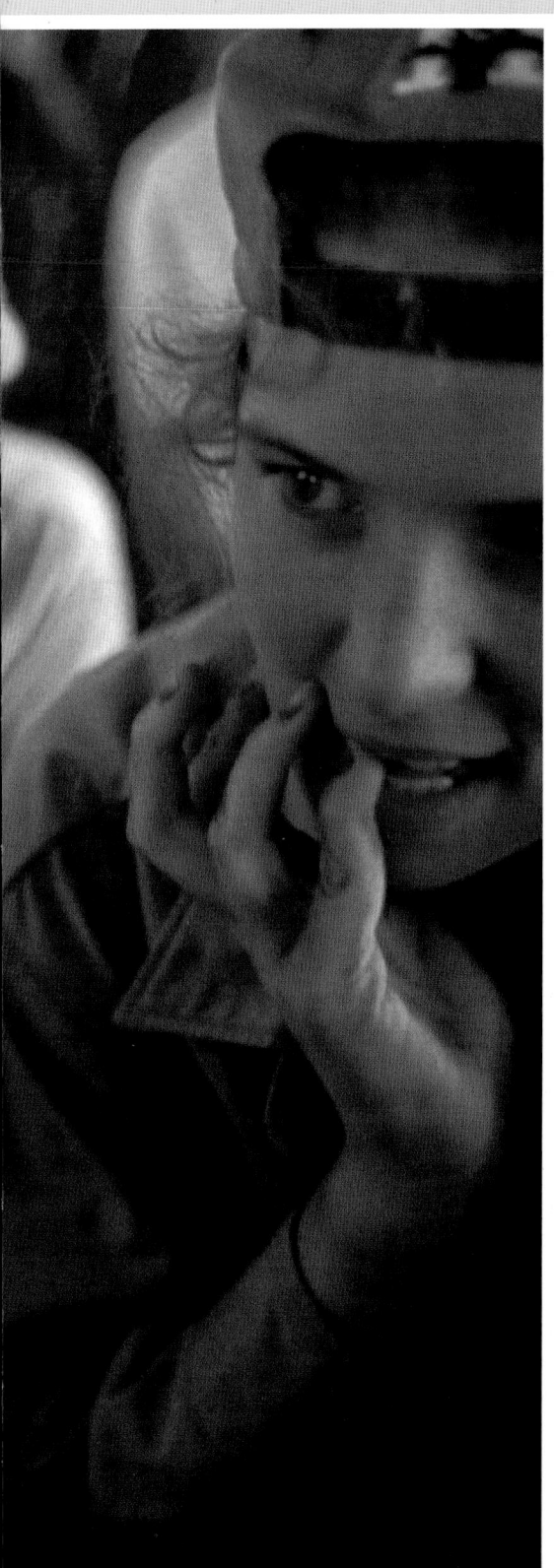

ANTICIPATION

This picture was taken on a bus full of kids who'd been hired to pull the tassels off corn during the summer. At the end of the day, they waited to hear how much they had earned. I boarded the bus with them and started photographing, open to whatever would come in the moments before, during, and after the big reveal.

CAPTURE A FEELING Anticipation is sometimes a more powerful emotion than the satisfaction or disappointment that may follow. As the kids wait, they're biting their nails, their lips; they're literally sitting on the edges of their seats. This is the moment that tells the story of their day of hard work, and the anticipation of the reward they have earned.

BE PRESENT The biggest benefit of practicing your skills is that once the technical stuff becomes second nature, it frees you up to be present in the moment. You can immerse in a situation and open yourself up to what your subjects are feeling, making pictures from a relatable space. This infuses an image with meaning, allowing viewers to tap into the emotional center of the scene.

DON'T STOP When you're trying to capture human emotion, start photographing before the feeling builds and don't stop until well past the payoff. As you review later, you'll discover that single frame that holds the most energy and delivers the greatest impact.

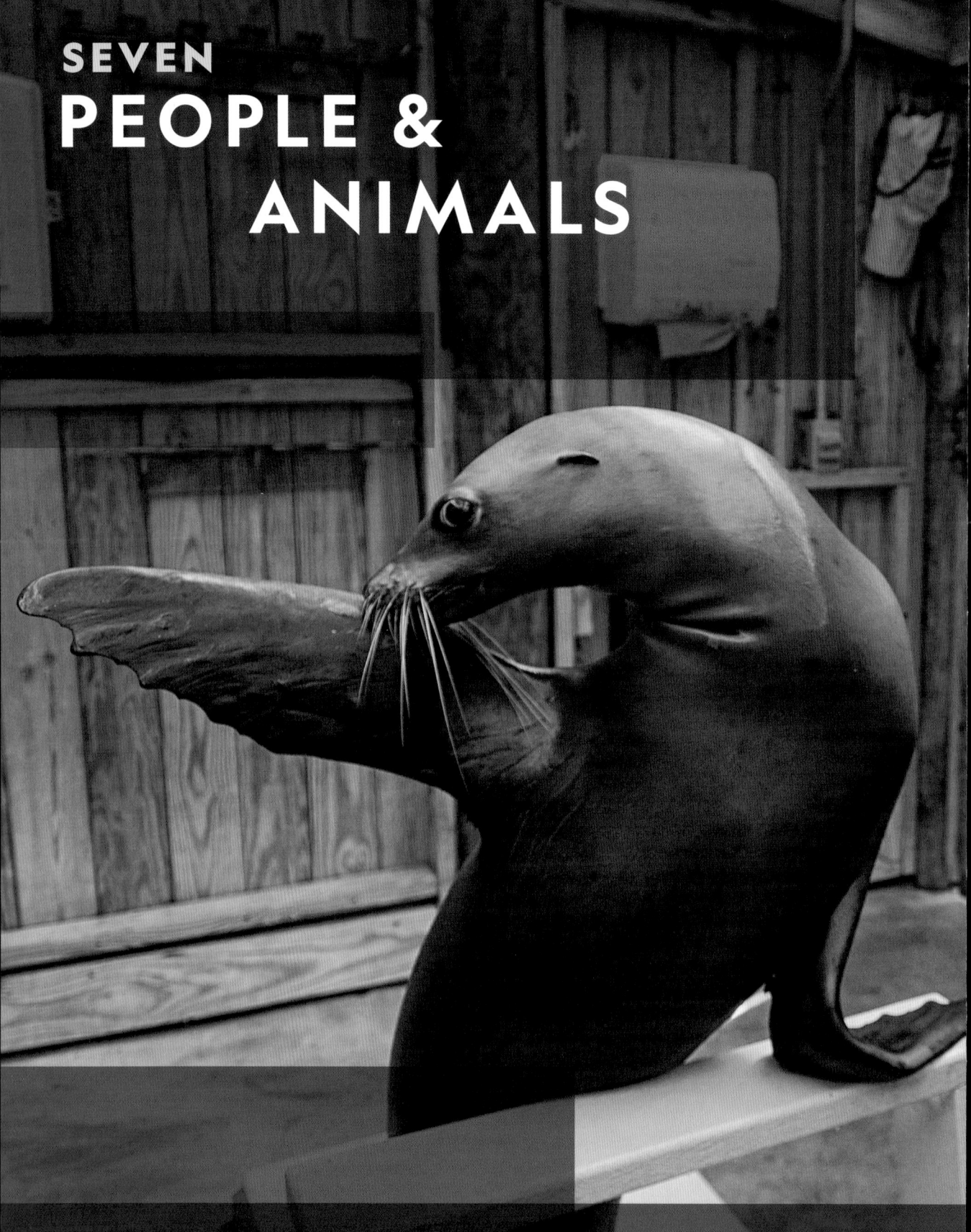

SEVEN
PEOPLE & ANIMALS

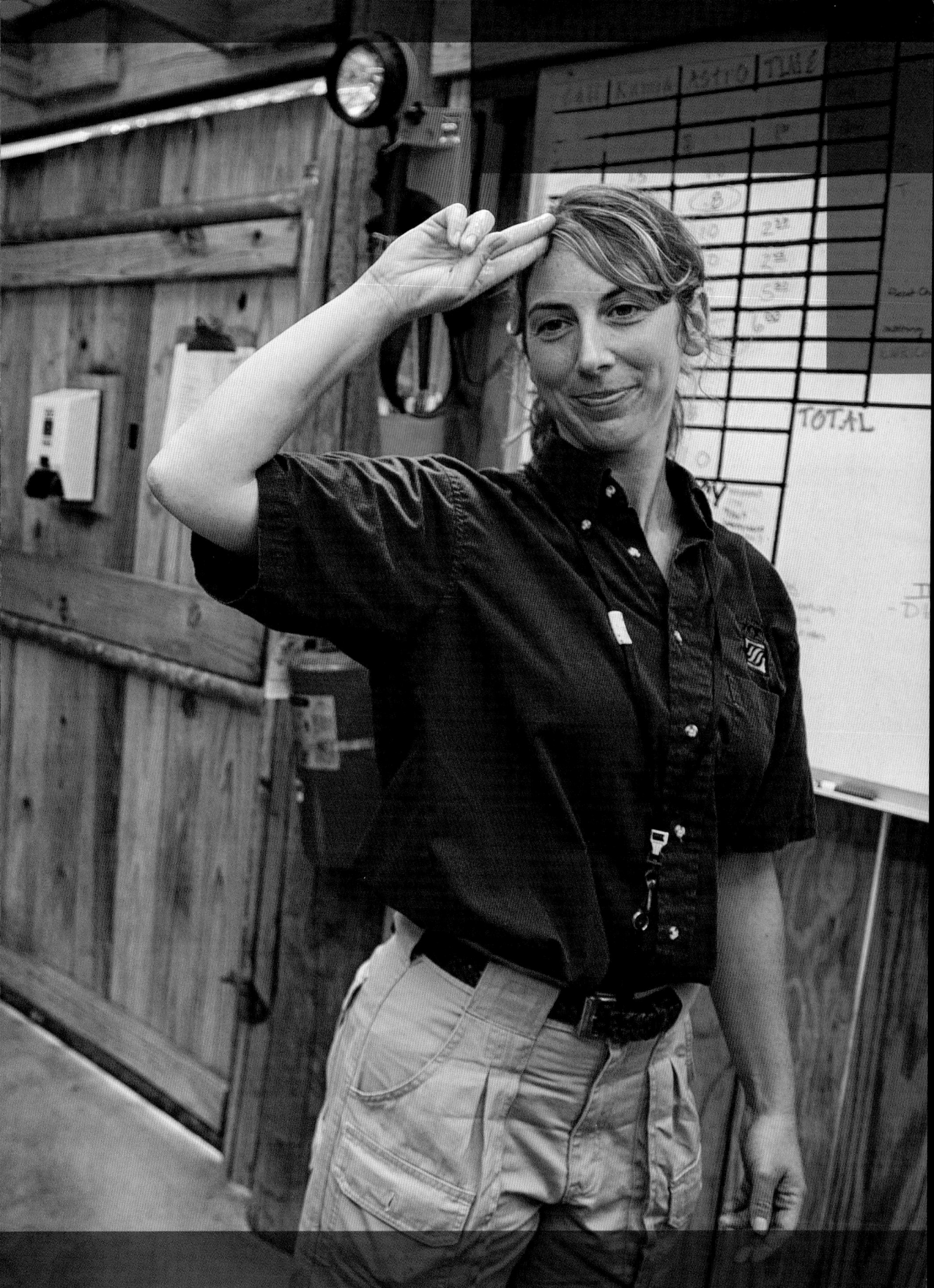

MAKING PORTRAITS

Photography freezes a moment in time: With just a click of the shutter, you preserve a split second of history. It's the reason that some photographs become iconic, why we return to some over and over again, why some stick with us long after we've stopped looking.

People and animals capture the attention of photographers around the world. From family photos to backyard wildlife, from foreign cultures to exotic safaris, you can tap into a nearly endless well of inspiration with the human experience and the animal kingdom. These relatable and compelling subjects are the reason so many of us get into photography, but it can take years to learn how to capture them in an authentically moving way. After all, they do have minds of their own. In this chapter, we'll explore some strategies for taking engaging and meaningful pictures of the people and animals around us. Whether you're photographing a staged portrait, a birthday party, or a selfie, these techniques will complement the technical skills we've learned so far.

The color, layers, and composition of this photograph of cowboys in Pantanal, Brazil, make it a beautiful and compelling portrait of men who work with horses for their livelihood.

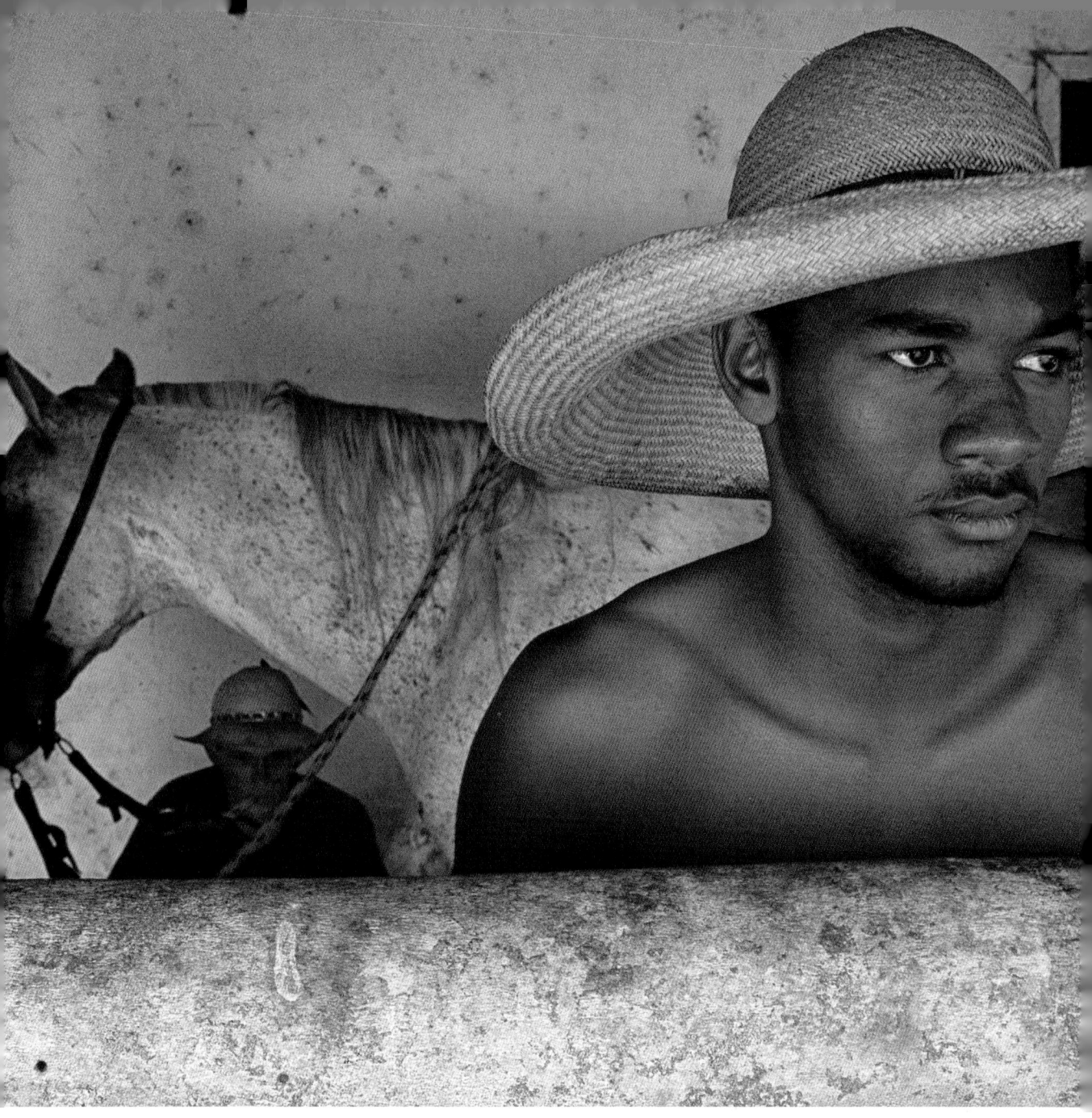

PORTRAIT BASICS

Even if the composition is simple, a portrait should still tell a story. Your connection with and the comfort of your subject can be a powerful tool in telling that story in a meaningful way.

A portrait is much more than a picture of someone. A successful one will say something about the subject's life, personality, or circumstance. Think of a portrait as a collaboration between you and your subject. Clothing, props, facial expressions, and even posture are all cues that will tell their story to your viewers.

APPROACH

Making a portrait is an intimate experience. It requires understanding your subject in a way that will allow you to see and capture something about her that feels personal or private. It requires trust between a subject and photographer, so if you're photographing someone you don't know well, plan for a little time together without a camera before you begin. When you start photographing, don't be afraid to get in close.

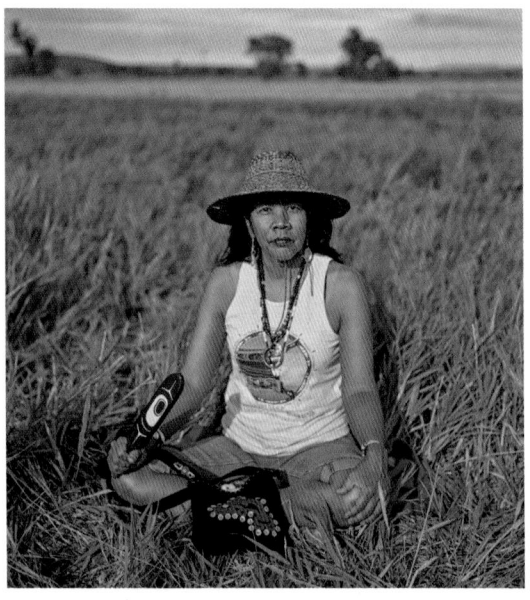

Sweetwater Nannauck is the executive director of Idle No More, a group that advocates for indigenous sovereignty. This portrait was taken at a protest against the Dakota Access Pipeline. Her posture and expression clearly communicate her position about the issue.

You can direct your subject a little, but focus on her natural moments. Letting her personality guide your approach will result in better portraits.

POSITIONING

Placing your subject in the center of the frame can be captivating with an arresting expression, but don't forget the rule of thirds. Test varying positions in the frame to see what resonates. One especially

| PRO TIP | GETTING COMFORTABLE |

The easiest way to put your subjects at ease is to look and listen. Before you start shooting, read the situation: Is it appropriate for you to put your camera in the subject's face, or is it better to wait off to the side for a candid moment? If you're photographing an animal, observe its behavior for signs of stress or aggression. Be still and respectful, letting your subjects get used to your presence so they look relaxed and natural in a photograph.

FOR MORE ABOUT INTRODUCING LIGHT, SEE PAGE 96.

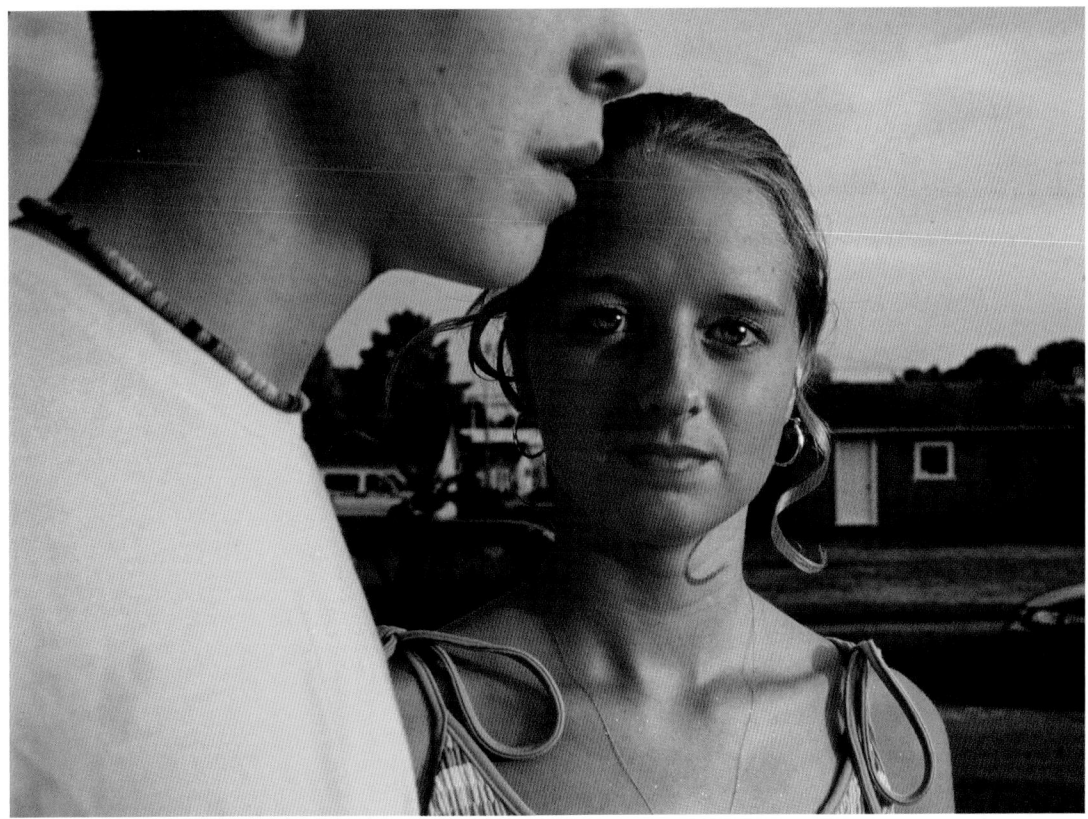

This portrait of a teenage girl in Ohio is a bit less traditional, but captivating nonetheless. The inclusion of just part of another person evokes an intimate connection between the two subjects without them even touching.

important rule in portraiture is that your subject's eyes should always, always, always be in focus.

Pay attention to the background. Consider details that will contribute to your portrait's story, or eliminate distractions by experimenting with aperture and depth of field. You might opt for a clean backdrop, which is typical in professional headshots.

WATCH THE LIGHT

Pay attention to how the light may reveal or obscure details of your subject's face. If the light isn't to your liking, do something to improve it—move a lamp, use a flash, grab a reflector. Good light means the difference between a decent portrait and a great one.

Start with people you know. Get so familiar with your camera that you don't waste time fiddling with settings—nothing makes a subject more uncomfortable than having to wait. Remember that being in front of the camera might feel like a vulnerable position for some. Do what you can to make them comfortable and create something that tells their story honestly.

ENVIRONMENTAL PORTRAITS

An environmental portrait is a picture in which details throughout the frame help tell the story of your subject.

When you're planning a portrait shoot, think about incorporating the environment into your image. Perhaps you photograph a horticulturist in her greenhouse, a bookseller among his bookshelves, or a mom making breakfast for her family. These techniques can apply to nonhuman subjects as well—the family dog in the backyard, a pigeon on a city sidewalk, a dolphin leaping from the sea.

Including the environment can enrich a portrait, adding depth and context to your subject's story. But be careful that the background doesn't steal the show—always try to keep your subject at the heart of the photo.

CONSIDER COMPOSITION

To find a good balance of subject and environment, try a few different approaches to the portrait's composition. A single approach won't work for every scenario, so try placing your subject in different parts of the frame and gauge the results. Look for elements within the scene that can help connect different layers and make it feel like a cohesive image. Leading lines can draw a connection between your subjects and their environment, or between elements of the scene.

SETTING THE SCENE

As with all portraits, your knowledge of your subjects and how they fit into their world will make for successful environmental portraits. Put some time in before sessions to consider creative ways to portray them in the context of their environment. Consider what you want to say, and scope out surroundings in advance, if you can, so you know any special equipment you might need—lighting for accent, a ladder for a different perspective, stabilization for an extended shutter speed.

ASSIGNMENT: CAPTURE SOMEONE IN HER ELEMENT

Think about a friend with an interesting job. Ask if you can photograph her in her workplace. Concentrate on creating a background that tells us more about your subject, without too much clutter or unwanted distracting elements. You can even try this with a pet—your dog with his favorite bone, your horse grazing in a field, your cat climbing around her cat tree.

And don't be afraid to think outside the box. Environmental portraits don't have to be literal—they can be conceptual for a more abstract and sophisticated portrait. Imagine using a trampoline to photograph an astronaut in the air to convey weightlessness, or using a fan to blow the hair of a race-car driver to convey speed.

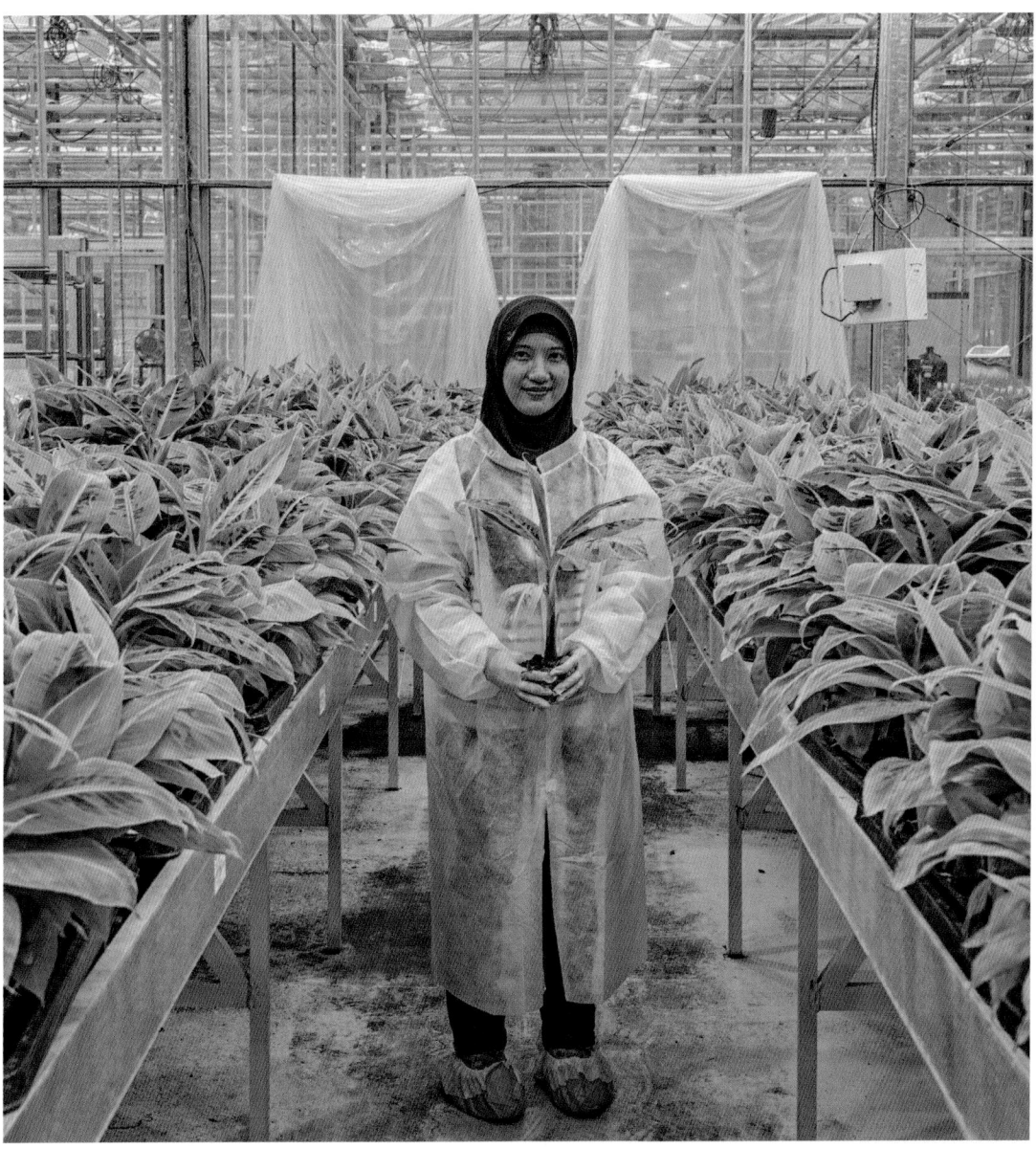

A student poses among her agricultural research in a greenhouse at Wageningen University and Research in the Netherlands. This portrait is well composed, and also describes her work—the leading lines of the tables draw our eyes right to her, the rows of plants help frame her, and the one in her hands ties her to her surroundings.

FAMILY & FRIENDS

Make portraits of the people you know best. Asking family and friends to let you photograph them will give you a solid place to start, and allow you to create important memories at the same time.

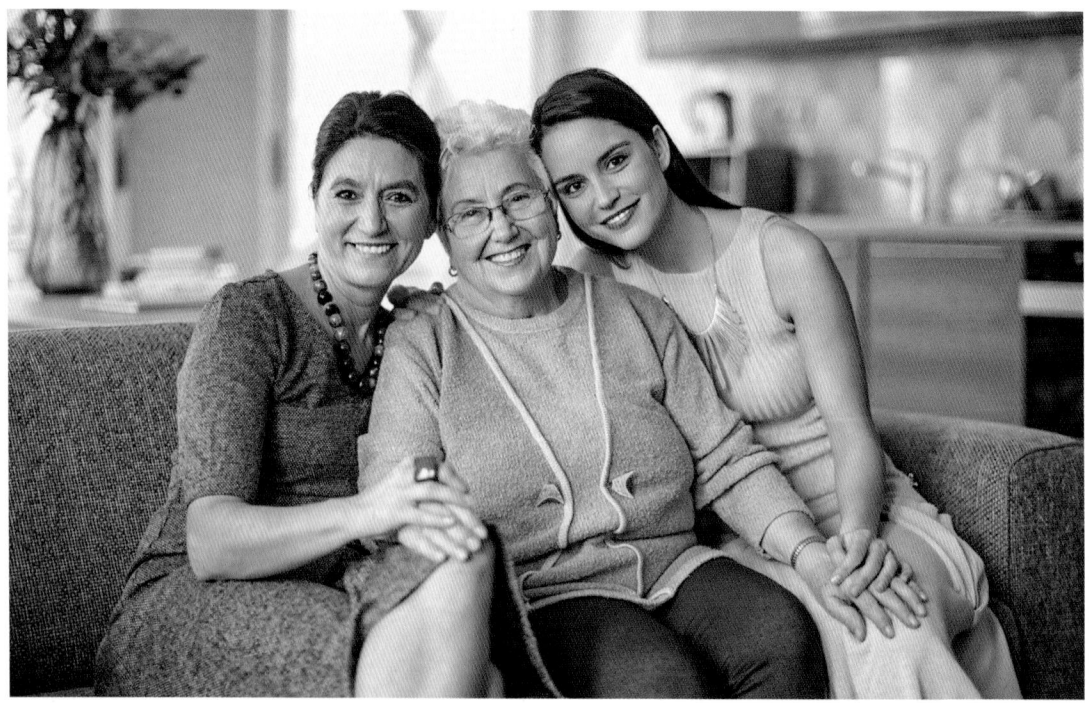

Natural light from a window and narrow depth of field help to capture this beautiful portrait of three generations of women sharing a loving, comfortable moment.

As you begin your journey into portrait photography, you'll find that working with family and friends provides the comfort of a preexisting relationship—this may allow you to experiment a little, try out some lighting techniques, or play with themes for environmental portraits. Ask for their patience, but remember that working efficiently will keep the session fresh. In the process, you'll refine your skills, gain confidence about exploring new ideas, and hopefully create photographs that are meaningful to them and to you.

CONNECTIONS

Start simple. Bring a loved one into a room with great window light. Sit him down and examine the way the light falls on his face. Add a reflector—anything white and reflective—to bounce some of that light back on to him from the other side. Take some test shots and make adjustments until you get

Organizing a group of people for a portrait can be a challenge, so here are a few tips:

- Be prepared. Being organized, confident, and direct will command respect from a rambunctious, possibly awkward crowd.

- Instead of tall people in back and shorter people up front, organize the group into a mountain shape, or even something more organic. Get them talking, laughing, but holding their positions. Let them know this is the goal.

- Stand on a chair. If all your subjects have to look up at you, you'll see more of their faces, and they'll be pleased with the flattering angle. Consider bringing a ladder for an even higher vantage point.

- Take a second before each shot to check that you can see each face and that no one is obscured.

- Once you've got all your subjects the way you want them, take several shots in a row to avoid anyone having closed eyes.

the exposure and depth of field the way you want.

Next, drop the camera for a moment and have a conversation with him and wait for him to get comfortable. Now you can begin to make portraits, keeping it light, maintaining that connection the whole time. Look for ways to draw out his personality and expressions of emotion. Look for the relaxed moments when your subject is most himself.

Experiment with the position of your subject in relation to the window, and repeat as the light changes throughout the day. In the pages ahead, we'll talk more about making portraits in less formal settings.

DON'T SETTLE

As always, keep what you know about good photography in mind. We love pictures of our family and friends because we love the people. Don't confuse your love for the person with love for the photograph, ultimately settling for a mediocre portrait. Instead, think about how you can make pictures of people you see all the time go from ordinary to extraordinary.

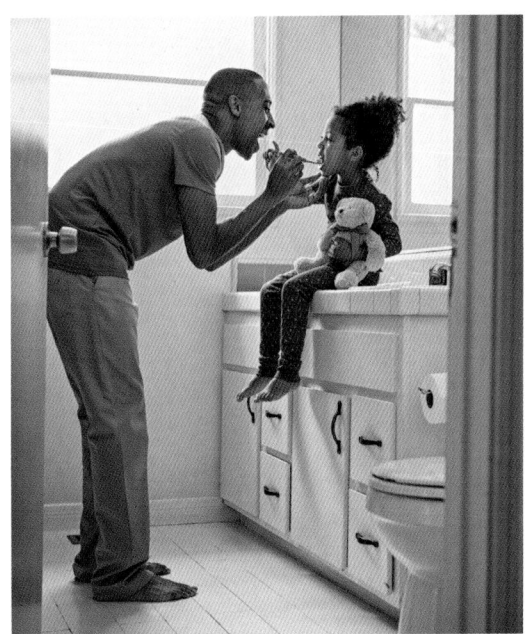

An intimate, everyday moment of a dad helping his daughter brush her teeth makes for a nontraditional yet meaningful portrait.

BABIES & KIDS

Portraits of babies and children should be as expressive as they are. Kids' high energy and range of emotions make photography a challenge, but good results carry great reward.

You can travel the world, take your camera into all kinds of crazy conditions—from mosquito-infested swamps to icy tundra—but it all pales in comparison to trying to get a good picture of a baby. Babies (and most kids) are always moving and they don't hold eye contact for very long. Getting a picture that's in focus often takes patience, anticipation, and a little luck. But when it all comes together, you have something to cherish.

BABIES

Look for spots where the light is soft and natural—maybe diffused through a curtain or bounced off a wall. Get on the baby's level—that may mean lying on the floor or on a bed next to her so that you can get direct eye contact.

Alternatively, you may want to shoot from directly overhead so that the floor or bed serves as a background. Remember

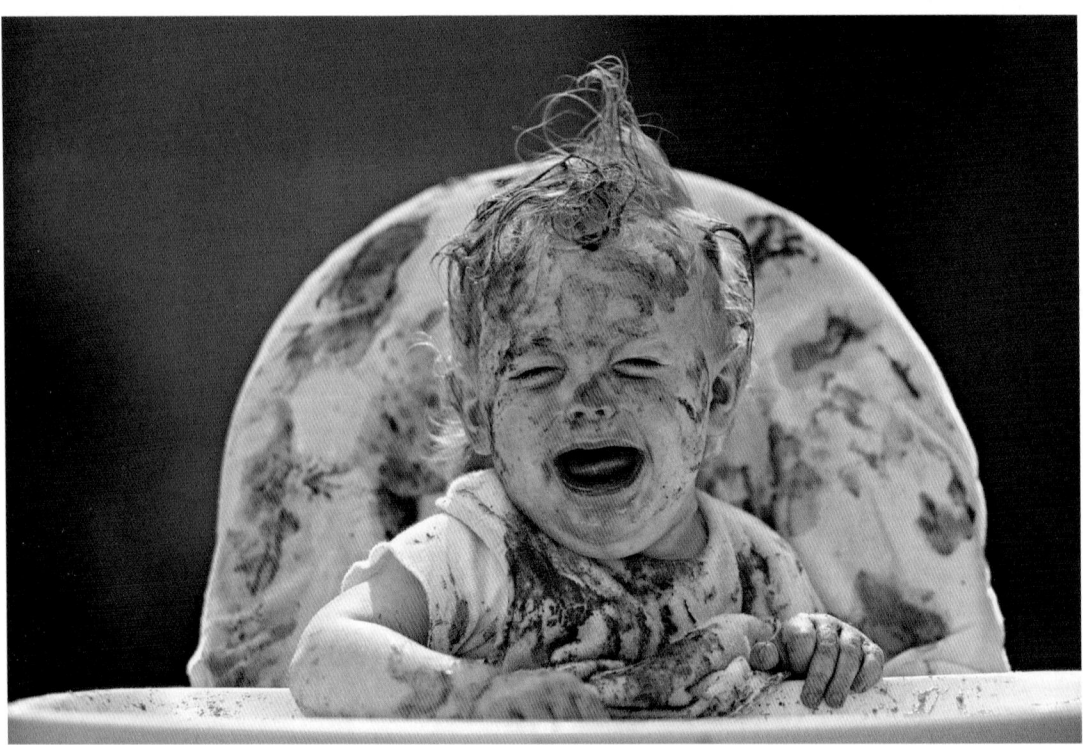

This child has had it with dinner—he's likely wearing more food than he ate. Grabbing a quick frame before cleanup may help lighten a frustrating moment, and the resulting image is one that anyone raising a child can relate to.

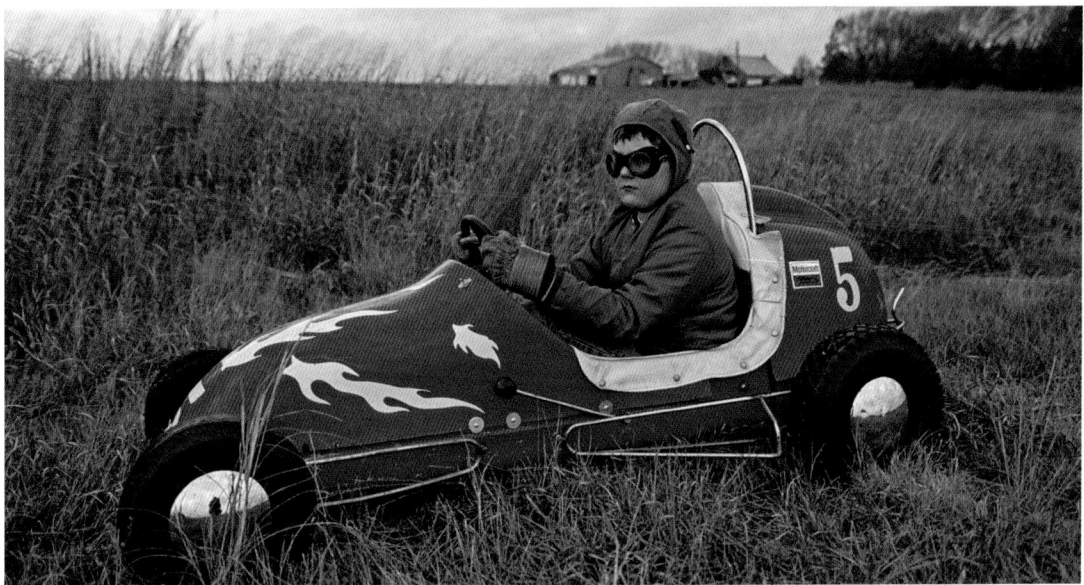

Here's a picture of my son Cole in a little race car called a "midget racer," a boyhood hobby of his. His outfit, his expression, the design on the car, and the prairie behind him say so much more about him at that age than if he were just looking into the camera and smiling.

the little details—tufts of hair, chunky thighs, wrinkly toes. Someday you'll look back and you won't believe how small your baby's hand once was.

KIDS AND EMOTIONS

Think about times your child shows genuine joy, whether playing with a favorite toy, running around a soccer field, or cuddling with the family dog. Try to anticipate those moments and have your camera ready. Consider as well the other emotions in the life of your child—fatigue, anger, sadness, and boredom can also make for compelling photos. When the inevitable happens, consider snapping a picture or two before soothing your upset child. Caveat: This is a tough balance to strike between parent and child, and only you can know when you can

grab a quick shot, or when he needs *you* and not your camera.

If you frequently photograph your kids, they'll likely learn to accept or just ignore it—meaning you'll get fewer posey moments, and more authentic, candid photographs.

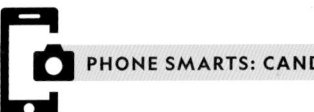

PHONE SMARTS: CANDIDS

Smartphones are ideal for capturing candid moments as you may not always have a DSLR on hand for milestones like a baby's first steps. Try to incorporate what you know about composition, but don't miss a special moment. Even if they're not the most technically impressive, these may be the photos you treasure most.

SELF-PORTRAITS

In spite of knowing yourself better than you know anyone else, a self-portrait might be the most challenging portrait you make.

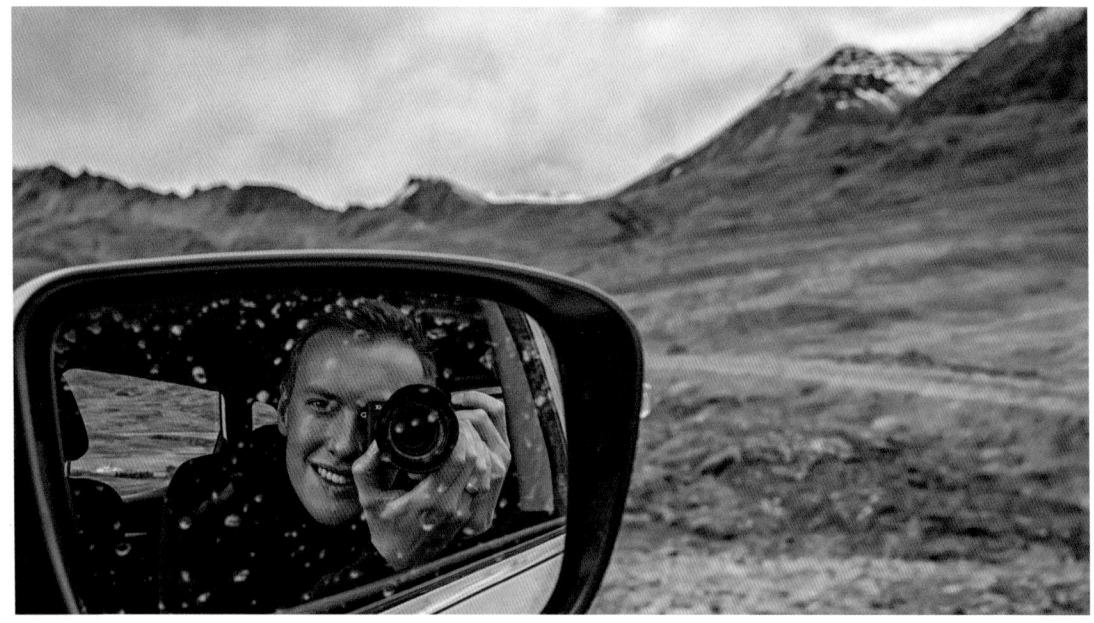

When taking self-portraits, remember your composition skills. This self-portrait does a great job of framing the photographer and clueing us in to his location and feelings about the adventure.

We live in the "selfie age," and, like me and everyone else, you've probably stretched out an arm to take a selfie with your phone. Some may say it's vain, but self-portraiture is a time-honored and beautiful tradition. At a minimum, a selfie is good practice, as you are always available as a subject! But how do you go from a selfie to an authentic, meaningful self-portrait?

INWARD REFLECTION

At first, photographing yourself might feel uncomfortable. Lean into whatever emo-tion you're feeling in the moment and start with the basics: What is the story you want to tell about yourself? Consider this as you sit in front of your own camera. Try an environmental self-portrait. Will it be literal—you in your office or home? Or something more abstract—say, a shadowy glimpse of just part of your face or a hazy reflection in a steamed-up mirror?

Spend a little time getting comfortable on the other side of the camera, then put your creativity to work. Try using your tripod and a timer or remote release. Exper-

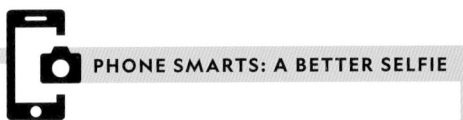
artist and the subject, you have total creative control.

BOTH SIDES OF THE LENS

Be brave. Experiment. If you're feeling self-conscious, focus on what you'd like the final portrait to communicate. Maybe write a caption for the picture you haven't taken yet. Inhabit that headspace, then make the picture that captures that story.

And one more thing: Subjecting yourself to time in front of the lens might give you a better idea of how your subjects may feel. Note how this influences your approach to others and the photographs you make.

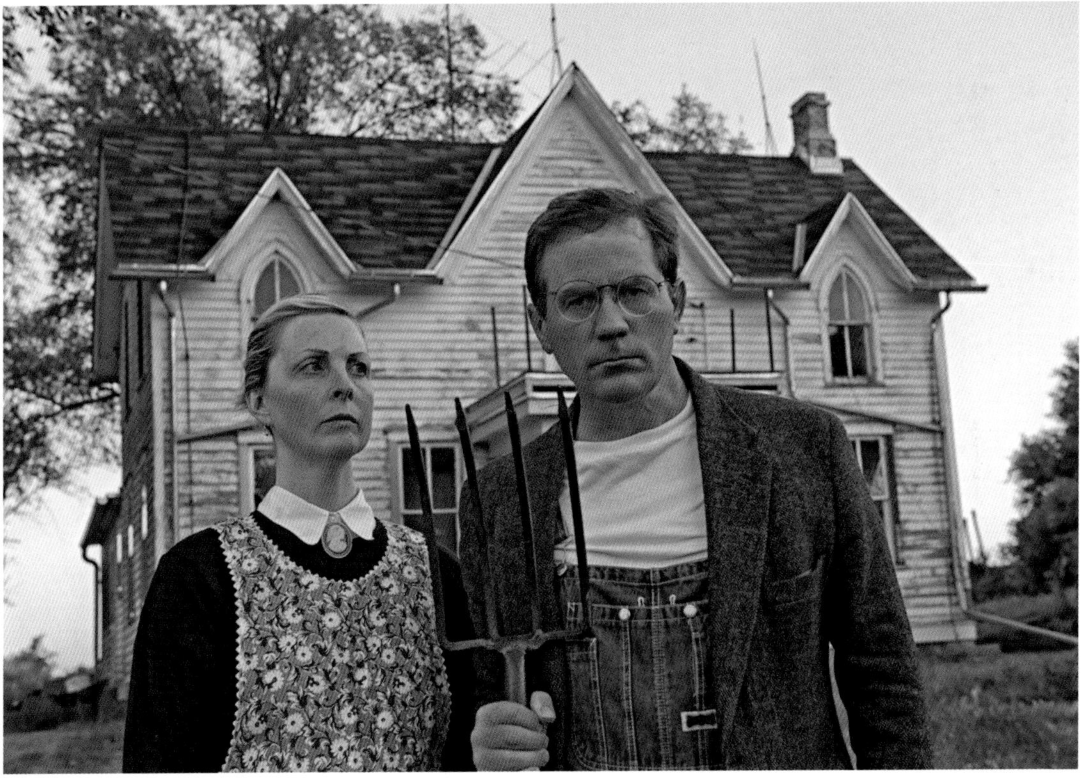

iment with different forms of lighting. Focus on one part of yourself, like your hands or your eyes. When you're both the

Self-portraits allow you to get highly creative with personality. Here, my wife, Kathy, and I reenact the famous 1930 painting "American Gothic" by Grant Wood.

CANDIDS

Good candid photographs have a special way of connecting with viewers but can be difficult to achieve. A candid photograph typically captures a scenario over which you have little control. You can improve your odds of success with the right approach.

By definition, *candid* means unposed, informal, impromptu, and natural. These photographs feel relatable because they usually document authentic, uncontrived moments when your subject is focused on something other than the camera. When you combine a genuine, unscripted moment with skilled composition, it makes for a moving photograph. Good candid photographs can be among the most powerful but challenging

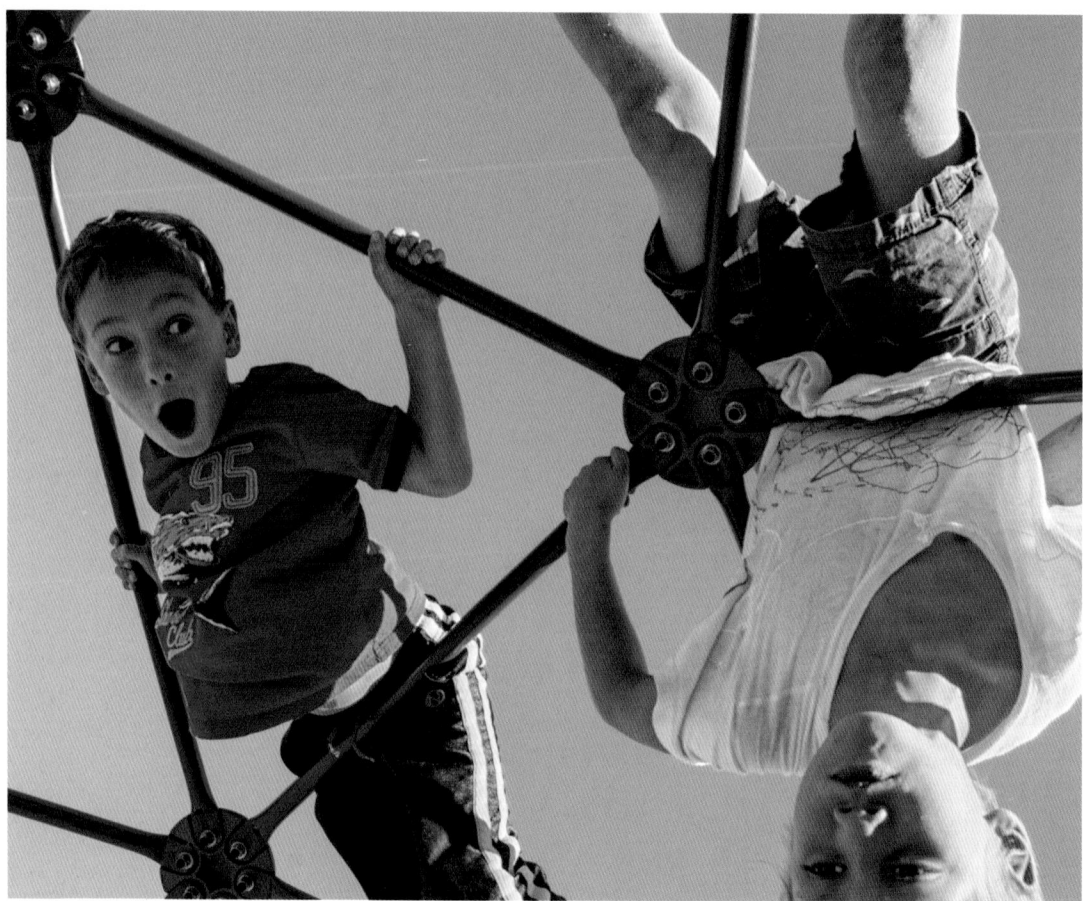

Hanging out under the jungle gym lets you capture the expressions of joy and excitement that accompany physical play. The metal bars add a pattern and frames for these energetic young climbers.

photographs to make. The best practice is to be ready at almost all times to capture the scene without compromising your standards for important photographic elements.

AT THE READY

Make it a habit to have your camera handy, with a charged battery and a clean memory card. Keeping it on aperture priority and at a midrange ISO is a good bet for shooting in most scenarios. Personally, I keep the camera on and the lens cap off to avoid obstacles between me and a fleeting moment.

When you see a scenario developing—a pillow fight between kids, or a dad reading to his child at bedtime—be stealthy and subtle. Pick up the camera and approach slowly and quietly without any fuss. Find your best vantage point and don't do anything to distract your subjects. Be a fly on the wall, equal parts observing and photographing.

Don't overstay your welcome—get several shots when a special or surprising moment occurs, and then set the camera back down. Don't prolong the shoot and risk annoying your subjects. Once they are aware of the camera, you risk losing the authenticity of the moment.

A WINNING STRATEGY

As you work, keep in mind the technical elements that make a good photograph: the quality of the light, balanced composition, and depth of field. Allow for separation between subjects and do your best to keep track of any distracting elements in the background. Avoid flash—it's often difficult to control in a candid scene, and a burst of bright light can interrupt a tender moment and make your subjects more aware of the camera than you'd like.

Anticipation is key. Focus on home plate and wait for a ballplayer to slide into it, or focus on the front door and wait for the birthday girl to walk in to her surprise party. Watch for patterns in how and where people move and use them to your advantage.

Candid photography is a place you can really prove your mettle as a photographer—you usually have bare-bones equipment and little control over the elements in the scene. Your photographer's eye and technical skills will be your best tools for capturing a special moment.

The more you practice, the more discerning you'll become about scenarios and elements such as light and background—a sure sign that both your creative eye and your photos are improving.

ASSIGNMENT: CAPTURE REAL EMOTION

Try to capture real emotion in a candid photo. Be respectful and discreet as you approach—be sure your subject is lost in the moment and not performing for the camera. Use composition in an artful way that lets the viewer be transported by the emotion of the scene without any other distractions.

SPORTS

Whether you're in the stands at a professional baseball game or in the bleachers at a kids' swim meet, there's lots of excitement at sporting events. The right gear and mind-set will help you capture the action every time.

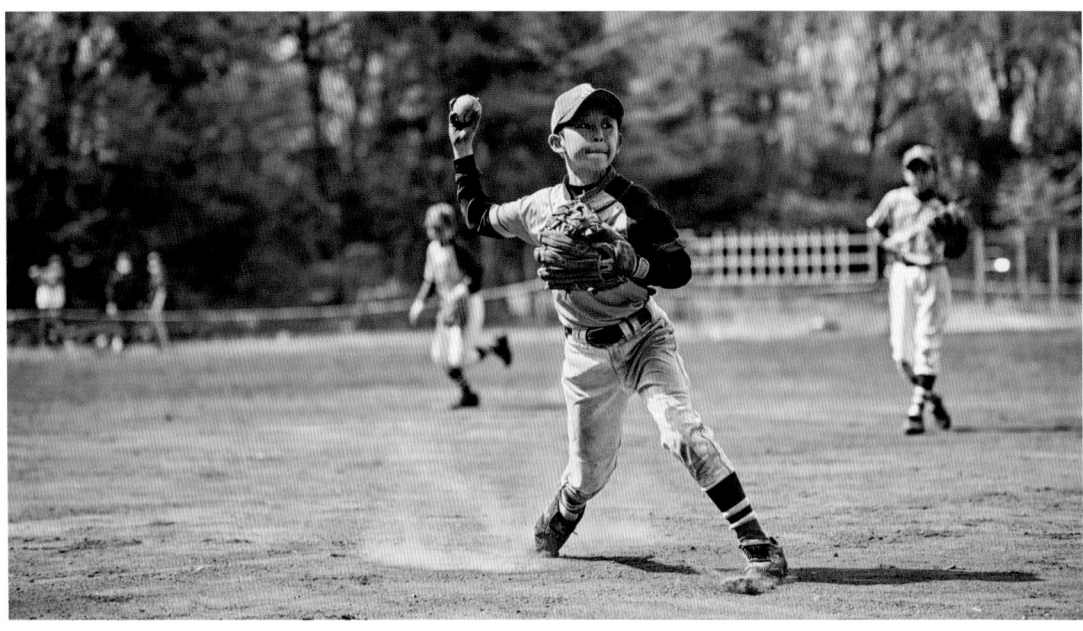

A fast shutter speed freezes the moment before this Little League pitcher hurls the ball. His determined expression and body position are captured perfectly here, and he's framed well by his teammates in the background.

Few things are more thrilling than watching athletes give their all in sport. Sporting events can yield wonderful photographs with a range of concepts on display—grit, camaraderie, strength, grace, joy, disappointment. And excitement, cheering, highs, and lows make for fantastic candids in the stands.

TIMING IS EVERYTHING

Good sports photography requires an obsession with timing. Get yourself to a great vantage point, whether in the end zone or on the pool deck, taking care not to compromise the flow of the action. With most sports, you should start to feel a rhythm emerge that will help you anticipate the most exciting moments. It helps to have a solid understanding of the sport, so you know what will happen and where to focus.

Shutter speed is your priority—set it fast to freeze the action (at a minimum of 1/350) or slower for a more abstract, artful blur. Get comfortable with your camera's autofocus so your subject stays sharp.

FOR MORE ON SELECTING FRAMES, SEE PAGE 232.

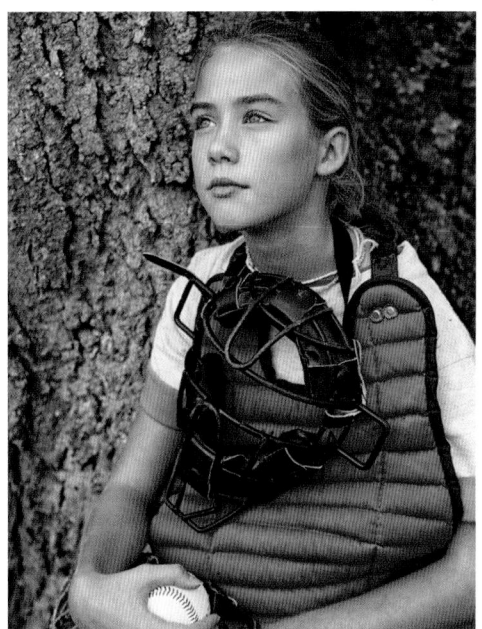 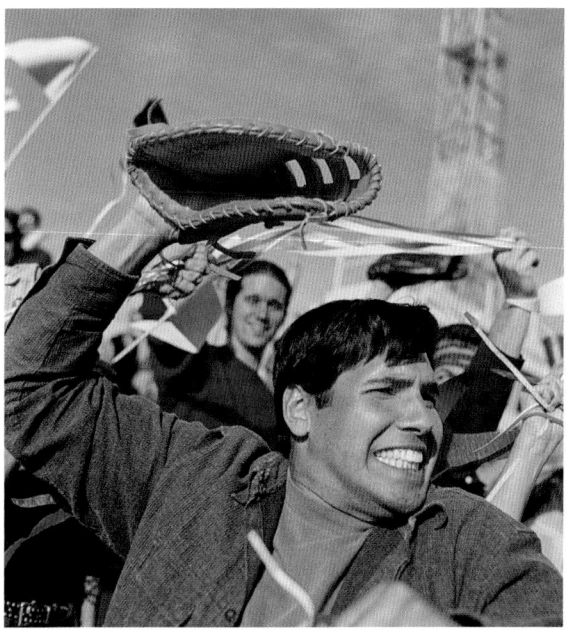

Not all sports photography has to focus on action. Make time for portraits of your favorite athletes with their gear to commemorate a great season (left). And not all sports photography has to be of the game itself! When you're in the stands, turn around and capture the excitement of the fans around you (right).

Think about composition as moments move in and out of frame. In general, it makes visual sense to have the action flowing into your frame rather than out of it, as the momentum will carry our eyes to the heart of the picture.

The rule of thirds is helpful here, giving your subject room to travel within the frame. Don't be afraid to take a ton of photographs, and try Continuous Shooting mode or Burst mode, which will allow you to take several shots at a time. You can pick out the best frames when you review later.

BE READY TO MOVE

You'll be slow on your feet if you're bogged down with gear, so a zoom lens is a good choice, since it's multiple lenses in one. A monopod can help support a heavy camera with a long lens, and be useful to steady your camera while panning as fast action moves past.

PRO TIP GYM LIGHTING

Gymnasiums often have terrible lighting that makes good photography challenging. The light is usually ugly and up high, and bounces all over yellow floors and off-white walls. Don't get discouraged—treat it as you would any other low-light situation. Turn your ISO up as high as you can without too much noise, and take a few test shots with different white balance settings. Check your LCD screen often, and you'll find the sweet spot.

WEDDINGS

Weddings combine happy, touching moments with beautiful decor and people looking their best—a great opportunity to make photographs you'll treasure.

Wedding photography is a very specific type of work—experienced professionals are not only expert photographers, but are also set up to distribute prints, albums, slideshows, and other products from the results of the big day's shoot. It's difficult, and the stakes are high—you only have one chance to capture most of the important moments. For that reason, it's best to leave the "official" photography of the event to the pros, and think about the special moments you can capture as a guest.

GUEST PHOTOGRAPHY

Unofficially photographing a wedding comes with some rules of etiquette:

- The bride and groom have likely hired a professional to photograph their big day. Respect their choice and be sure to stay out of the official photographer's way.
- If you'd like to take pictures during the ceremony, check with the couple, but also with the officiant or coordinator about where you can and can't be.

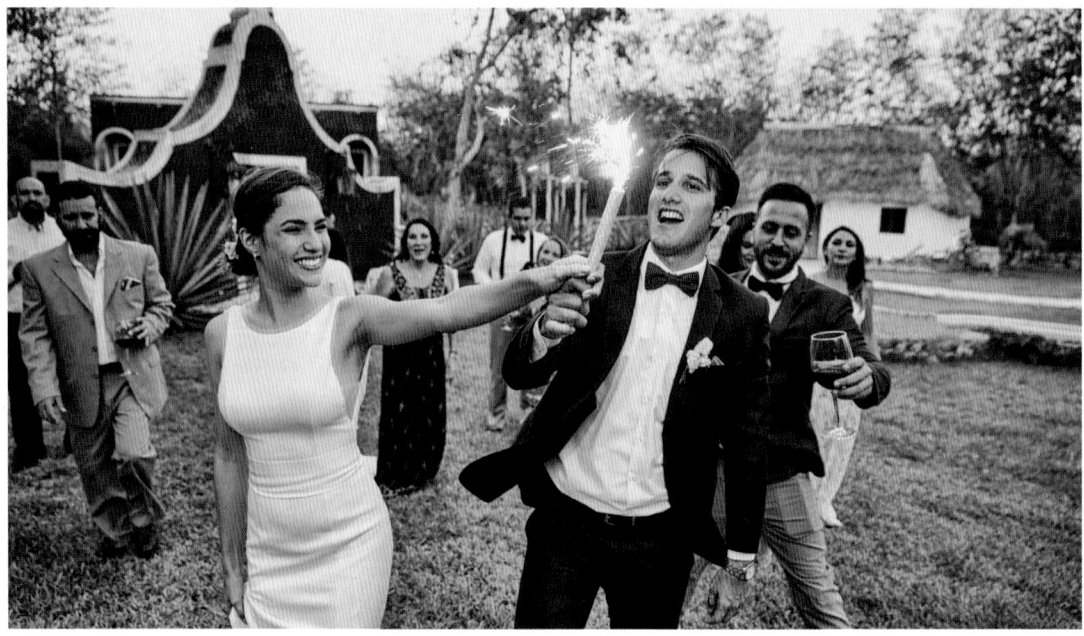

Your connection to your loved ones gives you an advantage when making photographs that capture their feelings in the moment. Putting what you know about candid photography to work on your friends' big day will usually result in an authentic photograph you'll all cherish.

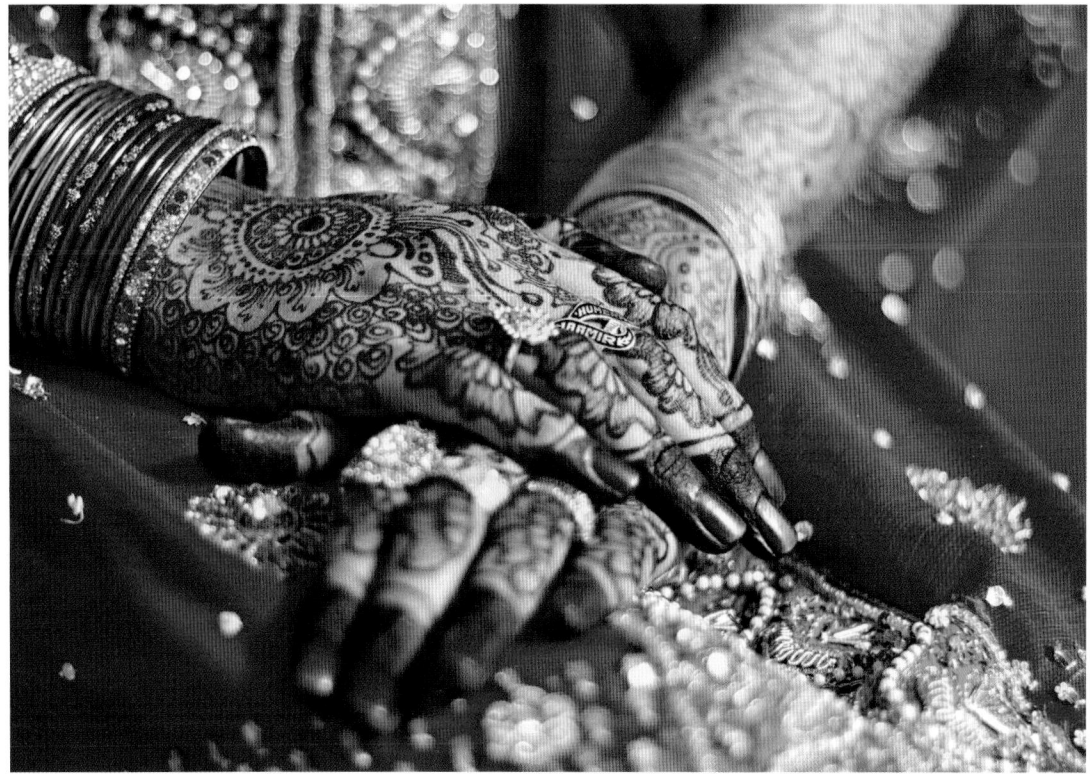

Every culture has its own unique rituals and traditions surrounding marriage and weddings. This image focuses on an elaborate henna decoration on the hands of a bride in India. Think about what practices are unique to your own culture.

- Use available light only. A flash will be disruptive and you probably won't like the results.
- Share your photographs with the couple, but check with them before sharing them anywhere else.
- Don't forget to dance! They invited you to help them celebrate, so be sure to put the camera down, take it all in, and have a good time.

INSIDER PHOTOGRAPHS

The wedding photographer will likely get photographs of the big, important moments as well as the small details, like venue decorations. Though you might find yourself drawn to creative elements like gowns, floral arrangements, and slices of beautiful wedding cake, consider what might set your photographs apart—you likely know the couple and other guests better than a hired professional.

Use that knowledge to look for all the moments that are distinct to them: reunions between old friends, silly dance moves, favorite songs enjoyed. Think about what you can add to a professional set of photographs, and remember to enjoy the party. Your friends will likely be grateful for your contributions to their big day.

CELEBRATIONS

Go beyond typical party snapshots to get the full story of a celebration. Important moments, reactions, and small details capture the essence of a birthday party or holiday celebration.

Like weddings, birthdays and holidays can be great opportunities for candid pictures of your friends and family members, but they can also be pretty chaotic. Think ahead as much as you can. Scout out rooms or areas with the best light or the cleanest backgrounds so you'll know where to focus your efforts. In most cases, you won't want to stop the action, so be prepared to improvise.

THE WHOLE PICTURE

If you can, go early and stay late. You'll be able to capture every detail of the party, from hanging decorations to cleaning up the mess afterward, and all the happiness and excitement in between.

Instead of posing people, be an observer—notice the way light lands on people in the room. Look for close conversations, laughter, greetings, and goodbyes. Set yourself up for success by getting into a good position, checking your camera settings, and shooting a lot of frames for the big moments, like blowing out candles and opening presents. Flash can be disruptive and difficult to do well in a party setting, so avoid using it, if possible. As always, look for clean backgrounds, interesting patterns, and opportunities to tell stories.

THE HEART OF THINGS

When the celebration is in full swing, pay attention to the emotional center—that may be the birthday boy, Grandma cooing over a new baby, or even kids fighting over who gets to play with the new toy first.

After you capture the big moments, look for little ones—dishes in the sink, half-eaten pie on the table, Grandpa dozing in his easy chair. Look around you and notice what else contributes to the story of the day, and commemorate it with your photos.

Finally, to fully engage with family and friends, don't try to get a picture of every little thing. Especially when food comes out, just put the camera down. You'll rarely get a good photograph of anyone eating—turn the camera off and have some dessert.

PRO TIP SET UP A PHOTO BOOTH

Sometimes the best-loved photos from a celebration are made with a little more intention. Offer to create a photo booth for a friend's gathering—find an out-of-the-way corner with great light (or set up lights) and fill the space with props and themed costume pieces. Ask people to come have fun while you make their portraits. Later, make them available to your host and fellow guests.

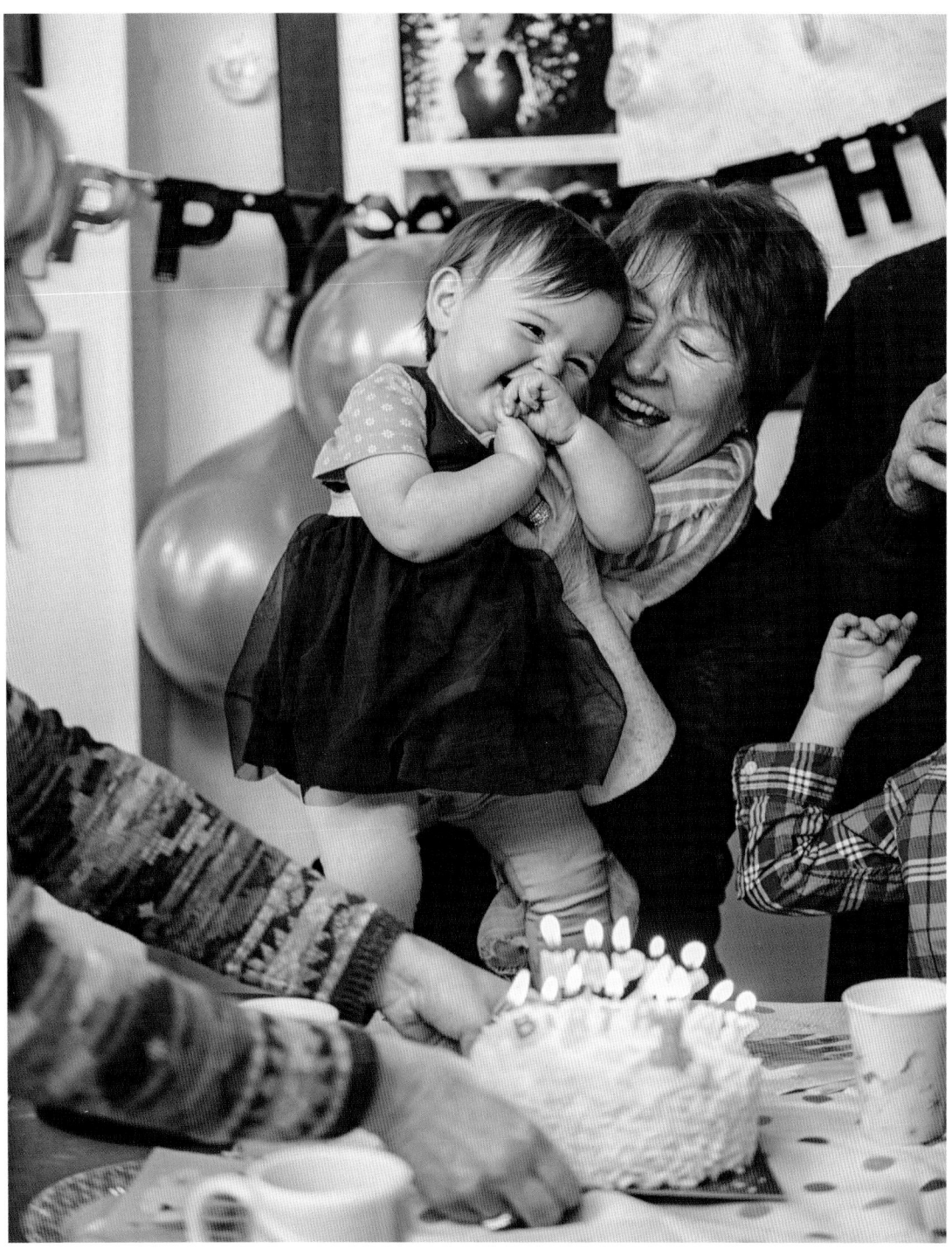

Instead of the classic candle-blowing moment, this is a great candid of the moment just before. Keep the spirit of the party at the front of your mind, and don't forget to enjoy yourself!

PETS

Just like friends and family, pets hold an important place in our hearts and family photo albums. Make portraits of your pet you'll cherish.

We love our pets, but making great photographs with them can be challenging, even when they're well trained. Secure the assistance of someone else who knows your pet well, and arm him with a favorite toy or treat, to direct your pet's attention to wherever you want it to be.

Remember to keep sessions with animals short, and reward them appropriately with treats, praise, and affection.

GET TO KNOW THEM

If you're photographing your own pet, you already have a good sense of her habits. Does your dog perk her ears up when you pick up her leash? Does your cat like to pounce when you wiggle your toes in bed? If you anticipate those moments and have your camera ready, you can get photographs that will convey what you know and love most about your pet.

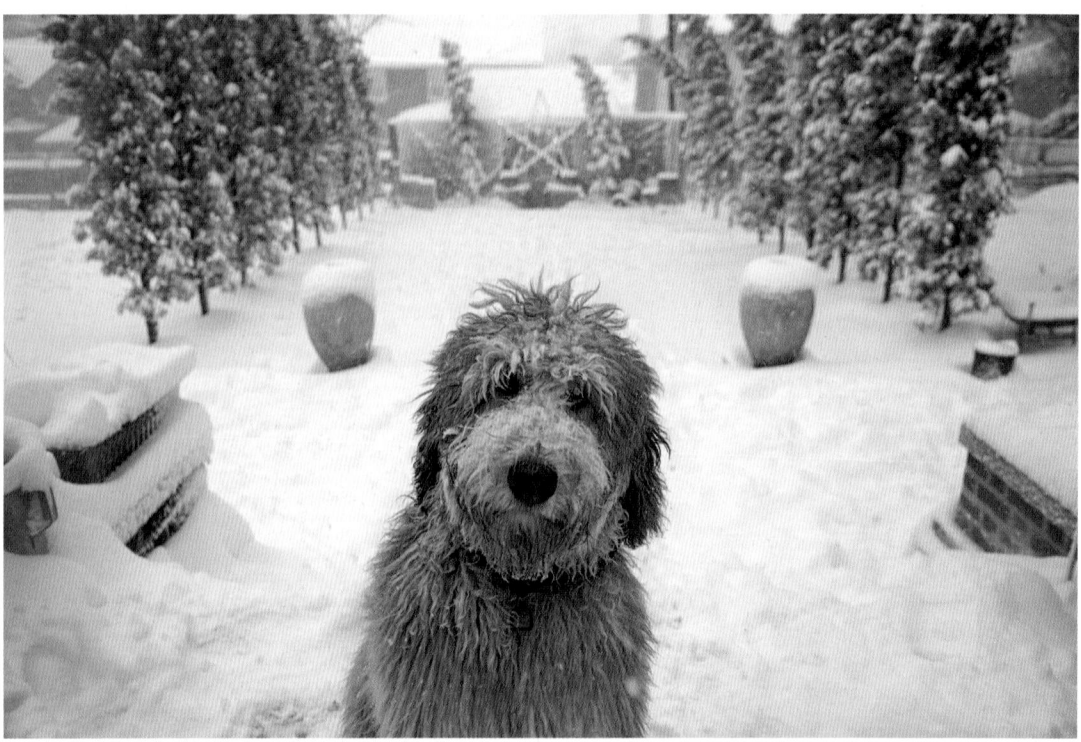

Just as you'd photograph a human friend, make portraits of your pets in their favorite settings. A clean background makes this dog easily stand out, and direct eye contact keeps you looking—both great ingredients for a portrait.

You know this move—your dog or cat hears your voice, or recognizes a toy or treat, and tilts her head. The animal head tilt can read as loyalty, curiosity, playfulness, or love. It's a moment when your pet's personality is openly on display. Do the thing you know elicits this response and take the picture for a portrait of your pet as you know her best.

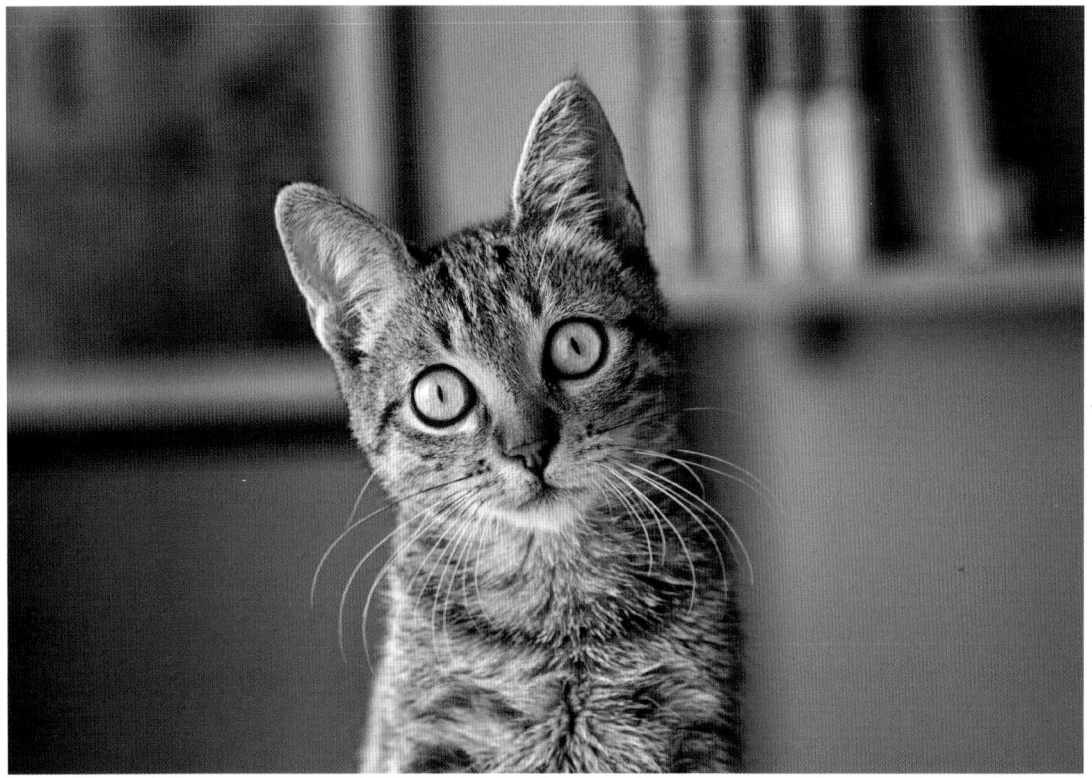

In what is often a fleeting moment, your pet may look at you in a way that is distinct to her and her relationship to you. Be ready with your camera and tap into your connection for a photograph that is different from the rest.

As with photographing children, it's helpful to get on the same level as a pet. Lie in the grass while your dog fetches a stick, or on the floor while the family hamster runs around in his plastic ball. Seeing eye to eye makes for a more intimate portrait, and being on your pet's level gives us a glimpse into his perspective.

Approach photographing a pet the same way you'd photograph a person. Find soft, flattering light, focus on the small details, and tell a story. Consider how he interacts with other animals or family members. Just like us, animals have their own personalities. If you can tap into that, you'll make a more compelling photograph.

WILD ANIMALS

Photographing wild animals can be a challenging but rewarding adventure. Whether you're on safari or in your own backyard, understanding the species you're photographing will increase your odds of getting a keeper.

Three key tools will help you get great wildlife pictures: knowledge, a zoom lens, and patience. In addition, photographing wild animals will test everything you've learned in this book—you'll also need research, planning, technique, anticipation, patience, and more patience.

UNDERSTANDING WILDLIFE

Spend time researching and observing an animal you want to photograph. Look for patterns and cues that will help you predict its behavior, and try to blend into the environment. Have your camera settings sorted out in advance—choose a wide aperture for a stately portrait, or a fast shutter speed for something on the move.

When you spot an animal, grab a shot from far away before you move closer—you'll have something to share even if it bolts before you can get proximity. Always think about safety for the animal and yourself—avoid risks that might make a wild animal feel threatened or angry, and be sure you have an exit strategy.

BACKYARD SAFARI

A great place to start wildlife photography is in your own backyard, where you can observe birds at a feeder or squirrels run-

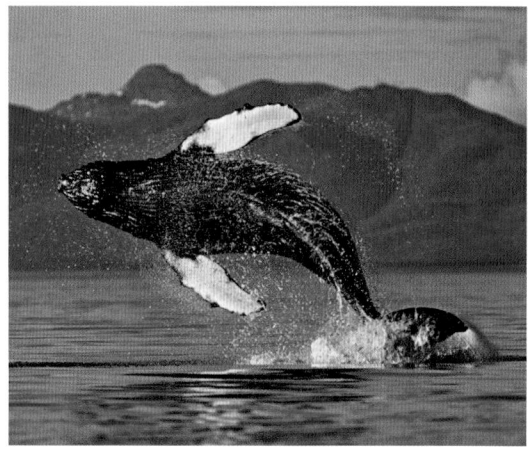

When photographing wildlife at sea, you'll really never know if or where they're going to surface. Your best bet is to have your camera preset and be at the ready for the moment you hear movement. Shooting on a Burst mode will give you multiple frames to choose from.

ning up trees. You'll have much more luck by settling in and letting the action come to you than by trying to chase it down, so pick a spot, set up, and wait quietly. A zoom lens is best here, so you can fill the frame without moving closer to your subject. When composing your photo, try to keep the animal's eyes in focus—it helps your viewer connect with the subject.

KNOW BEFORE YOU GO

If you decide to travel to photograph wildlife, do your research. Call local nature centers, zoos, or wildlife experts to learn about

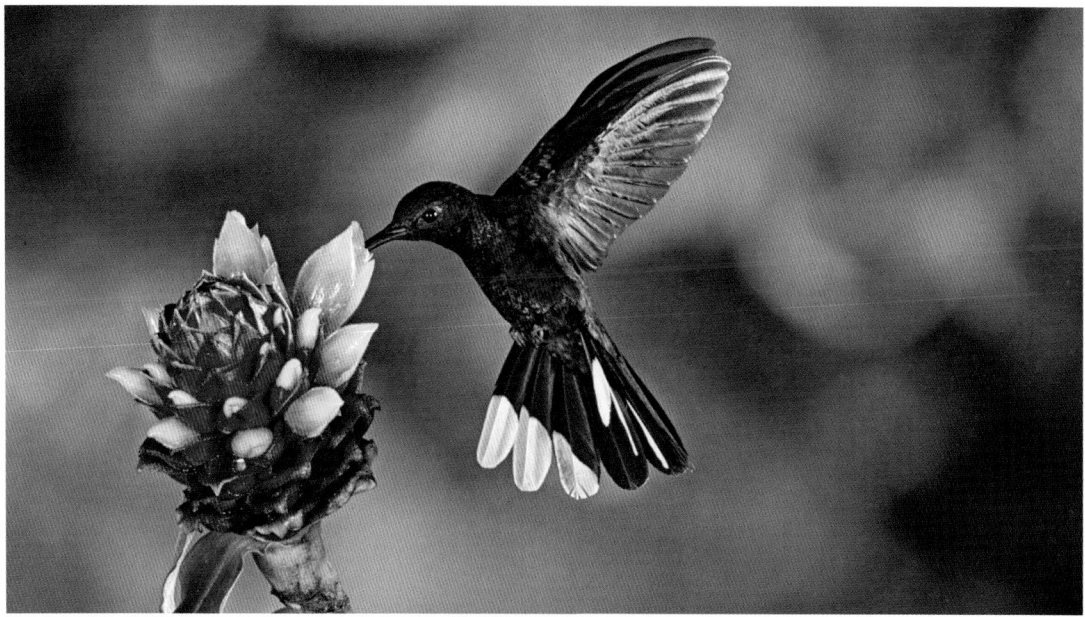

A hummingbird feeds on a ginger flower in Costa Rica. A super-fast shutter speed freezes the action of the bird's wings, and helps keep the eye in focus.

migratory patterns, restrictions, and best practices for working around a particular species or area. Know the seasonal patterns and peak activity times for the animals you want to photograph, and talk to other photographers who have had success in the area.

You should aim to show animals behaving naturally—sleeping, eating, playing—not stressed out or running from your camera.

Keep in mind that federal and state laws prohibit harassing animals in the wild or forcing them to abandon their nests or their young.

Wildlife photography is a marathon, not a sprint. It can take years just to have an opportunity to photograph a particular species. And even with ample opportunity, it will take much practice and patience to make a great photograph in the wild.

PRO TIP BLENDING IN

Professional wildlife photographers often try to eliminate a human presence in order to capture more natural behavior from their subjects. Here are some camouflaging techniques you can try at home:

- Make a backyard blind by hanging a piece of dark fabric over an open window. Cut a slit in the fabric for your lens to fit through. Frame the scene you want, set your camera accordingly, then wait. Consider setting up before sunrise when animals tend to move more freely.

- Create your own "camera trap" by setting up your camera near a feeder, or on a path where you know squirrels or deer regularly travel. Watch from your window, and use a remote trigger to take pictures when an animal comes near your camera.

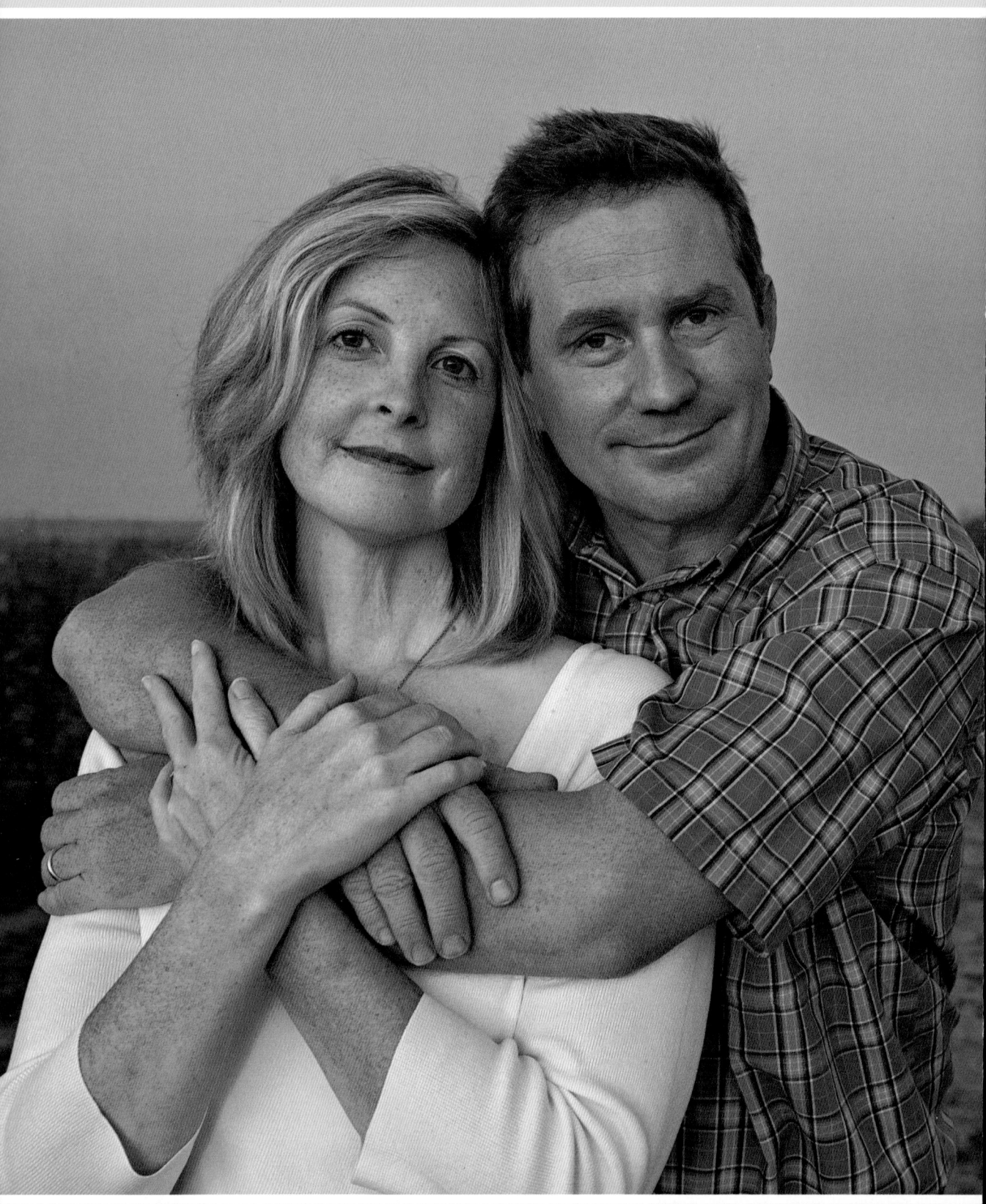

A SIMPLE PORTRAIT

I love this portrait that my son Cole took of my wife, Kathy, and me. While we were posing, a friend stopped to say hi. As he was about to drive off, he stepped on the brakes and the red from his truck's taillights reflected on us. I said, "Whoa! Whoa! Back up!" He was kind enough to stay put for a few minutes, and that's what lit us in this portrait.

REFLECTIVE LIGHT The sun had already set, and that little hint of red from the brake lights added a beautiful warm glow—reflective of the connection we have with each other and our son behind the camera. This is a great example of being open to circumstance, and being creative with light.

POSING Our pose here is natural and far more interesting than if we were standing side by side in the center of the frame. It's clear that we are both comfortable—with each other, in this setting, and, of course, with the photographer. This gives an intimate and honest feel to the portrait.

FRAMING ELEMENTS Cole did a nice job of framing this photo. Kathy and I fill the left third, the horizon hits the top third, and in the right third, there's a road leading away from us into the distance—a nice leading line, but also symbolic of the distance we've traveled together.

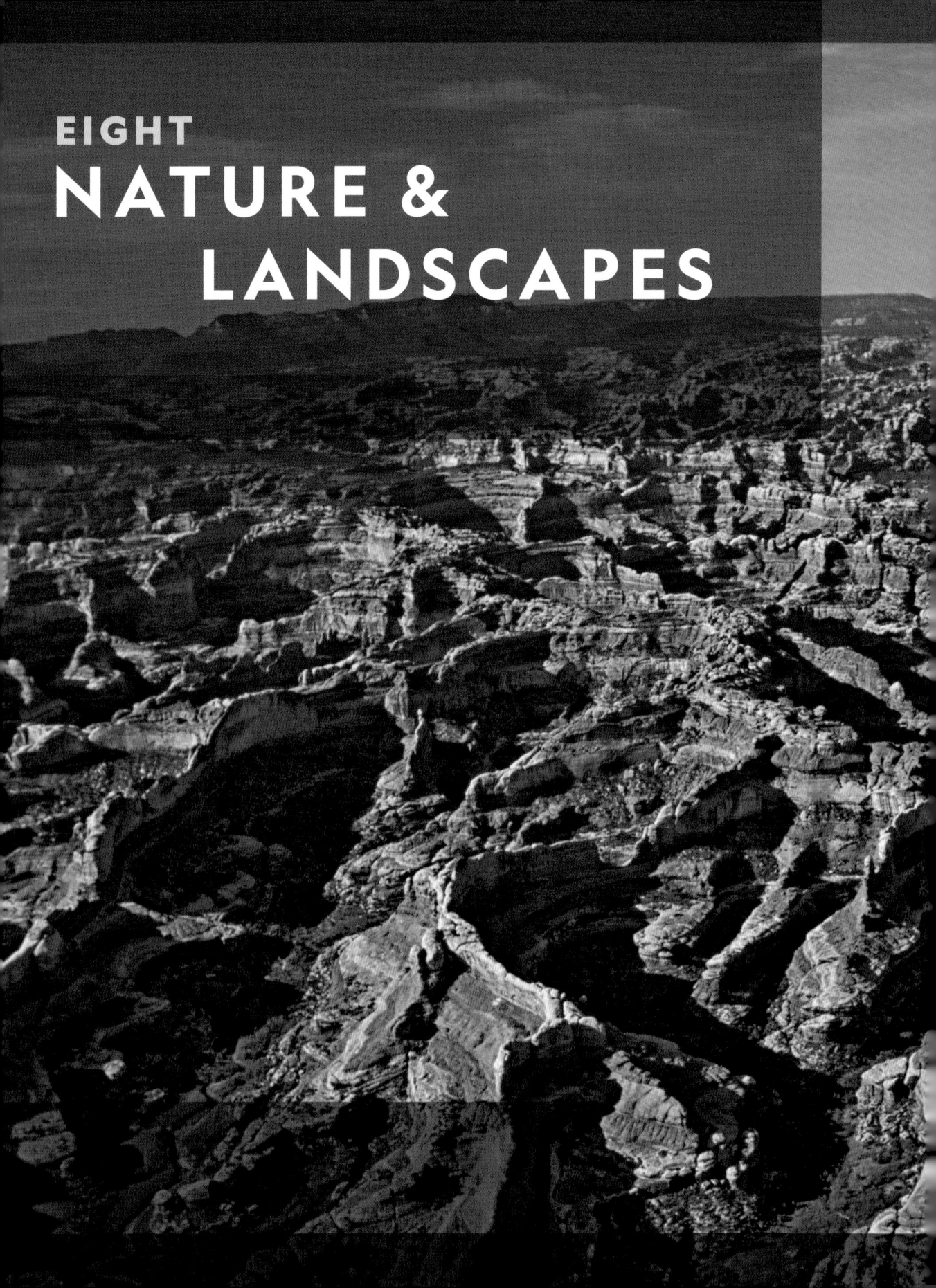

EIGHT
NATURE & LANDSCAPES

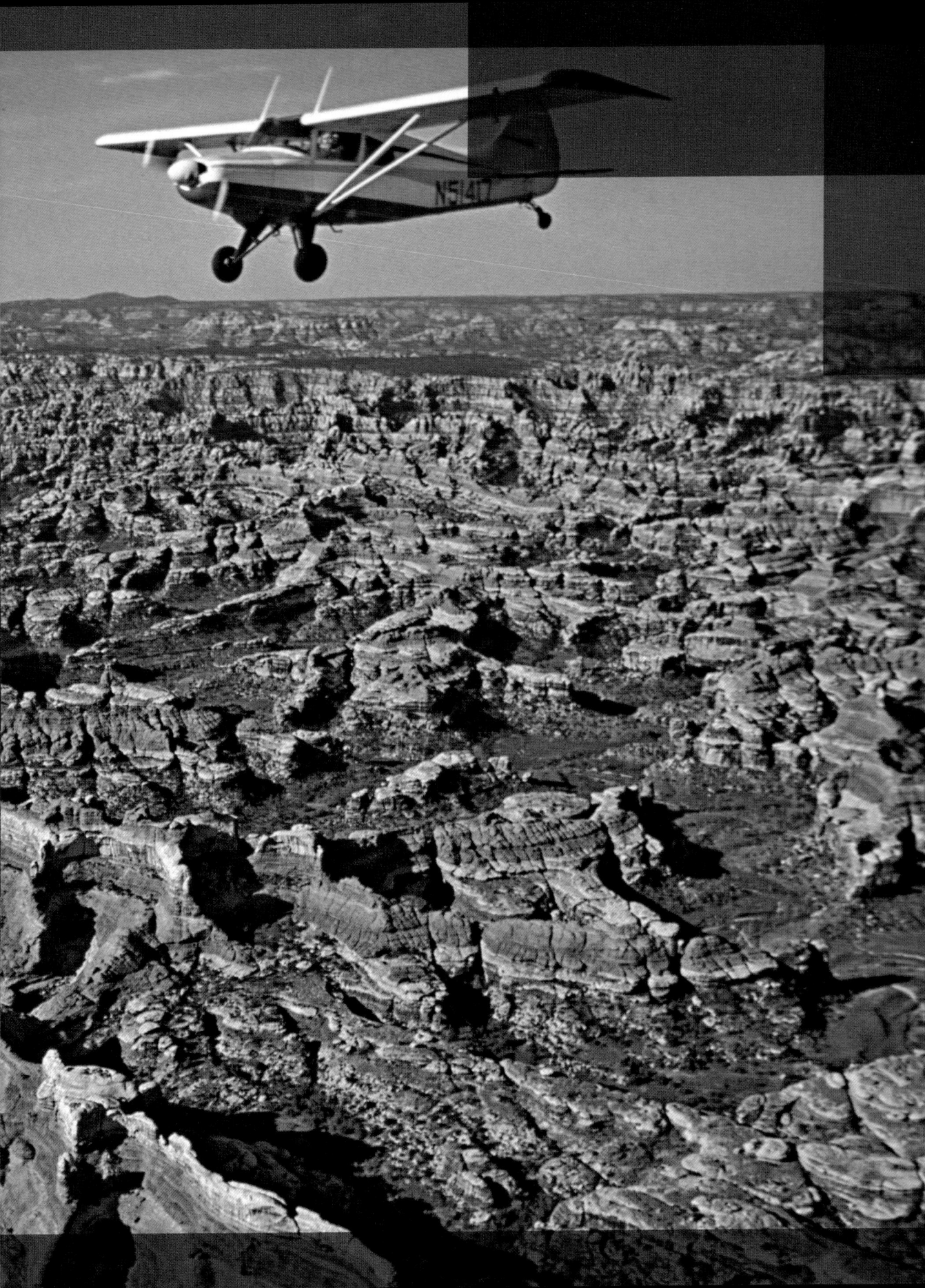

LEARNING LANDSCAPES

Whether on a prairie, at sea, among jagged mountains, or atop a sprawling city, landscapes are a draw for many photographers. When you don't have to worry about people or animals cooperating as your subjects, your only limitations are light and imagination. A landscape can be a canvas for your artistic vision, and the technical skills you've learned so far will help you create something beautiful.

But don't be fooled—just because landscapes don't move doesn't mean they're easy to photograph *well*. In this chapter, we'll talk about ways to enliven a landscape photograph, to make it sing in a frame the same way it sang to you in real life. We'll talk about challenges you'll face in different places, from difficult light to extreme weather, from shooting high above the ground to below the water's surface.

After reading through this chapter, go outside and practice. Your neighborhood, no matter where you live, qualifies as a landscape. How can you see it in a new way? Better yet, take this book on vacation with you, and refresh yourself on the lessons before heading out to the beach or on a hike. You'll begin to explore varying landscapes with a new eye, and be empowered to create compelling photographs to share.

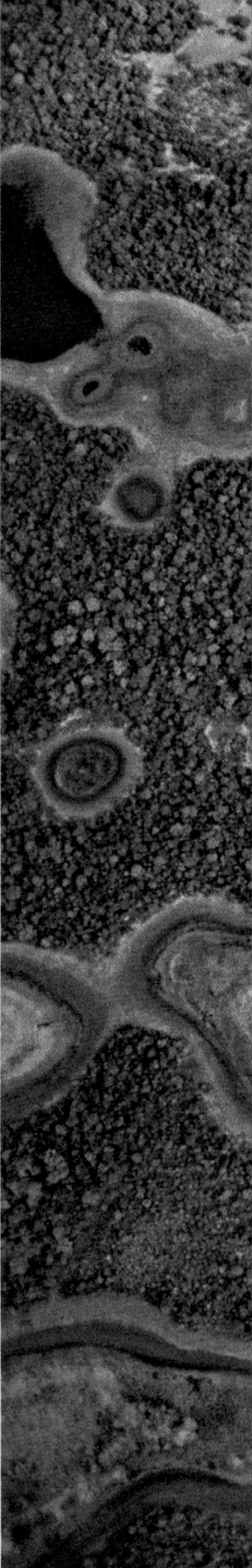

During the rainy season in Brazil's Pantanal, an aerial photograph of the flooded lowlands looks like abstract art.

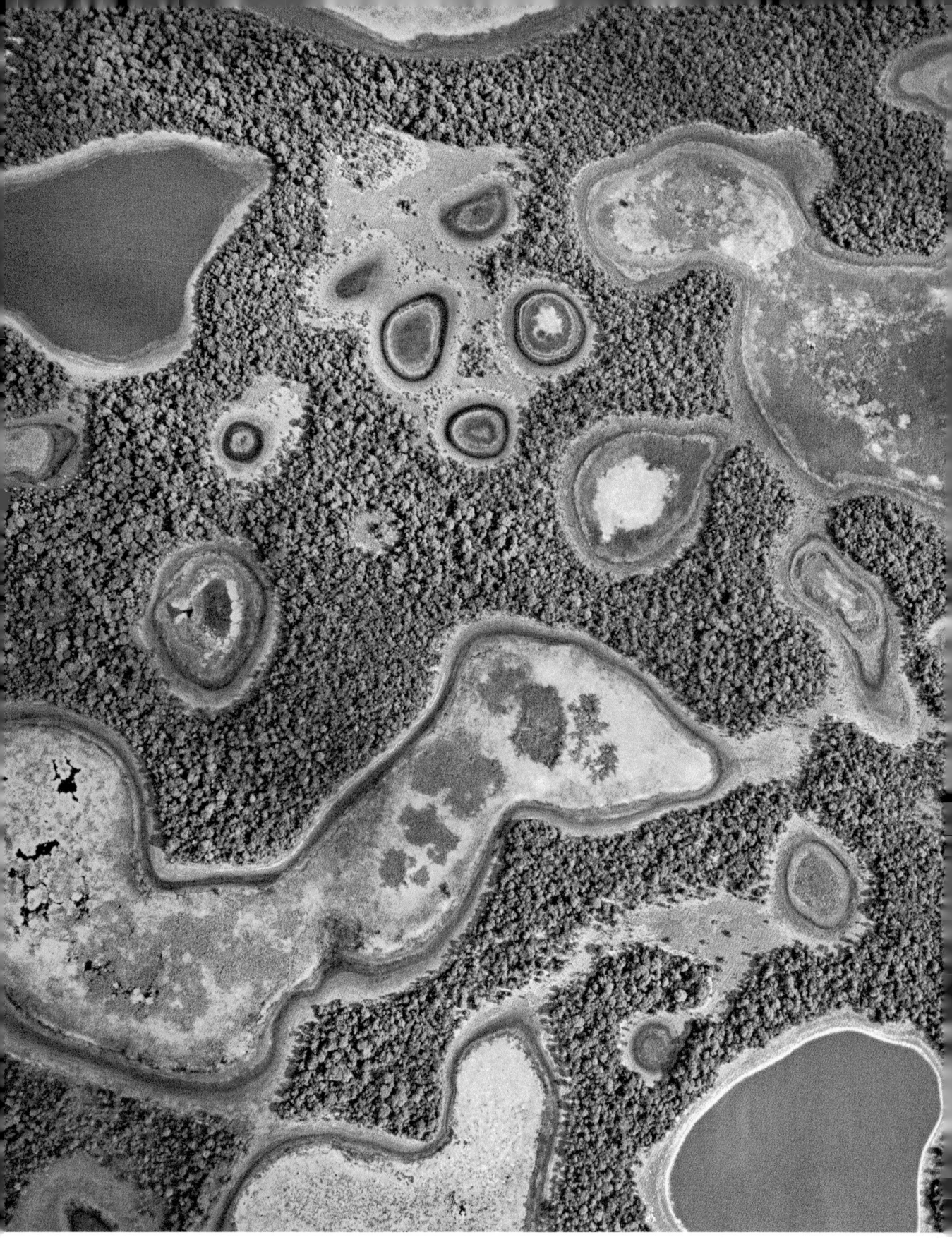

PHOTOGRAPHING LANDSCAPES

You can make a compelling landscape photograph anywhere—from an exotic destination to your own neighborhood. A few basic concepts will help you create the most impactful images of your surroundings wherever you are.

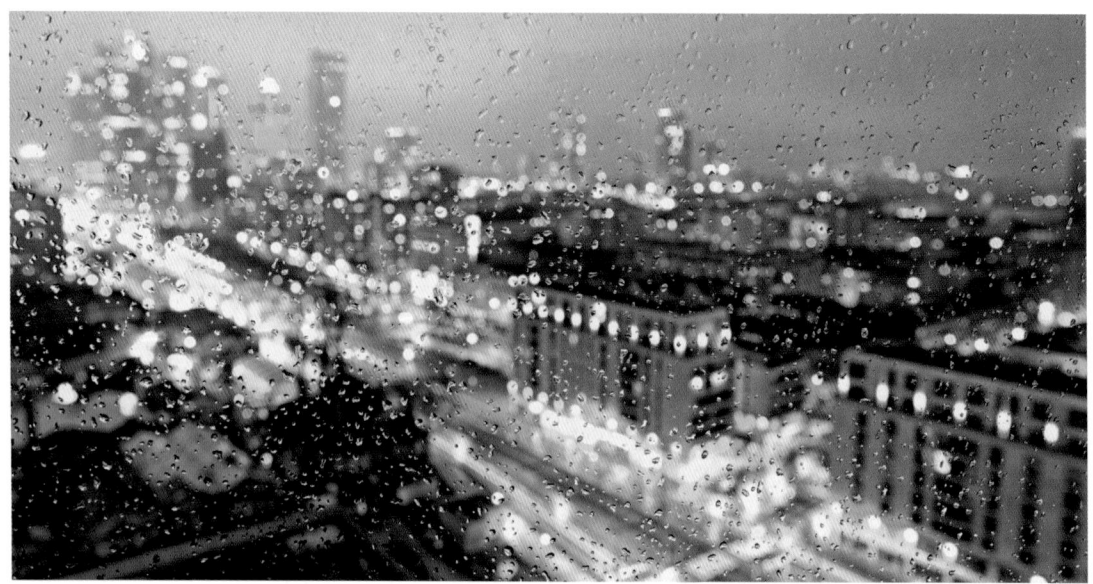

By focusing on raindrops on a window instead of the city skyline, we get the story of weather on this night, without losing the sense of what the city looks like.

Landscape surrounds you, no matter where you stand. Pavement or water, mountains or a city skyline, the landscape is quite simply the face of the Earth in your view. A landscape photograph takes a broad view, looking out, up, or down to tell the story of a place. As photographers, our mission is to synthesize the landscape in an artful and compelling way to show our audience a view they've never seen—or, better yet, didn't expect.

THE LIGHT

A landscape isn't going anywhere, so you can be choosy about light. The golden hour is often the best time to shoot. It can take time to get familiar with the quality and movement of light, so visit more than once if you can. The more you know a place, the better your photographs will be.

Many landscape photographers work with a tripod. When the light is low and diffuse, water can be softly blurred, or lights

FOR MORE ON THE GOLDEN HOUR, SEE PAGE 106.

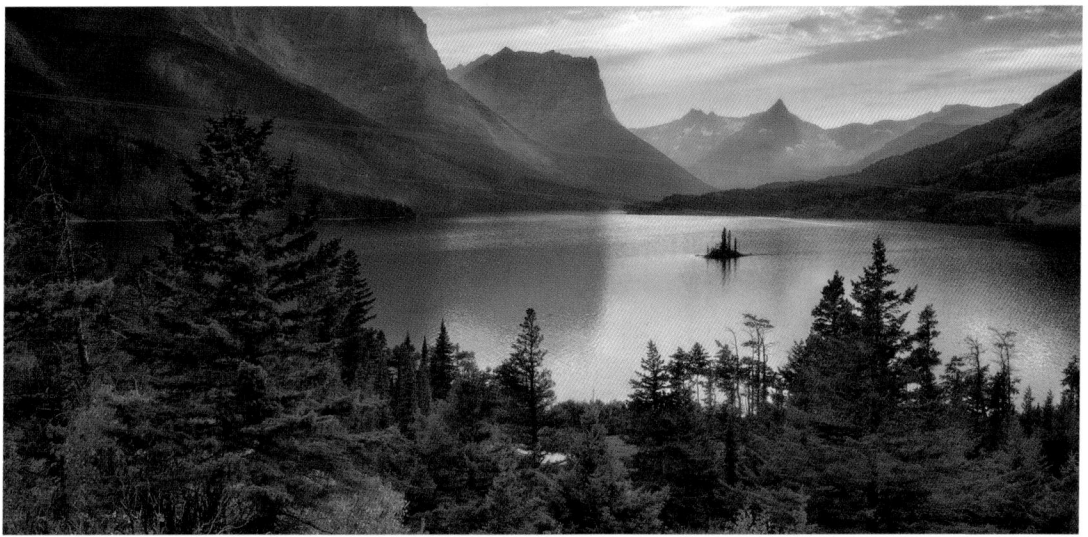

A sunset adds dramatic colors and soft light to this photo of Saint Mary Lake in Glacier National Park. Even when your subject is a majestic landscape bathed in nice light, good composition technique will make the photograph better.

from traffic can paint artful trails through a frame. A good landscape photographer often uses a tripod to stabilize the camera in low light, to allow for motion blur in water or stars, and to be able to use the highest aperture for greatest depth of field.

PERSPECTIVE

To some extent, perspective can change a landscape. Shifting just a few degrees can make a big difference. Say you're photographing a mountain range at sunrise. Standing, you may fill the frame with moun-tains bathed in warm light. If you crouch down low, you might shoot up at the mountains through a frame of colorful wildflowers. Your focus stays on the mountains, but colorful petals add a surprising element.

Try backing away from a famous monument to show the crowds of people around it. Maybe you want to shift a little to the left to eliminate a delivery truck on Main Street. Explore many different perspectives to find what best suits the landscape. Your choices will tell viewers what you want them to know.

ASSIGNMENT: ADDING TO THE VIEW

Don't limit your definition of *landscape* to empty scenes. Incorporating people and animals into the view can add context, color, and scale. Photograph fellow hikers wearing bright colors on a canyon hike, or capture your dog leaping over a creek. Try to add animate elements to a landscape to give viewers more information about a place.

THE SEASONS

Seasonal changes help tell the complete story of a landscape. Beyond foliage and snow, light quality, color palettes, and textures shift in a region as we travel around the sun.

Most landscapes undergo obvious changes with the seasons—from a ground cover of grass or snow, to the color of foliage, to the outfits of people walking around. But look for more subtle cues. Fold these features into your photographs to round out the story of a specific landscape and add variety to your photographs throughout the year.

LIGHT

Wherever you are, the Earth's rotation will change your position relative to the sun, meaning that light will come from higher or lower in the sky throughout the year. As we learned in chapter 4, the distance that the sun's light has to travel through our atmosphere impacts its quality and color temperature. Summer light is typically high and harsh through much of the day. Winter light, on the other hand, tends to be low in the sky and more diffuse, making it softer and casting longer shadows. In autumn and spring, the light may actually evoke a feeling of transition.

COLOR

Think in terms of color palettes—bright greens, blues, and yellows for summer; darker yellows, reds, and browns for autumn; cool blues, grays, and browns in winter, and the pastel greens, pinks, and whites of early spring. Even if these colors are in the background, they're important elements that can anchor a photograph in a particular place and time.

TEXTURE

Consider how surfaces change throughout the seasons. Winter often feels smooth, with sheets of ice and snow, while summer may be lush with leaves and grasses. Autumn appears dry and stark as leaves litter the ground, and spring may be fragile and prickly with new growth. Focus on these patterns and textures for a more intimate look at each season.

ASSIGNMENT: SAME SPOT, DIFFERENT SEASON

Find a location near your home with a distinctive feature—a field with a lone tree, a hill reflected in a pond, or the buildings of a city skyline. Pick a spot you can easily access with this view. Visit the spot once during the heart of each season—try to go at the same time of day—and make a photograph, using the same camera and lens each time. Compare the four photographs and make note of the differences. What changes can you see beyond the obvious signs of the season?

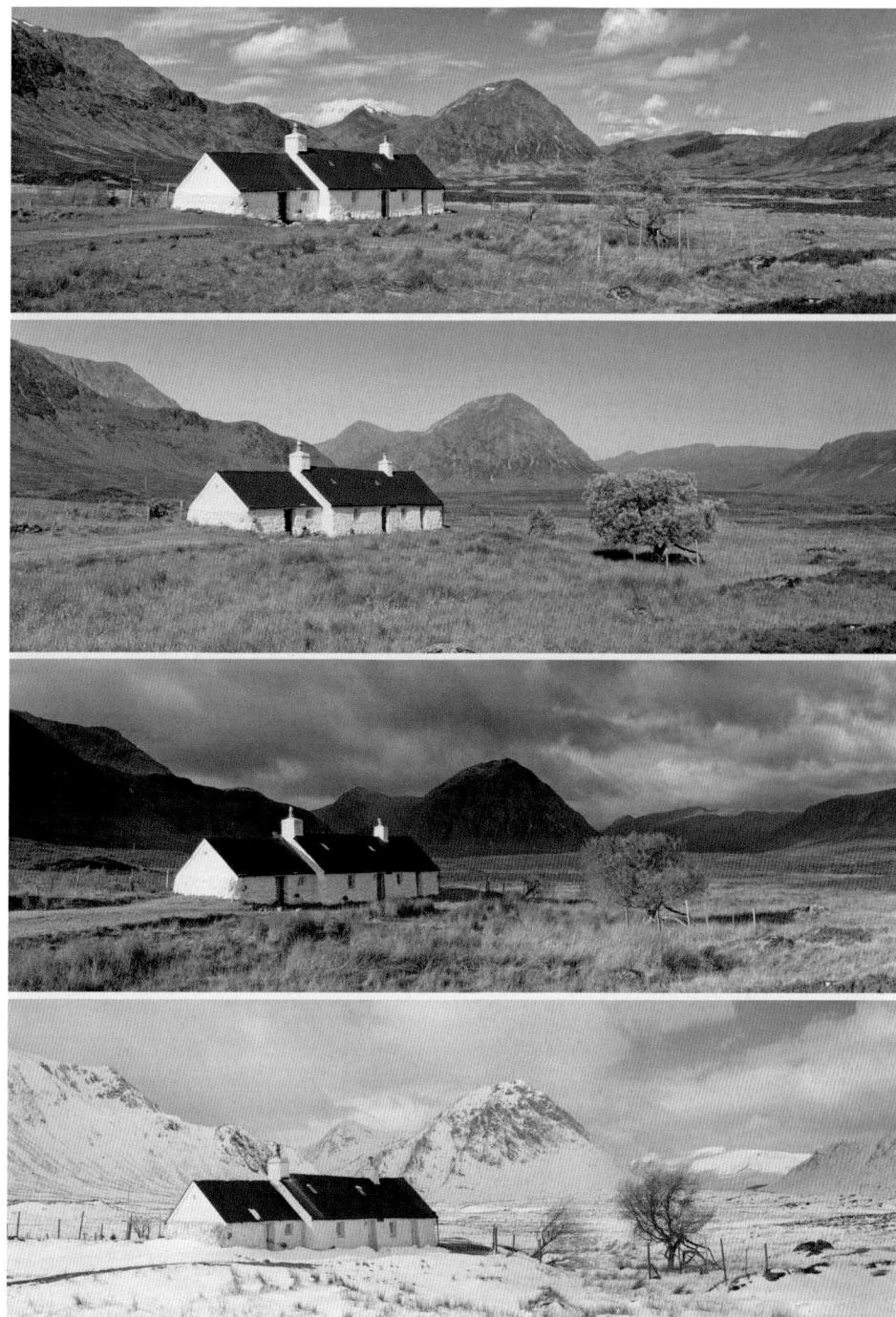

A cottage in the Scottish Highlands looks different in every season. Think about how you can communicate the weather and season of the place you're photographing. How do the colors and light differ from month to month?

WEATHER

Warm, sunny days are lovely for being outside with your camera, but clouds, fog, and storms make for stunning, dramatic imagery. Embrace wild weather to make some distinctive photographs.

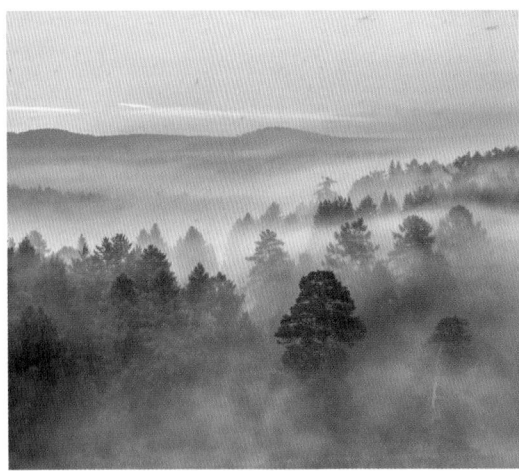 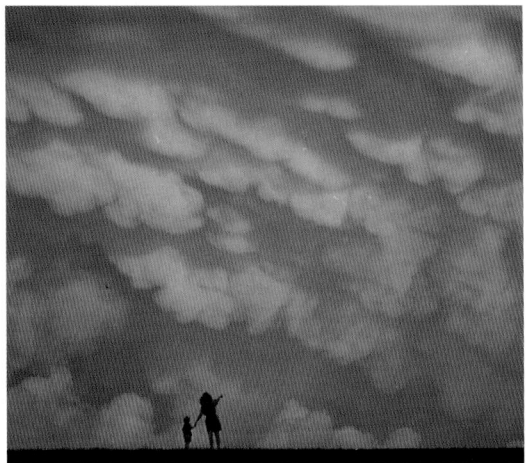

Fog rising through the trees (left) makes this picture of a forest much more interesting than it would be on a clear day. A storm makes a dramatic backdrop. Having people in the foreground offers a sense of scale for this impressive cloud bank (right).

Weather is the voice of nature, and we are usually at its mercy. More than just a backdrop, stormy, volatile weather, with its weird and dramatic light, tells a story all its own. It can be thrilling to photograph a change in the atmosphere, and the moments during and after a storm moves through. Calmer days of cloud cover or thick fog make for moody photographs.

PREPARATION AND SAFETY

If you're shooting in extreme weather, be careful with yourself and your equipment. For example, always take cover when lightning threatens. To protect your equipment, stand under shelter, if possible. If you'd rather be out in the elements, a trash bag or rain poncho works great for covering your camera—just be sure to leave a hole for your lens. Stay on your toes and keep abreast of rapid changes. Check your settings and results often to be sure you're keeping up with sudden shifts in available light.

WEATHER AND LIGHT

As we discussed in chapter 4, overcast days usually result in beautiful, soft light, because clouds work as a giant softbox or diffuser for sunlight. Shadows will be subtle and subjects will be wrapped in fairly even light.

The next time a rainstorm rolls around, suit up and go for a walk during and after the downpour. Keep a clean cloth in a dry pocket to periodically clear your lens. See how rain affects your scene, whether it's clinging to flowers, glistening on the road, or soaking the neighbor's dog—but cover your camera from the rain, exposing only the lens, protected by a filter.

Foggy and snowy days can be tricky to photograph, as moisture in the air and on every surface acts like a reflector. The bright white sky or ground can confuse a light meter, so take a reading on your subject to avoid underexposing your image.

STORMS

Even a dull landscape can make for a powerful image with a stormy sky above. A storm front moving toward your location is the leading edge of change—it can evoke uncertainty, upheaval, and the sense of something ominous headed into town. If you want to photograph lightning across the sky, you'll need patience and luck. A tripod, a wide-angle lens, and a long exposure can help.

As a storm moves away and the heavy rain clears, notice how things begin to glow—clearing skies behind a storm sometimes allow low, bright beams of light to illuminate the landscape against the dark receding clouds as a backdrop. The light feels crisp and polarized, making colors clear and vibrant. Play with exposure here, as you may want to stop down to keep the sky dark and highlight a glowing subject. Notice the ways a storm refreshes the landscapes around you, and look for rainbows, raindrops on leaves, reflections in wet streets and puddles.

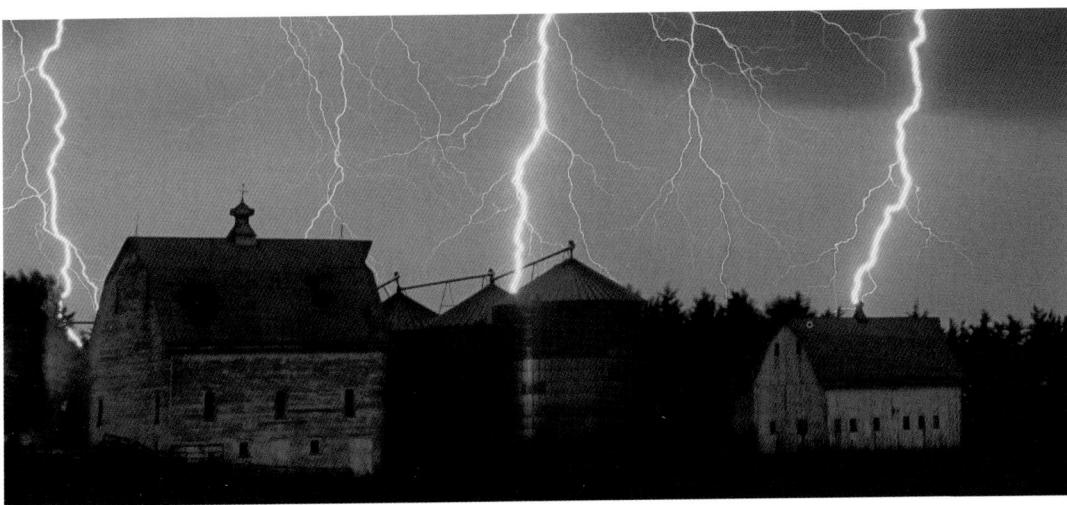

A time exposure of eight seconds captures the intensity of a nighttime thunderstorm rolling over a Nebraska farmstead.

SNOW SCENES

Snow can tell the winter story of a landscape, but it can also create a clean backdrop for your subjects. Whether falling from the sky or blanketing the ground, snow makes for tricky exposures, but can also make a magical photograph once you crack the code.

Unlike any other weather, snow can completely transform any landscape into a smooth, blank canvas. When falling, snow can take a portrait to another level, adding context, texture, and depth. It can be tricky to photograph snow successfully, but the payoff is big.

SNOWY EXPOSURE

Just like clouds and fog, a blanket of white snow can fool your camera's meter. There's so much light bouncing around that if you give the camera its say, your image may actually be underexposed. Whenever you have a subject against a field of white, you may want to intentionally overexpose the scene. Put your camera in manual mode, fill the meter zone with your subject, take a reading and adjust to that setting. Your light meter may protest with tick marks toward the plus sign (indicating too much light), but know that your subject will stand out as you see it.

Remember your histogram? You'll likely see a spike way over to the right, indicating a lot of pure white. You'll also hopefully see a smaller spike somewhere near the middle of the graph—this represents your subject, which should be more accurately exposed. Even if you've lost some detail in the high-

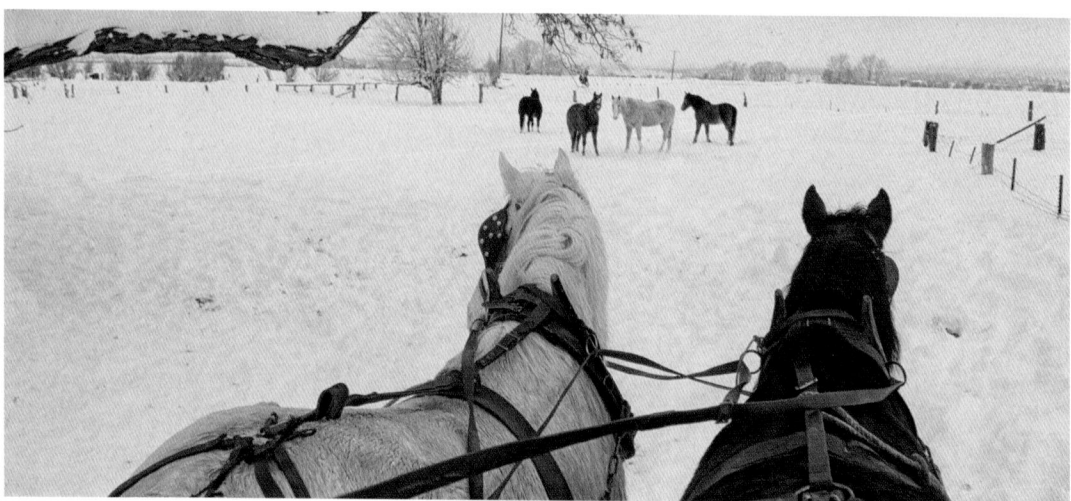

To correctly expose the horses in this field of snow, the settings used will result in the bright white snow being overexposed. Our eyes see details in the horses' coats, and our brains fill in the details we know about snow covering the ground.

FOR MORE ON HISTOGRAMS, SEE PAGE 95.
FOR MORE ON WHITE BALANCE, SEE PAGE 104.

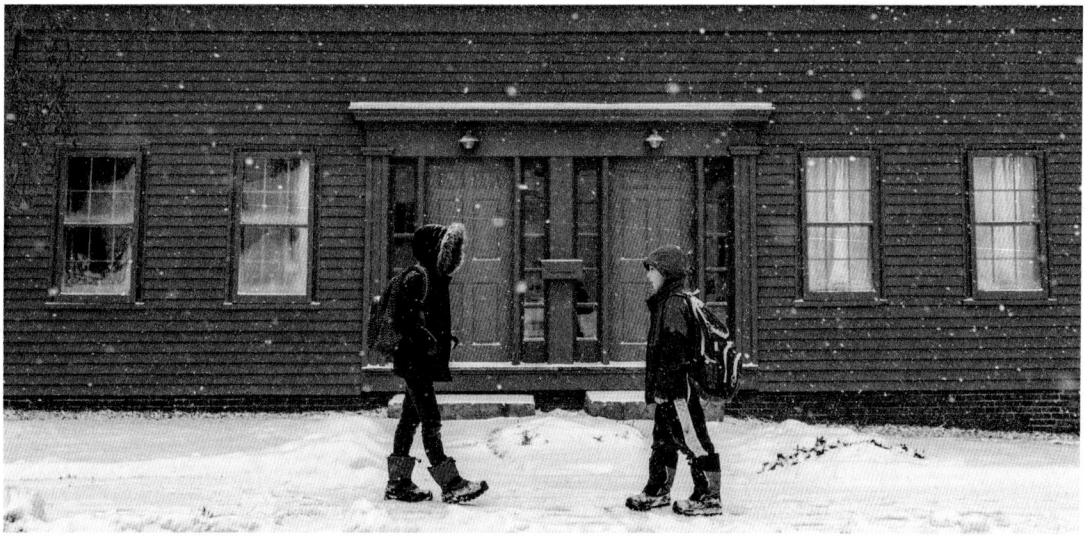

On a snowy day. two boys pause in front of a house on their walk home from school. A fast shutter speed freezes the snowflakes in midair, adding context and texture to the image.

lights (the snow), our brains fill in the blanks when we see a photograph of someone in a snowy scene.

WHITE BALANCE

Snow may present color temperature challenges. As we learned in chapter 4, our brains tend to autocorrect for surfaces we *know* should be white, but the camera sees the true colors. In a snowy scene, that might be a cool blue or gray. Blue light can add a peaceful, serene mood, but if you want to capture the white your brain reads, adjust the white balance settings on your camera.

Try the "flash" or the "cloudy" settings, and experiment with a few others before making your final frame.

FREEZING FLAKES

If snow is actively falling, play with shutter speed to see how the snowflakes look in your image. A fast shutter speed should freeze them in place, looking like a field of stars if it's snowing hard enough. A slower shutter speed might allow for white streaks falling through your frame. And be sure to have a dark background, or you'll never see the falling snow.

PRO TIP SPARE BATTERIES

Cold temperatures can mess with the life span of your batteries, making them drain more quickly than normal. If you're taking your camera out into snow (or anywhere especially chilly), bring spare batteries with you. If they die, putting cold batteries in your pockets to absorb body heat can be a good way to revive them.

PLANTS

Trees and flowers yield a lot of photographic bang for the buck. They're varied, beautiful, and they don't go anywhere. Experiment to find ways to get a fresh take on these commonly photographed subjects.

Many budding photographers love to work with plants—they are filled with rich patterns and textures and come in every color imaginable. Plants are a great subject for practicing technical skills; they don't complain or run away.

But you can't just let the pretty plants do all the work. Look deeper, stay longer, shoot more than you think you need, and try to create something that will stand out from other pretty flower pictures.

PLAY WITH PLANTS

Flowers seem like the reason macro lenses were invented. They allow you to fill the frame with a tiny bud or count the legs of an ant marching across a petal while letting the foliage fade into a soft background, thanks to a shallow depth of field. When things start to get interesting, push yourself beyond the obvious.

Run the aperture from wide to narrow and see what else comes into focus. Or grab a

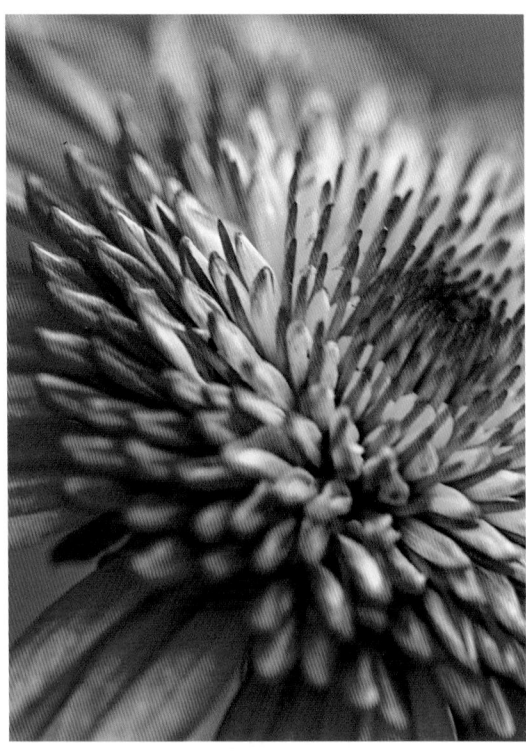

With a macro lens, you can focus tightly on the details of a flower in full bloom, like this echinacea.

wide-angle lens, wait for a windy day, and play with shutter speed—capture an

ASSIGNMENT: IN THE GARDEN

Pick one plant growing near you and tell its story as completely as you can. Get up close, far away, above, and below. Photograph its environment, and document any creatures that interact with it. Try different shutter speeds or apertures, making both obvious and abstract frames. For an extended project, come back to this plant in all four seasons.

abstract blur of color as plants wave in the breeze. Imagine tall grasses making ghostly paths across the frame.

Try introducing light with a reflector or even flash. Put your flash in a softbox or other diffuser and get in close for a soft light that will spill across bark, leaves, or petals.

Vary your perspective. Think about the difference between a picture of sunflowers at eye level and a picture of tall, colorful flowers shot from below against a blue sky.

EXPAND YOUR HORIZONS

Instead of the pretty parts of the plant, consider all the interesting details to be found in twisting branches, veiny leaves, and intricate roots. Look for mushrooms, mosses, fallen logs, and the bugs that inhabit them all.

Think about how plants fit into a larger story—it might be the story of your yard, the woods, a desert, or a swamp. How has a particular plant adapted to exist there, and how can you capture what sets it apart?

Take advantage of these reliable, vibrant, ubiquitous subjects and try something unusual. The possibilities are as rich and varied as any garden.

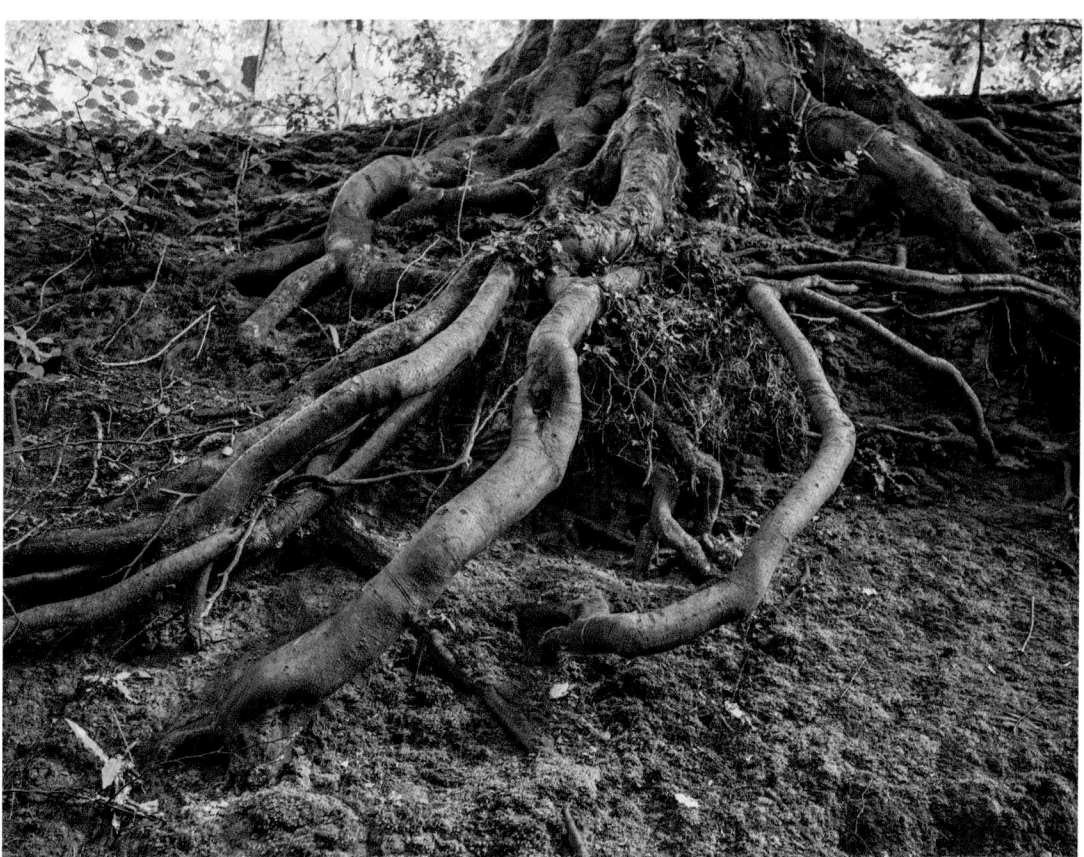

The mossy roots of this ancient yew tree in England line a path through the woods that is hundreds of years old.

THE NIGHT SKY

Astrophotography is photography of the night sky, and can be as complex as you're willing to get. You can also get some great results with a simple formula.

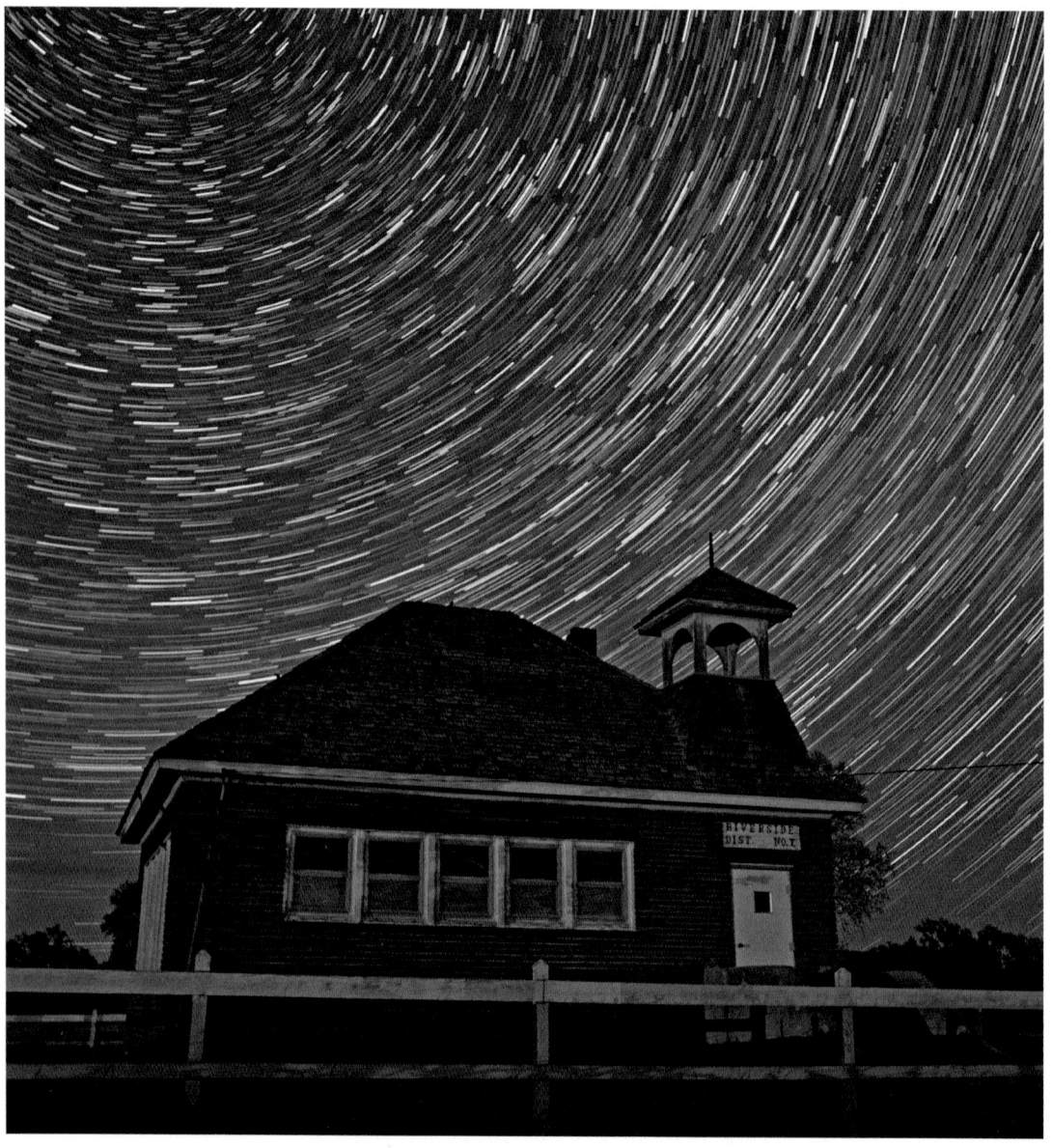

To photograph star tracings, you need a moonless night and no cloud cover. Use a tripod and cable release, and either do one long exposure or a series of images you later combine using downloadable Starstax software.

The night sky has always captivated us, from ancient navigation to modern space exploration. While astrophotography might seem intimidating, getting started is as simple as applying the principles of exposure and composition.

THE RIGHT CONDITIONS

The night sky has seasons, and the visibility of the densest part of the Milky Way will change depending on your location, the time of year, and the time of night. Stargazing apps can help you figure out where to point your camera. Once you know where you're aiming, find a place with little to no light pollution, and check the lunar calendar for a moonless night, or for nights when the moon will not rise until well after you're hoping to shoot. A clear sky is best, but you can get some beautiful results on a partly cloudy night, when soft clouds surround fields of stars.

THE GEAR

Stabilization is critical for astrophotography, and you can do this with a tripod and anything else that will hold your camera absolutely still for at least 30 seconds. Wide-angle lenses gather more light, so choose something at least 24mm wide, with an aperture of at least f/2.8.

If you want to delve deeper into astrophotography, you can buy all sorts of equipment, from lenses that photograph through telescopes to motors that allow your camera to track stars throughout the night.

THE FORMULA

A photograph of the night sky is like any other exposure—aperture determines the amount of light gathered; shutter speed determines for how long. A wide aperture and a long shutter period will allow the camera's sensor to catch tiny points of light coming from the stars. Given enough time, the sensor may register more stars than your eyes can—that's what makes astrophotography feel so magical.

With that in mind, start with this formula:
- A wide aperture, such as f/2.8
- ISO 3200
- Shutter speed of 30 seconds

Or just leave the shutter open and stop down to a narrower aperture.

If your image is too light or blurry, drop to a faster shutter speed or a lower ISO. If you're not seeing that magical glow of the galactic center, try a longer shutter speed or a higher ISO. Get comfortable in your night photography spot and enjoy this process.

PRO TIP THE WORLD BENEATH THE STARS

Once you get your star exposure down, try adding a few other things to your frame. Frame a sky scene near the water's edge and discover the soft, smooth look water will take on in your picture when exposed for that long. Or, include an object of interest—a tree, an interesting rock formation, an old barn—in the foreground of the frame. While the shutter is open, go up to it and "paint" it with light from a flashlight or even your mobile phone. Anything you've lit will appear in the frame, but it will look like you were never there.

BODIES OF WATER

Water can add something special to almost any landscape, and creates certain photographic opportunities and challenges in the process.

Oceans, lakes, rivers, ponds, and puddles—humans tend to gather at the water's edge, and it often inspires us. It also makes us want to take pictures. Waves crashing, water falling, ripples, splashes, even rain—landscapes that include water can yield beautiful photographs, and opportunities to convey moods from peace to power.

BEACH PHOTOGRAPHY

The beach has much to offer a photographer, from sunlight and seabirds to people at rest and play, to rhythmic waves crashing and retreating, all on a clean backdrop of sand.

Like snow, bright sand can fool your camera meter, which may suggest that you stop down to prevent overexposing. Take an exposure reading for your subject, then set the aperture and shutter speed manually. All that sand may be overexposed, but your subject will be exposed correctly.

Waves are dynamic, no matter what their size. From the shore, it's almost impossible to do justice to the size of a wave. Instead,

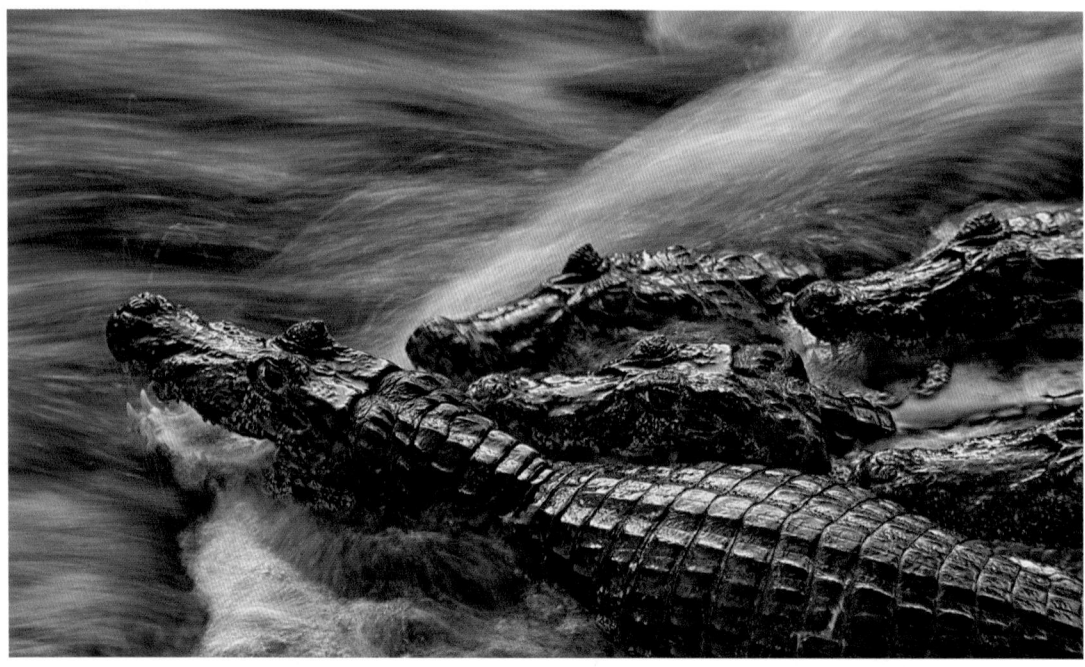

A group of caimans in Brazil wait for fish to be swept into their jaws. A slow shutter speed—1/2 second—allowed the water surging around them to blur.

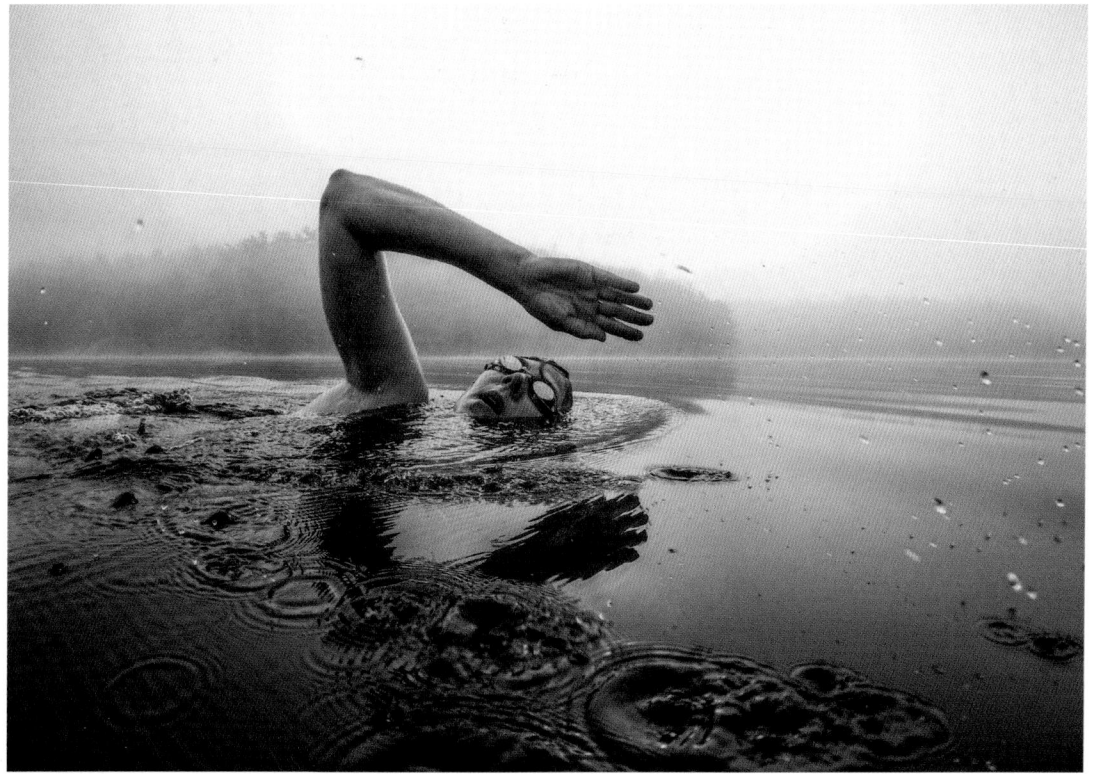

A woman swims across the surface of a pond on a foggy morning in Maine. A fast shutter speed freezes the droplets of water in the air as she goes.

focus on the impact of waves on people. Kids jumping waves, body surfing, and splashing add a spontaneous element and sense of scale. And don't overlook the artful impact that water has on sand. Ripples, holes, seafoam, and bits of flotsam provide endless inspiration.

MOVING WATER

Lakes, rivers, and waterfalls provide so much opportunity for creativity. Observe how a body of water moves—gently back and forth, in a strong one-way flow, or in crashing, splashing waves. Consider the ways you can use shutter speed to illustrate movement in a still frame. A fast shutter speed can freeze droplets in midair. Stabilization and a slow shutter speed will soften and smooth the edges of moving water. With each, consider exposure and adjust your aperture accordingly. Bear in mind that a fast shutter speed may be hard to use at dawn or dusk when the light is low and dim, and a slow shutter speed might not work on a bright, sunny day. As always, think about the image you'd like to create and pick your time of day for when the light you need for it will be best.

UNDERWATER

Even when exotic underwater locales and expensive equipment are beyond your reach, you can still create evocative underwater images that will make your viewers want to dive in.

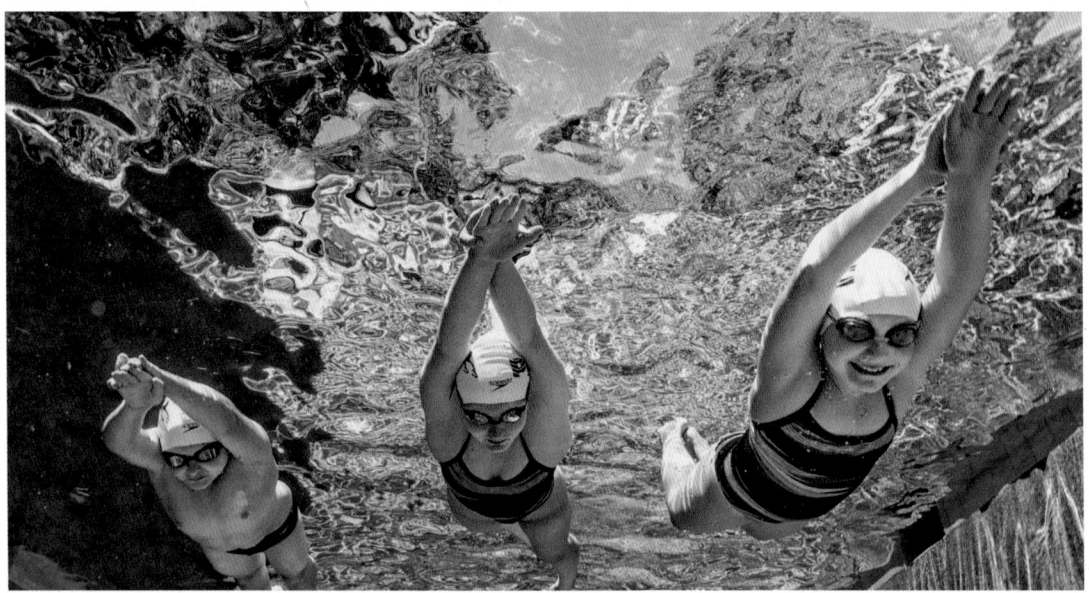

An inexpensive underwater camera can yield great results if you stick near the surface where there's more available light. Outdoor pools and the shallows of white sandy beaches, where light bounces back up at your subject from reflective floors, are perfect.

Coral reefs, kelp forests, shipwrecks—underwater environments hold otherworldly subject matter for photographers. A powerful underwater photograph can transport the viewer to another realm.

First, know that there are entire books, courses, and workshops dedicated to underwater photography. It can be an equipment-heavy endeavor, from scuba systems to camera housings and more. This might all sound intimidating and expensive, but you can do a lot with simple equipment just beneath the surface.

LIGHT AND WATER

Nothing can distort and change light quite like water. As light passes from air to the denser medium of water, it bends. This is called "refraction." The deeper light travels, the more it is absorbed. Remember how we dislike midday light, so high and harsh? Water's light-filtering properties make those ideal hours for underwater photography. Water also absorbs the color of light as it descends. Within the first 12 feet, reds, oranges, and yellows are swallowed up, giving everything a green-blue cast.

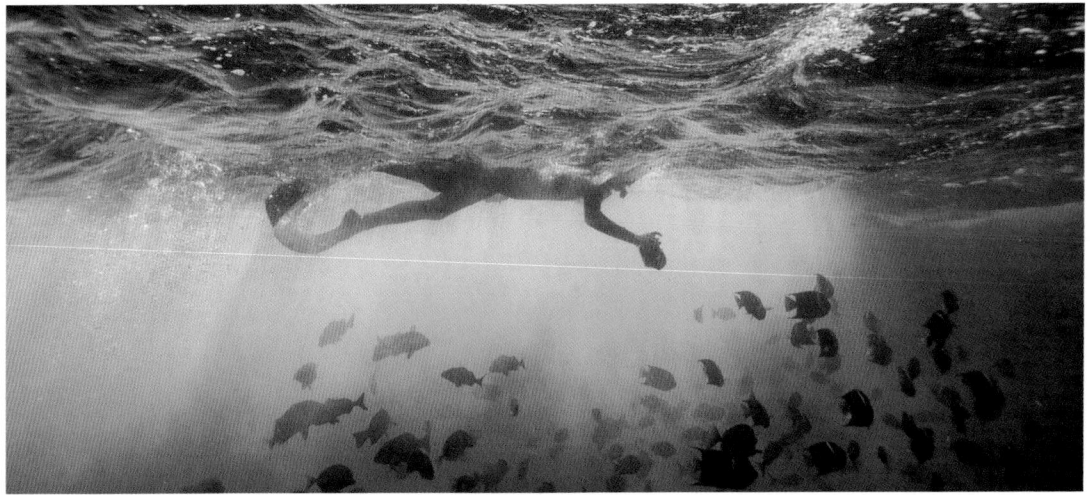

When there's not enough light to bring out the colors of your subjects, let them be silhouetted against the water. Here, a snorkeler swims above a school of fish in the Galápagos, where the water's surface creates a dynamic ceiling for the frame.

THE CUSP

Where air and water meet, everything changes, from how animals breathe to the way light behaves. The way the two mediums mix can be exhilarating: With a wave of your hand, droplets catapult into air, and bubbles glitter like jewels underwater. The water's surface is also a fantastic subject—dip below and look up at a liquid mirror, swirling and distorting the world above.

Split the view and catch the contour of a wave. Add a subject—a child in goggles, a swimmer with flowing hair. But before you throw your camera in the water, let's talk about the gear you should use for the job.

GEAR TO TRY

For your first forays in underwater photography, put away your DSLR. For about $30, try a disposable underwater camera. The photos may not be of the best quality, but it's a good way to test things out. The next step up would be a waterproof point-and-shoot camera. These are compact and great for travel, in the $200 to $400 range. Many are quite good, though you won't have much control over your settings. There are some fantastic small action cameras that are rugged and waterproof and offer HD video and stills. These can run anywhere from $100 to $600 and are great for sports and adventure.

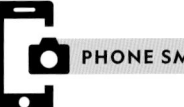
PHONE SMARTS: WATERPROOFING

More and more smartphones are water-resistant, meaning you can safely take them in the water for use at the surface. For those that aren't, there are waterproof cases that allow access to camera functions. Many of them make decent photographs in the water, and allow for quick and easy sharing once you dry off.

AERIAL PHOTOGRAPHY

From a vantage point above the landscape, whether atop a building, on a ladder, or standing on a chair, you can make a familiar place feel new.

With a view from above, a familiar place may look completely different. You can make out all sorts of patterns and lines that you may not see from ground level. All these patterns can make the landscape look abstract and alien, or orderly and epic—like a map of some grand plan. As you set out to photograph landscapes, be on the lookout for safe ways to get up higher.

UP IN THE AIR

If you're lucky and find someone to take you up in a plane, helicopter, or hot-air balloon, a few tricks will help you make the most of the opportunity. You'll be on the move, so choose a fast shutter speed of at least 1/350. It's best if you can be in an aircraft that moves low and slow, but if you're shooting out the window of a commercial plane, ascent and descent may be your best opportunities.

If you don't have access to such airtime, you can still gain a new perspective on a place by getting up above things. Find a building with roof access, climb an old fire tower, or even stand on a stepladder for a new view of a lovely table setting, a hotel

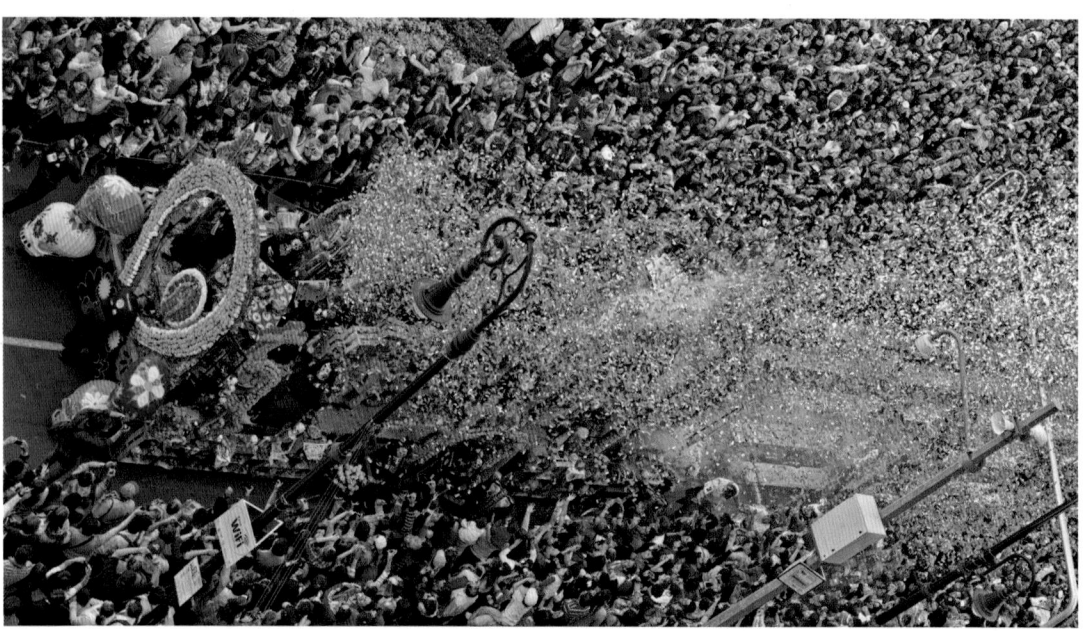

A parade takes on a whole new look when seen from above. Crowds of people lend a sense of excitement, and confetti or other dynamic features make it look like a party rolling by.

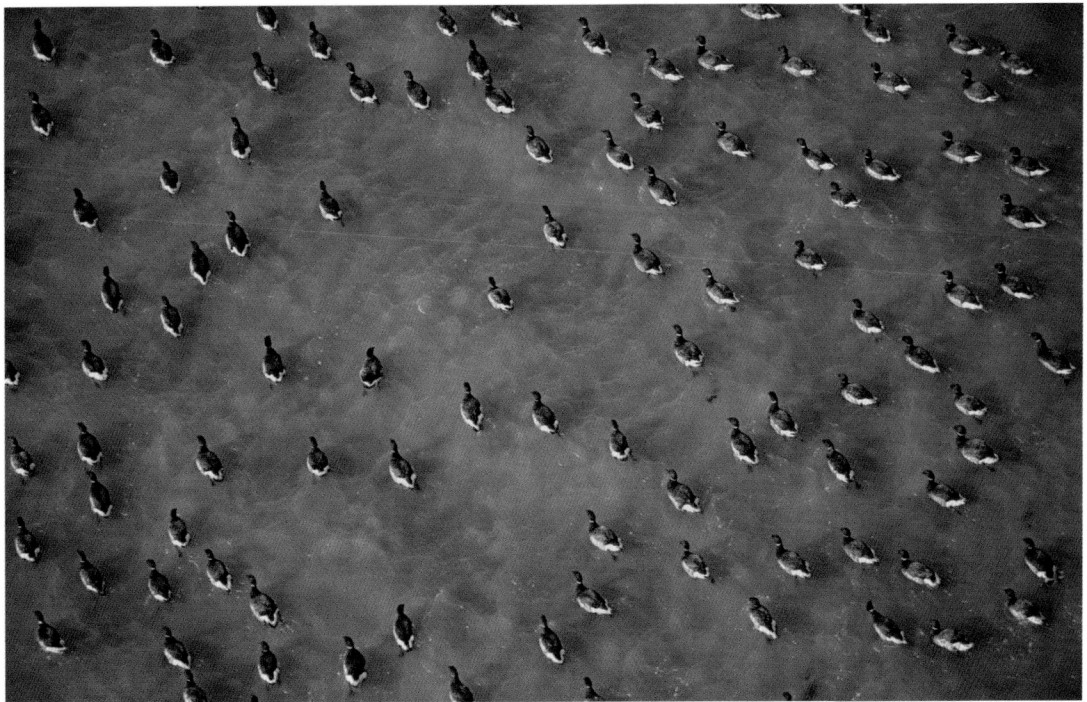

Teshekpuk Lake, Alaska, is home to the black brant, a type of goose. The green water serves as a background for an almost abstract but orderly photo. When you're looking down from above, look for interesting patterns and textures that emerge from the landscape.

swimming pool, or a parade down Main Street. Look for soft light, leading lines, and good composition. Just being in the air isn't enough—you still have to make compelling photographs.

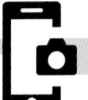 **PHONE SMARTS: STRAIGHT UP**

Selfie sticks aren't just good for getting group shots. With one of these special tools, you can trigger your phone's shutter from the end of an extendable pole—a great way to get above the crowd for a new angle on a scene when you can't find another way up.

DRONE PHOTOGRAPHY

Drones are a great development in modern photography. Now, we can get our cameras high up in the air without risking our lives (or our bank accounts). If you choose to go this route, be sure to research the laws and regulations about drones in your area.

If it's not prohibited, practice in your backyard, local park, or school football field until you're comfortable flying the drone and using its controls. Finally, pick a spot free of telephone wires and other obstacles—perhaps a natural area nearby. Set the camera and fly like a bird. You'll be amazed at how different a place you've always known will look from above.

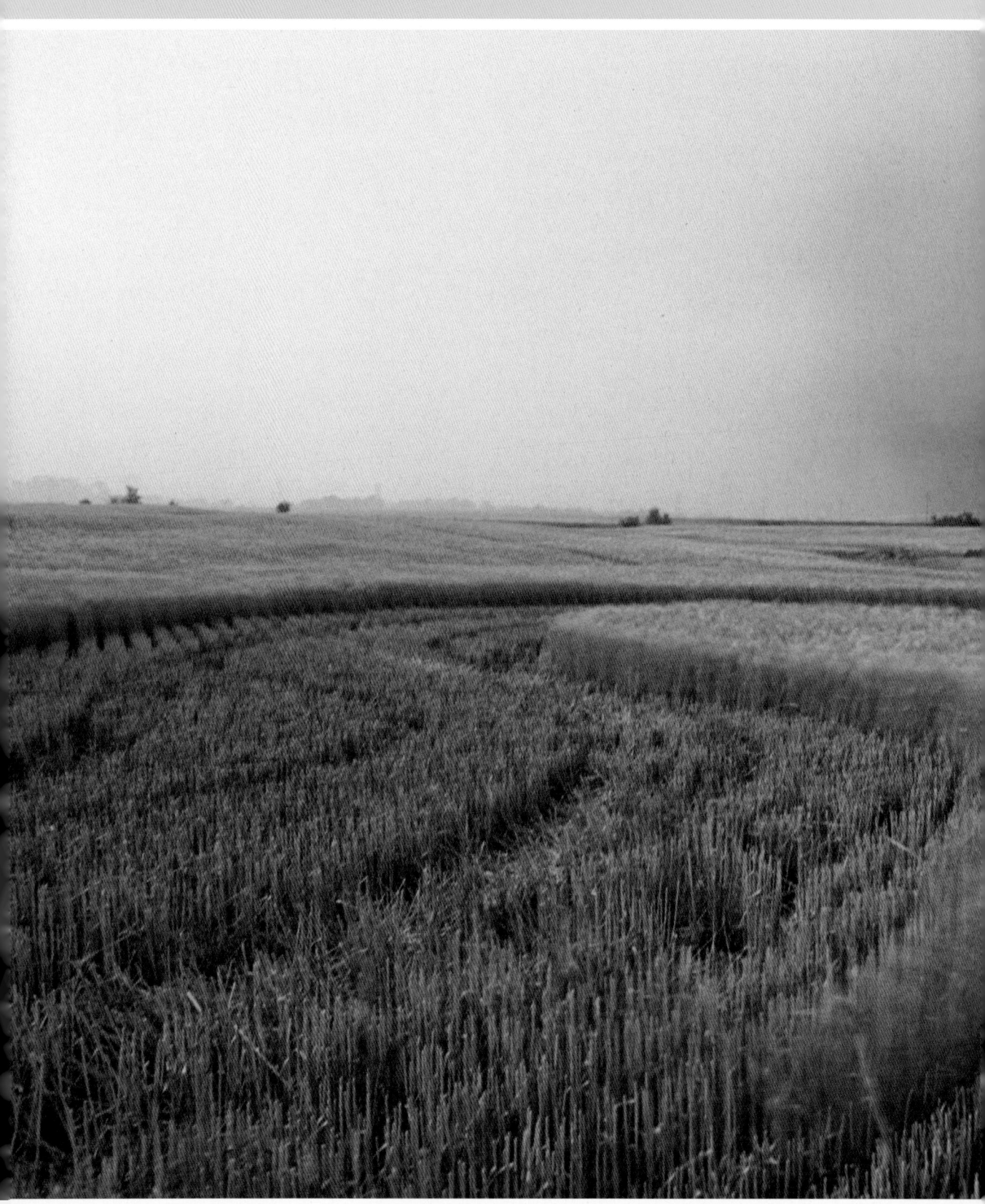

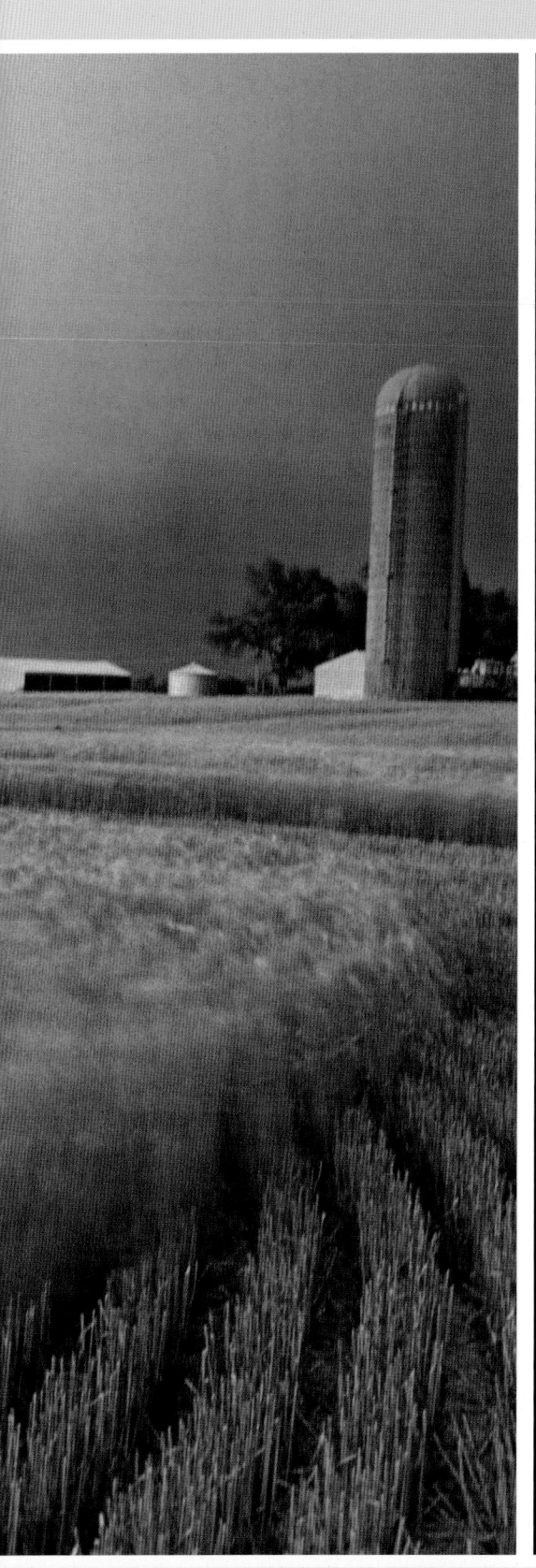

STORMY LIGHT

The weird, wonderful light of violent weather is so fleeting that it's easy to miss. I took this picture about 30 years ago near Haysville, Kansas. I was driving home and saw the storm coming, casting a greenish yellow light that meant strong winds and hail. I jumped from my car and set up a tripod to get the movement of wheat whipping in a partially harvested field, and remember missing a massive lightning bolt as I was mounting my camera. To this day, I wish I'd pulled up just 30 seconds sooner.

STRANGE LIGHT With or without lightning, the simplicity of this particular landscape sets up this stunning sky to steal the show. Good framing is always important, but beyond that, sometimes the light—when unique and magnificent—is enough.

COLOR After all these years, I've never gotten this kind of light again. The gradient from light to dark foreshadows what's coming, and the hue is otherworldly.

MAKE IT SPECIAL Moments like this in nature last just a few minutes but turn a common scene into something special. Especially when you're shooting something iconic and likely well documented—like the Eiffel Tower in Paris or Devils Tower in Wyoming—interesting light or a coming storm can set your photograph apart.

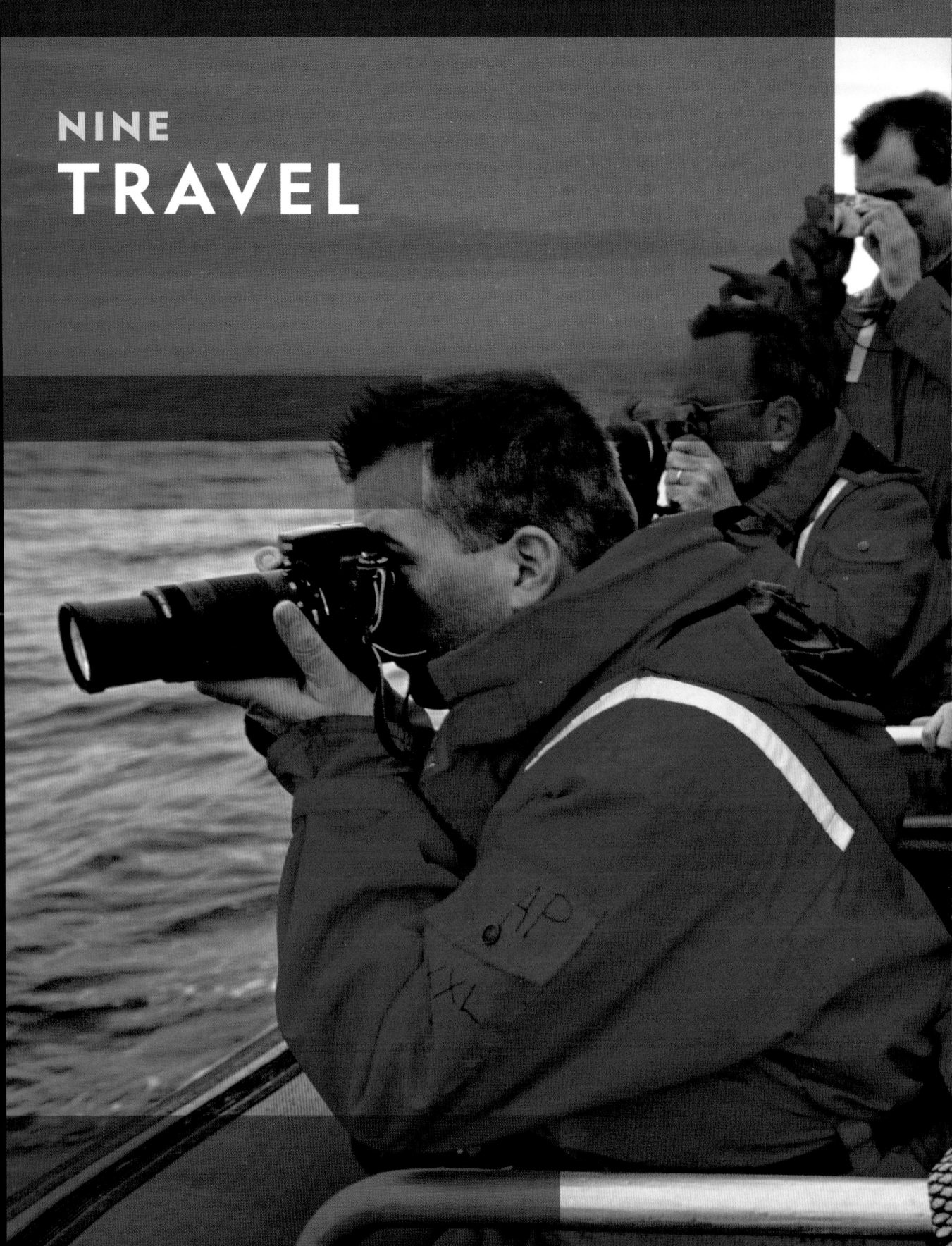

NINE
TRAVEL

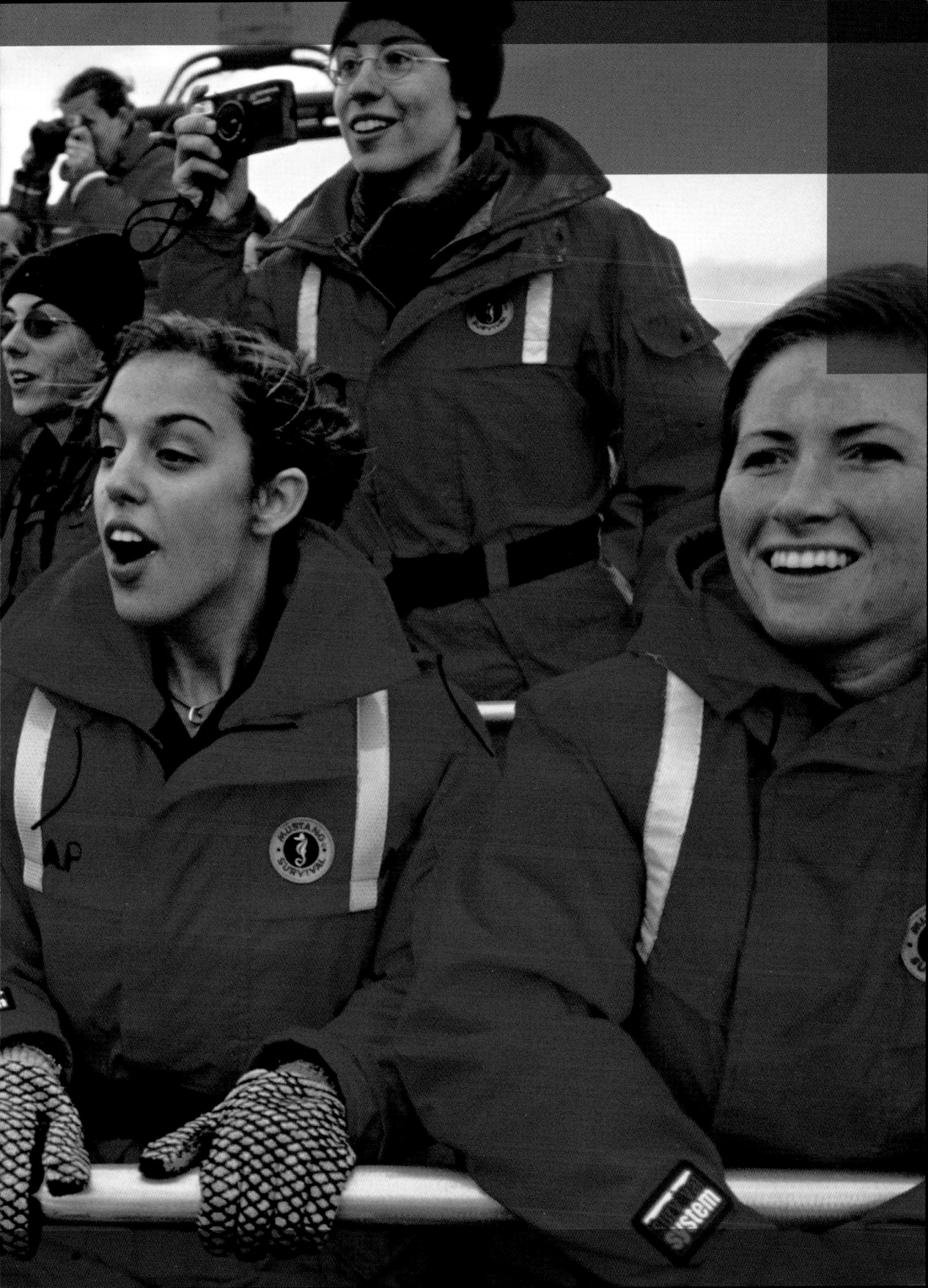

ROAM IF YOU WANT TO

Travel is the perfect opportunity for making pictures. Your eyes are open to a new experience, and all your senses are heightened. We all want to document those moments to look back on, to share and be transported back to that time.

Think about the travel photos you've seen—a family stiffly posed in front of Mount Rushmore, the Statue of Liberty, or some other monument. They don't feel all that special. You could swap in a different family and it wouldn't make much of a difference. Before you go, consider what makes your destination different from where you live. Is it the landscape? The faces of the people? The traditions? Prepare yourself and your gear to capture the type of photographs you'd like to make.

When traveling abroad, consider hiring a local guide to help you navigate the culture and language, and take you to unusual locations or events that tourists may generally not know about. These are the things that will help set your experience and your photography apart.

Above all, think about using photography to tell the story of your vacation and to show people new things. Don't shy away from traditional pictures, such as your family in front of a monument, to provide context. But then, do more. And if you cannot go abroad, or even leave the state, plan some trips close to home as opportunities for storytelling.

A rider and his horses follow a trail in central California's Sixty Lake Basin.

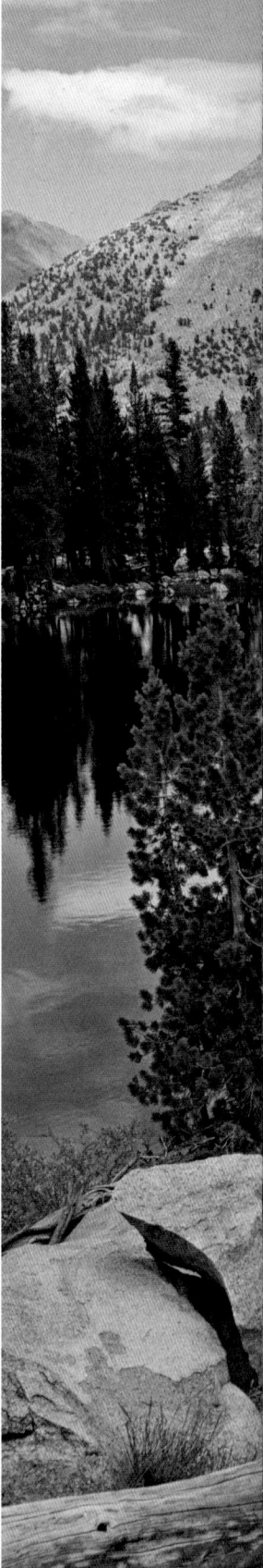

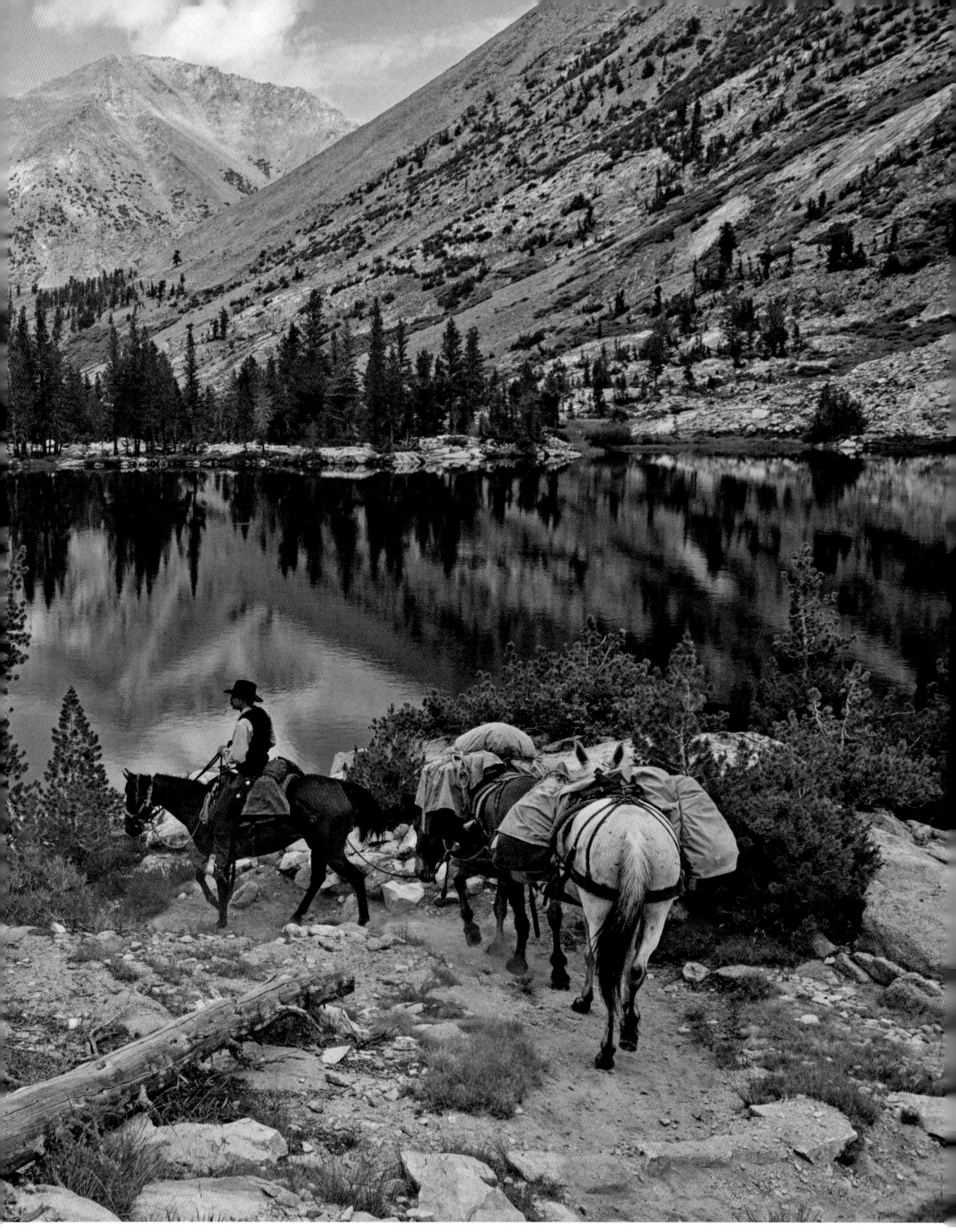

PACKING UP

Knowing what gear to bring is important before you take off on your next photography adventure. Think it through to have the most efficient kit for making photos away from home.

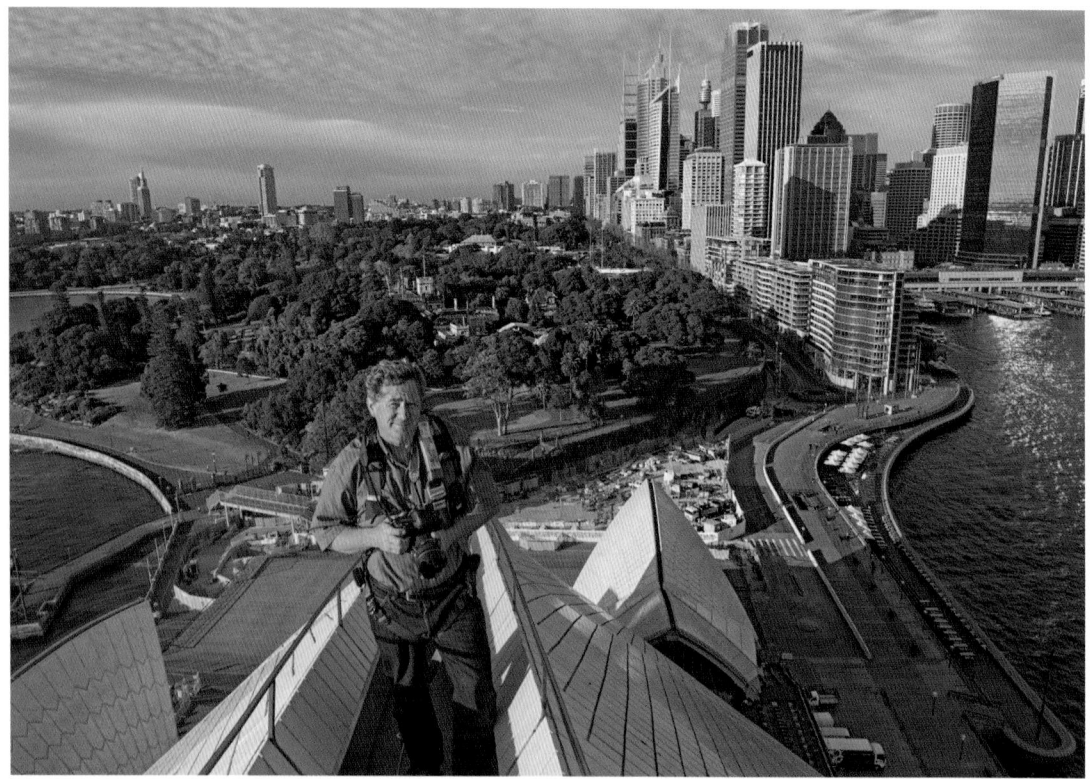

Traveling gives you the opportunity to visit some incredible places. Here, I'm standing on top of the iconic Sydney Opera House in Australia.

When you want to be prepared for anything from inclement weather to a night out on the town, packing can be tricky, and adding photography into the mix makes it even more challenging. As you assemble your gear, think about what you *really* need. Remember that your most important tools for making good photographs are your favorite camera, your best lens, and open-ness to the opportunities that arise. With these items and the knowledge you've gained, you should have all the tools you need to make a good photograph.

THE ESSENTIALS

You'll need your camera and at least one lens. A zoom is great for travel, as it is many lenses in one. Consider the subject matter you'll find: will it be scenic vistas, crowded city streets, or distant wildlife? Choose your lenses based on the scenarios in which you are most likely to find yourself. You also need two batteries and a charger, and plenty of memory cards, preferably in a protective case in which you can separate used from unused cards.

ACCESSORIES

Consider your lighting needs: Do you need an external flash, a reflector, or a tripod? Can you find other lighting or stabilization solutions once you arrive? Put these in a pile with your other bags and be sure you want to carry them. If you decide to bring them, wrap them in a bag with your clothing for protection and easier transport.

If you want to edit your photographs while traveling, you'll need a laptop and a portable external hard drive to back up your work. We'll talk about workflow and backups in the next chapter, but know that traveling with editing gear is a time and weight commitment, so be sure you *really* want it.

Finally, make a list of all the gear you take—including serial numbers—in case something is lost, broken, or stolen. Bring one copy of the list with you and leave one at home.

TRAVEL CONSIDERATIONS

A camera bag need not be expensive or complicated—any bag in which you can comfortably carry your gear will do. Consider a waterproof backpack for outdoor trips, and check that zippers and latches are secure. Make sure it fits your size and style, and that you can access your camera easily. Extra equipment, like chargers, card readers, computer equipment, and cords, can stay in a separate bag that you can leave in a hotel room or vehicle.

When flying, bring your most precious and essential items—the camera, your best lens—in a carry-on. Spare batteries, extra lenses, cords, and other accessories can be packed in your checked luggage, wrapped in soft clothing for protection.

No matter what you pack, it always feels like you have too much and not enough. But don't let packing concerns ruin the lead-up to your trip.

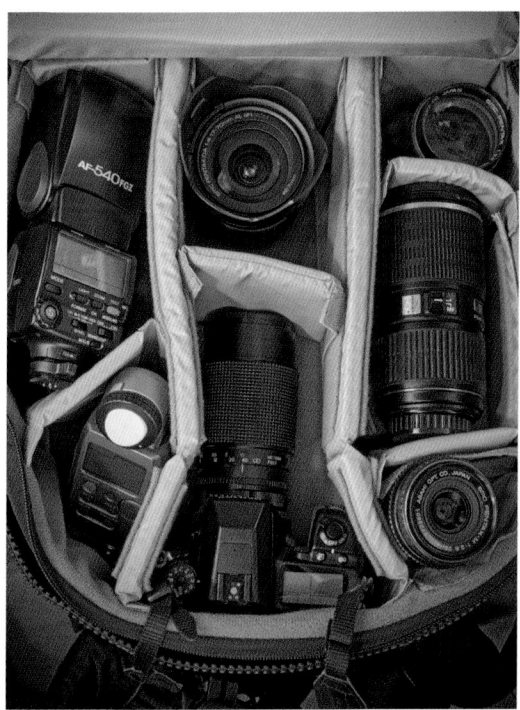

Think ahead to the pictures you want to capture, and pack the appropriate gear. Will you need a zoom lens, or a tripod for long-exposure photographs?

A SENSE OF PLACE

Photographers are often attracted to places they've never been. Identify the elements that make a place special and look for ways to incorporate them into your pictures.

We're often drawn to places because they're unfamiliar, and we want to document what makes them special. These elements—whether culture, heritage, or environment—communicate a sense of place. What is the essence, mood, or vibe of the place you're photographing, and how can you make viewers feel it, too?

DO YOUR HOMEWORK

As with portraiture, the more you know about your subject, the better your photographs will be. Research your destination before you even leave your house. Understand local traditions, climate, significant history, even the color palette of a place to form a vision for your photographs. Most important, try to get a sense for what is authentic, as opposed to tourist trappings.

A local guide can be a great asset—someone who will know the language and customs, and can steer you away from the veneer of a place and direct you to its heart. A simple internet search for LOCAL GUIDE and the place you are traveling to may surprise

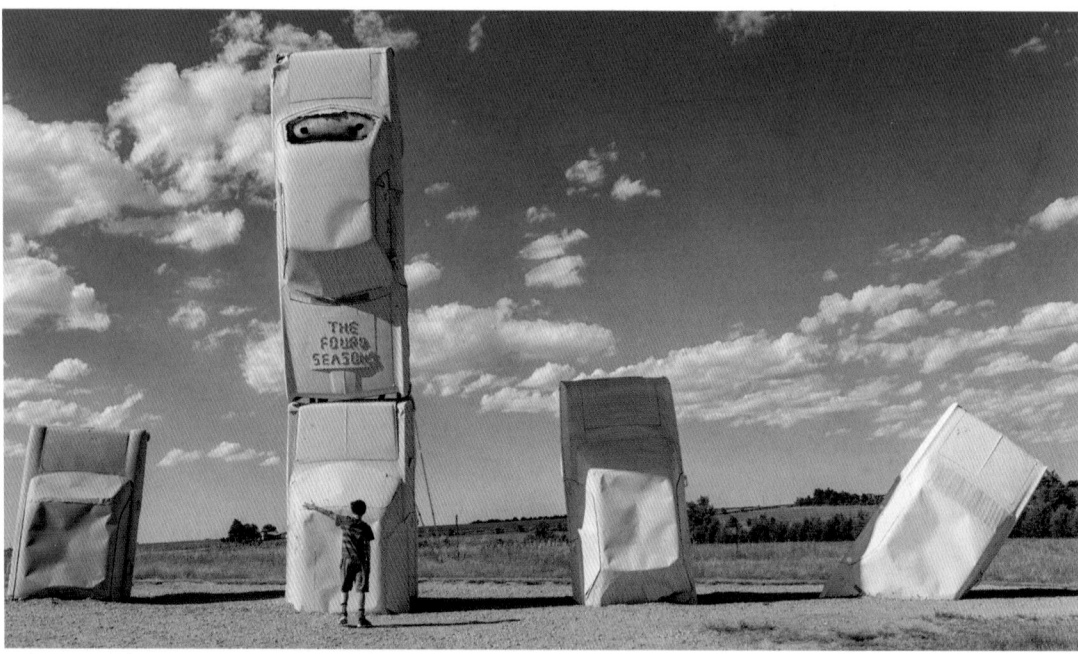

A boy stands in front of colorful sculptures made from old cars at Carhenge in Alliance, Nebraska.

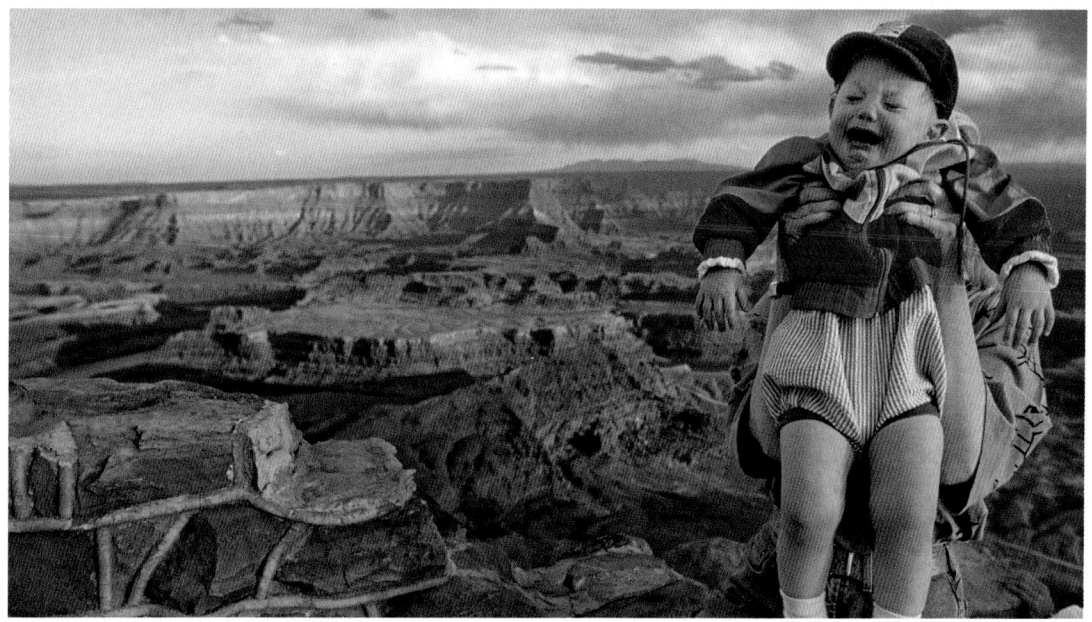

While the dramatic canyon landscape of Utah's Dead Horse Point State Park may have captivated his parents, this toddler has had enough. Adding a human element to a landscape, even an unexpected one, can evoke emotions beyond appreciation for nature.

you with reliable and knowledgeable options. Be sure to vet any company you might employ for this purpose.

It will also help to learn a few words in the local language, like "Hello," "Thank you," and "Please." This shows that you're operating in good faith, and will help you establish a rapport with the people around you. In turn, you'll gain trust, which will translate into more genuine and authentic photos.

THE HUMAN ELEMENT

One way to capture the essence of a place is to document all the different ways in which people interact with it. Perhaps you find a river where kids love to play in the water, or a market where vendors arrive in the wee hours of the morning to set up their wares. If you can capture people in their natural element, it will help tell a more complete story of the place you're visiting.

ASSIGNMENT: NO PLACE LIKE HOME

Every place has its own essence, even your hometown. It may feel familiar or even boring to you, but wander around with the eyes of a tourist. Try to answer these questions: What moments can you capture that express what the town is all about? What makes it unique? What traditions or events add to the story of your hometown? Make a list of relevant scenes in your town, and practice travel photography without even getting on a plane.

CULTURE

Culture is key to the fabric of a place. Document people and their traditions with integrity and respect, not as a gawking tourist with a camera. A smile cuts through all language barriers.

Travel pushes us beyond our comfort zone and gives us the opportunity to immerse in a different worldview. When you're planning to photograph cultures other than your own, it's essential to learn about customs, beliefs, and traditions. Culture influences everything from when the streets are busy to dress and body language.

Try to get a sense of how you'll be received, and how you can best approach a subject with a camera. Photography should be a means for documentation and building relationships, not intruding on a community.

PEOPLE

People are agents of culture and traditions, whether in their appearance, their dress, their gestures, or their activities. But photographing strangers can be tricky. It is considered rude in some cultures, and can be uncomfortable at first. When you approach people, always make an effort to be transparent and kind. Put in time getting to know them before you bring out your camera and you'll build foundations that will pay off in the long run.

Take care when photographing children. If at all possible, find a related adult who will give you permission. If you'll be spending a lot of time in one place, you want to establish trust and a good reputation.

PLACES

Culture lives in physical spaces. Look to where locals gather—urban parks, bustling city squares, crowded marketplaces. See how a space reflects its people. Look for what is put on display, what decorations are used, or how people interact with the space.

Holidays and special occasions are good opportunities to learn more about a culture. Research what is being celebrated or honored. If you can, join a family celebration, rather than a tourist version. Make friends. Building relationships will create opportunities for authentic photographs and gives you a connection to a place long after you return home.

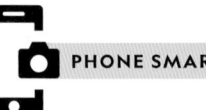

PHONE SMARTS: KEEP IN TOUCH

When you photograph someone, or if you get special assistance during a cultural event or ceremony, take down contact information for your subjects or your guide. Be sure to send them some photographs digitally or in print afterward. Sharing the product of your work will enhance the connection you've made.

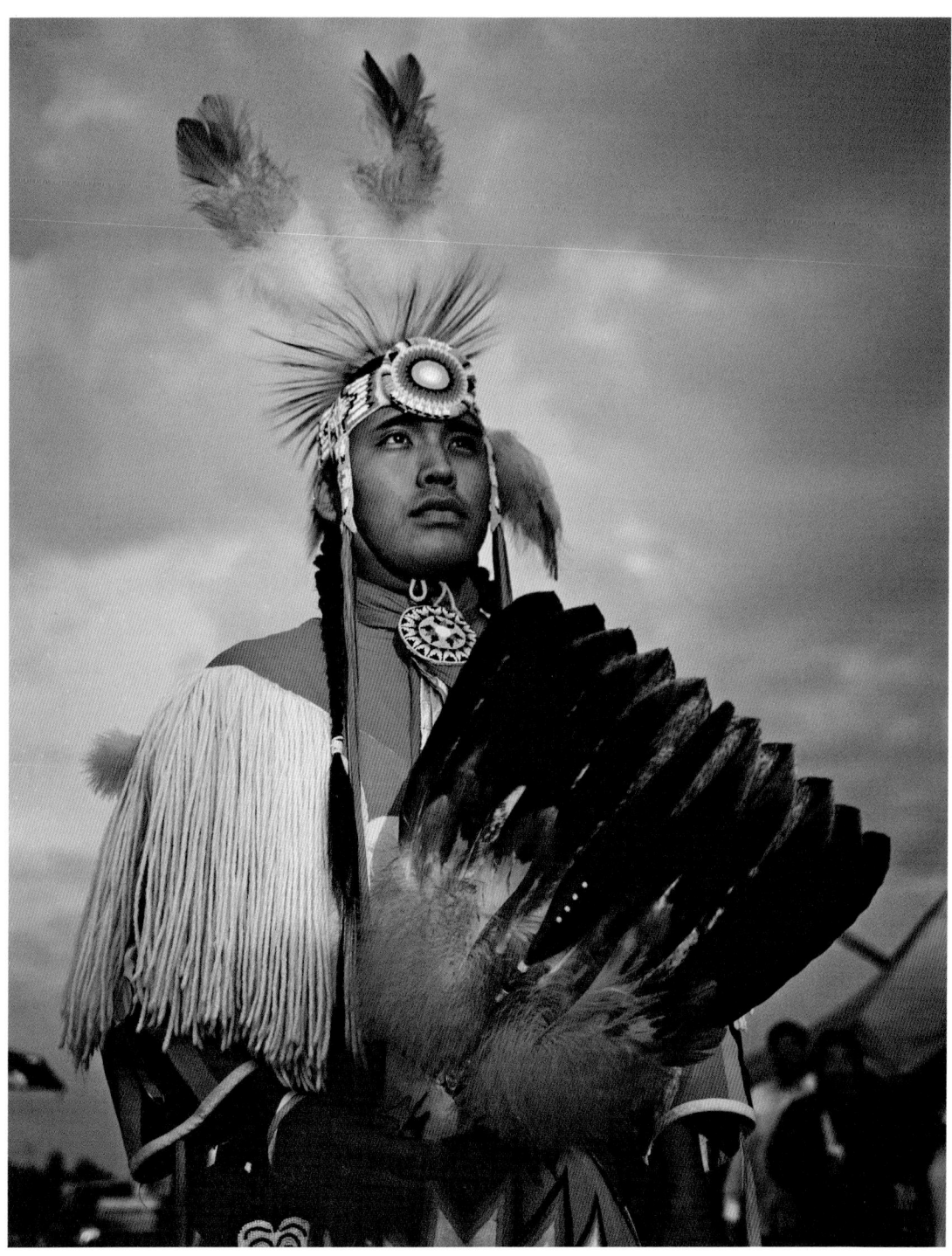

A young man wears traditional Navajo dance regalia in Window Rock, Arizona. Always be respectful when you're photographing cultures outside your own, especially when you're visiting for a significant cultural event.

ARCHITECTURE

From cathedrals and opera houses to homes and office buildings, architecture is often a defining aspect of a place.

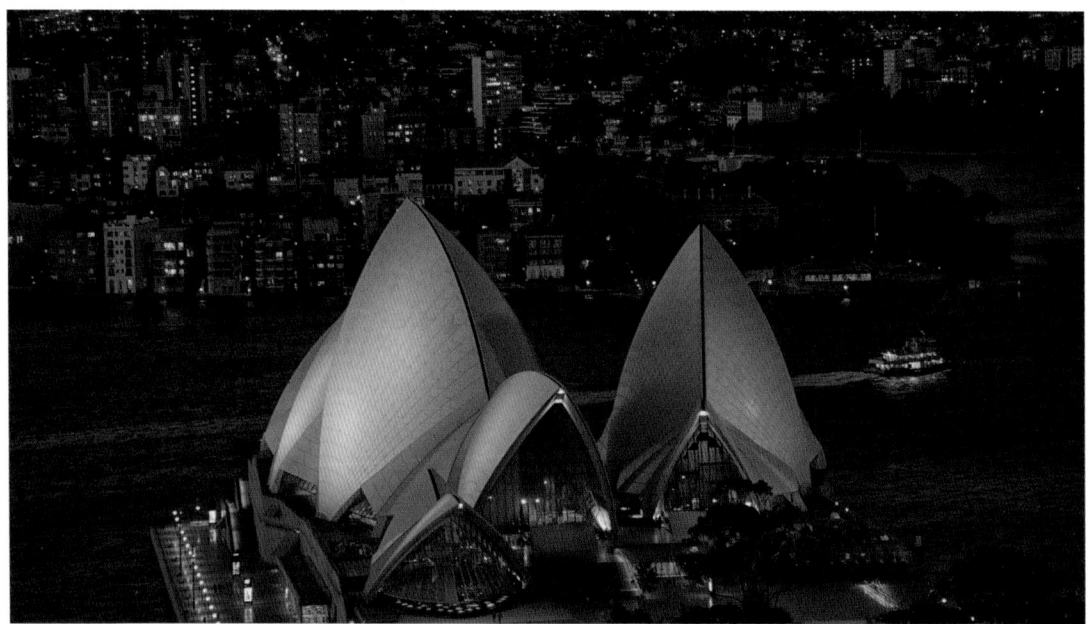

The Sydney Opera House is a familiar sight, photographed many times but most often from water level. An aerial view at dusk with a boat passing by yields something different: A new perspective shows how distinct the opera house is, perched and overlooking the city.

Architecture is a permanent part of a populated landscape and a major factor in defining a sense of place. Anyone can photograph a building, so your challenge is to capture it in a fresh or surprising way. Many buildings are designed with the environment in mind; take note of the way a structure inhabits and enhances a place, and try to incorporate some of those features into your photographs. Look for structures and materials that are unique to a place, or artful reflections.

TIMING

Plan for the golden hour—right after sunrise or right before sunset. Arrive early to pick your spot and frame your shot or set up a tripod. Then, wait. Observe how things change over time—lights coming on from within, people moving in and out, the way shadows move across a building's facade. Maybe the sun will flare between two buildings, or perhaps a person will enter your frame, walking up the steps, providing a sense of scale. With your subject fixed, you

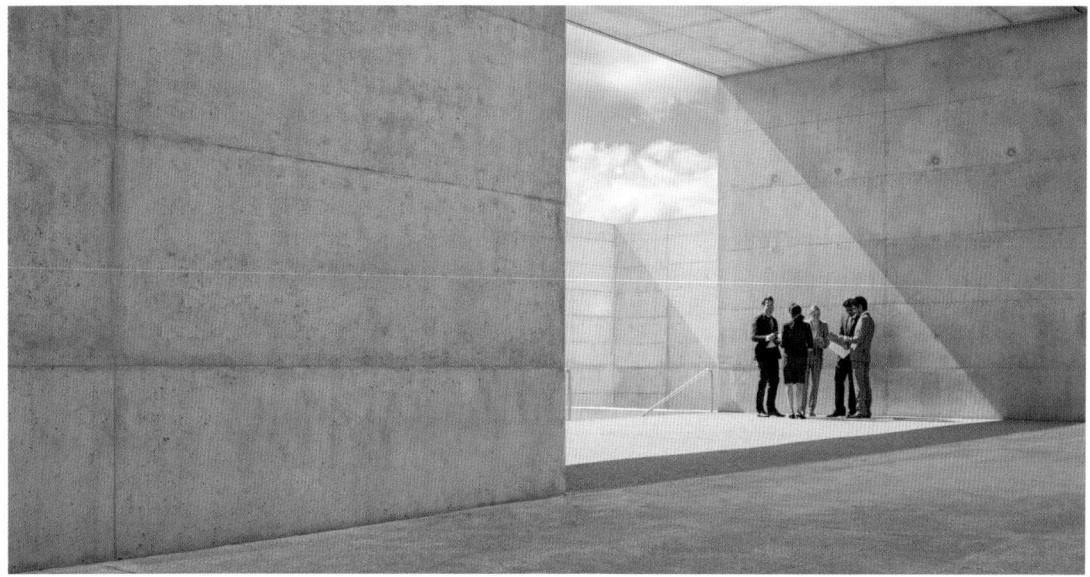

Photographs featuring architecture can be effective without revealing the whole building. Distill shapes, lines, and shadows by moving in closer, and include people in the frame to provide cultural context and scale.

can be creative with how you choose to photograph it.

COMPOSITION

Architecture lends itself well to compositional techniques like the rule of thirds, leading lines, and interesting framing. Experiment with perspective—lying on your back and photographing buildings against the sky, from mid-level in the stairwell of an adjacent building, or perhaps a view of the city from the top looking down. In addition to the whole of a building, look for interesting details, like patterns of bricks, intersecting rooflines, decorative features, or even the shadow it casts.

For a broader perspective of how a building fits into the landscape, head out of town to find an overlook with an unobstructed view of the skyline. As you would with any landscape photo, look for elements around you that will add interest, depth, or color.

PRO TIP | MONUMENTS AND LANDMARKS

When visiting famous landmarks, try to find ways to shoot them differently. For example, with icons such as the Sydney Opera House or the Colosseum in Rome, include people in the picture for a sense of scale. With Mount Rushmore or the Pyramids, use a long lens to let viewers see the texture of the stone. Or go totally abstract—photograph the back or underside of a monument, or tight frames of small parts of it. Photograph the surrounding areas that people don't often notice, or turn around and photograph the visitors taking it in, perhaps a reflection of it in their sunglasses. Work the area thoroughly to get a totally fresh look at something familiar.

FESTIVITIES

Special occasions, such as holidays, festivals, and celebrations, are rich in photographic opportunities, and a great time to practice your candid photography skills.

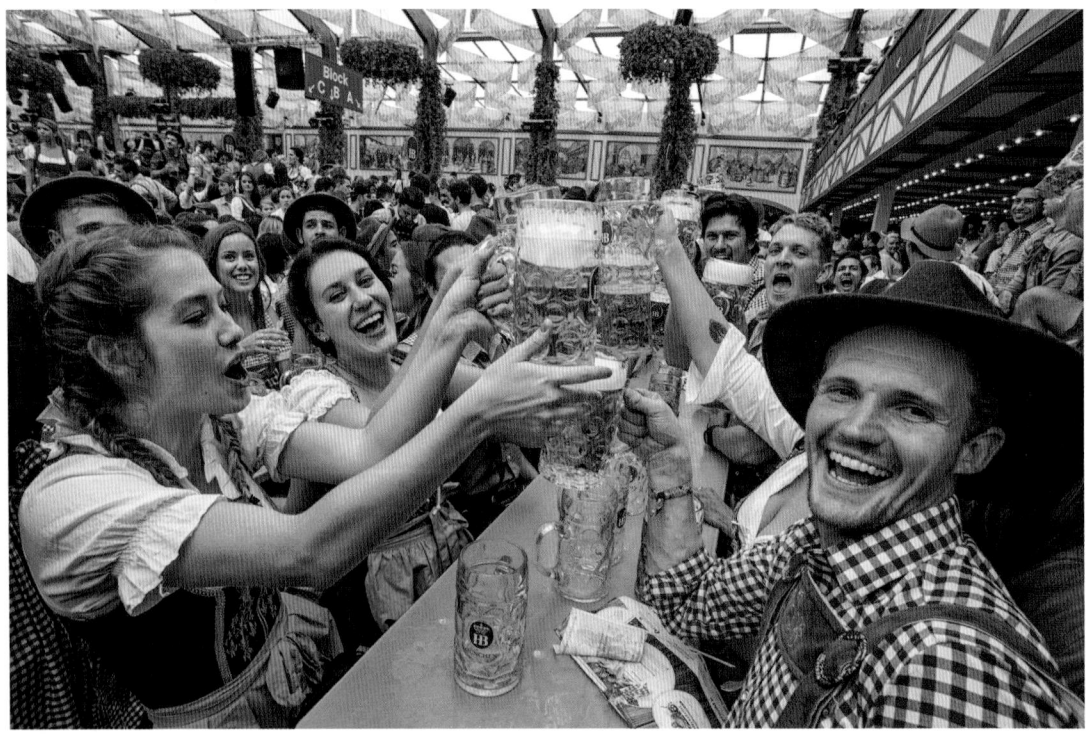

Citywide celebrations like Oktoberfest in Munich, Germany, can make for a memorable trip and stellar photographs.

Consider planning travel around an occasion—Mardi Gras in New Orleans, Oktoberfest in Germany, or Holi in India are popular examples, but plenty of small, lesser-known festivals take place all over the world. Look at the list of places you want to visit and investigate local celebrations that take place throughout the year. Research the historical significance of an event, and see what photographs you can make to convey the backstory of the occasion.

PARTY PLAN

Once you've settled on an event, consider the activity and situations you might encounter. Find places where locals celebrate the occasion, rather than venues set up for tourists. Pack your bag as light as possible so you can walk around, climb a wall, or kneel on the sidewalk without being weighed down. Show up early and stay late. Capture the setup and cleanup, if you can.

PARTY ON

Take a mix of portraits, details, and wide-angle shots. Throughout the event, document the way people seem to feel, and how they interact with the celebration and each other. Get in close. Look for tougher scenes, too—crying kids, a toppling display, a stalled parade float. These moments add authenticity and help tell the full story of the day, but be sure you're not intruding on a delicate situation.

Every celebration tells a story. Your job is to communicate it in a compelling way that makes your viewers feel as if they were there.

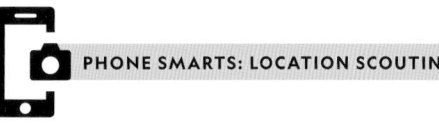

PHONE SMARTS: LOCATION SCOUTING

Your phone can be a digital notebook for advance scouting of locations you want to shoot during an event. Take test shots to note perspectives and where the light hits, then use a map app with GPS to add pins for any locations you want to cover on the big day.

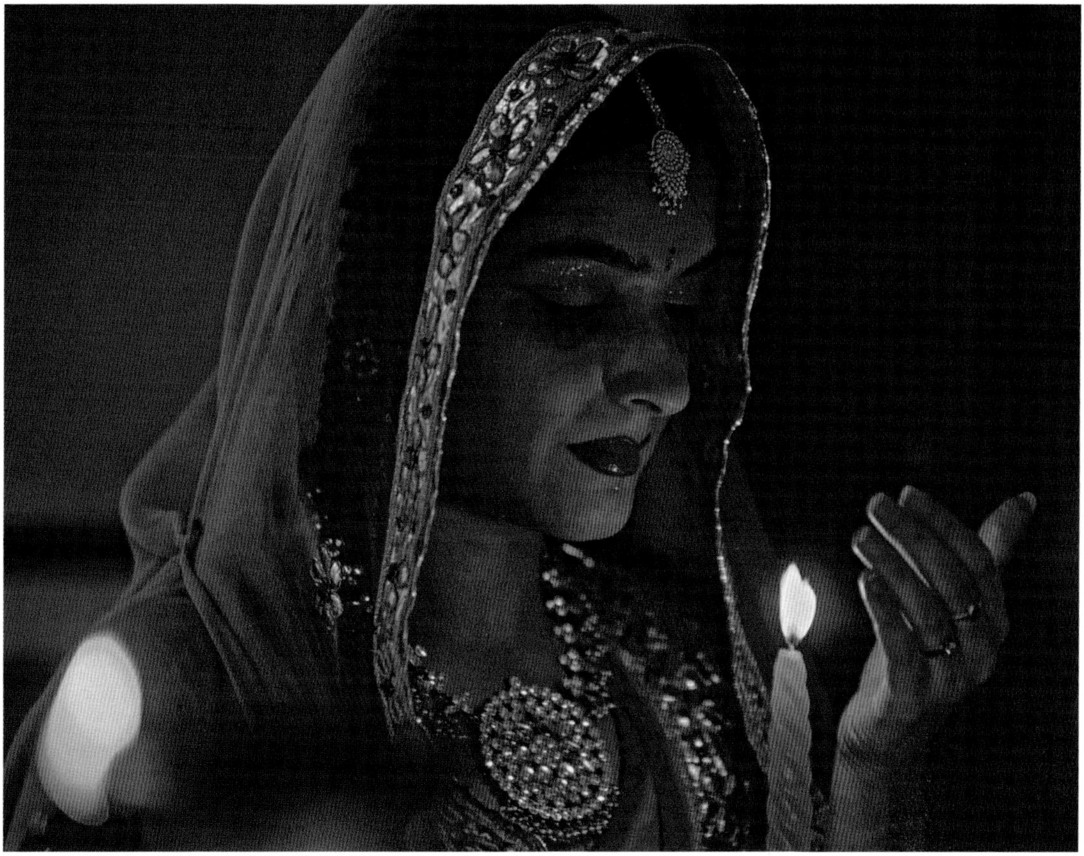

Not all pictures of festivities have to include large crowds. This lovely portrait captures a woman lighting a candle during Diwali in Jaipur, India, and evokes a sense of serenity and calm.

FOOD & DRINK

Don't be afraid to play with your food to make a great photograph. Natural lighting, clean backgrounds, and pops of color make for pictures that look good enough to eat.

No matter where you're headed, a wonderful part of traveling is trying out new foods. Photographing a meal is a great way to capture culture, tradition, and to preserve mouthwatering memories, even if you only get to experience the food once.

KEEP IT FRESH

The most important goal for food photography is to make the dish look appetizing. Natural light and bright colors are key.

Try visiting a food market with decent ambient light—plentiful, soft, and diffuse light is best. Look for baskets of colorful produce, or stalls where vendors cook fresh food for a crowd. Think about composition and the story you want to tell. Is the food—separate ingredients or combined in a dish—your main focus? If so, you might soften your background with shallow depth of field. Do you want to document the flair of a chef preparing and plating a local delicacy?

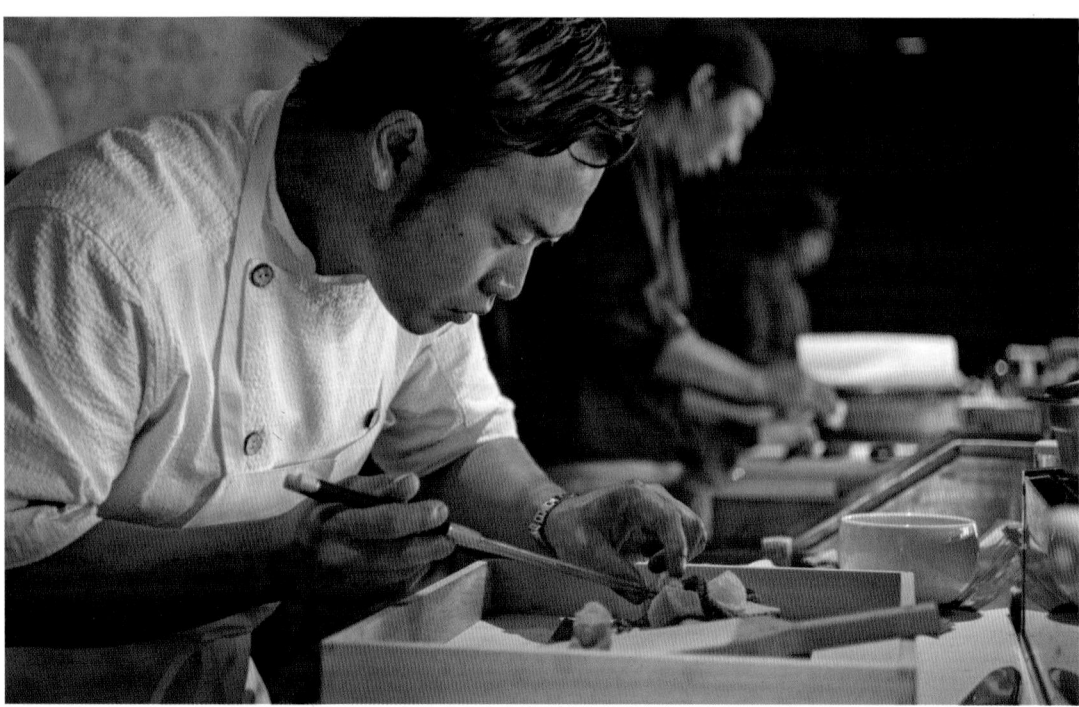

A sushi chef carefully plates a variety of sashimi at a restaurant in Manhattan Beach, New York. Sometimes the person making the food can be more interesting than the food itself.

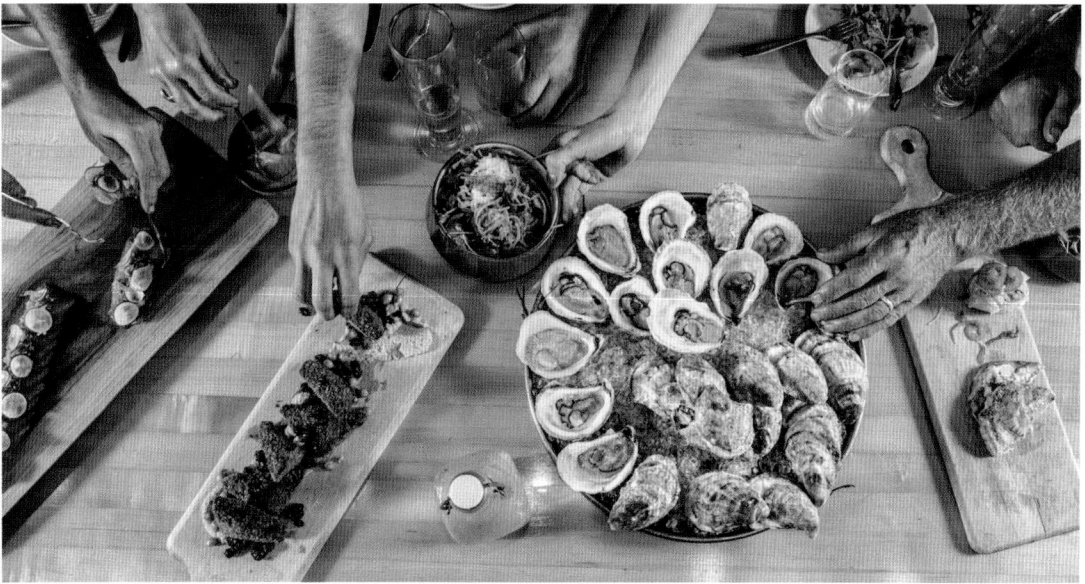

Shooting a table from above is most effective with a clean background, free from clutter and crumbs, that allows the shapes of plates and the colors of food to pop. Here, the food itself is the focus of the picture, while the hands add energy and action.

Shoot wide and use a faster shutter speed. And don't forget anticipation on the faces of hungry customers waiting for a bite.

SHOOTING IN A RESTAURANT

To photograph your meal at a restaurant, try to get a seat near a window. Soft, natural light will always make food look more appetizing. Avoid flash—it will make your food look flat or greasy and you'll disturb other patrons. Be ready as soon as the food is delivered to your table—capture the steam curling above your hot coffee, or a delicate arrangement the chef has created on your plate.

PRO TIP FOOD STYLING

A little thought for food can go a long way:

- **Clear the table** Before your meal is placed, be sure to move any unrelated or unappealing objects from the table—cell phones, car keys, wrappers, and dirty napkins can ruin a scene, while hands and utensils add context and scale.

- **Consider composition** A simple, clean background allows the food to be the star. Try shooting from directly above, or from a soup's-eye view, making that burger or meringue pie stand proud and tall.

- **Highlight action or texture** Hang on to your ice cream for a minute, and capture a drop melting down the cone; give your sandwich a little squeeze to catch gooey, melted cheese oozing out the sides.

ACTION & ADVENTURE

Whether you're a participant or a spectator, action and adventure make for an exciting travel experience. Plan ahead, keep your wits about you, and you'll leave with a great story and dynamic photos.

Unless you're planning to sit by the hotel pool for a week, your vacation is likely to include some sort of adventure. Whether tubing down a river or snowboarding, rock climbing, or sailing, capturing the action will add liveliness to your travel photos so be ready for it.

YOUR ADVENTURE

Think about how you can safely photograph your experience. If your whole trip is a backwoods adventure away from standard amenities, be sure you can keep your equipment dry, and pack enough batteries to get through a few days without an outlet.

Consider a small action camera rather than your DSLR, and some sort of accessory to strap it to your body. Photographing from the center of the action will give your viewers a great feel for what it was like to experience it firsthand.

SPECTATOR SPORTS

If you'll be along the sidelines, set yourself up with what you need to be comfortable while you wait, and have your camera set to capture the event from your position. You'll likely need fresh batteries and a fast shutter speed. A zoom lens is your best bet for activities that might rapidly change in distance. Consider a tripod or a monopod if you need to support a long lens over time.

THE ADVENTURERS

No matter what the activity, focus on the human story. Whether you're snowboarding with your friends or watching a professional rodeo, think about the people at the heart of the adventure. Try to capture the feel of the scene through the details that highlight the emotions of the participants and spectators. Focus on faces and capture the struggle or elation they're experiencing.

And don't forget the environmental details, such as tables with cups of water for exhausted marathoners, referee hats covered in snow, empty stables waiting for racehorses to return. A varied series of images will better tell the complete story of an adventure and its participants.

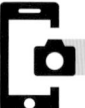

PHONE SMARTS: UP CLOSE AND PERSONAL

One advantage of a smartphone is its size. Since it's smaller than a DSLR, you can get a phone camera right in the middle of the action by attaching it to the handlebars of a bike or holding it in the center of a group of fishermen. Just make sure it's secured and protected against any elements it might encounter.

FOR MORE ON PHOTOGRAPHING SPORTS, SEE PAGE 164.

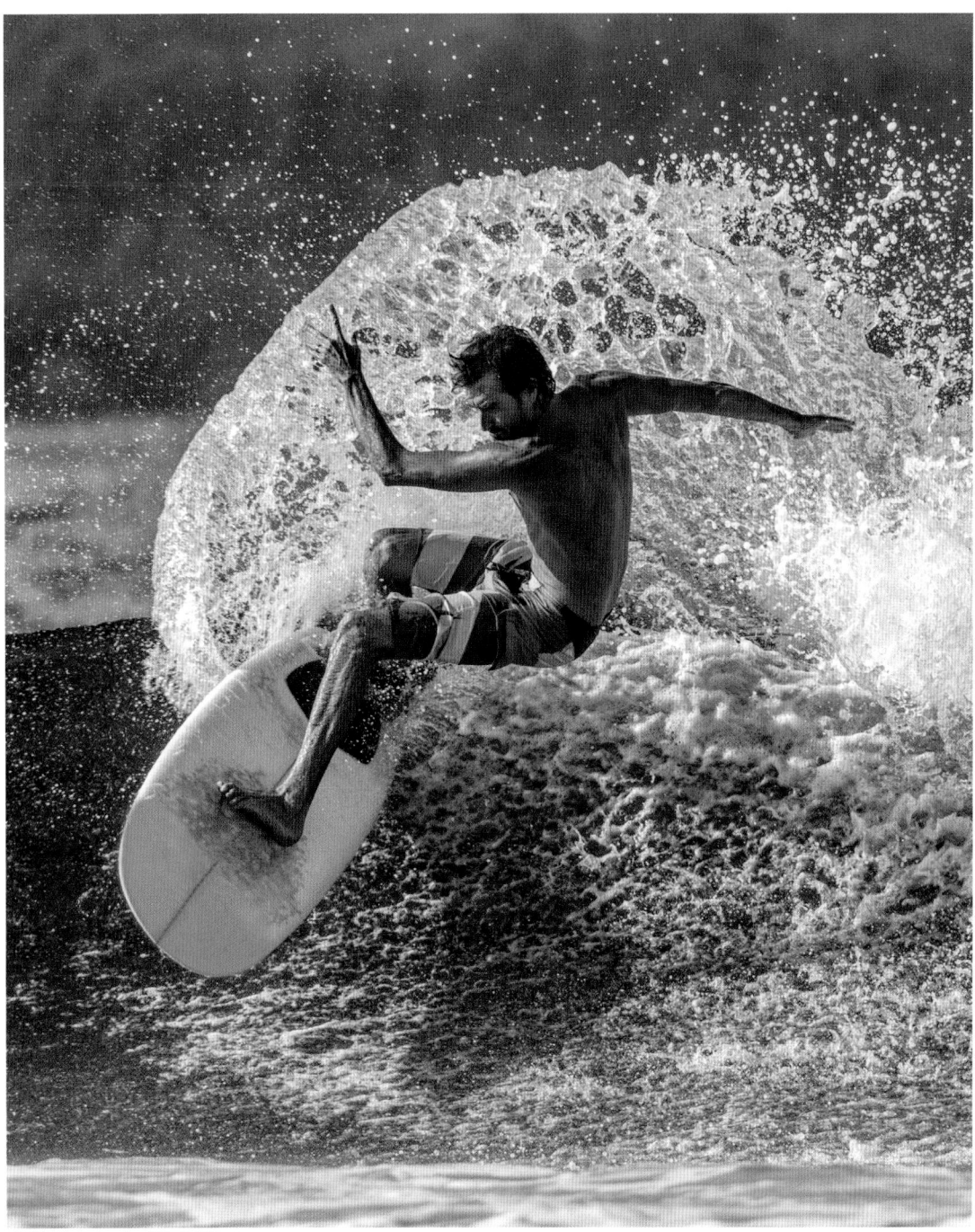

This photograph of a surfer makes good use of a telephoto lens and a fast shutter speed. The long lens makes us feel close to the action, and the shutter speed freezes the water as his board cuts across the wave.

OUTDOORS

Whether you're hiking through wilderness or deep sea fishing, playing in the great outdoors is an opportunity to infuse your photographs with your passion for nature and adventure.

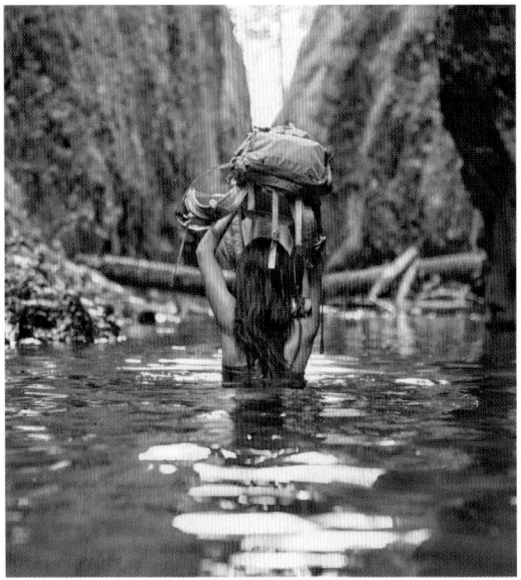 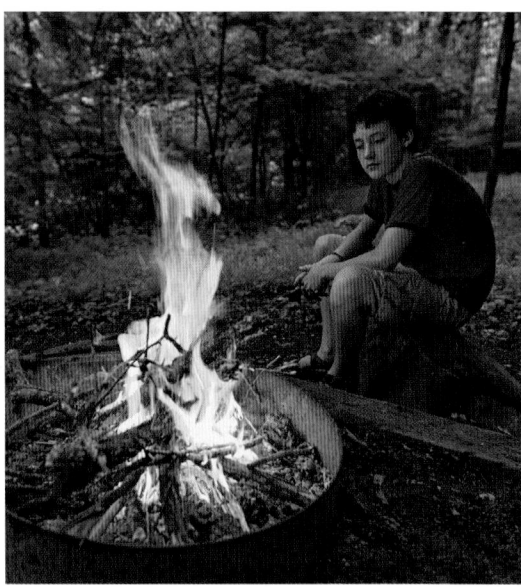

Whether your vacation involves water adventures or relaxing around a campfire, make sure you pack the right gear for your comfort and for the type of photographs you want to make.

Outdoor travel combines the opportunity for great landscape photography and adventure photography. The challenge lies in incorporating photography into an experience that might already push you to your limits. Pack light, and pare your gear down to one camera, a good zoom lens, and a few extra batteries and memory cards. You'll have a world of natural light to tell the story of your adventure.

SEARCHING FOR LIGHT

As always, try to photograph your surroundings when the light is low and diffuse, but be flexible when conditions are less than optimal. You may wind up reaching the summit of a mountain at high noon, or roasting marshmallows around a campfire after the sun has set. These moments are just as important as the ones with easy light, so embrace the challenge. Adjust ISO, white balance, aperture, and shutter speed until you get results you're happy with. Use your meter and histogram in challenging light, adjusting your exposure accordingly. For example, to capture the group sing-along around the fire, lock in the exposure for faces gently illuminated by firelight.

GROUP PHOTOGRAPHER

When adventuring with a group, it may be wise to break away from the pack to get the photos you want.

Jog ahead so you can photograph your fellow adventurers with the scenery in the background. Head off to the side so you can capture their silhouettes against the sky as they scramble along a ridge or paddle down a river. You may get quite a workout while you seek out good vantage points of your group, so be prepared for some extra activity.

Be careful to protect your equipment by keeping gear free of moisture, dust, and sand, and have a clean, dry place to store any memory cards that you've filled up during the trip.

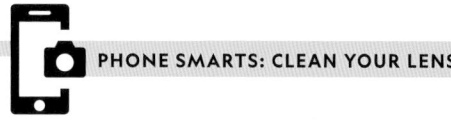

PHONE SMARTS: CLEAN YOUR LENS

Many of us carry our phones in our pockets, or in a bag filled with lots of other things. In everyday life, and especially if you're roughing it in the great outdoors, it can get dirty and dusty very easily. Clean off that tiny phone lens with a microfiber cloth or a clean T-shirt—you might be surprised at the difference it makes.

Most important, know when to put away the camera. Don't be so distracted by getting the perfect picture that you forget to look up and around at the beauty the world has to offer.

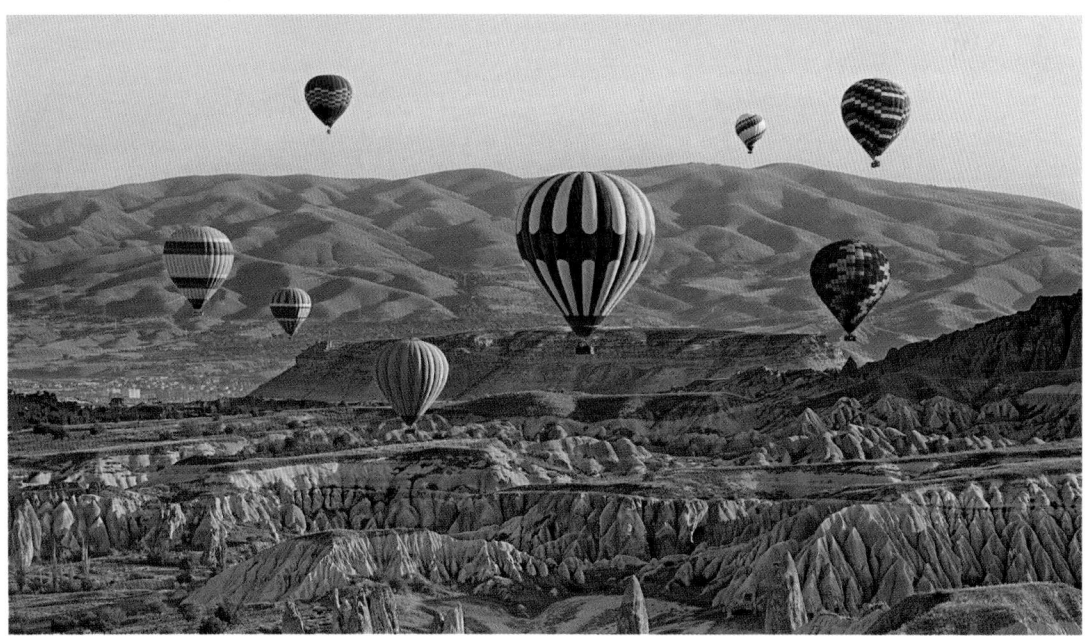

These hot-air balloons in Cappadocia, Turkey, look stunning from the perspective of another hot-air balloon. Whether you are lucky enough to enjoy a balloon ride or have your feet firmly planted on the ground, don't forget to put down your camera and experience the wonder of the world in front of your eyes.

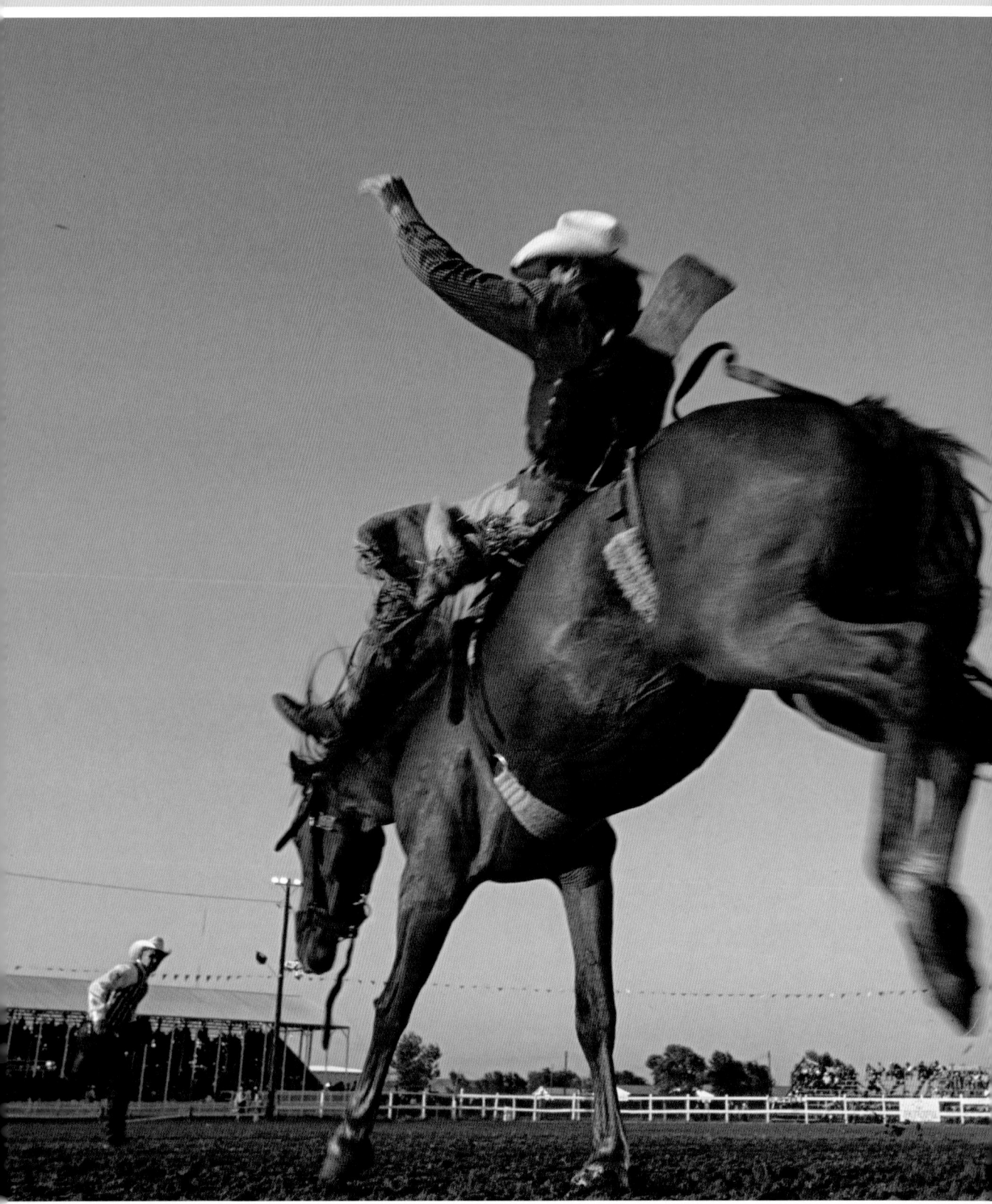

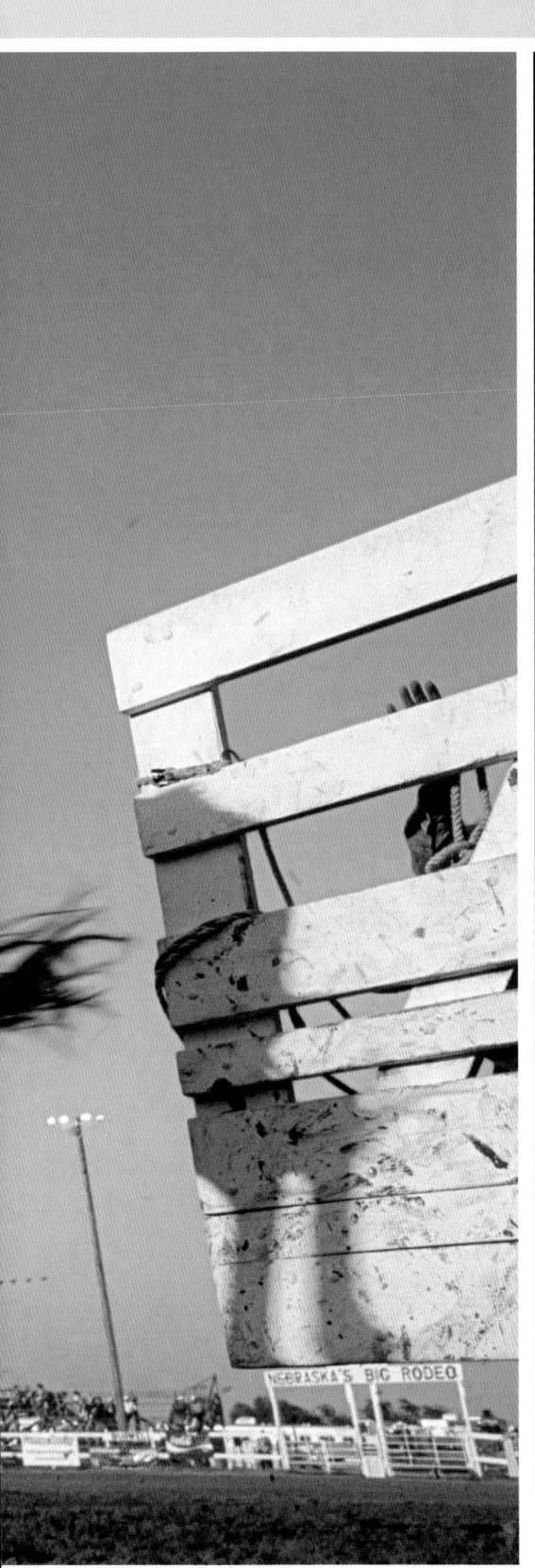

AT THE RODEO

Just because the action you're shooting is inherently interesting doesn't mean you can forget what makes a good photograph or disregard your own safety! I took this picture of a bucking bronco at a rodeo in Burwell, Nebraska, about three hours from my home in Lincoln. Although I like the way it turned out, getting the shot nearly cost me my camera—and my consciousness. If you're going to be getting close to the action or photographing high-risk adventures, it's especially important to be aware of your environment.

GET WIDE I used a wide-angle lens to frame the action with context—the crowds in the stands, a rodeo clown in the background, the way the gate is flinging open at the wild start of the ride.

BE SAFE Crouched low to the ground, looking through the viewfinder with a wide-angle lens, meant that I couldn't gauge how close I was to the action. For safety, I appointed a "holder"—someone to stand behind me and pull me back by my vest if the bucking bronco came too close for comfort.

USE A REMOTE Now I know: Electronic remote triggers for cameras are easy to use and can yield dramatic results, especially in quick-changing or dangerous situations. Buy one.

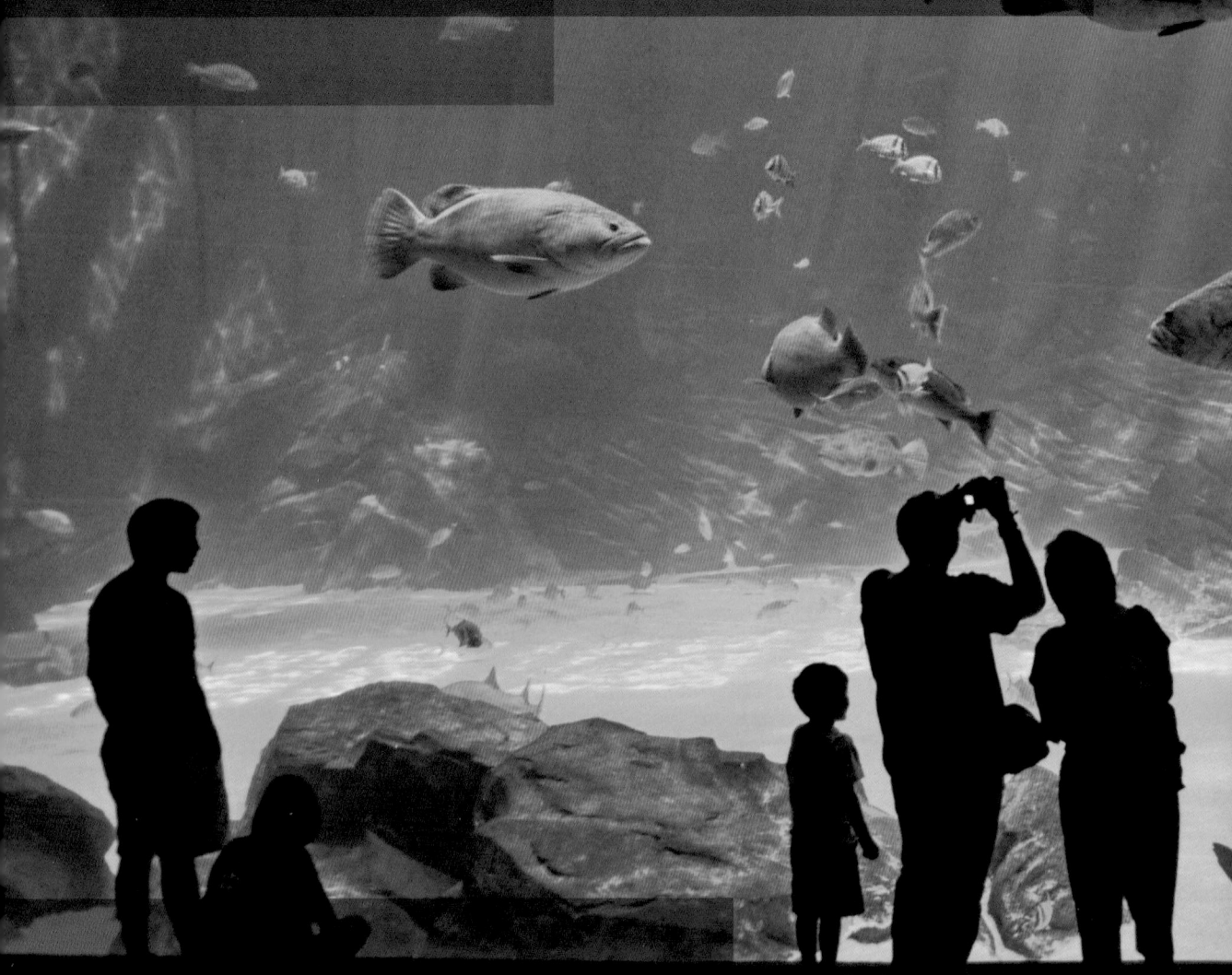

TEN
EDITING

THE BACK HALF OF PICTURE MAKING

Editing. One word encompasses so many steps in the photographic process, from organizing to selecting to polishing up. The concept of editing might seem daunting, intimidating, or even dry and boring—not nearly as much fun as pushing the button! But what you do after taking a picture is every bit as important as capturing it in the first place. Whether you are working on a Mac, a PC, or a smartphone, using photo-editing software or simply organizing your work, planning and consistency will be your best assets in the editing process. Without them you can't effectively share what you've made.

Editing is more than labeling, organizing, and selecting—you'll still need to use your creativity to finish your picture. There are entire books, courses, even professional degrees that cover postproduction techniques, from creating presets for common, global alterations on your photographs to sophisticated retouching, advanced dodging and burning, layers, masks, and more. Some creative professionals make careers out of editing and retouching photographers' work. In this book, we'll focus on how to develop a consistent, efficient workflow that will carry you through capturing, storing, enhancing, and sharing your work in a way that will keep you excited about what you've created. So put your gear away and get comfy by your computer. It's time to review what you've done so far.

A man rests against a lovely yellow wall after a day in the Tuscan sun.

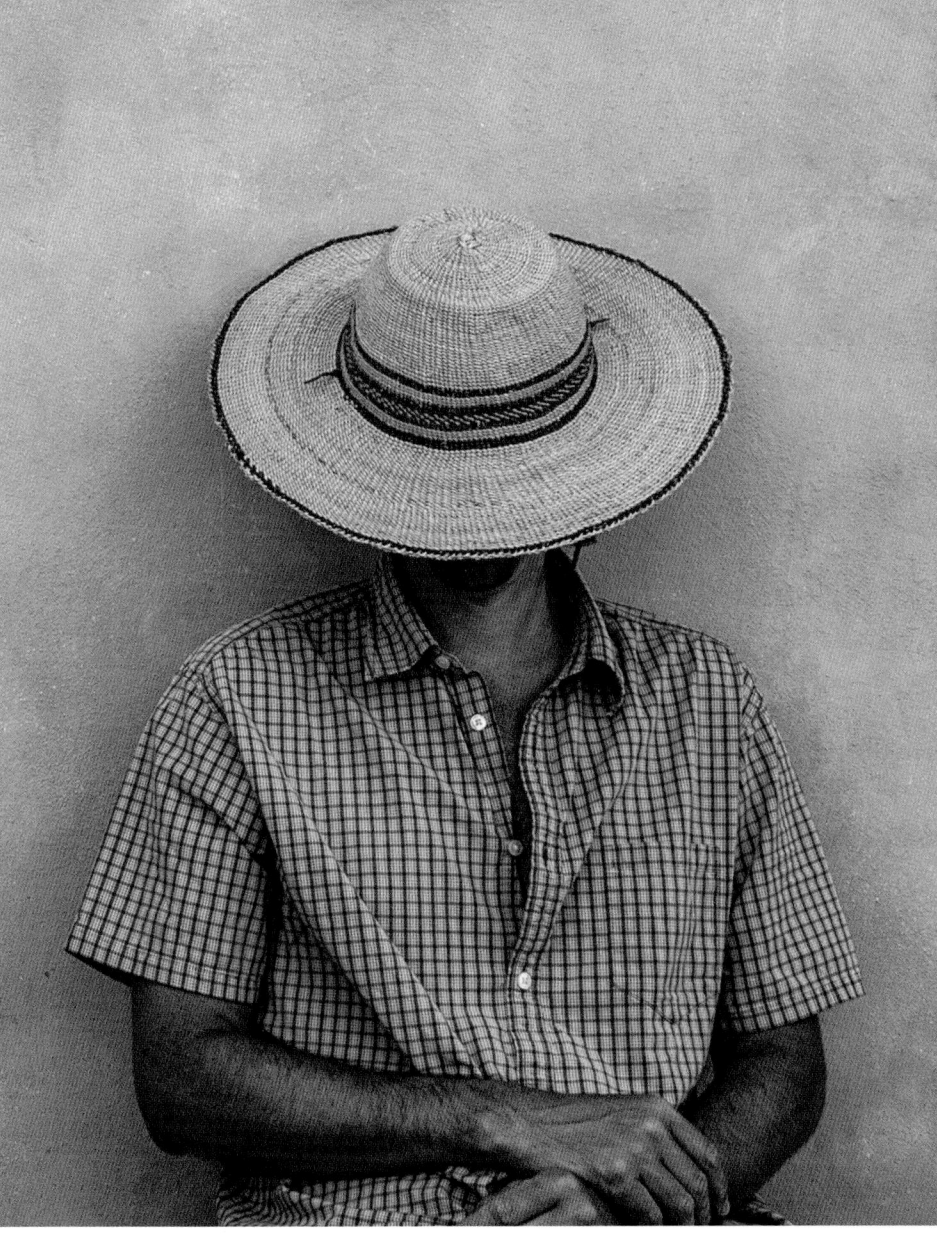

WORKFLOW

Developing an efficient workflow will take the mystery out of the editing process, and help you make the most of the images you've worked so hard to create.

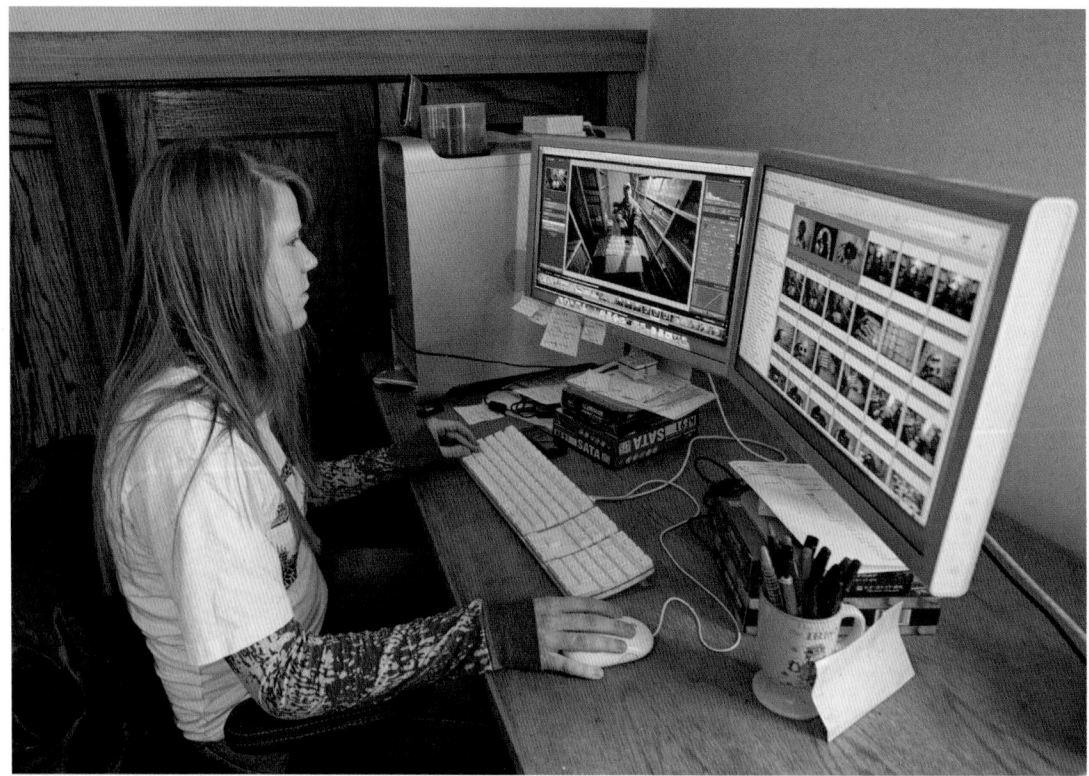

Photo software, like Adobe Lightroom, will let you look at thumbnails of your images all at once. This comes in handy for making quick decisions while you're editing a batch of photos.

You've just come back from a great day photographing something you're passionate about. You put your gear away and find yourself with a handful of memory cards. What next?

The best approach to a smooth workflow is to have the framework for it set up in advance. Once you have a solid understanding of what your process will be for getting your photographs from camera to audience, you'll be much more likely to create, archive, and share the fruits of your labors.

FILE TYPES

Let's back up for a minute. When you turn on your camera for the first time, one of the first things you should do is select your image file type. This option will be

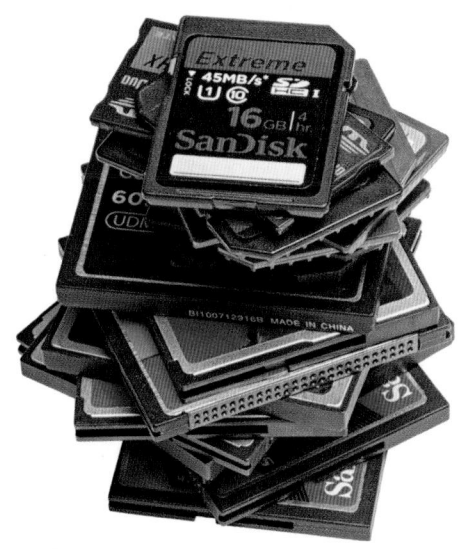

There are many types of memory cards and they come with various storage capacities. Be sure you know which type your camera uses, and have extras on hand.

somewhere in your shooting menu, but check your manual for specifics. Typical file options are several sizes of JPEGs and RAW. Both types have pros and cons. In JPEG, you'll find that you can fit many photographs on your memory card and hard drive—JPEGs are compression files, so they don't take up a lot of space. But they are much less flexible for editing, and every time the file is opened and re-saved, some pixels or visual information is lost. This means that, over time, your JPEG photograph will have less and less of the precious information you worked so hard to capture, and you'll have less data to work with in your editing process.

Enter the RAW file format. RAW files retain every bit of information originally captured in the picture, giving you the ability to make lots of adjustments later on. The cost is that RAW files are very large and take up a lot of hard drive space. They also require photo software to be viewed and edited—this software is fairly common, and the photo programs bundled with the latest operating systems of both Mac and Windows will handle it, but it's still a consideration. The fact is that RAW is the best way to make a photograph you'd like to work with, share, and keep for a long time.

THE SETUP

For a typical DSLR workflow, you'll need the following:

- Your camera
- Memory card
- A card reader or a cord that connects your camera to your computer
- A computer
- Photo-editing software
- An external hard drive for storing and backing up files

Essentially, you make photographs with your camera, which writes them to the memory card. You transfer those images to your computer, where you will organize, edit, and store them. You'll want to back everything up onto an external hard drive for security, and then share your edited images as you wish—to social media or to a lab for printing. We will cover the details of these steps in the upcoming lessons, but understanding this general flow will help you work with your images efficiently.

FILE ORGANIZATION

Like filing important papers, your photographs should be stored in a way that will keep them organized, safe, and easily accessible, long after you make them.

The more photographs you make, the better your odds of getting a keeper or two. But with a high volume of photographs comes the significant issue of storing and organizing them. Here, we'll discuss an approach to organization of your photographs on a computer system. One overarching tip: Your system for storage will be most effective if you set it up and use it well right from the start. We often think we'll go back and organize the work from our last shoot, but once you move on to the next one, you almost never will. Not being able to access your photographs later is almost the same as never having made them at all. Start out with habits that will serve you well as long as you're making pictures.

FILING SYSTEM

If you want to keep things basic and simply store your digital image files on your computer, devise a system of nesting folders that makes sense to you and the type of photos you are taking. Generally, it's most useful to organize your photographs by date and location, in a series of folders. For example, you may have one folder labeled with the year. Within that, you may have one for each month, and within those, folders for specific days or locations, like a birthday or a beach vacation. If you photograph a distinct location or event frequently, you may want to have a folder with that name and subfolders for different dates. You'll deposit the image files for the corresponding days into those folders.

If you decide to work with photo-organization software, these types of folder systems will be part of the import process. Most photo applications—from the ones bundled with your computer's operating system to more sophisticated programs, such as Adobe Lightroom or Photo Mechanic—will enable you to customize your filing system to suit your preferences.

METADATA

When you make a photograph, the camera writes the information about your settings into the metadata of the image file. This gets imported along with your pictures, and both Mac and Windows operating systems will allow you to view that information easily, which can be useful in reviewing which settings worked in various scenarios.

IDENTIFIERS

One benefit to organizing with photo-editing software is that most of the programs have GPS reading and facial recognition functions, which can tag your pho-

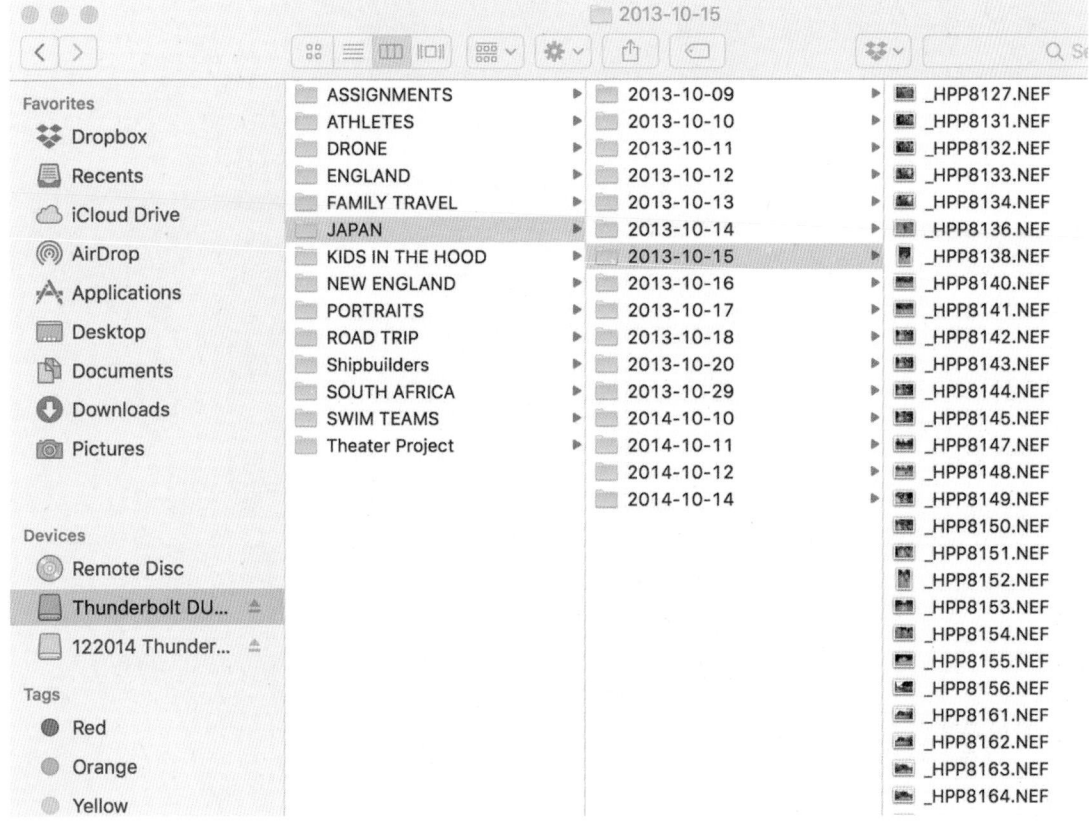

These folders are organized by subject or location, and contain folders identified by date, containing all the image files from that day of shooting. Nesting folders are easily searchable and can be expanded for the organized addition of future shoots.

tos with location information recorded by most cameras, or identify the people who appear in them. These programs allow you to search across dates or events for photographs with matching information—handy if, for example, you want to find all photographs with a certain person in them, no matter where or when they were taken.

Most of these programs also allow you to add other specific keywords to the metadata of your images, either in batches on import or individually.

Other information you might want to embed into an image file is a descriptive caption, and contact information for your subject or anyone else important to the shoot. These identifiers will further refine your searches for images later, but don't let the work of it deter you from moving on to the selection phase. If you stick to a thorough organizational system with dates and locations, it's likely you'll always be able to find what you're looking for, even years later. As technology continues to improve, the workload of successful image organization is gradually being reduced.

BACKUPS

Backing up your work is as essential as creating it. Period.

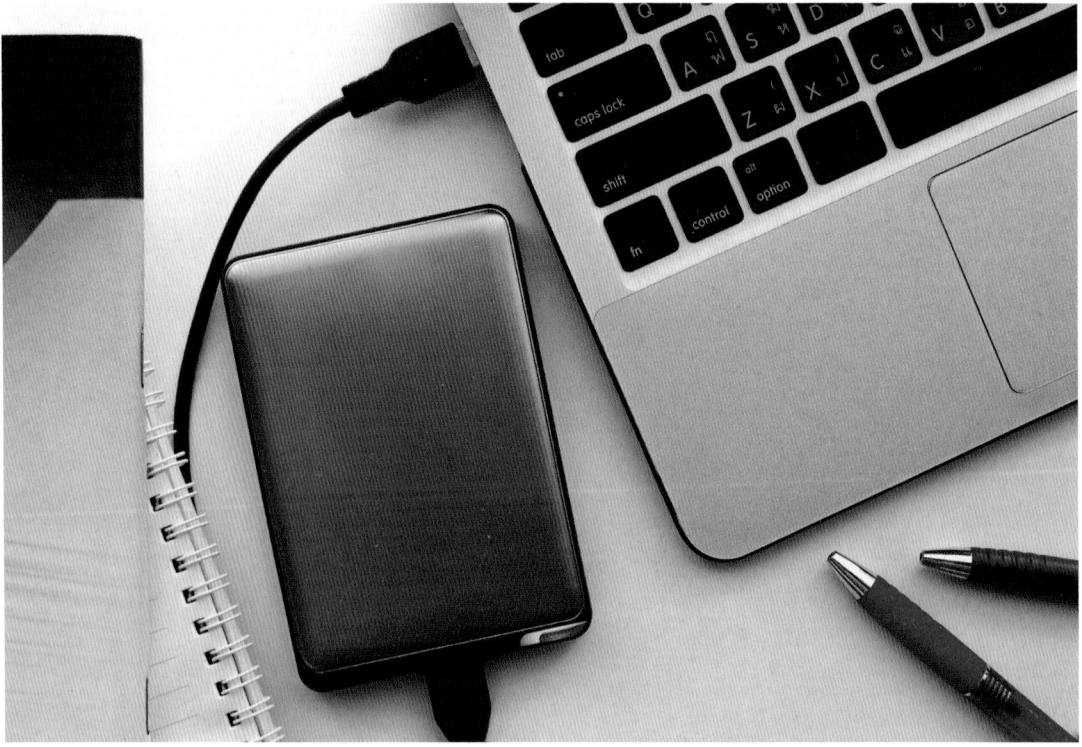

Small hard drives are relatively inexpensive and easy to carry in your gear bag. Backing up while in the field is especially important, as equipment gets moved around and can be exposed to elements that could cost you important photographs.

One of the many excellent things about working in a digital medium is that backing up your work has never been easier. Replicating files is often a matter of clicks, and you can't do it too soon or often enough. After capture and as soon as possible, your images should live in at least two places. At a minimum, you should invest in an external hard drive to back up the photographs that live on your computer, and make sure you do so after each time you sit down to work with them.

INCREMENTAL BACKUPS

To start, never reformat (erase) a memory card until you are sure that the images on it have been copied into two places that do not occupy the same disk or drive. Get in the habit of doing this immediately after you've imported and organized them. Creating a backup system can be as simple as copying your nested image folders to a separate hard drive, or asking your photo-editing software to do it for you whenever you download images.

When you use photo-editing software, like Photos, Adobe Lightroom, or Photo Mechanic, be sure to back up a copy of the application's library—where your edits and other metadata live—in addition to the original photo files. This ensures that your editing work will also be preserved. Always label your backup copies clearly to avoid overwriting original files.

Backup media may include CDs, DVDs, or flash drives, but keep in mind that as technology advances, these get more and more difficult to burn and read. Having separate, clearly labeled hard drives to house copies of your organization system is, for now, the most accessible solution. Cloud storage may not be the most practical solution for housing all your original images, but it is a good option for backing up your most important photographs once they've been edited.

REDUNDANCY

Digital storage space is fairly inexpensive and easy to acquire—an online search for EXTERNAL HARD DRIVE will yield many options. Invest in a few and use them wisely by making multiple copies of your image storage system, and doing so both after capture and after your editing process is complete. This will minimize your chances of losing images, or winding up with only low-resolution versions.

BACKING UP ON THE ROAD

If you're on location for more than a day, it's smart to bring a portable hard drive and a laptop. At the end of each day, you can transfer the images on your memory cards onto a hard drive, then store the cards in a safe place and start with new ones the next day. Pack the hard drive and memory cards in separate bags during air travel, and keep one set in your carry-on. This ensures that you'll have your images in two places until you're ready to work with them.

Backing up is something that causes every photographer a fair amount of anxiety—no matter how many copies you have in how many places, it never feels like enough. Give yourself peace of mind by developing a system that makes sense to you, provides redundancy, and is integrated into your workflow.

PRO TIP | STORING ORIGINALS ON AN EXTERNAL DRIVE

An external hard drive is essential for backups, but also consider housing your initial storage system on a hard drive connected to but separate from your computer. Most photo-editing programs can work with "referenced files"—meaning the originals are stored on a connected, separate drive—leaving only a library of metadata and adjustments housed on your computer. This technique will save your computer's hard drive from being filled up too quickly, and will make transition to a new computer much easier.

SELECTING A PHOTO

When you have hundreds of frames in front of you, developing a system for eliminating the duds and evaluating what's left will help you sort through it all to find your favorites.

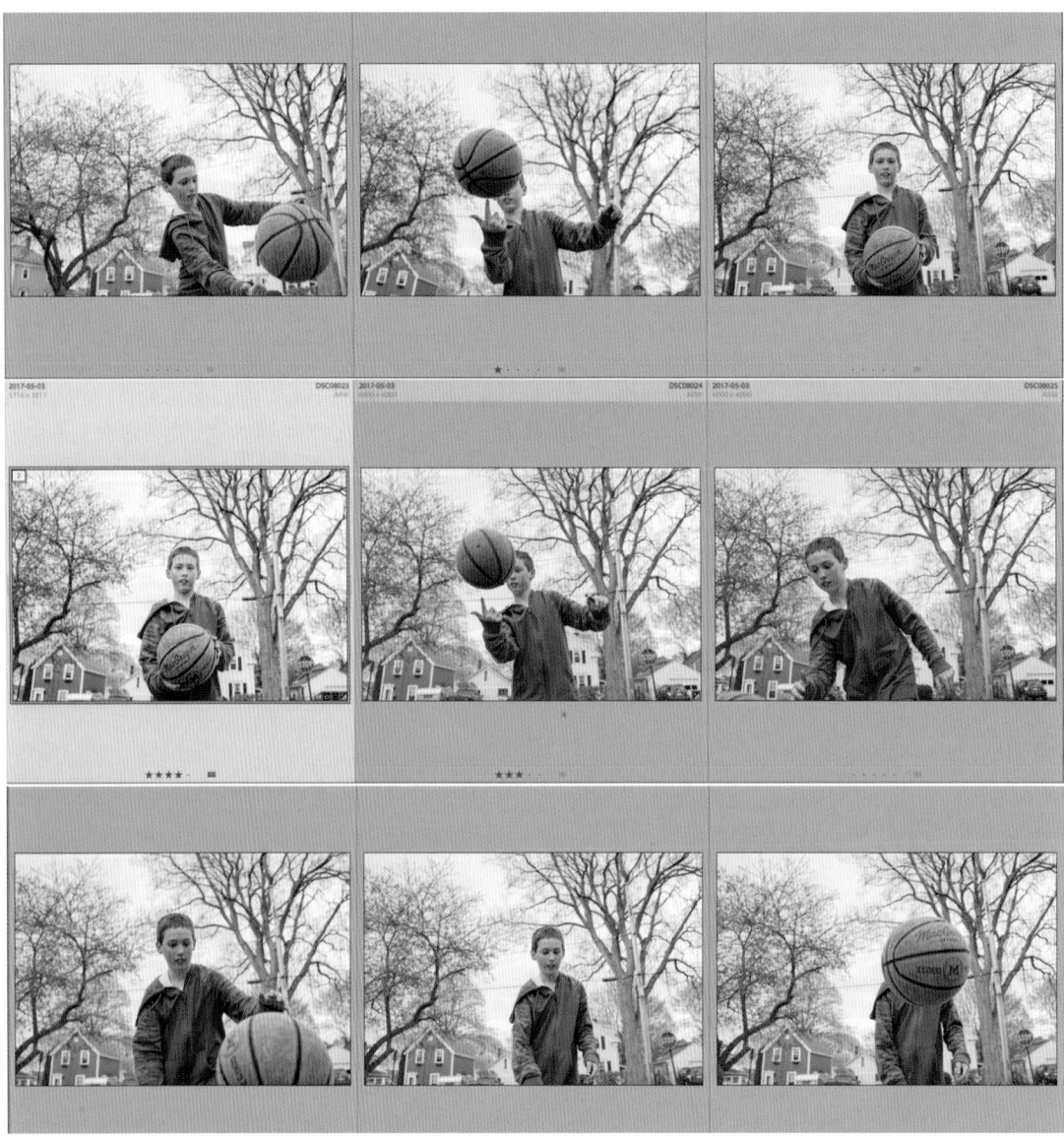

This grid shows a small portion of a photo session with a boy and his basketball. On the first pass, anything that stood out got one star. Subsequent passes narrowed the set to fewer frames with two, then three stars. A final frame was selected and is marked with four stars and has been labeled red.

While you often need to make hundreds of photos to get one or two good ones, you shouldn't share them all. The goal of good photo selection is to distill your work to the handful of frames that tell a story completely, and in the most compelling way. Just like photography itself, the editing process takes time, practice, and a solid understanding of what makes a good photograph.

MAKING PASSES

The easiest way to approach facing a large number of images is to flip through them all several times, fairly quickly, with a more discerning eye each time. Your first pass may be an elimination round, where you mark the obviously "bad" shots for deletion—frames that are out of focus, exposed incorrectly, or have missed the subject altogether. You may put these files in the trash, or some editing programs will allow you to mark throwaways with an X to later discard in bulk. Through this first pass, you'll develop an overview of your work, a reminder of which scenes you photographed and roughly how many variations you have within each scene.

On your next pass, mark anything that catches your eye with one star, or perhaps label it with a certain color. If you're not working in editing software, simply drag these favorites into a first-round folder. Next, start at the beginning of your first-round picks, and upgrade the images that stand out from the rest to two stars, with another label color, or into a new folder,

and so on. Make one or two more passes until you've distilled the work into a handful of the most special, meaningful frames. In the end, this selection should cover the scenarios you photographed thoroughly, with each frame making a unique contribution.

By now, you've had experience with exposure and framing, and what goes into making a good photograph. And while you will apply these same principles to your selection process, you can also lean on your gut reaction—note which images evoke a response in you, which feel compelling—without thinking too much about technical details. After all, this is the way your audience will be seeing your images—they will be most attracted to the frames that grab their attention, without being aware of your camera settings or why you chose them.

BE RUTHLESS

As you look at your work with an editor's eye, you'll need to put your heart on hold. As photographers, we have a personal connection to each scenario we shoot, but objectivity is key here. Ask someone else to review your choices. Apply your understanding of what makes a good photograph (and not your love of the subject) to your selection process. Use a critical eye and your gut to determine which frames will best tell the story. Think of your images as a way to give viewers an experience of their own, rather than simply sharing yours. Intrigue them with a compelling selection that will leave them wanting more.

EDITING BASICS:
ADJUSTING FRAME

Capitalize on a good capture with some simple adjustments to help an image reach its full potential. Tweaking your framing is a good place to start.

When photographing action or something happening quickly, it can be tricky to get the horizon straight on capture.

Try to make the most of an image on capture—it's good practice to be conscious of composition and exposure while you're shooting, rather than relying on tricks to correct mistakes later. That said, even a well-composed, well-exposed image can use a little enhancement, and sometimes an image with minor errors is worth saving. Think of your postproduction practice like working in a digital darkroom. You're not changing the facts of a photograph, simply bringing out the best version of it. We'll explore some simple, global enhancements you can make to an image in this section and the next.

STRAIGHTENING

In chapter 2 we discussed the importance of horizon as the foundation of your photograph. A slanted horizon will make your viewers feel off-kilter, and unless that's your goal, a level horizon is essential. Capturing a level horizon can be challenging when holding your camera, but straightening it in postproduction is simple. Nearly every photo-editing software program has a straightening tool. Usually, it will drop a temporary grid over your image that will help you line things up horizontally and vertically. Many applications will also allow

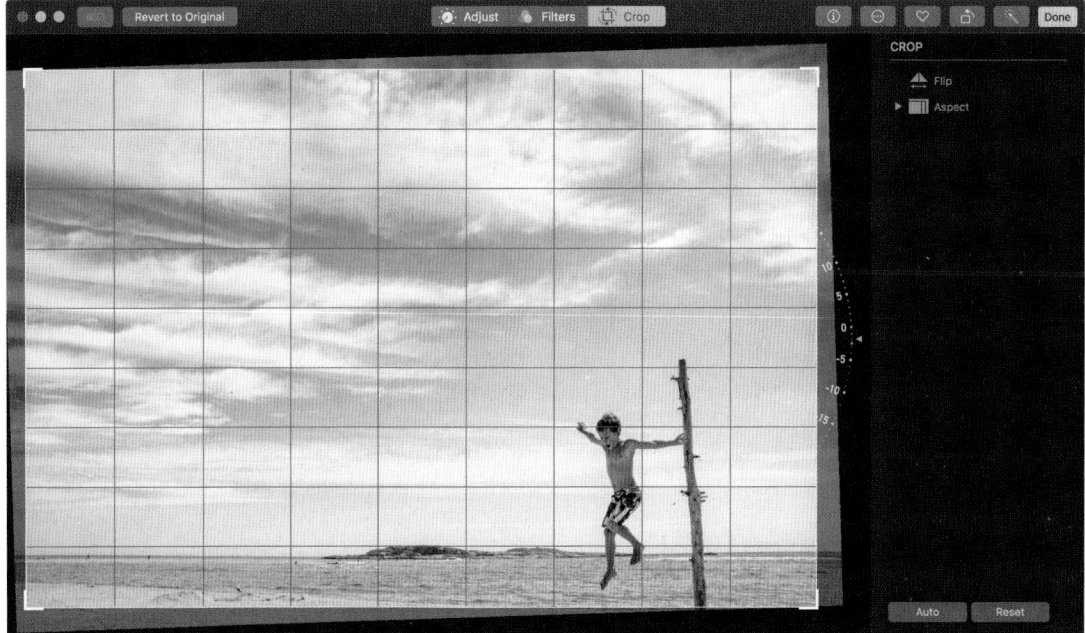

Straightening the horizon is fairly simple in most photo-editing software programs. Most drop a temporary grid over the photograph that allows you to rotate the frame until the horizon is level.

you to correct with both vertical and horizontal distortion—useful when photographing buildings at an angle—when your camera lens plane doesn't match that of your subject.

CROPPING

Cropping is usually necessary to "trim" an image after adjusting the horizon or lens distortion angle, but can also cut distracting details at the edges of your frame. You can crop either freehand or by maintaining a specific aspect ratio. Using the cropping function to digitally "zoom" in on a subject is not a great idea, as it will reduce resolution. It's also possible to change the orientation of a photograph with careful cropping—making a horizontal frame vertical or vice versa. Unless you are working

with very large digital files, this is not recommended. Reserve these tweaks for fixing small mistakes. The better you are at framing your photograph as you're taking it, the less time you'll need to spend editing it.

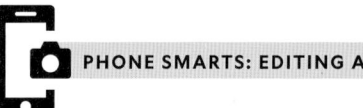

PHONE SMARTS: EDITING APPS

Most smartphones come with a photo-editing function that can straighten and crop images, as well as make slight color and exposure adjustments. Most also offer an array of preset filters designed to give your images a particular look. Find your favorite app and practice with it to give your images a look that is distinctly your own.

EDITING BASICS:
ADJUSTING EXPOSURE AND COLOR

Slight adjustments to the color, tone, and exposure of your images can help make a photo pop, so that the scene is as vivid as you remember it.

Sometimes you'll have a frame that captures just the right moment, but has just missed the mark on exposure, or maybe the colors aren't quite right. Postproduction is the time to correct these minor mistakes. Most photo-editing programs have a set of basic, global adjustments you can make to a photograph. These are typically controlled by sliders that will allow you a range of alteration. Here are a few of the most common tools.

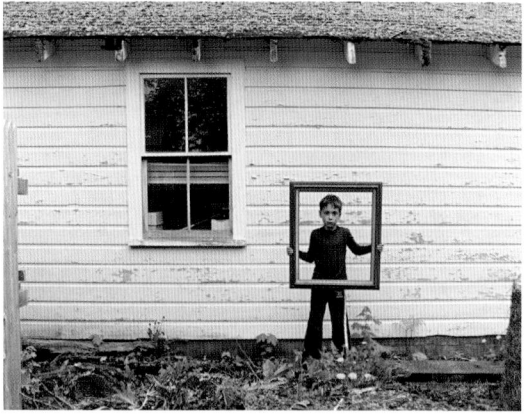

The RAW version of this photo looks underexposed and lacks the vividness of the scene as seen in person.

EXPOSURE

This will adjust the exposure of your image by lightening or darkening the entire frame, just as adjusting your camera settings would have. The whole numbers on the slider equate to exposure "stops." This is generally a good place to start and is typically at the top of your adjustment panel. This tool is sometimes called "Light."

CONTRAST

Contrast helps define light and dark areas in your image. The more contrast you apply, the more defined these areas become. Adding a little contrast will often make a subject pop against a background that is lighter or darker.

SHADOWS AND HIGHLIGHTS

These will affect the brightest and darkest parts of your image. Moving them one way or the other will increase or decrease the targeted areas. If you're hoping to reveal details in the highlights, decrease that slider. If you're hoping to reveal details in the shadows, increase that slider. An area that is completely overexposed or underexposed will not have any detail to reveal.

TEMPERATURE AND TINT

Remember when we talked about white balance and color temperature? These tools will give you another crack at it. Click on the eyedropper tool—this is your white balance selector. Drag it to an area of the image you know should be neutral gray and click again. The program will adjust the color temperature of the photo accordingly. You can also nudge the temperature and tint sliders manually. Temperature will go from cooler (bluish) to warmer (yellowish), and Tint will add or remove green or magenta casts.

SATURATION

This adjustment controls the intensity of the color, either boosting it up or toning

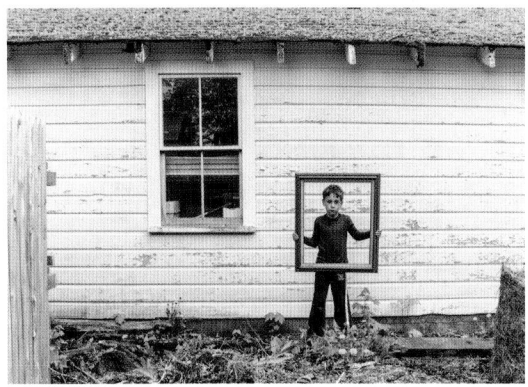

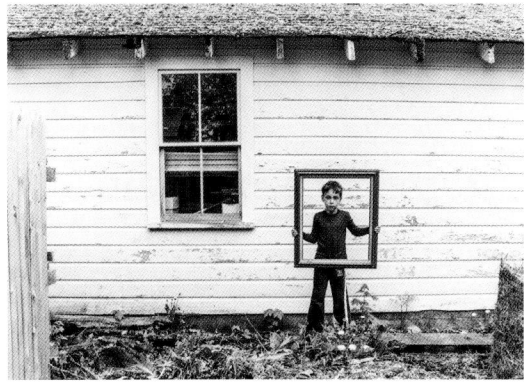

A few minor adjustments can make it more vibrant. In both versions the contrast and sharpness were adjusted, then saturation was increased in the top photo, while a black-and-white filter was applied to the bottom.

it down. Use it very subtly to avoid an unnatural look. You can also move it all the way down to completely remove color from the image for a quick conversion to black and white that will include all of your earlier adjustments. This tool is sometimes called "Color."

SHARPENING

You can make small adjustments to the focus with the "Sharpen" slider. This will bump up the contrast where light and dark areas meet, bringing out texture by making the edges pop. It cannot make up for bad focus or low resolution, but it can add some definition to important details. Small boosts are best here, as too much will make your picture look overprocessed.

BLACK AND WHITE

To convert a color photograph into black and white, many programs have an adjustment that will apply various black-and-white looks. These will vary in contrast and shades of grays. Try several out and see which one suits your preference for the image.

Your photo-editing software may have even more options. See how those options alter an image. It's sometimes helpful to push the slider far to one side or the other to see what changes, then dial it back for a subtle enhancement.

Beware of overusing these tools—it's easy to go from just enough to way too much. Overprocessing can cause distortion, which takes your viewer out of the moment. A light touch is usually all you need.

SHARING YOUR PHOTOGRAPHS

Telling your story in photographs isn't complete without someone to experience it. Share what you've created to bring your photographic journey full circle.

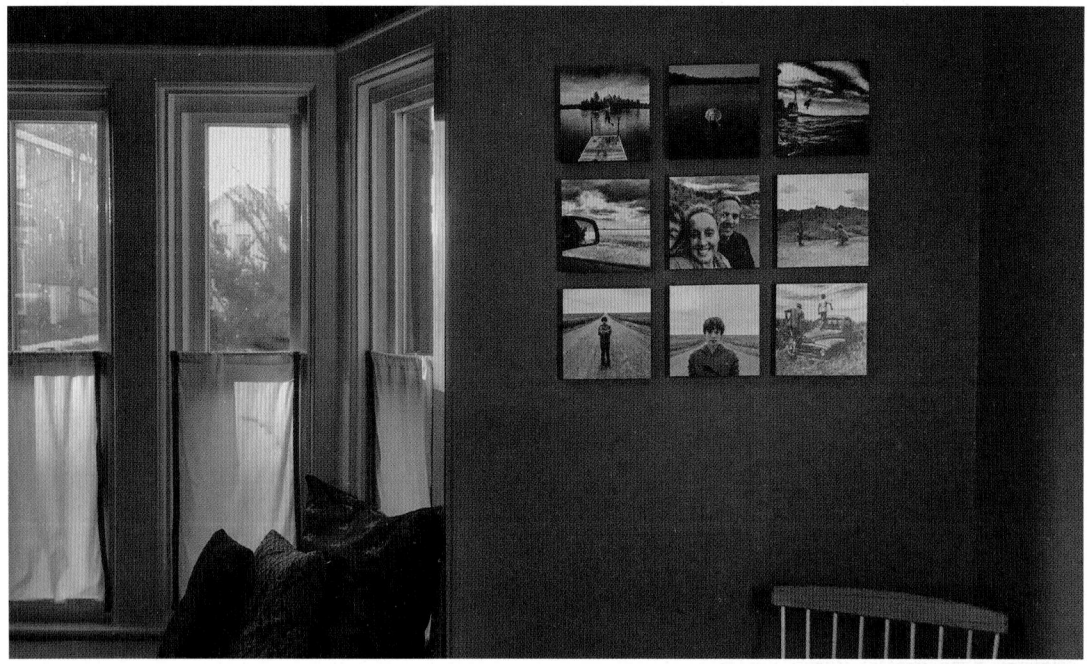

No matter how technology changes the process of making photographs, the joy and fulfillment of sharing them never goes away.

The work is done. The preparation, planning, seeing, shooting, reviewing, selecting, enhancing—you've done it all, and now you have a set of photographs that you've poured yourself into. These pictures tell the story of your neighborhood, your vacation, your family, your pets, or your friends that you can share with the world. To maximize your sharing options, be sure you have an understanding of how to export your edited photographs, and the ways in which you can share them easily between your computer and smartphone.

ONLINE SHARING

The easiest way to share your photographs with a large audience are the various and ever changing social media outlets available online. Most of these require you to have a personal account and a level of comfort with a digital connection to the world. As of this writing, Instagram is the go-to for sharing photography, and allows you to share a published photo to multiple other platforms with a single click. Many social media channels offer style filters that can be applied to your photographs before sharing. As with presets in photo-editing software, these are designed to give your image a certain look. Again, beware of applying too many postproduction layers. If you know you have a favorite Instagram filter you'll want to use, consider skipping alterations earlier on in the editing process. Some platforms make posting from either a computer or a smartphone equally easy, though others, like Instagram, require a smartphone for publishing.

Think about who you are trying to reach with your photographs and why. Consider order, arrangement, and words to accompany your images before publishing. Once you've shared your work, be open to the responses you receive—let these guide you in your future projects.

If you'd like to share your photographs as a portfolio and in a less interactive way, consider creating a website to showcase them. With so many template-based platforms with reasonable subscription fees, having a website has never been easier. Squarespace, Wix, and Virb are a few of the most widely used, but find the one that works best for your personal needs.

PRINTS AND MORE

Nothing beats hanging a print of one of your favorite images or creating a photo album of a complete project. There are many options for printing your digital images. You can upload digital files from your computer to some local drugstores for printing. These are typically machine-generated and often have a magenta or green cast. But a Google search of CUSTOM PHOTO PRINTING will lead you to many professional labs that offer excellent print services at reasonable prices, and deliver right to your home. These labs will print any size on a variety of media—from photo paper to canvas to aluminum. Some smartphone apps let you order prints, photo albums, and more from your phone. The quality and efficiency of these apps is impressive. You can easily get into a routine of creating prints or albums from finished projects, ensuring a lasting way to share your work.

FROM CAMERA TO VIEWER

A photograph freezes time. The moments we capture—the good ones and the tough ones alike—are preserved for as long as the medium lasts. This alone has intrinsic value. But sharing these moments with loved ones, friends, or an even greater audience offers an opportunity for connection, understanding, perhaps even effecting change. No matter how technology changes the process, photography will always be a form of meaningful communication.

The more you practice, the more your process will become second nature. When you know how to use a camera well, you can begin to work more creatively, with more heart and soul, to tell your story. These are the images that will really move a viewer. You picked up this book because photography is the way you want to share what you see. Give it the practice, patience, and passion it deserves.

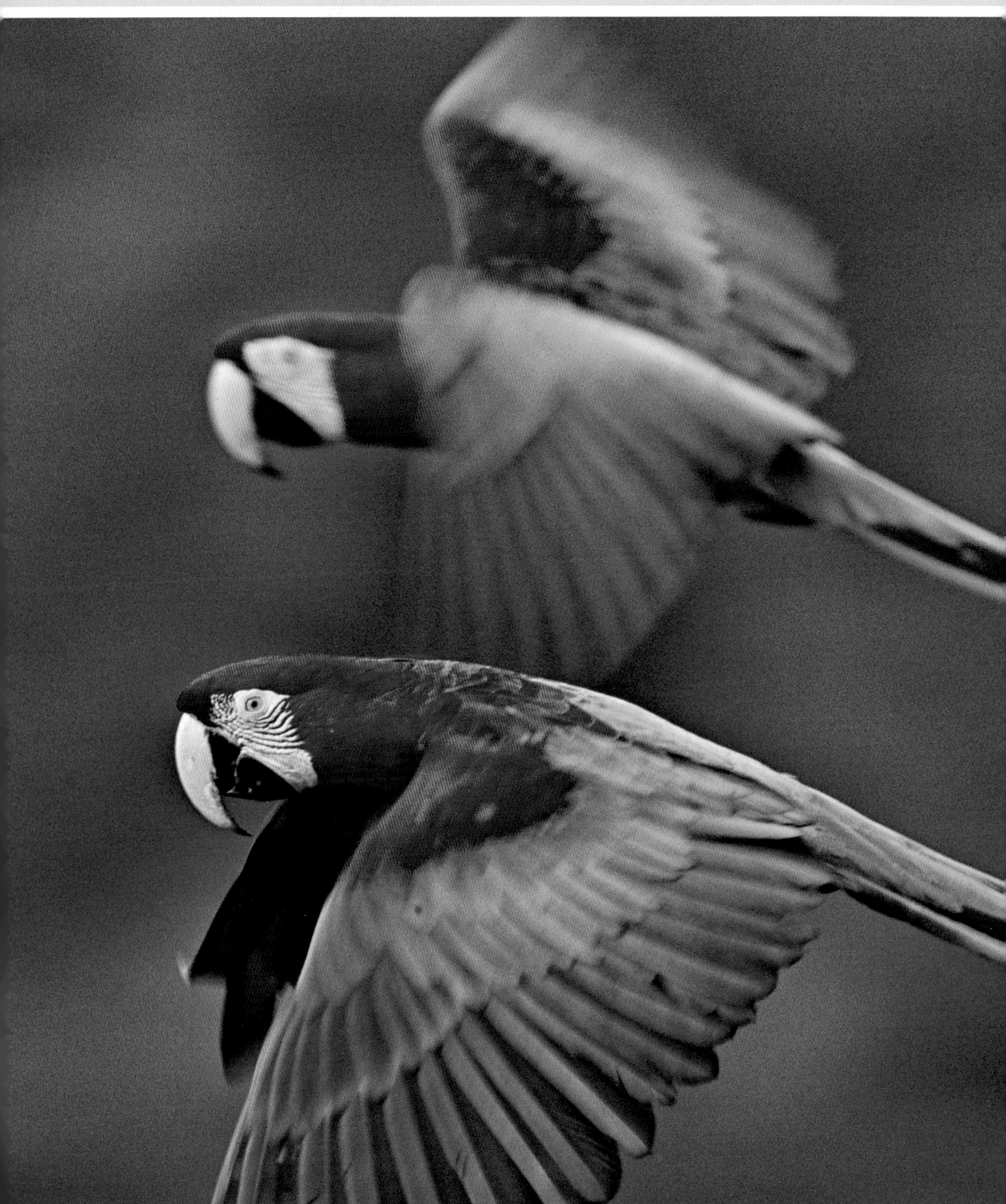

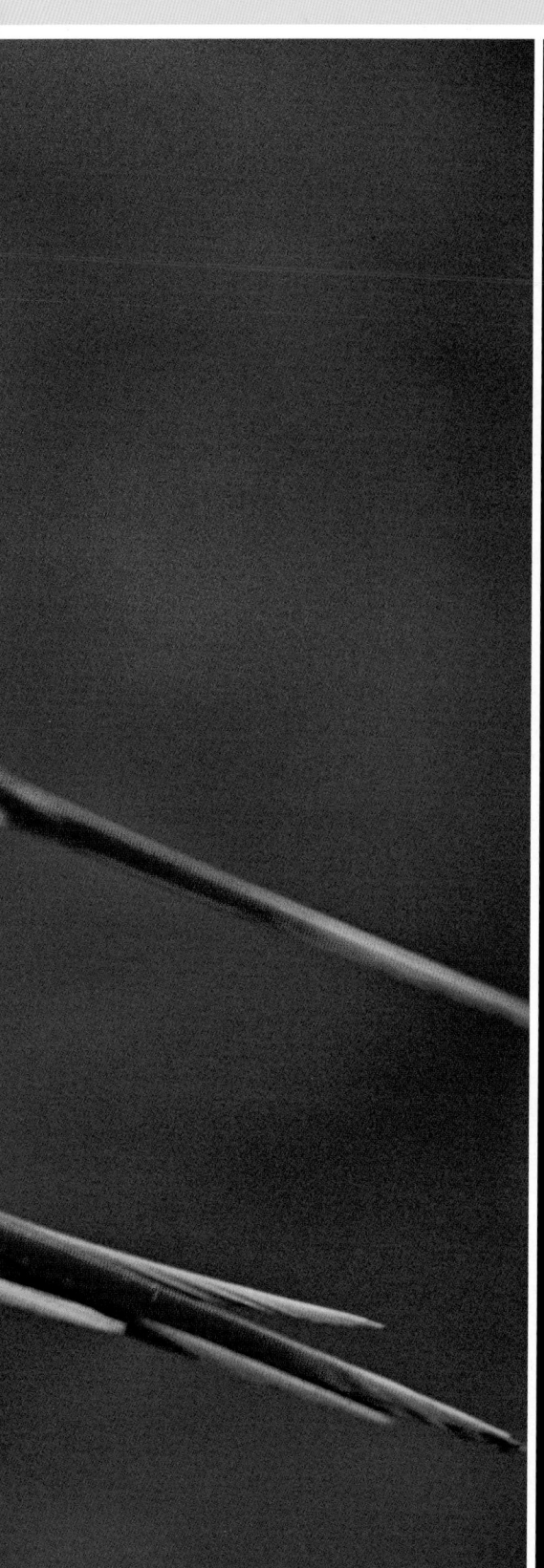

IN FLIGHT

I took this picture of macaws in Bolivia's Madidi National Park while on assignment for *National Geographic* magazine. I was photographing the incredible diversity of wildlife there, and the macaws flying over the park were a highlight. Photographing them was a tremendous technical challenge—getting close enough, finding good light, and capturing them in flight. This called for the best of my photographic and problem-solving skills.

VANTAGE POINTS I knew that the only way to capture the macaws well and from up close was to be above them or, better yet, at eye level—on high scaffolding towers and the edges of cliffs where my guides told me the birds had been.

BE PATIENT I spent two weeks, on and off, waiting to see a few bursts of color out over the green canopy. The climbing and patience all paid off with this picture—the lines, the symmetry, the clean background, the vivid colors, the front macaw's eye in sharp focus. This image was featured on the cover.

MAKE AN IMPACT More than getting a good photo, I was excited that people would see the macaws of Madidi and feel moved to protect them. Whether or not you go pro, photography will enrich your life and give you a new appreciation for the beauty of the world around us. In turn, your photography will bring joy and understanding to the people around you. That's why I do what I do.

GLOSSARY

ANGLE OF VIEW The amount of any scene that a lens "sees," measured in degrees; the shorter the focal length, the greater the coverage. Also called "field of view."

APERTURE The opening inside the lens that allows light to pass through to the sensor; this is adjusted in size (except in mirror lenses and a few others) by the diaphragm and is expressed in f-stop numbers, such as f/8. The aperture also controls depth of field.

APERTURE PRIORITY (A OR AV) A semiautomatic camera mode where the user sets the aperture and the camera sets the corresponding shutter speed for correct exposure, based on information collected by the in-camera exposure meter.

ASPECT RATIO The ratio of width to height in an image or image sensor.

CAPTURE FORMAT In digital imaging, the format used to save or record photographic data—JPEG or RAW, for most digital cameras.

CENTER WEIGHTED METERING A metering system where the camera meter evaluates the light in the center of the frame and its surrounding areas, ignoring the tones in the corners.

COLOR TEMPERATURE A measurement of the color of any given light source, expressed in degrees kelvin. "Warm" light, such as the light at sunset, has a low temperature, whereas "cool" (bluish) light, as on a heavily overcast day, has a high color temperature on this scale.

COMPRESSION The process used to decrease the size of a digital image file by combining or averaging data.

CONTRAST The range of brightness of a subject; the difference between the lightest and darkest parts of an image. A scene with high contrast includes both extreme highlights and very dark shadows.

DEPTH OF FIELD The zone or range of apparent sharpness in a photograph. While the focused subject (and other objects at the same distance) is truly sharp, acceptable sharpness extends in front of and behind the focused point, its range determined by the aperture.

DEPTH-OF-FIELD PREVIEW A control found on some cameras that lets the photographer preview the depth of field of a particular aperture before making an exposure.

DIAPHRAGM The mechanism inside a lens that controls the size of the aperture, using overlapping metal leaves.

DIFFUSER A translucent material generally held between the subject and the light source (ambient or flash) to soften the illumination. Can be handheld or an accessory to use with a flash.

DSLR (DIGITAL SINGLE-LENS REFLEX) An electronically operated camera that uses mirrors to show the potential image through the viewfinder. When the shutter opens, the mirror lifts away, and the same view strikes the sensor.

EXPOSURE COMPENSATION A control found on most cameras with automatic mode that allows the user to overexpose (+ factors) or underexpose (– factors) from the metered value.

FAST A term used to describe either a lens with a very wide maximum aperture or a highly light-sensitive ISO. Both allow for faster shutter speeds (than their "slow" counterparts) to make a correct exposure.

FILTER A piece of coated or colored glass or plastic, placed in front of the camera lens, that alters the light reaching the film or sensor. Filters can modify the color or quality of the light, change the relative rendition of various tones, reduce haze or glare, or create special effects.

FLARE An artifact or quality in an image created by stray light that reduces contrast or forms patches of light. Caused by reflections inside the lens that come from light striking the front element from a certain angle. Flare can be reduced by special factory coatings on all elements, other internal technology, or the use of a lens hood to prevent light from striking the front element.

F-STOP A numerical value to denote the size of the lens aperture. Regardless of lens size or focal length, the same f-stop number allows the same amount of light to be transmitted to the sensor. Wide apertures are denoted with small numbers, such as f/2; small apertures with large numbers, such as f/22.

GRAIN Refers to the random optical texture apparent on film exposures when magnified. The faster the film (higher ISO), the larger and more noticeable the grain. This effect can be applied in digital photography, and is similar to, though technically different from, noise.

HISTOGRAM A bar graph showing the relative number of pixels in different brightness ranges in a digital image.

ISO A standard for image sensor rating. ISO is an abbreviation for International Organization for Standardization, which sets the standards used to rate the speed, or light sensitivity, of a camera sensor. Common sensor ratings range from ISO 25 to 1600, but many digital cameras reach as high as 10,000 and more.

JPEG A standard file format where digital information is compressed so that the file takes up less storage space when not open. JPEG files usually have the suffix .jpg

KEYWORD A label added to data attached to a digital image (metadata) to help with computer searches. Keywords are also called "tags."

MACRO The close-focusing ability of a lens, or a lens with such capability. Strictly defined, the term is used to describe when a subject is reproduced five times life-size (or larger) in the frame.

MATRIX METERING (NIKON)/EVALUATIVE METERING (CANON) A metering system that reads the intensity of light by dividing the scene into zones that are then assessed by light and dark tones; the default metering mode on most DSLRs.

MEGAPIXEL (MP) One million pixels. The higher the number of pixels, the greater the resolution of a digital image. More megapixels equal more data.

METADATA Information automatically attached to each image by a digital camera.

NOISE The patterned texture created by artifacts in a digital photograph. Appears as specks of color showing up as distortion in images that should have a smoother, more unified color. Noise occurs when photographs are shot with a high ISO in low light. The size and resolution of the image sensor also affect noise levels.

PANNING: A technique used when photographing fast-moving subjects in which the camera is moved at the speed of the subject. This keeps the subject sharp, while blurring the background.

PIXEL Abbreviation for picture (pix-) element (-el). These are the smallest bits of information that combine to form a digital image. The more pixels (current cameras are measured in megapixels), the higher the resolution.

PRIME LENS A lens with a fixed focal length, as opposed to a zoom lens.

RAW A type of image file that captures the maximum amount of data possible, allowing photographers to process the image as they like.

RED-EYE Light from a camera's flash reflected by the retinas in a person's eyes. This effect is easily corrected by using an off-camera flash, photo-editing software, or, more commonly, by functions within the digital camera itself.

RESOLUTION A measurement of fine detail. With digital cameras, a measure (in pixels) of the amount of information included in an image, which determines the clarity and sharpness of a printed photograph.

SENSOR An electronic chip containing pixels that are sensitive to light. The larger the sensor and the more pixels, the more information the sensor collects.

SHUTTER The mechanism built into the lens or camera that regulates the length of time that light reaches the sensor through the aperture to produce an image.

SHUTTER PRIORITY (S, Tv) A semiautomatic camera mode where the photographer sets the shutter speed and the system sets the f-stop required for a correct exposure, based on information collected by the in-camera exposure meter.

SHUTTER SPEED The length of time the shutter remains open to allow light to hit the sensor. This is expressed in seconds or fractions of a second, such as 1/60 or 1/250.

SPOT METERING A metering system that reads the intensity of light reflected by only a very small portion of the scene.

STABILIZATION Techniques and technologies that reduce camera movement at slow shutter speeds, thus decreasing blur in photographs.

SYNC SPEED The fastest shutter speed of a camera that can be used to ensure that the burst of flash is synchronized with the time that the shutter is open.

TELEPHOTO A specific lens design that offers focal lengths longer than the standard, although this term is now used for any long lens. Any focal length longer than 200mm is generally referred to as a telephoto.

VIEWFINDER An optical system that allows the user to view the image area that will be included in the final picture. Types vary significantly. Some allow for viewing through the lens that will actually take the picture, whereas others are near the lens and offer only an approximate view of the actual image area.

WHITE BALANCE An in-camera or postproduction control used to balance the color temperature of a light source in an image so that the picture looks natural.

WIDE-ANGLE LENS A lens with a focal length shorter than normal for the format. Any lens of about 35mm or shorter is typically referred to as a wide angle.

ZOOM LENS A lens that allows its focal length to be varied, shifting between longer and shorter focal lengths.

RESOURCES

BOOKS ABOUT PHOTOGRAPHY

Ang, Tom. *The Complete Photographer,* 2nd Edition (2016).

——. *Digital Photography: An Introduction,* 5th Edition (2018).

——. *Photography: The Definitive Visual History* (2014).

Carroll, Henry. *Read This if You Want to Take Great Photographs* (2014).

Hoy, Anne H. *The Book of Photography* (2005).

Getting Your Shot: Stunning Photos, How-to Tips, and Endless Inspiration From the Pros (2015).

National Geographic Complete Photography (2011).

National Geographic Ultimate Field Guide to Photography (2009).

Sartore, Joel. *Photographing Your Family* (2008).

BOOKS OF PHOTOGRAPHY

Abell, Sam, and Robert E. Gilka. *Stay This Moment: The Photographs of Sam Abell* (1990).

Allard, William Albert. *Portraits of America* (2008).

——. *William Albert Allard: Five Decades, A Retrospective* (2010).

Allard, William Albert, and Thomas McGuane. *Vanishing Breed: Photographs of the Cowboy and the West* (1982).

Cobb, Jodi. *Geisha: The Life, the Voices, the Art* (1998).

Davis, Wade. *Wade Davis Photographs* (2018).

Doubilet, David. *Water Light Time* (2006).

Harvey, David Alan. *Cuba: Island at a Crossroad* (1999).

Johns, Chris. *Wild at Heart: Man and Beast in Southern Africa* (2007).

Leibovitz, Annie. *Portraits 2005–2016* (2017).

Liittschwager, David, and Susan Middleton. *Archipelago: Portraits of Life in the World's Most Remote Island Sanctuary* (2005).

Nichols, Michael, and Mike Fay. *Last Place on Earth* (2 volumes) (2005).

Nicklen, Paul. *Polar Obsession* (2009).

The Pictures of Texas Monthly: 25 Years (1998).

Salgado, Sebastião. *Genesis* (2013).

——. *Migrations: Humanity in Transition* (2000).

Sartore, Joel. *The Photo Ark: One Man's Quest to Document the World's Animals* (2017).

——. *The Photo Ark Vanishing: The World's Most Vulnerable Animals* (2019).

——. *Rare: Portraits of America's Endangered Species* (2009).

Sartore, Joel, and Noah Strycker. *Birds of the Photo Ark* (2018).

Skerry, Brian. *Ocean Soul* (2011).

——. *Shark* (2017).

Zwingle, Erla. *William Albert Allard: The Photographic Essay* (1989).

BOOKS OF PHOTOGRAPHY FROM THE
NATIONAL GEOGRAPHIC ARCHIVES

In Focus: National Geographic Greatest Portraits (2004).

National Geographic Image Collection (2009).

National Geographic: The Photographs (2008).

Through the Lens: National Geographic Greatest Photographs (2003).

Wide Angle: National Geographic Greatest Places (2005).

Women: The National Geographic Image Collection (2019).

ONLINE RESOURCES

Digital Camera World: Tutorials and gear reviews
www.digitalcameraworld.com

Digital Photography Review: Tutorials, buying guides, and discussion forums
www.dpreview.com

Joel Sartore: The author's website, with photos and videos representing his entire career
www.joelsartore.com

National Geographic Instagram: A curated collection of National Geographic photographers' work (@natgeo)
www.instagram.com/natgeo

National Geographic Photography: The online home for photo stories and advice
nationalgeographic.com/photography

PetaPixel: Detailed tutorials and photography news
www.petapixel.com

The Photo Ark: Joel Sartore's growing archive of photos of all the world's animal species under human care
www.nationalgeographic.org/projects/photo-ark/

Your Shot: National Geographic's online photography community
yourshot.nationalgeographic.com

NATIONAL GEOGRAPHIC GREAT COURSES
IN PHOTOGRAPHY

www.thegreatcourses.com

Bob Krist, Fundamentals of Travel Photography

Joel Sartore, Fundamentals of Photography I & II

Joel Sartore, The Art of Travel Photography: Six Expert Lessons

National Geographic Guide to Landscape and Wildlife Photography

National Geographic Masters of Photography

ILLUSTRATIONS CREDITS

Joel Sartore: Front cover (LO LE), 2-3, 4, 6-7, 8, 9, 27 (UP LE), 27 (UP RT), 36-7, 40-41, 44, 46, 47, 48 (RT), 49, 52, 54, 55, 56, 58-9, 60-61, 62-3, 68, 73, 74, 82, 84-5, 86-7, 88-9, 98-Photo Ark image photographed at Lemur Island, Madagascar, 101 (ALL), 102, 103, 110-11, 112-13, 114-15, 120, 126-7, 128 (CTR), 129 (UP CTR), 129 (LO RT), 130-31, 132-3, 134, 136, 142, 143, 145, 146-7, 148-9, 150-51, 158, 159, 161, 170, 174-5, 176-7, 178-9, 184 (RT), 185, 186, 190, 192, 195, 197, 198-9, 200-201, 202-203, 204, 207, 210, 220-21, 222-3, 226, 240-41, 254 (UP), back cover (UP RT), back cover (LO RT).

Heather Perry: 24 (LO LE), 24 (LO RT), 28-9, 45, 48 (LE), 50, 69, 70, 71 (ALL), 77, 80, 81, 83, 92, 93, 94, 95 (ALL), 99, 104 (ALL), 137, 162, 187, 189, 193, 194, 206, 215, 224-5, 229, 232, 234, 235, 236, 237 (BOTH), 238.

Front cover: (UP LE), aabeele/Shutterstock; (UP RT), Mauricio Handler/National Geographic Image Collection; (CT LE), Image Source/Getty Images; (CT RT), Ben Pipe/Robert Harding/National Geographic Image Collection; (LO RT), Manuel Sulzer/Cultura/age fotostock. Back cover: (UP LE), Elena-studio/Getty Images; (LO LE), Rawpixel/Getty Images. 12 (UP LE), Corinna Dumat/EyeEm/Getty Images; 12 (UP RT), Fabio Tomat/Shutterstock; 12 (LO LE), DuKai photographer/Getty Images; 12 (LO RT), Henrik Sorensen/Getty Images;

12-13, Andrei Kuzmik/Shutterstock; 13 (UP LE), Westend61/Getty Images; 13 (UP LE INSET), Ismailciydem/Getty Images; 13 (UP RT), foto by Chandler Chou/Getty Images; 13 (CTR), Michael Forsberg/National Geographic Image Collection; 13 (LO), Jimmy McIntyre/Getty Images; 14-5, perkmeup/Getty Images; 16-7, Mint Images/Cavan Images; 19, Canon USA, Inc.; 21, Bhanupong Asatamongkolchai/Getty Images; 22 (UP), Scanrail1/Shutterstock; 22 (CTR), seen0001/Getty Images; 22 (LO), ParabolStudio/Shutterstock; 23 (UP), Bet_Noire/Getty Images; 23 (LO), Dominionart/Shutterstock.com; 24 (UP), Patrick J. Bagley; 26 (UP LE), Canon USA, Inc.; 26 (UP RT), PhotoPlus Magazine/Getty Images; 26 (CTR LE), Nikon, Inc.; 26 (LO LE), Canon USA, Inc.; 26 (LO RT), Kitch Bain/Adobe Stock; 27 (CTR LE), Blaine Harrington III/Corbis Documentary/Getty Images; 27 (CTR RT), LedyX/Shutterstock; 27 (LO), slobo/Getty Images; 31 (UP LE), Andriy Prokopenko/Getty Images; 31 (LO LE), Andriy Prokopenko/Getty Images; 31 (UP RT), creativesunday/Shutterstock; 31 (CTR RT), Utha/Shutterstock; 31 (LO RT), yevgeniy11/Shutterstock; 32 (UP), Digital Camera Magazine/Getty Images; 32 (CTR), Ilya_Starikov/Getty Images; 32 (LO), PhotoPlus Magazine/Getty Images; 33 (UP), Elnur/Getty Images; 33 (CTR), Constantine Pankin/Shutterstock; 33 (LO), sanapadh/Getty Images; 34 (UP), Art65395/Shutterstock; 34 (CTR), Kaesler Media/Shut-

INDEX

CONTRIBUTORS

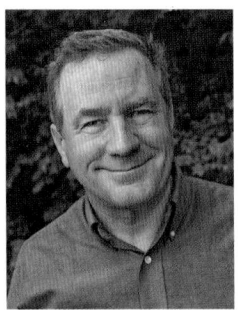

JOEL SARTORE is a photographer, author, teacher, conservationist, National Geographic fellow, and regular contributor to *National Geographic* magazine. His hallmarks are a sense of humor and a Midwestern work ethic. He specializes in documenting endangered species and landscapes around the world. He is the founder of the Photo Ark, a 25-year documentary project to save species and habitat. In addition to the work he has done for *National Geographic,* Sartore has contributed to *Audubon, Sports Illustrated,* the *New York Times, Smithsonian,* and numerous book projects. He is always happy to return from his travels around the world to his home in Lincoln, Nebraska, where he lives with his wife, Kathy, and their three children.

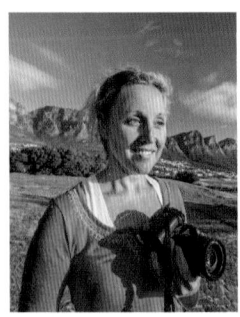

HEATHER PERRY is a freelance photographer and writer whose first passion is photographing people in and around water. Her work has been published in *National Geographic*'s magazines, books, and online content, as well as in the *New York Times, Smithsonian,* and other publications. She has done commercial photography for National Geographic Channel, South African Tourism, and Sony. She's photographed stories on immigration issues, refugee populations, fishing communities, shipbuilders, and neighborhood kids in her home state of Maine, and has worked with swimmers in pools and oceans around the world. Perry is a photo expert with National Geographic Lindblad Expeditions and enjoys sharing her photographic knowledge with travelers.

MELODY ROWELL served as a contributing writer on this book. She lives in Washington, D.C.

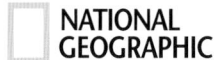

PHOTO BASICS

Since 1888, the National Geographic Society has funded more than 14,000 research, conservation, education, and storytelling projects around the world. National Geographic Partners distributes a portion of the funds it receives from your purchase to National Geographic Society to support programs including the conservation of animals and their habitats.

National Geographic Partners, LLC
1145 17th Street NW
Washington, DC 20036-4688 USA

Get closer to National Geographic explorers and photographers, and connect with our global community. Join us today at nationalgeographic.org/joinus

For rights or permissions inquiries, please contact National Geographic Books Subsidiary Rights: bookrights@natgeo.com

Library of Congress Cataloging-in-Publication Data
Names: Sartore, Joel, author. I Perry, Heather, author.
Title: National Geographic photo basics : the ultimate beginner's guide to great photography / Joel Sartore with Heather Perry.
Description: Washington, D.C. : National Geographic, [2019] I Includes bibliographical references and index.
Identifiers: LCCN 2019008959 I ISBN 9781426219702 (pbk.)
Subjects: LCSH: Photography--Handbooks, manuals, etc.
Classification: LCC TR146 .S327 2019 I DDC 770--dc23
LC record available at https://lccn.loc.gov/2019008959

Printed in China

23/HHC/5

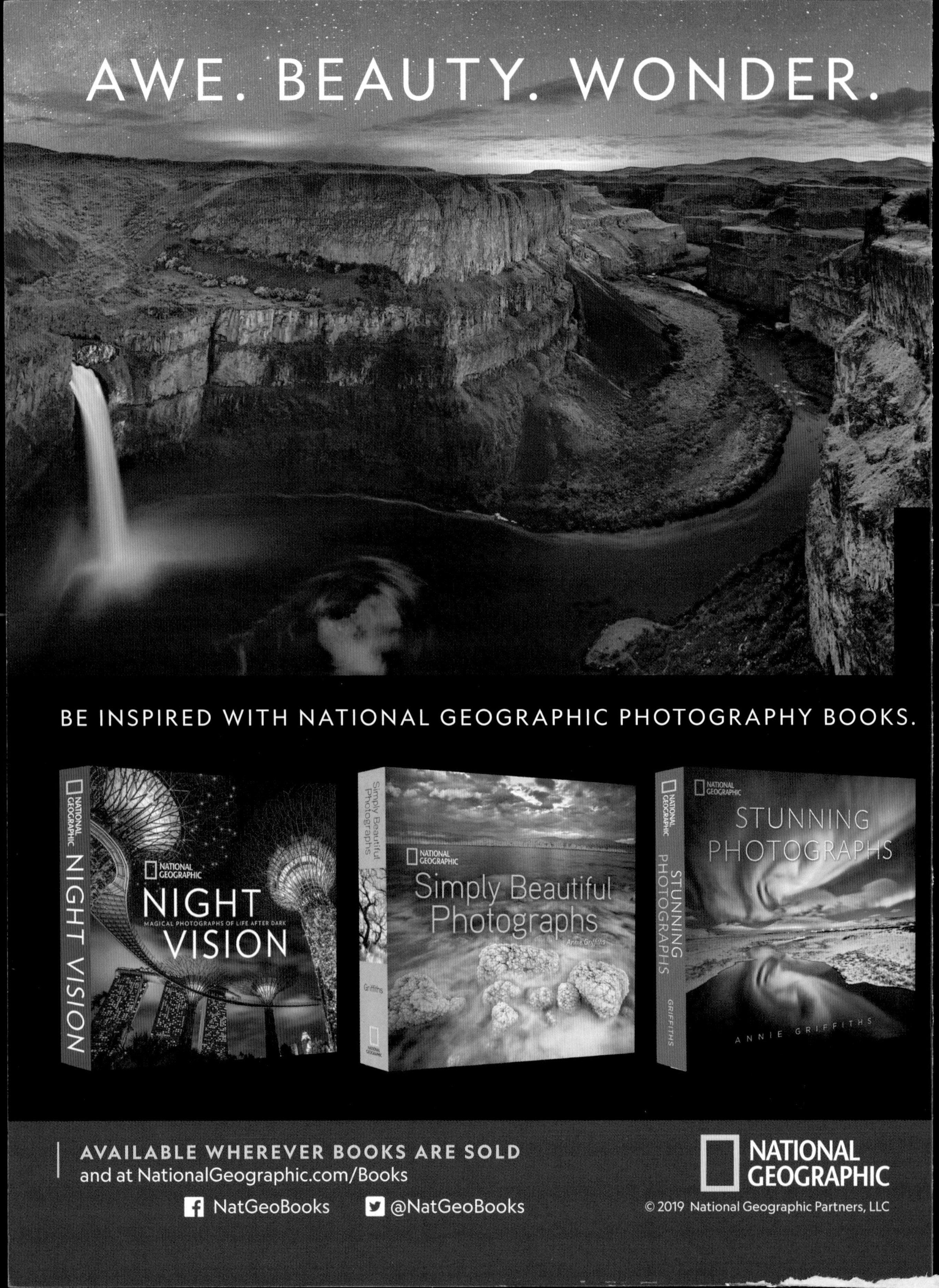

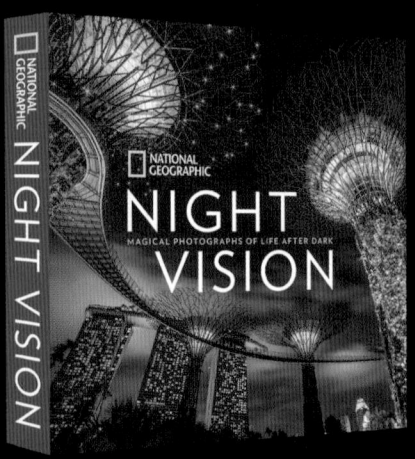
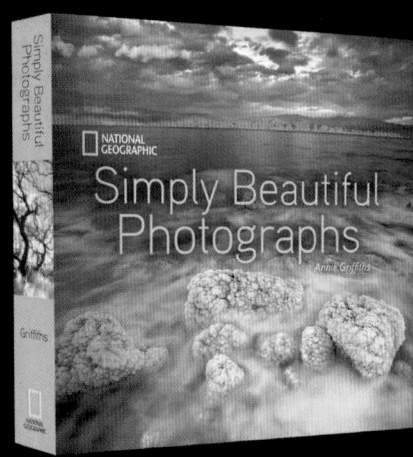
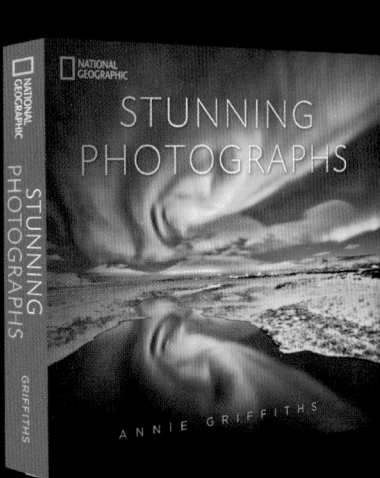
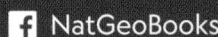 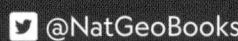
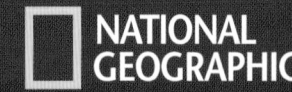